Classics in Western Philosophy of Art

Classics in Western Philosophy of Art

MAJOR THEMES AND ARGUMENTS

Noël Carroll

Hackett Publishing Company, Inc.
Indianapolis/Cambridge

Copyright © 2022 by Hackett Publishing Company, Inc.

All rights reserved
Printed in the United States of America

25 24 23 22   1 2 3 4 5 6 7

For further information, please address
    Hackett Publishing Company, Inc.
    P.O. Box 44937
    Indianapolis, Indiana 46244-0937

www.hackettpublishing.com

Interior design by E. L. Wilson and Elana Rosenthal
Composition by Aptara, Inc.

Library of Congress Control Number: 2021946253

ISBN-13: 978-1-64792-061-6 (cloth)
ISBN-13: 978-1-64792-060-9 (pbk.)
ISBN-13: 978-1-64792-062-3 (PDF ebook)

The paper used in this publication meets the minimum requirements of American National Standard for Information Sciences—Permanence of Paper for Printed Library Materials, ANSI Z39.48–1984.

∞

To Paul Guyer
My Teacher
Who will always be younger than me

Contents

Acknowledgments	ix
Introduction	xi
Chapter 1 Plato's *Hippias Major*, *Ion*, and Books 2, 3, and 10 of the *Republic*	1
Chapter 2 Aristotle's *Poetics*	58
Chapter 3 Francis Hutcheson's *An Inquiry Concerning Beauty, Order, Harmony, and Design*	99
Chapter 4 David Hume's "Of the Standard of Taste"	126
Chapter 5 Immanuel Kant's *Critique of Aesthetic Judgment*	155
Chapter 6 G. W. F. Hegel's *Introductory Lectures on Aesthetics*	199
Chapter 7 Arthur Schopenhauer's *The World As Will and Representation*	227
Chapter 8 Leo Tolstoy's *What Is Art?*	246
Chapter 9 Clive Bell's *Art*	275
Envoi	309
Index	311

Acknowledgments

I would like to thank the following for their help in the composition of this book: Joan Acocella, Margaret Moore, Aaron Smuts, Sheila Lintott, Susan Feagin, Gary Iseminger, Jeff Dean, Richard Eldridge, Nicholas Pappas, Iakovos Vasiliou, Nancy Worman, Daniel Malick, John Gibson, Jason Cutmore, Marilynn Johnson, Frank Boardman, Ni Sheng, Peter Kivy, Sibyl Swarzenbach, Omar Dahbour, Paula Gottlieb, Jesse Prinz, Robert Clewis, and Chloé Cooper Jones. This book is dedicated to my former teacher Paul Guyer who has advised me on all things scholarly and professional and who never fails to remind me that he will always be younger than me. Paul was particularly generous in his close reading of four of the chapters in this book.

Finally, since all these very smart people have given me so much advice regarding this project, I cannot be sure that I am solely responsible for its imperfections, although I think that I am probably guilty of most of them.

Introduction

Why "Classic" and for Whom?

This book is an introduction to and commentary on a series of classics in the philosophy of art, specifically in the philosophy of art in the West. These books, or excerpts from them, often appear as the primary readings in introductory courses in the philosophy of art, both at the undergraduate and graduate levels. Thus, this text can be viewed as a companion to such courses. It is designed to be a resource for both the students and instructors of such courses.

As such, it does not presuppose any previous knowledge of the philosophy of art on the part of its readers. But in addition to covering the elementary nuts and bolts of the readings it canvasses, I have also tried to pursue certain selected topics more deeply in order to give more sophisticated readers the opportunity to further ponder various subjects. Although some readers may find parts of the book familiar, I hope they will find other parts that explore new ground.

In addition to introducing various texts, this book also is designed to introduce readers to various tools and techniques of philosophical analysis through their application in the interpretation and criticism of the works under review. Moreover, although I have suggested so far that the readership for this book is primarily academic, I have attempted to write it in such a way that it will also be accessible to serious art lovers who are curious about the philosophy of art, especially in terms of the ways in which it can augment their appreciation of art.

Beginning with Plato, the book examines seminal works by Aristotle, Francis Hutcheson, David Hume, Immanuel Kant, G. W. F. Hegel, Arthur Schopenhauer, Leo Tolstoy, and Clive Bell. One reason that these books belong together is that they talk to each other. Aristotle answers Plato, Kant engages ideas associated with Hutcheson and Hume, Hegel responds to Kant, while drawing upon Aristotle; whereas Schopenhauer borrows freely from Kant as well as from Plato. Moreover, Tolstoy comments on Kant and Hegel, while arguably being influenced by the latter, and, as I shall argue, Bell can be best understood as "Schopenhauer-without-Wagner."

Of course, there are classic writings on the philosophy of art from non-Western cultures. They are not included in this survey because they are not part of this conversation and not because they are not worthy of philosophical discussion. They are. As the philosophy of art as practiced in the English-speaking world becomes more cosmopolitan, as it will inevitably become, works such as the ones reviewed here will come into conversation with the classics of other cultures. The result will be a new conversation that embraces an enlarged canon and that will mandate the need for a new introduction.[1]

One way in which these texts are classic is that they have raised what have become, undoubtedly through their influence, perennial topics in the philosophy of art, especially for the Anglophone tradition. Plato challenges the intellectual and moral credentials of art, a challenge to which in effect Aristotle replies, though it is an issue that remains hotly contested by living philosophers into our own times. Hutcheson counters the ancient conception of beauty with a subjectivist account, popularizing the notion of "disinterestedness" that will mutate via Kant and his successors into the most highly influential view of aesthetic experience embraced by contemporary philosophers. Hume attempts to clarify the problem of aesthetic disagreement that is still with us, as does Kant. Contemporary philosophers, notably Arthur Danto, have returned to Hegel for inspiration, while George Dickie has focused attention on the evolution of modern aesthetic attitude theory from the contributions of Hutcheson, Kant, and Schopenhauer. Tolstoy is a pioneer in the development of the expression theory of art, while Bell performs a comparable service in terms of the competing tradition of formalism. Both Tolstoy and Bell explicitly take up the task of defining art, thereby initiating one of the dominant programs in the philosophy of art in the twentieth century and beyond.

Thus, these works are classics in the sense that they are touchstones for some of the major debates that continue to embroil contemporary philosophers of art, especially in the Anglophone tradition. Indeed, they are more than that. They are continuing resources. That is, they are still part of the conversation.

Moreover, as is probably evident, a number of the aforesaid issues are concerns not only for the meager audience of professional philosophers; they are important for the culture at large. These issues include questions concerning the ethical and cognitive status of art initiated by Plato and echoed in various ways throughout succeeding classics as well as the problem of aesthetic disagreement wrestled with by Hume and Kant. John Maynard Keynes once observed that every time you hear some businessman hawking some idea about the economy, he is probably spouting the views of some dead economist. A similar point can be made about the many of "assumptions" that are frequently taken on board in statements about art; they echo the views of dead philosophers of art, often the ones being explored in this text. This trickle-down effect is another reason to study these philosophers. Forewarned is forearmed.

---

1. A similar observation should be registered with regard to race and gender. All the authors I discuss herein are white and male. As historians of philosophy survey the past and identify women and nonwhite thinkers who engaged issues of art and aesthetics in the past, the conversation will need to be reconceived, enlarged, and revised. In that respect, this anthology, it is to be hoped, is at best an interim report.

Finally, these texts are also classics of the philosophy of art because they are part of the self-understanding of the Anglophone tradition. As already mentioned, they are frequently anthologized in the textbooks that are used to introduce students to the discussion; articles about them frequently appear in leading scholarly journals in the field such as the *British Journal of Aesthetics* and the *Journal of Aesthetics and Art Criticism*; and they are recurring topics of dissertations. Anglophone philosophers of art are expected to be familiar at least to the ideas of these authors, although admittedly to varying degrees. Plato, Aristotle, Hume, Kant, and perhaps Tolstoy and Bell are probably referred to more often than Hegel and Schopenhauer.[2] Nevertheless, all these philosophers and their views comprise something like the shared "vocabulary" or "memory" of contemporary, Anglophone philosophers of art.[3]

In that respect, this book can be regarded as an invitation to join that conversation.

Chapter Overview

The earliest systematic theoretical writing that we have on art in the West is found in the works of Plato. This writing concerns poetry, primarily dramatic poetry, but Plato also suggests approaches to the visual arts and music. What, of course, is ironic about considering Plato to be the first philosopher of art is that he comes not to praise art, but to bury it. He is extremely critical of what we call art and artists. He is especially worried about whether art can serve the needs of society, and he suspects instead that art will disrupt it. Thus, many of Plato's concerns have to do with regulating or censoring art. The first philosopher of art, then, is a censor. Plato is interested in determining the nature of dramatic poetry, painting, and art not for the abstract academic pursuit of pure knowledge, but in order to show that they should be subject to social control.

---

2. One important philosopher of art who does not have a chapter in this book is Nietzsche, although he is briefly discussed in the chapter on Schopenhauer. The reason for this omission is that I do not think that he fits into the ongoing conversation of the philosophy of art as neatly as do the other authors. Similarly, I have vaulted over the medieval period in Europe altogether because I do not think it is immediately relevant to the tradition of the philosophy of art as currently practiced. Both Nietzsche and medieval aesthetics are worthwhile topics for philosophical research. But they are not part of the story that I am telling.

For the record, in terms of the contrast drawn between artistic autonomy and heteronomy in this book, Nietzsche is on the side of heteronomy.

3. As I hope this paragraph signals, in this book, I am primarily interested in the way these texts figure in the history of the philosophy of art, and I am less concerned with reading them in their cultural context or in fitting them into overarching oeuvres of the authors in question.

One of the first dialogues by Plato that we consider is called *Ion*. Ion is the name of a rhapsode. A rhapsode is a kind of singer—a person who recites and interprets poetry in public. Ion is a rhapsode who specializes in reciting Homer. He is rather like a rock star in ancient Athens. Plato, however, is as suspicious of Ion as many present-day political commentators are suspicious of the rock stars, rap artists, and movie actors who presume to make pronouncements about current affairs.

Plato believes that the authority they have in society is ill founded, and in this particular dialogue Plato, through the character of Socrates, is out to show that the rhapsode is an exceptionally ignorant and mindless sort of person who does not deserve a hearing on matters of substance. Indeed, Plato not only attacks the rhapsode—the singer or performer of poetic texts—but he also extends his assault to the authors of those texts, including Homer. Poets in Greek society were often regarded as educators, and in his *Ion*, Plato is at pains to argue that poets should not be accepted as teachers because they have nothing to teach anyone.

In his *Republic*, Plato continues his assault on poetry and the arts. Having established in his *Hippias Major*, the first Platonic dialogue that we will examine, that beauty is beneficial pleasure, in his *Republic*, Plato demands to be shown what benefit poetry, and by extension the arts, can provide for the commonwealth. In his *Republic*, his arguments heat up, surpassing the intensity of his *Ion*. In the *Republic*, Plato goes further than merely alleging that poets have nothing to teach; he charges that what they pretend to teach and the way they present it are literally dangerous to the well-being of society. Thus, he says in Book 10 of his *Republic* that unless the friends of poetry can rebut the charges he has leveled at it, we have grounds to censor artists and even to banish some of them from society.

One way of understanding Aristotle's *Poetics* is to regard it as taking up Plato's challenge to meet the objections against poetry that he so forcefully advanced in his *Republic*. In order to do this, Aristotle argues that poetry, or at least tragic poetry, does have something to teach its audiences. Narrative, Aristotle argues, is an instrument for obtaining knowledge about human affairs. In order to sustain this claim, Aristotle embarks on a penetrating analysis of the nature of narrative—indeed, one of the most important and foundational discussions of narrative in the Western tradition. Furthermore, in opposition to Plato, through this discussion, Aristotle, in effect, justifies the narratives of the poets by connecting them to knowledge.

One of Plato's most striking objections to poetry is that it excites the emotions, arousing them to a pitch that is bad for society in general. The emotional intensity of poetry, like the emotional intensity of rock music according to some contemporary commentators, threatens social stability and for that reason, Plato maintains, it should be regulated, if not suppressed. Aristotle, in contrast, contends that there is a positive way in which the emotions are engaged by tragic poetry. For, according to Aristotle, poetry not only arouses emotions but also leads to the *catharsis* thereof, a process that putatively has an altogether good effect on audiences.

Thus, Aristotle, the student of Plato, agrees in part with his mentor—that is, he belongs to the school of Plato—in that he believes that poetry incites the emotions. *But* he argues that Plato's analysis is incomplete since poetry does something salutary to the emotions in addition to exciting them. Consequently, for Aristotle, it would appear, Plato's argument for the suppression of poetry in particular and art in general is too hasty a conclusion. For poetry not only arouses the passions but also causes catharsis in audiences—that is to say, it purges or purifies or clarifies the emotion that it ignites and this is to the good of society in general. So, Aristotle's argument implicitly rejects Plato's brief for the repression of poetry and the arts.

After discussing Plato and Aristotle, we turn to the philosophy of art in the modern period. One thing that is striking about the discussion of art in the ancient period is the emphasis that the ancients place on the relation of art to knowledge. Their debate, in large measure, is over whether art yields knowledge. In this, their preoccupations may strike you as missing something important. They do not seem overly concerned with the aesthetic pleasure to be had from artworks. They are primarily concerned with the utilitarian value of art. So obsessed with the use value of art are they that they pay scant attention to its aesthetic value.

That focus, however, changes dramatically as we shift our attention to the modern period. For questions of aesthetic pleasure are central to the writings of Hutcheson, Hume, and Kant. Hutcheson and Hume address it in terms of the notion of beauty, whereas Kant adds the broader concept of the aesthetic to the conversation.

The first modern philosopher in our review is Francis Hutcheson. Hutcheson is interested in the nature of beauty which he claims is really sensation of disinterested pleasure that we undergo when we are moved by what he calls the compound ratio of unity in diversity in stimuli that range from artworks to landscapes to mathematical formulae. The notion of *disinterestedness* that Hutcheson defends remains a bone of contention into the present. Many politically disposed artists regard this idea as it figures in contemporary calls for a return to beauty for its own sake as a repudiation of socially engaged art.

Hume doesn't spend so much time analyzing beauty. He agrees that beauty is connected with subjectively felt pleasure. But he is vexed by the implications of this. He worries about a problem that is related to the kind of subjective characterization of beauty that had been articulated by people like Hutcheson. Namely, if beauty is reducible to a sensation (of pleasure) that we feel as a result of encountering an object—if it has grounds in nothing more than our feelings—how can our judgments that this or that object is beautiful be in any way objective? That in which each of us takes or feels pleasure is highly variable, isn't it? Our taste appears very subjective—don't people say that there is no disputing judgments of taste? And yet, on the other hand, we do *argue* about our judgments of taste, and that suggests that we think that there are objective standards of taste—objective standards that we can use to adjudicate our diverging and often conflicting judgments about beauty.

So, according to Hume, we find ourselves in a paradoxical situation. On the one hand, we think that our judgments of taste are subjective and yet on the other hand, we behave as though we think they are objective. Hume tries to resolve this paradox; he tries to explain how our judgments of taste—our judgments that such and such is beautiful—can be objectively grounded at the same time that they are rooted in subjective feelings of pleasure.

In his *Critique of Judgment*, Immanuel Kant returns to this problem from a different direction. Exploiting the concept of disinterestedness that we encountered in Hutcheson, Kant proposes an ingenious theory of the way in which we can make judgments that this or that is beautiful in what he calls a universal voice—that is, in a way that our pronouncement commands the assent or agreement of everyone. For Hume, the objectivity of aesthetic judgments or judgments of taste is grounded in the joint verdicts of what he calls Ideal Critics. That is, when you and I disagree about whether a particular painting is beautiful, what we need to do is to compare our judgments with the verdict that these Ideal Critics endorse. If your judgment more closely approximates the verdicts of the Ideal Critics, you are right; if my judgment converges on the views of the Ideal Critics, then I am right.

But on Kant's theory, we have no need for recourse to critics, ideal or otherwise. Kant maintains that we can issue objective judgments of taste—aesthetic judgments—without adverting to Ideal Critics. Instead, under the appropriate conditions, aesthetic judgments can be objectively grounded in our own experience. But how can one be justified objectively in alleging that something is beautiful solely on the basis of a single response, namely my own? We certainly cannot make objective empirical judgments on the basis of a single case. So, the burden of Kant's enormously elaborate *Critique of Judgment* is to show how on the basis of my experience of a sunrise, I am entitled to say that the sunrise is beautiful, not just for me, but for everyone else as well.

Hegel is a successor of Kant's in the tradition of German philosophy. He rejects the Kantian approach for reasons that many contemporaries find sympathetic. For, whereas Kant appears to de-emphasize the relation of aesthetics to ideas and concepts, Hegel takes the relationships between these factors to be central. Hegel develops a conception of art that considers art to be the sensuous embodiment or manifestation of ideas and concepts. In this, Hegel considers art—or at least art of certain periods—to be on a par with religion and philosophy in terms of the communication of knowledge, whereas Kant tends to set off pure aesthetic experience as a realm apart.

For Hegel, art is a matter of sensuous or concrete universals—ideas and concepts embodied in sensuous forms. In this way art contributes to cognition whereas Kant seems to contrast pure aesthetic experience with cognition properly so called.

Whereas on the Kantian-derived approach, especially as it has been traditionally developed, art is compartmentalized—set off from other precincts of society—the Hegelian approach attempts to situate art as an integrated, functional contribution to the life of the culture.

Hegel's most determined but unsuccessful rival was Arthur Schopenhauer. Returning to the Kantian perspective and mixing it with ideas drawn from Plato and various traditions of Indian philosophy, Schopenhauer argues that art is important because it lifts us out of everyday life and mundane human affairs. Art is not valuable because of its contribution to social life but as an avenue of escape from all-too-human concerns and desires. Indeed, in Schopenhauer we find articulated the notion that the point of art is to afford aesthetic experience understood as something valuable in itself, divorced from the claims of life.

Schopenhauer's emphasis on art as a means to transcend the realm of utility and desire—Schopenhauer's psychologized version of Kant's notion of disinterestedness—moreover, had profound influence on twentieth-century aesthetics, particularly on the development of formalism. Clive Bell's book *Art* is perhaps the clearest statement of this tendency.[4] Combining Kant's suggestion that the aesthetic response is primarily one to the form of the work with Schopenhauer's claim that such a response lifts us out of the flow of life, Bell hypothesizes that in virtue of its form—what he calls its significant form—an artwork engenders a specific emotion in percipients, namely, the aesthetic emotion which itself is valuable for its own sake in a way that transcends mundane preoccupations by transporting us to an ecstatic realm.

For Bell, the essence of art is form, or, as he puts it, significant form. This feature of artworks raises an aesthetic emotion in spectators, an emotion, as Hutcheson and Kant would have agreed, is marked by disinterestedness. For Bell, art of necessity stands outside the nexus of utilitarian or use value. Artworks are valuable in virtue of their form and for the disinterested aesthetic emotion or experience the form is said to provoke. Bell's position amounts to a powerful statement of the view that is sometimes referred to as *art for art's sake*. That is, art is not valuable because it produces knowledge, or because it provides moral education, or because it purges, releases, or purifies ordinary emotions. Rather it is valuable for its own sake and for the uniquely aesthetic feelings it is believed to engender.

According to Bell, that which makes something art is its possession of form or, at least, of significant form. Significant form is a feature that anything must have

---

4. Some might object to the inclusion of Bell in a book like this. I have several reasons for including him. First, he is typically among the readings assigned in introductory courses in the philosophy of art where those readings constitute something like the memory and, in that sense, the subconscious of Anglophone philosophers of art. One of the reasons for that is that he gives twentieth-century philosophers one of their primary directives: define art. Moreover, as I will argue, Bell represents an important turning point; through his adaptation of certain of Schopenhauer's ideas, he paves the way for the theory of art's autonomy.

if it is to count as an artwork rather than something else. In technical language, significant form provides a necessary and sufficient condition for the status of artwork. But this conception of art, generally called formalism, has never gone uncontested. Even in the early twentieth century, there were dissenters.

One line of dissent notes that formalism does not appear to capture what is arresting about much art. For what seems essential to most, if not all, art is not its display of form, but what it expresses. Art, on this view, is not merely a vehicle for exhibiting formal properties; rather, it is primarily a vehicle for expression. But what gets expressed? The most common candidates on this view are emotions, feelings, points of view, and the inner experiences of the artists.

Because of its emphasis on expression, this philosophical persuasion gets called the expression theory of art. Throughout the first half of the twentieth century, these theories were probably the most popular ones. Indeed, it is probably still the most commonly held view of art among most people. Certainly, the images of the artist that we most frequently encounter in popular fictions like movies are underwritten by variations on the expression theory of art.

Most often artists are portrayed as trying to get in touch with and then expressing their own unique feelings, emotions, and visions. These popular images of the artist are arguably the residue of expression theories of art and the romantic philosophies that presaged them. They are an example of the trickle-down effect mentioned earlier, whereby philosophical ideas seep into the common understanding.

Expression theories of art are rivals to formalist theories. We will examine expression theories before we explore Bell's *Art* because historically, they arrive on the scene earlier.

The expression theory of art that we will discuss in the penultimate chapter of this volume is the one developed by the great Russian novelist Leo Tolstoy in his book *What Is Art?*[5] Tolstoy locates the essence of art in the artist's expression of his or her own feelings, emotions, and points of view. But Tolstoy requires that the artist not only express her emotions, but also that she arouse the self-same feeling she has undergone in her audience. Tolstoy argues that a genuine work of art not only articulates the artist's emotional experience but also transfers or communicates a comparable affective experience to its audiences. For Tolstoy, art properly so called communicates feeling. Moreover, good art is that which communicates the very best or most progressive feelings to its audiences. Thus, where we began

---

5. Some may object to the inclusion of Tolstoy in this survey on the grounds that he is not a philosopher. This seems unjust to me. If you read his book, you are struck by his comprehensive command of the relevant philosophical literature and of the penetration of some of his criticism of it. Moreover, he is a representative of a major type of art theory, the expression theory, which remains extremely popular, especially among art lovers. Indeed, I will argue even something like his version of the expression may still have resonance among political progressives. And finally, like Bell, he appears regularly on introductory reading lists and merits interrogation for that reason.

with Plato, who suspects that all art is a detriment to society because it arouses the emotions, we find a contrasting view in Tolstoy, who, insofar as he is committed to the existence of socially progressive feelings, endorses art as a good that contributes to forging a bond of solidarity between people, exactly the sort of worldly function rejected by Bell.

Thus, the book ends with a face-off between Tolstoy and Bell, between expressionism and formalism, or, more broadly speaking, between the view that art is heteronomous—that is, an altogether embedded and inseparable part of its environing culture—versus the view that art is autonomous—utterly separate and distinct from every other social practice.

An Underling Narrative

Previously, I suggested a series of different ways in which various of the texts under consideration were in conversation with certain other texts in my canon of classics. But there is also a larger conversation that I think echoes throughout the volume. It concerns the just mentioned dialectic between the heteronomy versus the autonomy of art. Virtually every philosopher in the West from Plato through the early modern period, including Hume, thinks of art as connected to cultural interests like ethics. What begins to emerge gradually in the early modern period—with the appearance of what has been called the Modern System of the Arts[6] and the notion of aesthetics[7]—is a view that art is a realm unto itself, apart from the claims of utility, morality, politics, religion and so forth, a realm of art for its own sake.

This view comes together in stages. The notion that aesthetic pleasure is disinterested is championed by Hutcheson and Kant, who believe that disinterestedness is a condition for aesthetic pleasure. That is, in order to judge an artwork as a source of free beauty, one has to have a disinterested attitude toward it. However, in the hands of various subsequent commentators, like Schopenhauer and Bell, disinterestedness becomes the very purpose for experiencing art, not merely a condition for experiencing it as beautiful. That is, the purpose of art is to free us—to liberate us—from the practical and moral demands of everyday life.

So, there is a narrative that underpins this book. The beginning of the book charts a time from when it went virtually without saying that art was embedded in social life to the time of the emergence of the view that art is autonomous. The complications that take shape as the story moves forward then take note of the

---

6. Paul Oskar Kristeller, "The Modern System of the Arts," *Journal of the History of Ideas* 12 (1951): 496–527.

7. J. Colin McQuillan, *Early Modern Aesthetics* (Lanham, MD: Rowman and Littlefield, 2016).

appearance of resistance to the rise of the affirmation of autonomy in the work of Hegel and Tolstoy.

Nevertheless, I conclude this telling of the tale with Bell not because the kind of autonomism he defends, namely formalism, has conquered but because I think it sets the stage for what will be one of the most important debates in the philosophy of art in our own day, the debate between the autonomists and the heteronomists of which autonomism has, so to speak, a head start.

To a certain extent, this book is a history of the philosophy of art. However, it should not be mistaken as having the same aim as Paul Guyer's recent, magisterial *A History of Modern Aesthetics*.[8] For one thing, this book discusses the ancients, not only the moderns. Furthermore, Guyer's book is far more comprehensive. If he doesn't cover every modern philosopher of art, there aren't many he misses. My account is far more selective. Also, a different dialectic underlies Guyer's narrative than underlies mine. He contrasts philosophers who place the value of art in cognition with those who place it in play. I emphasize the contest between autonomy and heteronomy. I do this not only because I find Guyer's use of the antipode of play a bit too broad, slippery, and sometimes strained, but also because there is a moral to my story: that by the time Bell publishes *Art*, Anglophone philosophy is on the brink of what will become the continuing debate over the value of art—that of whether it is autonomous or enmeshed in the cognitive, moral, historical, spiritual, and political life of society.

My Agenda

This book is a selective history of the philosophy of art in the West.

History, it goes without saying, is retrospective. We write about the past from the perspective of the present, which, of course, was in the future of the historical figures we go on about. We know something they did not, namely how their contributions would impact what was to come—the future us. So, when we write about the past, we typically emphasize those aspects that are relevant to our own present situation. We weave a narrative of how things have evolved to get us to where we are now. Thus, we choose episodes that we think belong to our narrative in terms of what we think got us to where we are now.

And that is how this book was constructed.

As I see it, two major issues in the philosophy of art in the last decades of the twentieth century and the first decades of the twenty-first century are (1) determining whether art is an autonomous practice or a heteronomous practice, and

---

8. Paul Guyer, *A History of Modern Aesthetics*, 3 vols. (Cambridge: Cambridge University Press, 2015).

(2) answering the question "What is art?" Moreover, these two questions are often interrelated.[9]

Autonomism, as articulated by Bell, is one way of getting a particularly tidy theory of what art is. For autonomism separates art from everything else by definition. Thus, autonomism has been a constant source of temptation for subsequent philosophers interested in finding a theory of art that would cleave art from every other social practice. One way of reading the narrative in this book is as an archaeology of the emergence of autonomism. However, that would be an incomplete reading, inasmuch as the alternative view, including coverage of resistance to autonomism, is also chronicled. In that respect, what I have excavated are the earliest strata of the major debates now pressing philosophers of art in the Anglophone tradition—not only the question of what constitutes art, but the relation, if any, between art, cognition, morality, politics, history, and so on.

The works canvassed in this book have been elevated to the status of classics in virtue of their formative influence on philosophical discourse today. They have not only set the stage for our debates. They contain insights that may even help us resolve them.

---

9. See my "Beauty and the Genealogy of Art Theory," in Noël Carroll, *Beyond Aesthetics* (Cambridge: Cambridge University Press, 2001), 20–40.

Chapter 1

Plato's *Hippias Major*, *Ion*, and Books 2, 3, and 10 of the *Republic*

It is in the work of Plato—a citizen of the Greek city-state of Athens in the fifth century BCE—that we find the first sustained writings on the philosophy of what we call art and related issues of aesthetics in the Western tradition.[1] In the course of his writing, Plato addresses questions about the nature of poetry, painting, representation, the pleasures to be had from art, and the role that art should play in the good society. In this chapter, we will survey Plato's views about art and beauty, beginning with his early dialogues, notably the *Hippias Major* and *Ion*, and then proceeding to what is probably his most famous dialogue, the *Republic*, and to what it has to say about art (primarily about the art of poetry).

The *Hippias Major*

Many scholars consider Plato's *Hippias Major* to be one of his earliest dialogues. It is relevant to the philosophy of art because it is an investigation into the nature of *kalon*, a Greek word that is often translated into English as "beautiful." Of course, for centuries, even millennia, the concepts of art and beauty went hand in hand in the Western tradition. In French, the group of arts that we consider to be the Arts with a capital *A* (poetry or literature, drama, music, painting, sculpture, and dance) was called the *beaux arts*, that is, the "beautiful arts." In the eighteenth century, it was held that membership in this constellation of the fine arts, properly so called, required that the art form in question imitate the *beautiful* in nature. The association of art and beauty ran so deep in Western culture that in the beginning of the twentieth century, many viewers denied that the works of modern art, like the creations of the German expressionists, the cubists, and the Dadaists, could be art at all on the grounds that the works in question were not beautiful. Thus, the question of "what is beautiful" has a bearing on important debates in the history of the philosophy of art.

Plato's *Hippias Major* is not a piece of dry argumentation. Like most of Plato's other writings, it is set out characteristically in the form of a dialogue with the character of Socrates, Plato's actual teacher, representing Plato's side of the debate.

---

1. Plato did not have our concept of art, but rather wrote about various arts—notably, poetry, drama, painting, and music.

One could imagine this dialogue mounted like a play in a theater. Moreover, the kind of theater we find staged in the *Hippias Major* is comedy. Socrates and his interlocutor, or rather, straight man, the sophist Hippias, play roles reminiscent of the characters in the Greek tradition of what is called Old Comedy, the comedy of authors like Aristophanes.

For Plato, the target of comedy is vice, notably that of self-unawareness. That is, we laugh at people who fail to realize the Delphic adage—"know thyself"—and who instead deceive themselves, imagining that they are smarter than they are, or stronger, or taller, or more attractive. Hippias is full of himself. He is, not to put too fine a point on it, a know-it-all. He is boastful and swaggering about his abilities, and a substantial part of the dialogue involves taking Hippias down more than one peg and unmasking his foolish overestimation of himself. Self-centered, obstinate, and unenlightened, Hippias patronizes Socrates, failing to acknowledge that Socrates has the upper hand in every exchange.

Hippias is what in Greek comedy is called an *alazon* or boaster, whereas Socrates is an *eiron*, an ironic man whose wit often takes the form of saying one thing while meaning its opposite. For example, when Socrates commends sophists for putting fine thoughts in fine words, the reader gradually comes to recognize that the excessiveness of Socrates's compliments signals the degree of his disdain for sophists like Hippias. For, as we will see, in their pretension to tutor virtue through rhetoric for money, Plato believes that they are false teachers, as unworthy to perform the role of educators of the Greeks as Plato will later argue that the poets are.

Strictly speaking, the topic of this dialogue is *kalon*, a Greek word which, as mentioned previously, can be translated as "beautiful." But *kalon* can also be rendered as the *fine*, or the *excellent*, the *admirable*, the *noble*, the *useful*, or any of a wider range of terms of praise. Since Socrates's aim in the dialogue is to define *kalon* and since *kalon* can be used in various different ways, the task of getting straight about the meaning of *kalon* can become quite complicated. Nor can it be simplified by supposing *kalon* to mean nothing more than "the beautiful" in English, since, in English, the notion of the beautiful is almost as diverse as the word *kalon* in Greek.

In English, "beautiful" can refer to that which pleases the eyes and/or the ears, as do Brad Pitt and Angelina Jolie and the song *Amazing Grace*. But beautiful can also mean "well done," and this usage would often diverge from the previous sense, as when the director of a horror movie commends the makeup artist by saying of the zombie's putrefying wounds, "beautiful," or when we shout "beautiful" after one of our teammates executes a bone-crushing tackle. And, like *kalon*, "beautiful" in English can simply mean *excellent*, as occurs when, after you get a huge tax return, you exclaim "Excellent!" With so many different possible senses of *kalon* and "beautiful" in play, it is easy, as we shall see, to get bogged down. Indeed, by the end of the dialogue, Socrates himself is not even convinced that the definition he ends up defending is the correct one.

The dialogue begins with Hippias bragging about how busy he is—how he's so much in demand. His extreme vanity marks him immediately as an *alazon*. Throughout the dialogue, he serves as Socrates's comic butt. Hippias is so enamored of himself that he fails to recognize that Socrates is talking about himself when he, Socrates, complains about that abusive fellow who is always badgering him for a precise definition of *kalon*. Furthermore, Hippias appears to have no idea of who Socrates is—not a glimmering of Socrates's reputation for tying his interlocutors into conceptual knots in conversations like the one in which Hippias and Socrates are now engaged.

Undoubtedly you are wondering why Hippias deserves the merciless ridicule that Socrates and Plato heap upon him. As a sophist, he is a person who teaches others for money. This includes teaching people to speak in public—in particular, teaching them to speak persuasively. A sophist is a rhetorician who trains his clients how to represent their cases in courts and assemblies. Because they are in it for the money, the sophist will take on any customers, even if their case is disreputable, and the sophist will help those clients prove anything by means of whatever rhetorical tricks are available. In short, the sophist is willing to supply the student who is paying him with the forensic strategies, whether fair or foul, that the student needs to win; the sophist doesn't care about teaching what is true. And this appalls Socrates and Plato as philosophers—that is, as lovers of knowledge (i.e., justified, *true* belief, according to Plato's *Theaetetus*).

Socrates and Plato maintain that teachers should teach what is true, not what gains rhetorical advantage. Thus, they do not think that sophists are real teachers, although that is how the sophists advertise themselves. So, Socrates and Plato strive to unmask sophists like Hippias as hypocrites. They distrust the sophists, and as we will see, they also distrust the poets, because they think the sophists and the poets alike pander to what people want and not what they need—which is first and foremost the truth.

One extratextual indication that Socrates holds the sophists in particularly low esteem is his emphasis on the reluctance of the Spartans to hire Hippias as an educator. This signals Socrates's contempt for sophists like Hippias inasmuch as Plato is known to have had a very high regard for Spartan society, which was organized like an army and which some have said was a model for Plato's ideal Republic. Consequently, that the Spartans would not purchase Hippias's services as an educator and that Socrates makes such a big deal about it is a telling wink to the reader that Plato/Socrates thinks this guy is damaged goods.

The dialogue begins at a leisurely pace. It introduces Hippias, lets us know who he is, and does a nice job establishing how conceited he is. For example, Socrates tricks Hippias into boasting about how he and other contemporary sophists are superior to the wise men of the past. Hippias reveals how shallow he is by claiming his superiority in terms of the amount of money he rakes in. This leads to the discussion of the Spartans and their lack of interest in Hippias's services. In this section (line 284d), Socrates introduces the notion that a genuine law is one that *benefits* the people. This will be important at the end of the dialogue when Socrates defines beauty or *kalon* as *beneficial pleasure* since it offers insight into half of that definition.

The discussion of Sparta ends with Socrates leveling a telling putdown at the expense of the ever-oblivious Hippias. Hippias remembers that the Spartans are willing to pay him to do one thing—recite stories about the past. To this, Socrates dryly replies, "Oh, that's right, I forgot, you have the art of memory. So, I understand the Spartans enjoy you predictably, because you know a lot of things and they use you the way children use old ladies to tell stories for pleasure" (286a). Clearly, this is intended as an insult; its sexism notwithstanding, Socrates is saying, "Oh yeah, about all you have to offer are little bedtime stories."

The real subject of the dialogue only emerges around 286b–286d, when Socrates says, "Teach me enough about what the fine (*kalon*) is itself and try to answer me with as much precision as possible." Socrates claims to need to know this because an aggressive interlocutor embarrassed him recently by demanding a definition of the fine in a highly insulting way (286c). This is a superb piece of Socratic irony because we know—although Hippias never seems to get it—that that abusive interlocutor, later re-identified as one of Socrates's relatives, is none other than Socrates himself.

Even if the topic of the fine is not introduced explicitly into the dialogue until we are approximately five and a half pages into the dialogue, its entrée has been prepared for from the beginning of the dialogue by means of certain literary devices, the leading one of which is the virtually obsessive use of the notion of the *fine* from the first sentence onward—recall: "Here comes Hippias *fine* and wise!" The patent overuse of the idea of the *fine* makes it ripe for discussion. For, if you need to use the concept so frequently, then it appears to be advisable to get a handle on it.

Hippias lets on that this won't be very difficult. Again, he's out to lunch.

Thus begins the interrogation of the concept of *kalon*—the structure of the rest of the dialogue being a series of proposals about the nature of *kalon* in which all but the last one is rejected dialectically by Socrates in argument after argument.[2]

What it is that Socrates wants specifically from Hippias is a definition of *kalon*—the beautiful, the excellent, and/or the fine. That is, Socrates is asking, "What is *kalon*—what is the fine, the excellent, the beautiful?" But this question is somewhat ambiguous, and Hippias misunderstands it. Hippias at first seems to think that Socrates is asking for a list of the beautiful or fine things; so he says women, mares, lyres, and even pots and kitchen utensils, although Hippias is not

---

2. It is worth noting here that since *kalon* can mean not only "beautiful" but "noble," in the moral sense, Plato's notion of beauty would appear to be opposite the influential view of free beauty that we will encounter in the chapter on Kant. For Plato, unlike Kant, beauty, it appears, can be connected to morality in a way that Kant and his followers would deny.

quite comfortable with saying pots can be fine. However, this is not the kind of answer that Socrates is after.

This is what nowadays we might call the extension of *the fine*—the set of all things that belong to that category. Socrates wants the intension of the concept of *the fine*, the specification of the criteria that sorts some entities rather than others into the category or set of *the fine*—that is, what we might call the *meaning* of "the fine."

Socrates attempts to express this desire to know in the following exchange:

> *Socrates*: "Then all fine things, too, are fine by the fine, isn't that so?" (287e)
> *Hippias*: "Yes, by the fine."
> *Socrates*: ". . . by that being *something*?"

where the "something" in question is a meaning or a definition.

Hippias has a hard time getting his mind around the intellectual project Socrates is pressing on him. He persists with his list, and Socrates persists with the ironic fiction that there is some (other) really nasty guy who stands ready to eviscerate Hippias's every answer.

One argumentative strategy that Socrates levels at Hippias's use of a list as a plausible answer to his question is to note that all of the things that Hippias has listed are only fine relative to certain comparison classes. What does that mean? Well, a woman may be fine or beautiful when compared to a pot, but not when compared to the goddess Aphrodite. Even Helen of Troy, allegedly the most beautiful woman ever, is not beautiful when compared to Aphrodite. What Socrates is getting at here is this: when you define what is fine or excellent, you should tell us what it is for something to be excellent in itself, that is, non-comparatively or absolutely. One cannot answer the question of what is fine on its own terms with a list of examples that are only fine relative to certain comparisons. Socrates makes this point to Hippias by saying, "tell me what fineness is itself" (292d). That is, Socrates explains, he wants to know what property it is that, when added to something else, makes that something else fine. For example, what property do you have to add to a horse to get a fine horse, what property do you have to add to a pot to get a fine pot, and so on.

Hippias, dimwit that he is, takes Socrates's metaphor of addition here quite literally and answers "gold." Gold is what you have to add to a pot, for instance, to make it a fine pot. Socrates dismisses this proposal quickly, since there are obviously many fine things to which gold can't be added, such as fine laws.

But Hippias still doesn't understand, so he tries something else, although it is just another example. Hippias says that what is fine is a fine life, adding what he thinks goes into having a fine life. One of the things he includes in the inventory of things that make for a fine life is the ability to construct a memorial to one's parents when they die. That is part of what constitutes a fine life, perhaps along with other things, such as having children, friends, one's health, and so on.

But Socrates counters that this is clearly not a necessary condition for having a good life, since it would entail that the children of the gods cannot have a good life. For, since the gods are immortal, their children could never erect memorials for them when they die. Thus, Socrates defeats Hippias's suggestion by offering a counterexample to Hippias's idea. And, as we'll see, the counterexample technique is one that Socrates has honed to perfection.

At this point in the dialogue (around 293e), something important happens—Socrates increasingly takes over. That is, rather than relying on Hippias to propose attempted definitions of the excellent, henceforth, Socrates is going to propose the hypotheses himself. Instead of attempting to elicit definitions from Hippias, Socrates is going to introduce ideas about the nature of excellence himself and then interrogate them. This is an important transition because it marks a frequent shift in Plato's dialogues. Basically, Socrates comes to do almost all of the talking, as we'll see when we come to discuss Plato's *Republic*. And this is also what happens at the aforesaid juncture in the *Hippias Major*. Socrates proposes and criticizes a series of definitions of excellence as Hippias simply stands by and agrees with whatever Socrates says.

We will turn to those proposals shortly, but first, it is useful to say something about Socrates's method and its potential shortcomings. Some people think that the way in which Socrates argues involves a fallacy, which they call the Socratic fallacy. What is the Socratic fallacy? To explain that, first consider what Socrates's arguments presuppose. Socrates appears to believe that you cannot know that to which a concept, such as the fine or the beautiful, applies unless you know what these concepts mean—that is, unless you possess a definition of the concept. For instance, Socrates seems to think that you cannot know how to apply the concept car unless you can define what a car is. But this seems to presuppose that I can't know that something, say x, is a car without knowing the definition of a car, which, in turn, is tantamount to being in a position such that I know that I know that x is a car—that my application of the concept is correct in virtue of some definition that I know.

Yet, this strikes many philosophers as too excessive. I can know that I'm in a classroom right now without knowing that I know that I'm in a classroom. As Descartes pointed out, I may be dreaming that I'm in a classroom or that an evil genius with magical powers may be causing me to suffer the illusion that I am in a classroom when I am really somewhere else. Nevertheless, we are very often in the position to know something is the case—for example, that we're all in a classroom—while at the same time, it is not the case that we know that we know this. Second-order knowledge of this sort is too stringent to require as a condition for first-order knowledge.

With this in mind, let us return to the issue of definition. I may know that the *Mona Lisa* is a work of art without knowing that I know this in virtue of some definition of art that I possess in my cognitive stock and know to be true. Even though there may be some hard cases, in general, we are all probably pretty good at picking out works of art, but, equally, it is unlikely that many, if any, of us knows how to define art. Were Socrates here, he would deny that we know how to apply the notion of art to the pertinent works because we don't have the sort of definition that would be required for us to know that we know we are applying the concept correctly.

It is this demand for knowledge of a definition that supports our application of concepts that Socrates uses again and again against his opponents. But whether this is a reasonable expectation is open to debate since, in addition to the previous objection, it may be pointed out that we apply most of our concepts in everyday life—concepts like chair and game—without being able to formulate a strict definition of them—a point made by the twentieth-century philosopher Ludwig Wittgenstein and his followers.

Having alerted you to this issue with respect to Socrates's methodology, it is now time to return to the text and to observe that methodology in action. Socrates, as I've said, has taken over the dialogue. With respect to definitions of the fine or the beautiful, he is the proposer. And his first proposal is that what is fine is that which is appropriate (*prepon* in Greek). Something is excellent, fine, or beautiful just in case it is appropriate (290c–290e).

But no sooner does Socrates offer this definition than he rejects it. Why? Because on Socrates's view, the appropriate can *seem* to make things fine that are not really fine. For example, Julius Caesar performed certain rituals when he installed himself as the dictator of Rome. These were the appropriate rituals according to Roman custom. But Caesar's performance of these rituals, although the rituals were appropriate, was not fine or admirable because, in performing them, Caesar, in fact, was usurping the Roman Republic. He was doing something ignoble rather than something noble. That the rituals were appropriate gave his seizure of power the appearance of being excellent, yet his seizure of power was anything but excellent. Or that, at least, is the kind of thinking that leads Socrates to abandon the idea that what is excellent, fine, or beautiful is that which is appropriate.

Here, of course, you might want to object that there is a sense of the notion of *appropriateness* according to which something is appropriate just in case it really is fine and not merely seems fine. But then the definition does not appear to be particularly informative because "the appropriate" and "the fine" would be synonymous, and this would be circular—you would have to know the definition of *the fine* in order to know what is *appropriate*.

Moreover, although it is not advanced by Plato, there is another objection to thinking that the fine or the beautiful is a matter of appropriateness. We may call a sunrise fine or beautiful, but it doesn't make much sense to call a sunrise "appropriate." That is, appropriateness is too narrow a concept to cover all the cases where we think that the concepts of excellence and beauty apply. The notion of appropriateness is too tied to human social behavior, whereas there are things that are fine or beautiful—like sunrises—that are outside the realm of human social behavior.

Since appropriateness does not get Socrates an adequate definition, he tries another candidate. He proposes the useful (295c), which he then refines in terms of the idea of the beneficial. But Socrates quickly rejects that alternative. Why? To follow his reasoning, it is helpful to remember the origin of the English word "beneficial." It comes from the Latin *bene facio*, which means "to make good." If something is beneficial it is a means for producing some good. What is beneficial is a cause of what is good—it is an instrument for bringing about something good. And that is how Socrates understands what it is to be beneficial—as that which brings about goodness.

But this then prompts Socrates to the conclusion that the beneficial cannot define what is excellent. For, he argues that if the beneficial is what brings about goodness, then it is not goodness itself. But surely the fine is good. So, the fine cannot be defined by the concept of the beneficial, since what is beneficial is only a means to what is good and is not good itself. That is what Socrates is getting at when he says that the father is not the son (297b–297c).

Another way to see this is to think that there are two kinds of value—two ways in which things can be valuable. That is, there are (1) instrumental values and (2) intrinsic values. Something is instrumentally valuable because of its consequences. A mousetrap is valuable because of what it brings about. It is not valuable for itself. Something that is valuable for its own sake and not for the sake of anything else is intrinsically valuable. Good health is intrinsically valuable.

On Socrates's view, the good is valuable intrinsically. The beneficial is valuable instrumentally—it brings about the good. Socrates presupposes that the fine would belong to the category of the good and, therefore, be intrinsically valuable. Hence, since the beneficial is only instrumentally valuable, it cannot serve to define the excellent. Another candidate must be found.

Socrates's next definition accords nicely with the sense of beauty we use in English when we call Brad Pitt and Angelina Jolie beautiful people. It is what we might call the "aesthetic sense of beauty," where *aesthetic* means something like "pertaining to the senses." At 297e, Socrates suggests that the beautiful is "whatever makes us glad, not with all the pleasures, but just through hearing and sight." The beautiful, in other words, is that which provides pleasure to vision and audition—that which gives us delight or causes joy simply by our looking at it or hearing it. The beautiful is what is good looking or good sounding—what engenders pleasure in us through sight or hearing, like the starry sky at night or Mozart's *Jupiter* Symphony.

You might think that Socrates distrusts this alternative because it is too narrow. It will not cover the full range of things that are fine or excellent. Even if it works for the beautiful in terms of beautiful people, beautiful artworks, and beautiful natural vistas, it will not apply to many other things that are fine, like fine laws. Fine laws do not cause pleasure in virtue of the way they look or sound. Nevertheless, this is not the objection Socrates raises.

Instead, he worries that this definition is arbitrary. What justifies limiting the beautiful to only two senses—vision and audition? What about taste, what about smell, what about touch? That is, what makes the pleasures of just some of the senses fine, but not the pleasures delivered by other senses?

By the way, the association of the beautiful with sight and hearing runs deep in Western culture. Philosophers continuing into the nineteenth century treat vision and audition as privileged senses. Some, like Hegel, think that taste, smell, and touch are less theoretical than sight and hearing. And later, when we discuss Kant, we'll see that his distinction between the agreeable and the beautiful is drawn in a way that favors vision and audition. My point here is not to endorse the distinction between seeing and hearing, on the one hand, and the rest of the senses on the other, but only to note that the division is long-standing, perhaps due to the traditional conviction that sight and hearing are supposedly more closely connected to the ideational aspects of our makeup than are the other senses, or, perhaps relatedly, because sight and hearing operate at a distance whereas the other senses involve direct, intimate physical (fleshy) contact with their objects. Moreover, the theme of disparaging the flesh will continue in Western culture abetted by certain interpretations of Christianity.

In any event, Socrates is dissatisfied with the definition of the beautiful in terms of that which causes pleasure through sight and sound.[3] So he makes one last attempt. He hypothesizes that the fine is correlated to beneficial pleasure. He seems happy with the idea that the fine is somehow connected to bestowing pleasure—perhaps because pleasure is something that we appear to value intrinsically. But pleasure is not enough to define the fine, since not all the things that can be pleasurable are excellent. Taking methamphetamine might give you pleasure, but it would not be fine; in fact, it would be bad because overuse of it would

---

3. Socrates reaches this conclusion after a complicated argument that goes like this: because other senses give rise to pleasure, it cannot be by being a particular sense that a sense is the source of beauty. Thus, it cannot be by seeing that something is beautiful. Ditto for hearing. So, it must be the combination of seeing and hearing that makes for beauty. But Socrates finds absurd the notion that the conjunction of seeing and hearing could be beautiful while each alone is not beautiful. But is this absurd? Each stick may be weak, but when combined in a bundle, the bundle may be strong. And, in any case, Socrates seems to be overlooking the possibility that something is beautiful if it is the product of hearing or seeing or the combination of hearing and seeing where this disjunction is inclusive rather than exclusive. Socrates would probably respond that focusing on hearing and seeing to the exclusion of the other senses is arbitrary; however, there may be a nonarbitrary distinction to be drawn between these two senses and the rest, perhaps in terms of the way in which these two senses typically involve appreciable bodily distance, whereas the others do not.

compromise your health. So, Socrates has to figure out how to qualify "pleasure" in his definition so that the definition will apply to all and only the excellent.

At this point, Socrates returns to the idea he rejected earlier of the beneficial, which we might understand as what is useful. Thus, Socrates commits himself to the definition that x is fine if and only if it is pleasurable and useful. A horse is fine just in case it is both a source of pleasure and is useful as well.

Hippias thinks that this nails it. Socrates, on the other hand, seems a bit worried. He voices his apprehension that that abusive interlocutor will return to hector him.

Although he isn't so clear about the basis of his anxiety here, perhaps it has to do with the problem broached earlier about the beneficial being only instrumentally valuable. Undoubtedly, Socrates would prefer to avoid altogether mixing up the fine with instrumental value. But, on the other hand, by including pleasure in his formula, he would appear to have made contact with something that is intrinsically valuable and, therefore, his definition does meet a desideratum that he feels any definition of the fine must respect. Because of this, he appears willing to live with the definition of *kalon* as beneficial or useful pleasure.

Moreover, as we'll see, this notion plays a very important role in the *Republic*, where Socrates lays down the requirement that if the exiled artists ever expect to be allowed to return to the ideal city, their works must be shown to be "beneficial as well as enjoyable" (*Republic*, 607e). Thus, despite the nervousness Socrates exhibits about the definition of *kalon* at the end of the *Hippias Major*, he does not abandon it—maybe because of the work he intends for it further down the line.

Furthermore, it is very significant for the history of the philosophy of art that Socrates does not segregate beauty in a purely aesthetic realm that is ontologically distinct from morality and use, since this provides a telling contrast to much modern philosophy. In this, perhaps Socrates is responding to the multiple meanings already implicit in *kalon* which can mean the *excellent* and the *fine* (in the moral sense) and *useful* and *beneficial* (in the instrumental sense) as well as the *beautiful*.

Plato and the Poets: A Preview

Earlier, I identified Plato as the first philosopher of art. Yet perhaps the operative preposition here should not be *of* art but *against* art. That is, Plato's philosophy *of* art reads more like the case of philosophy *against* art, most particularly against poetry or literature, with glancing barbs thrown at painting as well. Through Plato's writings (e.g., *Republic*, 607 b), we learn that there is an ancient quarrel between poetry and philosophy (although some commentators suspect Plato of opportunistically attributing longevity to a debate that he himself initiated).

Plato thinks that poetry and art are dangerous and that they need to be censored, if not banished altogether from the good city. However, in order to criticize poetry and art, Plato needs to say what they are, and he also must be able to isolate those of their *essential* features that he believes to be dangerous and misleading. Thus, for these reasons, he backs into a philosophy of art, although he comes not to praise art but to bury it.

In order to understand Plato's *Ion* and the pertinent sections of his *Republic*, it is useful to begin by explaining what is at stake, from Plato's point of view, in this alleged quarrel between philosophy and poetry. Plato's philosophy of art is not detached or academic; it is engaged and committed. A great deal rides on it for Plato. In both the *Ion* and the *Republic*, Plato is at pains to prove that poetry, and by extension what we would call art, is not a source of genuine knowledge. The major theme of the *Ion* is that neither the poet nor the rhapsode really knows anything. Why is this issue so important for Plato?

Here it is important to recall the status of the poet and poetry in Greek society. Poets, especially Homer, were called the educators of the Greeks (*Republic*, 606e). This is what especially rankled Plato since Plato thought that philosophers, not poets, should be the educators of society. Thus, the supposedly ancient quarrel between poetry and philosophy concerns authority—who should the Greeks look to as teachers: Homer or Socrates, poets or philosophers? Socrates, of course, had been Plato's teacher. And what was good for Plato, Plato prescribes for everyone else.

It may sound strange to our contemporary ears that poets were ever considered for the role of educators. But here it is important to remember the place of poetry, especially that of Homer, in Greek culture. Poetry, notably oral poetry, was the primary means of acculturating citizens. The Greeks treated Homer and Hesiod in the way that Jewish culture treated the Bible, and the way Christian culture later treated the New Testament. They read portions of it aloud and commented on it. Language and reading were taught through poetic texts. When a topic for discussion arose—from medicine to charioteering—one first recalled what Homer had said of it. For entertainment, people might read poetry to each other at home as we might watch TV, or they might attend poetry performances as we might go out to the movies. Poetry was a primary source of social information in Greek life. And just as contemporary intellectuals bewail the fact that TV or the blogosphere rather than themselves are the "educators" of contemporary industrialized societies, philosophers, like Plato, resented the influence that the popular culture of their day—namely, poetry—exerted on their fellow citizens.

In Plato's writings on art, the recurrent theme is that poets do not really know anything. This is connected to the question of whether poets should be the educators of the Greeks in a fairly straightforward way. For if the poets truly know nothing, then obviously they have nothing to teach. In Book 10 of Plato's *Republic*, we come across the line that we are "sometimes told that they [the poets] understand not only all technical matters but also all about human conduct and religion." But note that the crucial word here is *told*. It signals that people *say* that the poets have this authority, this knowledge, but it further insinuates that even though people say this, it is not really true. Throughout these dialogues, starting with *Ion*, Plato argues that poets do not have the authority to be the educators of the Greeks because they lack the requisite knowledge or mastery. Ion, we will see, does not really have mastery of any of the professions or skills about which Homer writes, nor, Plato believes, does Homer, himself. And, of course, if poets lack the requisite knowledge or mastery, it makes no sense to treat them as educators of the Greeks or of anyone else.

Moreover, if poets lack the capacity to be the legitimate educators of the Greeks, the question naturally arises as to who is left to fill this role. In the course of these Platonic dialogues, perhaps needless to say, it becomes painfully clear that the answer is *philosophers*. That is, the subtext that underlies Plato's dialogues about the philosophy of art is that there is a rivalry between poets and philosophers for the coveted title of the educator of society, and the conclusion that Plato reaches is that the title belongs to the philosophers. In short, we might read these dialogues as a protracted nominating speech, albeit one of self-nomination.

Furthermore, although the argument against poetry is generally conducted in terms of every sort of knowledge, Plato, through Socrates, makes very clear that the education that most concerns them is moral knowledge. In *Ion*, Socrates notes that what Homer writes about most is "how people deal with each other and men" (*Ion*, 531c). Thus, it is the poet's presumption to teach ethics that most vexes Socrates, and it is Plato's contention that that role belongs to the philosopher.

Throughout, there is an implicit master argument that underlies the *Ion* and the *Republic* (especially Book 10). Stated formulaically, it looks like this:

(1) Either the poets (including rhapsodes like Ion) or the philosophers should be the legitimate educators of the Greeks. (There are, of course, other competitors, such as sophists and rhetoricians, but Socrates eliminates these possibilities in other dialogues.)

(2) Whoever is the legitimate educator of the Greeks must have genuine knowledge. (That is, in order to teach, you need to have something—obviously knowledge—to teach.)

(3) The poets do not have genuine knowledge of anything. (A premise to be substantiated by tons of argumentation.)

(4) Therefore, the poets are not the legitimate educators of the Greeks.

(5) Therefore, philosophers are the legitimate educators of the Greeks.

This might be called Plato's master argument against poetry. It approaches the question of the value of poetry solely in cognitive terms—in terms of questions of knowledge. This may seem peculiar; however, remember that Plato's analysis of poetry occurs within the context of the question of who should be society's teacher. And where the context is that of education, it would seem natural that knowledge—particularly *teachable* knowledge—be the appropriate measure of value.

The energy of these Platonic dialogues about poetry is channeled toward dislodging poets from their role as educators of the Greeks—and to installing philosophers in their place. Moreover, by the end of these dialogues—in Book 10 of the *Republic*—we will see that the poets have not only been disenfranchised as the educators of the Greeks, but even more radically, Plato is prepared to argue that poets, or at least some of them, should be excluded from society altogether.

Here it is tempting to interpret Plato's motives as at least partially tinged with a desire for vengeance. For Plato, it's personal. For Athenian society, abetted by poets like Aristophanes, who satirized Socrates in his comedy *Clouds*, put Socrates on trial and condemned him to death by ingesting hemlock. Plato's verdict on poets, in turn, one supposes, exacts delicious retribution by consigning poets like Aristophanes to exile. Whereas the Athenians attempted to banish Socrates, Plato expels the poets whose position as cultural leaders and educators, once evacuated, can be assumed by philosophers—those whose very name means "lovers of knowledge," in contrast to the poets who, as far as Plato is concerned, could be called mere pretenders to knowledge.

Ion

The *Ion* is considered to be an early Platonic dialogue. As already indicated, the dialogue was Plato's preferred form of exposition. It involves a dramatic staging of debates in which the central figure, usually Socrates, is generally taken to reflect Plato's opinions. Socrates was a real person, Plato's teacher, whose condemnation by public trial in Athens led to his death. It is at least maliciously satisfying to imagine that Plato takes his revenge on Athenian society in dialogues like *Ion* by enabling Socrates to savage the "received wisdom" of Greek culture as represented by figures like Ion.

Ion is a rhapsode, a person who recites poetry—poetry composed by others—in public. In this, one might think of him as akin to an actor or a singer, although, unlike present-day actors and singers, the rhapsode also commented on the texts that he recited. So, in this respect, the rhapsode is not only part actor/performer but also part critic. Therefore, we may interpret Plato's arguments as applying to literary critics as well as to artists. (And thus begins the ancient quarrel between the Philosophy Department and the English Department.)

Ion's specialty is the work of Homer. Of all the Greeks, Ion is reputed to be the best singer of and commentator on the *Iliad* and the *Odyssey*. Socrates never disputes this claim, but rather repeatedly presses the question of what accounts for Ion's stellar performances. Is it based on knowledge or something else? And, if they are based on something else, exactly what? Socrates's candidate here is divine madness.

Plato's *Ion* is not simply a dry piece of argumentation; like the *Hippias Major*, it is also a piece of theater, specifically a comedy. And also, as with the *Hippias Major*, Socrates and his interlocutor play roles reminiscent of standard figures in what is called Old Comedy. For Plato, as mentioned earlier, the object of comedy is vice, particularly the vice of self-unawareness. Ion's vice is that he thinks that he is smarter than he is. He is vain with respect to his abilities, and a large part of the comedy in the dialogue involves Socrates revealing Ion's foolish overestimation of himself. Like Hippias, Ion is an *alazon*, a braggart or a boaster. Self-centered, obstinate, unenlightened, and benighted, he patronizes Socrates, unaware that Socrates is toying with him. Undoubtedly, Plato took special, diabolical delight in casting the representative of poetry in this way, since in Aristophanes's *Clouds*, a comedy that indelibly influenced Athenian views of Socrates, it was Socrates who was portrayed as the *alazon*.

In Plato's *Ion*, Socrates is not an *alazon*, but rather is again an *eiron*, a figure we defined earlier as an ironic man whose wit often takes the form of saying one thing while meaning its opposite. Early in the dialogue, Socrates says that he envies rhapsodes like Ion; by the end of the day, however, we realize that Socrates is speaking with a forked tongue, his verbal cleverness functioning to unmask Ion. That Ion is only confusedly aware of this is a further measure of his foolishness, his myopic self-unawareness, occluded, as it is, by his laughably inflated ego. Thus, Plato's assault on poetry in *Ion* is not only logical, but comic, or more exactly, wickedly satirical.

There are many arguments about several apparently different issues in *Ion*. So, it is easy to get lost in the give and take. However, despite all the subarguments and side arguments, there is a master argument here as well into which these subsidiary arguments flow. Stated schematically, Plato's master argument against Ion is this:

(1) If rhapsodes recite poetry beautifully, then that is the result of either knowledge or madness, albeit divine madness.
(2) Rhapsodes do recite poetry beautifully.
(3) The rhapsode's beautiful recitation of poetry is not the result of knowledge.
(4) Therefore, it is the result of madness, albeit divine madness.

This is the conclusion toward which all the argumentation in *Ion* is aimed. Throughout, it is accepted as a matter of fact by Socrates that rhapsodes like Ion do recite poetry beautifully; their recitations give pleasure to audition, they sound delightful. That is, the second premise of the preceding argument is taken as given. Moreover, it also seems to be the case that in the debate with Ion, the first premise exhausts all the alternative sources for the beauty of the rhapsode's performance. Consequently, it is the third premise of the argument that is the locus of controversy. Thus, it is the third premise—that the beauty of the rhapsode's performance is not based on knowledge—that the subarguments and side arguments in the text are intended to substantiate. Or, in other words, all the dialectical action is in advancing the third premise of the master argument against Ion.

The conclusion of this argument is that the origin of the rhapsode's accomplishment is madness or, more specifically, divine madness. The rhapsode is possessed by the gods whose messages he channels, like a kind of human transmitter. The rhapsode, in other words, makes no cognitive contribution of his own. Moreover, though this conclusion pertains primarily to rhapsodes, it is evident from the text that Socrates also believes that it applies to the poets who compose the text the rhapsodes recite. For, poets function as magnets in the story of divine madness. And further evidence for this elision is the seamlessness with which, throughout the dialogue, Socrates moves from discussing rhapsodes to discussing the poets the rhapsodes represent (e.g., 532d). Ion, that is, plays the role of a stalking horse for Homer, a device that Plato adopts, perhaps since it was not historically feasible to stage a debate between Socrates and Homer.

Thus, the conclusion of *Ion* is not just that the accomplishment of rhapsodes is the result of divine madness, without any cognitive contribution from the human channelers, but also that the same is the case with respect to the poets who supply the rhapsodes with their lines. Homer no less than Ion is possessed. Art, whether that of the rhapsode or the poet, is a matter of ecstasy, not cognition or knowledge. And this, of course, implicitly poses the question of whether we should entrust the education of society to such madmen.

There are several reasons to surmise that if rhapsodes and poets are conduits of the gods (or muses), they are not fit to be the educators of the Greeks.

First, teaching requires knowledge that Plato understands as justified, true belief. If the poets are merely channeling the gods, even if they believe what they are saying, they cannot justify it. So, they have no genuine knowledge to dispense. Furthermore, how can they pretend to teach anything since they know not how they came to the things they propound.

Indeed, arguably, the poets may not even be said to have beliefs—that is, things that they are prepared to assert. Why? Because the gods inspire them to say many things—some true, some false (e.g., characters in poems may contradict each other)—without giving the poets the wherewithal to say which is which.

Moreover, it cannot be by means of knowledge that the poets create their admittedly beautiful compositions because the poets do not know how to compose beautifully—they are simply channeling the gods. This, by the way, is why poetry cannot be a craft according to Plato, since, for him, a craft is a knowledge-based skill—in fact, that is why crafts are teachable. But poetry is not a craft—it's all inspiration, construed as a form of madness.

Socrates describes this madness as divine, thereby supplying Western culture with one of its leading formulas for poetic inspiration. But however flattering "divine madness" sounds, it is still *madness*. The god takes away the poet's intellect. Thus, it is hard to resist the suspicion that "divine madness" drips with irony when uttered by Socrates—that the concept is, so to say, a poisoned pawn.

Of course, nowadays, when people speak of artistic inspiration in terms of divine madness, they generally mean it to be complimentary. This is how Percy Bysshe Shelley[4] took the phrase. And in the ancient world, Greek poets began by invoking the muse, thereby ostensibly acknowledging divine provenance of their songs. But the attribution of poetry to divine madness in *Ion* scarcely seems harmless.[5] Socrates appears to be praising the rhapsode and the poet, but in context, we surmise that he is conning Ion. One reason to believe that Socrates's remarks are ironical is that Ion himself is not exactly happy with this conclusion and only accepts it grudgingly. Ion seems dimly aware that if poets lack knowledge and at best transmit mad flashes from the gods, their status will be demoted. Who would seek out madmen to be teachers?

Most of *Ion* is devoted to showing that rhapsodes—and by extension poets—lack knowledge; basically, Plato wants to prove that they do not know what they are talking about (hence, the possession metaphor). Socrates gets the first argument moving by eliciting certain admissions from Ion, almost in the way that a comic sets up a straight man. Socrates persuades Ion to agree that his beautiful recitals of Homer are based on his understanding of what Homer is talking about (530c)—that is, Ion agrees to Socrates's observation that "A rhapsode must come to present the poet's thought to his audience; and he can't do that beautifully unless he knows what the poet means." That is, Ion concedes that

(1) The rhapsode's beautiful recital of the verses is the result of his understanding of what the verses are about.

But then Ion also concedes that

(2) His understanding only extends to Homer (and not to other poets) (531a).

---

4. Parenthetically, it is worth noting that with the notion of divine madness, Plato introduces Western culture's long-standing association of artistic creativity with madness and intoxication (via alcohol or some other controlled substance). It is difficult to think of a popular movie of an artist (or singer) that does not involve the artist's descent into some form of loss of mental control. Indeed, check out the film about Janis Joplin entitled *The Rose*.

5. In his *Laws*, Plato maintains that the poet is not of sound mind. However, in his *Phaedrus*, Plato takes a more sanguine view of inspiration and connects it to craft. It is beyond the scope of this chapter to deliver a resolution to this apparent tension in Plato's corpus. Thus, it is best to regard the present commentary as simply an interpretation of the position in Plato's *Ion*.

Socrates finds this puzzling. Why? Because Homer and Hesiod often write about the same things, and if you understand what the verses are about, say farming or divination, then you ought to understand equally what the verses are about whether it is Homer or Hesiod who is doing the writing. That is, if you understand farming, then you will be in a position to understand and to evaluate what anyone discoursing on farming writes. So,

> (3) If you understand what the verses are about, then you will understand any poet who writes on the subject in question.

Nevertheless, when we combine (1), (2), and (3), we arrive at a contradiction. That is, we realize that not all these propositions can be true at the same time. Why? Because (1) and (3)—along with the assumption that Ion recites Homer beautifully—imply that Ion understands a great many poets. And yet (2) says—and everyone apparently agrees—that Ion only recites Homer beautifully. So, (1), (2), and (3) appear to be incompatible or inconsistent. In order to relieve this inconsistency, Socrates realizes that we must deny one of the premises, and the premise he explicitly denies is (1). He denies that the beautiful recitations of rhapsodes are a consequence of the rhapsode's understanding and knowledge, thereby opening the way for his own hypothesis that it is the result of divine madness.

But is this argument compelling? For Socrates's argument to go through, we must be sure that the three putatively incompatible propositions are genuinely incompatible. Yet whether these propositions are incompatible depends on how we interpret the phrase "understanding what the verses are about." It is clear how Socrates understands this phrase. Let us call his understanding I1 (where "I" stands for interpretation). Socrates, then, believes:

> I1: "to understand what the verses are about" *means* to understand the topic to which the verses refer.

So, if the verses are about divination, then one understands the verses, only if you understand the topic of divination. And, of course, if you understand the business of divination, then you should be able to understand and evaluate what anyone says about it. And that is what (3) asserts.

However, is this the sense of "understanding the verses" that we should apply to (1)? Does what we mean by the poet's understanding of the verses when we take (1) to be true coincide with the Socratic interpretation of that phrase in I1? Or is there an alternative reading of the notion of "understanding the verses" such that when we apply this alternative interpretation to premise (1), it does not lead to an inconsistency with premises (2) and (3). That is, if we can find an alternative interpretation that makes (1), (2), and (3) compatible, then we will be able to undercut

Socrates's argument since that argument depends on reading "understanding the verses" in a way that makes (1), (2), and (3) incompatible.

Here is one possibility. Let us call it I2.

> I2: "to understand what the verses are about" *means* to understand the poet's words in the sense in which the poet intends them and to understand how the poet intends to move the audience by the way in which the words are used.

If Ion embraces I2, perhaps he can evade Socrates's argument. Why? Because if I2 expresses what "understanding what the verses are about" comes to, then saying that a rhapsode has such understanding does not entail that his understanding of Homer's verses on warfare implies an understanding of warfare or any other topic in general; nor does it entail that Ion must understand other authors as well as he understands Homer, since they may be using words and intending to seek effects different from Homer's. That is, in the sense articulated by I2, understanding Homer on farming does not entail understanding Hesiod on farming because Hesiod may intend to use some of his words in a way that is different than Homer and that the rhapsode does not comprehend.

Plato makes Ion's claims sound pretty scandalous. But it is not obvious that they are as counterintuitive as they appear. After all, we do not find it hard to say that some musicians are better at playing the work of some composers rather than others, or that some composers are better at working in some musical forms rather than others. Might not that be because they are better at detecting the effects those composers are after and the distinctiveness of their chosen forms? Perhaps when Ion claims that he understands Homer better than he understands other authors, he is saying no more than that he is more attuned to Homer's intentions than he is to the intentions of other authors.

Whether one agrees that Socrates's first argument against Ion is successful may depend on whether you think that I1 or I2 is the most reasonable interpretation of Ion's claims concerning understanding what the verses are about. If you find I2 more acceptable or just plausible, then you may be disposed to discount Socrates's argument. Of course, Socrates might respond to this by alleging that one cannot really understand a set of verses in the sense of I2, unless one understands them in the sense of I1—that is, you really cannot be said to understand the formulas in a chemistry textbook, unless you understand something about chemistry in general. But even admitting this, could not the friend of Ion nevertheless maintain that it makes sense to say that while Ion's understanding of Homer's words gives him *some* understanding of Hesiod's words, he still does not understand what Hesiod is up to with his use of those words? And it is that he understands what Homer is up to that enables him to recite Homer beautifully, but not Hesiod.

Socrates follows this first argument about the rhapsode's claim to knowledge with another that also rests upon catching Ion in a contradiction. Ion agrees that he knows of Homer in comparison with other poets that "he's good, and they're inferior" (532a). But Socrates finds this hardly compatible with Ion's earlier claim that he, Ion, doesn't really understand other poets. Socrates insists that it does not make sense to claim that you can know that x is inferior to y if you only understand x but not y. That is, it is unfathomable for Ion to claim that he only understands Homer *and yet* that, at the same time, he, Ion, knows other poets are inferior to Homer. Socrates is arguing:

(1) If anyone knows that one writer is inferior to another, then he/she must be able to compare knowingly the writers in question when they write on the same subject.

The justification for (1) is that being knowledgeable of both terms in a comparison is a necessary condition for judgments of inferiority. That is, if you cannot knowingly compare two things, on what could your judgments of inferiority possibly be based?

(2) Ion cannot knowingly compare other writers with Homer even when they write on the same topic that Homer does. (This is what Ion himself concedes.)

Therefore, Ion cannot know that other writers are inferior to Homer.

So, once again, the rhapsode is shown to be lacking the sort of knowledge he claims to possess—here, knowledge of Homer's superiority. Thus, whatever talents rhapsodes have, they do not originate in knowledge. They must come from elsewhere (such as divine madness).

But one wonders whether these opening Socratic conclusions are ultimately satisfying. Undoubtedly, the argument against Ion's claims to know that Homer is superior to other poets is solid as it stands. But perhaps this conclusion might be averted if we modified Ion's claims. The two arguments against the rhapsode so far rely on Ion's assertion that he understands only Homer and no other poet. Taken literally, this is a strange claim. Even Ion seems aware of its anomaly; he admits that he's never met anyone who could explain why Daedalus's statues are well made but not why the statues of other sculptors are well made (533b). So perhaps we should not take Ion literally. When he says he only speaks well about Homer, perhaps that is his hyperbolic way of saying that he speaks best about Homer (because he understands Homer best, and not because he understands *only* Homer). People often exaggerate in this way in order to make a point. And even if Ion does not realize he is speaking figuratively, we might charitably interpret him that way. And if we abandon the unlikely claim that rhapsodes can understand one and only one poet, then the arguments that Socrates has offered so far are undermined. Call this "saving Ion from himself." Moreover, this interpretation, of course, entails that if Socrates is going to make his case against Ion stick, he will need some further arguments—ones that do not ride on Ion's bizarre and somewhat obstinate assertion that he understands only Homer and no one else.

Indeed, there is also a consideration in the text that suggests that at this point in the dialogue, Socrates needs a new argument against the rhapsodes, actors, and poets. Socrates has hypothesized that the beautiful productions of the rhapsode and the poet issue from divine madness—that they result from a kind of frenzy.[6] However, as Ion himself points out, this does not appear to square the facts. When he recites, he does not appear possessed—that is, out of control in the manner of a Dionysiac celebrant. And, as Socrates agrees, the rhapsode must be self-possessed (rather than divinely possessed) at least to the extent that he is able to shape and to modulate his audience's responses on a moment-to-moment basis. So, the hypothesis of divine madness requires further support.

One line of argument that Socrates broaches to this end is that when the rhapsode recites frightening subject matter, he, himself, is gripped with fear. And certainly, there is something crazy about being gripped with fear about monsters, like Cyclops, from long ago and far away (537a). However, Socrates's main line of attack from here on is to develop new and more powerful arguments to the conclusion that rhapsodes and poets lack knowledge, thereby rendering the hypothesis of divine madness unavoidable.

In order to prove that rhapsodes and poets lack knowledge, Socrates needs a conception of what knowledge is and where it comes from. Clearly, throughout the dialogue (and indeed elsewhere), Socrates thinks of knowledge as rooted in practices—practices like farming, medicine, sailing, divination, charioteering, the martial arts, and the like. The people who have knowledge of farming, medicine, divination, and so on are the farmers, the doctors, the prophets or oracles, the charioteers, and the warriors and generals. Knowledge is technical knowledge or professional knowledge—knowledge connected to a profession (*techne*). Knowledge is

---

6. According to Socrates (533d–535a), the god acts on the poet as a magnet acts on an iron ring, pulling it in the direction predetermined by the divinity. The poet, in turn, pulls the rhapsode and/or the actor in the same direction and then the rhapsode and/or the actor pulls the audience likewise. What is notable about this account is not only that it denies the relevant artists any cognitive or intellectual involvement with their performances—since they are quite literally out of their minds—but it also treats the audience in like manner. The audience member is another ring in the circuit of divine madness, automatically taking on the frenzy/ecstasy of the poet/actor/rhapsode. This is probably the first theory of audience identification in the philosophy of art. It not only has the spectator identifying with the pertinent artist but also represents that process as irrational. This understanding of the audience's relation of identification to poetry and its performance will be developed in further arguments by Plato in his *Republic*.

intimately related to a practice and the exercise of a skill. Only the people with the skill, training, and experience in question really know about, for example, medicine or military strategy. The knowledge of x—say farming—is connected with the skill and training of the practitioner of x—the skill, training, and experience of a farmer. Only farmers really know about farming; only doctors really know about medicine; only sea captains know about navigation; only generals know about strategy and warfare. Knowledge is based in practices, understood as professions. To have knowledge of an area means to have working knowledge—the knowledge of a practitioner, the knowledge of an expert, the knowledge of a professional.

Given this view of knowledge—to which Ion assents—the question becomes what the rhapsode and the poet really *know*. Poets may speak of strategy and farming and statecraft, but they cannot do so with authority and knowledge because they are not practitioners in these matters—they lack training, skill, and experience—they are not generals or farmers; they are not lawgivers or politicians. And neither are the rhapsodes who recite what the poets have written on these matters.

Socrates maintains that neither rhapsodes nor poets can have knowledge about things like charioteering or naval matters because they are neither charioteers nor sea captains. Moreover, on Socrates's view, knowledge is connected to practices, practices which are distinct from each other. A doctor knows about medicine and a general knows about strategy, but doctors do not know about strategy (unless they are also practicing generals). People may talk about drugs, the way the elderly often speak about their medications. But only trained and experienced physicians really know about medicine. The rest of us are kibitzers.

Given this conception of knowledge, Socrates claims that each profession or craft is the source of understanding for a given activity. The craft of chariot driving is the source of knowledge about charioteering. Moreover, each profession or craft is distinct. A rhapsode is not a charioteer, nor is the charioteer a rhapsode. So, it is the charioteer and not the rhapsode who will really know about charioteering. To illustrate this point, note how often professionals complain that the way in which Hollywood represents them is usually ridiculous—for example, police often make fun of the fact that in a movie like *Lethal Weapon*, the characters use their sidearms more frequently than the average cop is likely to do over an entire career. (That movies like *Lethal Weapon* "work" for the general audience, but not for the real police, bespeaks the degree to which popular fictions rely on the ignorance of the general audience, a point, we shall see, that Plato emphasizes in his general attack on poetry in Book X of his *Republic*.)

Poets write about everyday practices like medicine and the law, but since they are not practitioners of the crafts in question, they cannot offer genuine knowledge of these activities; thus, they are not situated in such a way that they could truly teach us about the practices about which they write. Indeed, poets typically write about many different practices. Perhaps one might be tempted to evade Socrates's objections, as Ion does, by saying that the poet and the rhapsode are really masters of all the crafts that he or she represents. But this is absurd. Not only is this obviously refuted by the facts—we know that Homer was not a practitioner of every craft about which he wrote—but, furthermore, it does not seem possible that one human could be a master of all the crafts, professions, practices, and occupations that are discussed in his epic poems the *Iliad* and the *Odyssey*. That is, we cannot save the poet or the rhapsode from Socrates's argument by saying they are the masters of every craft because it seems humanly impossible that one person could be the master of every craft and profession.

The charge that poets and rhapsodes lack knowledge then really comes down to the charge that they have no craft knowledge. The discovery of craft—the discovery of the link between practice and knowledge, between theory and practice—was one of the great discoveries of Greek culture. It was a powerful insight, and the Greeks often tried to understand everything else on the model of crafts—for example, politics was understood as a craft, that of statecraft, and in Plato's *Timaeus*, even the demiurge is figured as a sort of craftsperson. Given this predisposition, Socrates claims that poets and rhapsodes lack knowledge and, therefore, have nothing to teach because they were not practitioners of any of the crafts about which they wrote.

Of course, one might think that there is an obvious gap in this argument. It may be true that the poets and rhapsodes were not practitioners of the multitude of crafts of which their verses sing. But nevertheless, they still might have knowledge—knowledge based on a specific craft, namely, the craft of poetry.

But Socrates explicitly denies that poetry is a craft. He notes that poets write about other crafts; they do not write about the craft of poetry. Moreover, one suspects that Socrates does not think this is merely an accidental oversight. For, he believes that if anything is a craft, it must trade in *teachable* knowledge. But like many today, Socrates appears to believe that poets are born, not taught, inspired, not tutored—and this is further evidence that poetry is not a craft, but something else, remote from knowledge. It is a matter of divine madness, not craft. A craft comprises a body of skills, techniques, and knowledge, and Socrates presumes that no one can identify a body of specialized knowledge for poetry. Indeed, that is why poets talk about everything else; they have nothing of their own about which to speak.

Summarizing, then, the present argument, Socrates alleges:

(1) If poets have any knowledge, then it must be craft knowledge. (This is perhaps justified by the idea that any sort of knowledge is really craft-based knowledge; but it might also be justified by the view that since poets write about crafts, this requires craft knowledge.)

(2) If poets have craft knowledge, they must be masters of some of the established crafts (medicine, martial arts, government, shoemaking—i.e., all the recognized crafts, excluding poetry), or they must be masters of all the established crafts, or there must be a craft of poetry.

(3) The poets are not masters of any of the established crafts.

(4) The poets are not masters of all the established crafts.

(5) There is no craft of poetry.[7]

(6) Therefore, the poets do not have craft knowledge.

(7) Therefore, the poets do not have any knowledge.

And, of course, from this it follows that the poets have nothing to teach; so much for the supposed educators of the Greeks.

This argument is a deductive argument. Its conclusions logically follow from its premises. Furthermore, it is a valid deductive argument. That means that if the premises of the argument are true, the conclusion must be true. The logic of the argument is airtight. So, if there is something wrong with this argument—that is, if the argument is not sound; if the conclusions are false—that is because one or more of the premises are false. In order to refute an argument like this, what is required is to refute one or more of the premises.

And that, of course, is what Ion attempts to do. At one point, he tries to refute premise (4), claiming that rhapsodes and poets are masters of all the professions. But this is rather silly. His more serious challenge to Socrates is his denial of premise (5). He attempts to argue that the poet and the rhapsode do have a craft, that they are professionals, and, therefore, capable of conveying knowledge. But, of course, in order for this to fly, Ion must be able to say of what that craft consists. What sort of craft knowledge is it that the poet and the rhapsode possess?

Ion says, "My opinion, anyhow, is that he'll [the poet and/or the rhapsode] know what it's fitting for a man or a woman to say—or for a slave or a freeman, or for a follower or a leader" (540B). But what does this mean? Perhaps this: in the movie *The Hunt for Red October*, the leading rhapsode, Sean Connery, who plays the Soviet submarine commander, will know how it is fitting for a submarine commander to bark out an order. And Tom Clancy, the "poet" who wrote *The Hunt for Red October*, will know what it is appropriate for the commander of an American aircraft carrier to say—for example, when the aircraft carrier commander tells his assistant to cut the character named Ryan some slack.

Socrates responds to this conjecture by asking: "What should a leader say when his ship is hit by a storm—do you mean a rhapsode will know better than a navigator?" (540b). This is a rhetorical question. Socrates expects that our response will be no. Ion claims that the poet knows what it is fitting for people to say and, by extension, that the poet knows how they will act in any situation and, moreover, that the poet can portray this by writing descriptions of actions and by writing

---

7. Indeed, poetry and the recitation thereof is an affair of divine madness. No craftsperson could proceed in a state of madness. But the poet and the rhapsode perform while literally out of their minds.

dialogue for the actors. But Socrates, predictably, denies that it is the poet who is the expert on what people will say and how they will act in given situations. Socrates argues that when a storm strikes a ship, it is the captain who knows what to say, how to say it, and to whom to say it as well as it is the captain who knows what to do.

But has Socrates really addressed Ion's point here? Why think that he has not? Socrates's counterargument basically turns on how one interprets the phrase "what it is fitting to say." Socrates has one interpretation, but Ion may mean something else by it. Perhaps Socrates's rebuttal of Ion actually depends on Socrates's neglect of Ion's intended meaning.

There are at least two different senses of what might be intended by saying that someone x knows what it is fitting for someone else y to say in situation z. One sense may be called the *veridical sense*. According to the veridical sense, x knows what it is fitting for someone else, y, to say in situation z if and only if x knows what it is correct for y to say in z. When there is a storm at sea and the captain shouts "batten down the hatches," that is fitting in the sense that that is the correct procedure to initiate in that kind of situation, and it is the captain or the seafarer who knows when it is fitting to issue that command. This, of course, is what Socrates has in mind when he says that it is the captain who really knows what it is fitting to say.

But there is another sense of what it is for someone to know what it is fitting for someone y to say in situation z. Call this the *imitative sense*. On the imitative sense, x knows what it is fitting for someone else y to say in situation z if and only if x can *imitate* the way or manner in which y would speak or act in situation y. That is, knowing what it is fitting for someone to say is a matter of being able to imitate how the captain of the ship would issue the command to "batten down the hatches"—that is, how the captain would state the command, and perhaps how he would look when he did so. For example, the poet or rhapsode would know that the captain would utter "batten down the hatches" in a strong, firm voice rather than saying it tentatively. What Ion may be claiming is that the craft of the rhapsode, the actor, and ultimately the poet is the activity of imitating or representing the words and deeds of people involved in other practices.

Socrates appears to miss this possibility. If this is so, then when he responds with his example of the ship captain, he may be committing a fallacy of equivocation. If I argue that "all and only men are created equal; women are not men; therefore, women are not created equal," my argument fails because I am exploiting an ambiguity or equivocation in the word *men*. In the first premise, it pertains to human beings; in the second premise, it pertains to persons of the male gender. The argument shifts between these meanings as it proceeds; "men" is not used univocally—that is, with a single meaning. Therefore, the argument is not really coherent, though it may sound so. Likewise, Socrates appears to be changing the meaning of "what it is fitting to say" mid-debate since Ion is probably using it in the imitative sense, whereas Socrates responds by using the veridical sense.

But if this is what is going on—if Socrates has committed a fallacy at this point in the debate—then his larger argument to show that the poet lacks craft knowledge stalls. For it looks like Ion may actually be in a position to refute one of Socrates's premises—specifically premise (5), which maintains that there is no craft of poetry (and, therefore, no knowledge for the poet or rhapsode to convey).

Ion, then, seems to be making the at least plausible point that there is a craft of poetry, namely imitation, a craft highly relevant to education.[8] Socrates either misses the distinction between the veridical and the imitative sense of "knowing what it is fitting for someone to say" or he ignores it, fallaciously acting as if it is the veridical sense that is at issue. But this leaves a loophole in the Socratic argument through which the friend of Ion can slip.

Although Ion in the actual dialogue may be bluffed by Socrates, readers can see that Ion might have stood his ground and challenged Socrates's conclusion that poets lack knowledge by responding that poetry is a craft—the craft of imitation—and that, consequently, the poet has genuine craft knowledge which, in turn, is pertinent to education. If rhapsodes and especially poets have this sort of knowledge, then their claim to be educators remains at least plausible. For, imitation may be a source of a certain kind of knowledge that is especially germane to education. Therefore, the arguments in Plato's *Ion* have not yet ejected the poets from the field.

Perhaps Ion appears to accept Socrates's conclusion when he says that it is lovelier to be thought divine. Yet it is not certain that he fully accepts Socrates's view since he does not say that it is lovelier to be thought to be divinely *mad*. Arguably, Ion holds back, maybe on the grounds of the considerations raised in the preceding paragraph.

Inasmuch as such a loophole remains outstanding at the end of the *Ion*, Plato appears alert to the dialectical need to close it. Thus, imitation (*mimesis*), a possible basis for claiming that poets have knowledge, becomes the focus of his philosophizing about art in his *Republic*. That is, the unresolved issue of imitation is the bridge that takes Plato from *Ion* to his speculations about art in his *Republic*. In Books 2 and 3 of his *Republic*, Plato questions the extent to which the craft of imitation is one befitting a real educator, for there he alleges that there is something unsavory and even dangerous about much of it. By the end of Book 3, if Socrates grants some educational role to poetry, it is a seriously limited one. And in Book 10, Socrates apparently denies that imitation involves knowledge at all, which, of course, returns us to the master argument that poets are not worthy of the role of

---

8. As we will see in the next chapter, Aristotle regards poetry to be a craft (*techne*), one involved in imitation in a way that is important to education. Perhaps we can conjecture that Aristotle's defense of poetry may be a development of some of the notions first suggested against Socrates's onslaught by Ion. That is, Aristotle may be adumbrating the nature of poetic imitation suggested by Ion and explaining its relevance to education.

educators of the Greeks. Books 2 and 3 of Plato's *Republic*, in other words, represent stage one of Plato's assaults on poetry. Book 10 is stage two.

Republic, Books 2 and 3

Plato's discussion of art in the *Republic* occurs in the context of larger debates—the pursuit of the question of the nature of justice and the argument that it is better to be just than to be unjust. This latter issue is motivated by the Myth of Gyges (359d). Gyges of Lydia had an ancestor who discovered a ring that enabled him to become invisible at will. He used it to seduce the king's wife who, in turn, helped him murder the king and take over the kingdom. The question is: If one had such power to do wrong with impunity, would it be better to behave as Gyges's ancestor did or would it be better to behave morally? Ultimately, Socrates wants to argue that one is better off being moral—that is, being just rather than being unjust.

These problems are initially framed in terms of the individual person—what makes one just and why should one be just rather than unjust. However, Socrates suggests that the answers to these questions are best approached by probing the nature of the just society. In part, he introduces this shift of focus on the somewhat fanciful grounds that it will be easier to observe the nature of justice in the state than in the individual because the state is larger. The state is but an individual writ big, a veritable body politic. Indeed, this vision of the state as a giant, a leviathan as Hobbes would have said, is displayed on many of the covers of Hobbes's famous treatise in political philosophy. Thus, justice in the state affords us, so to speak, a magnifying glass with which to investigate the nature of justice in the individual.

Nevertheless, Socrates also has a more prosaic reason than this conceit for regarding justice in the state as relevant to the question of justice in the individual. Namely, Socrates believes that a just state is characteristically a precondition for the emergence of just citizens. In other words, statecraft is, in part, soul craft.

The just state, the Republic, that Socrates goes on to outline is an idealization, presumably because he did not believe that any existing states were truly just and because genuine justice in the individual typically only emerges in a genuinely just state. Thus, Socrates begins his account by sketching the way in which an authentically just state would evolve.

Key to its evolution is the division of labor. Although all of us may start out doing the same thing, say hunting and gathering or farming, in short order, it will become evident that the most efficient way to organize our productivity will be specialization. Some will continue to farm, but rather than making their own clothes and farm tools, many will use their surplus crops to acquire by exchange clothes and tools from others who specialize in weaving and plow making.

As barter becomes more and more complex, merchants and stallholders will appear in order to facilitate exchange, including foreign trade. Where there is prosperity, desires will become more refined; satisfaction with basic foodstuffs will give way to desires for more rarefied fare—wines, cheeses, spices, and the like—and, as well, a taste for finery will emerge. These new desires will give birth to further specializations—vintners, haberdashers, and more merchants and traders of every variety will begin to appear.

As a community becomes richer, the prospect of warfare arises. Other communities, envious of the wealth of their neighbors, may be tempted to invade and plunder them, and, in truth, the richer communities may be greedy for the resources of the adjoining lands. Also, as populations get larger, our state will require more land, while the same process is going on in neighboring states. We need more of their land, and they need more of our land. Thus, the possibility of war spurs further specialization: the development of a military class.

The military class will have the responsibility not only to wage foreign wars, but also to quell conflict within the borders of the community. Thus, the military class also comprises the police. The military/police class will have as their charge defending the community from without and within. The military defends both the borders and the laws of the community. Inasmuch as the military/police class administers the laws of the land, it is natural for Socrates to speculate that the rulers of the community will be drawn from this class.

According to Socrates, the division of labor is the foundation of the state. In order to be the best state possible, the optimal situation is one in which each person in the division of labor be allotted the role he or she is best suited by nature to discharge. Common sense would appear to dictate this. The best possible doctors should dispense medicine, the best possible blacksmiths should man the forges, and the best possible warriors should wage war and patrol the community.

Each person, Socrates presupposes, is best suited for one and only one social role. It is crucial for the community to match citizens with the right roles, and to make sure that people stay in the role that most suits them. It will not do for people whose natural talents are best realized as merchants to be soldiers; that will only result in a society whose resources are being misspent; and it may also lead to disaster if folks with little or no talent for warfare are cast in the role of generals. Surely Hitler's incompetence as a military strategist hastened the defeat of Germany in World War II. Hence, essential to the best society is a strict maintenance of the division of labor. Indeed, so essential is it that it will be written into law and upheld by the military/police class.

Because Socrates believes that the health of the best society depends vitally on filling each slot in the division of labor in the best way possible, Socrates must identify a mechanism for allotting social roles. He envisions that this will be done by the educational system. Teachers, philosophers drawn from the ruling class, will observe children, closely on the lookout for their various natural talents, and then they will track them into the appropriate courses of study—both mental and physical—which are maximally suited to bringing said talents to fruition. Of central importance to this tracking procedure is the identification of the rulers of the best society. These will be of two sorts: the military/police class, called auxiliaries, and those, called guardians, with the executive authority to direct the auxiliaries.

Initially, perhaps all the children will arrive at school together. As the teachers, who belong to the guardian class, observe them, a process of social meiosis occurs. Children with different abilities are channeled into different tracks. The more spirited, stronger students are selected out and their training as auxiliaries begin. And then, from the auxiliary class, those more thoughtful and intelligent—more, shall we say, philosophical—students with evident qualities of self-discipline are then further selected out for training as guardians.

The theme of education not only returns us to the issue of the quarrel between poetry and philosophy, but since education is so important to the functioning of the ideal republic, it is not surprising that Plato devotes a great deal of attention to it. He is particularly interested in the education of the auxiliary and guardian classes since it falls to them to ensure that the ideal republic runs smoothly. Indeed, most of what Plato has to say about education in the two books now under discussion appears to pertain to the guardian/auxiliary class.

It is the responsibility of the educational system as run by the guardians to assure that people are tracked into the right social enterprises, and it is up to the auxiliaries to make sure that, once assigned roles, people stay in those roles. Therefore, since the guardians and the auxiliaries are the lynchpins of the entire system, the education of the ruling classes is a primary concern of Socrates's outline of the just state.

How are the rulers to be educated? This is the abiding question that straddles Books 2 and 3 of Plato's *Republic*. Since, as we saw earlier, poetry and, by extension, art were traditionally core elements in Greek education, the question arises as to the role of poetry in the education of the rulers of the Republic. Moreover, this focus enables Plato to return to the purportedly ancient quarrel between philosophy and poetry and to the unfinished business of *Ion* since here Plato, through Socrates, is prepared to confront head-on the claims of poetry to be an imitative craft or practice, and, as such, a potential source of education.

In Books 2 and 3, Socrates is, at first, disposed to allow poetry some role, albeit highly constrained, in the education of the rulers. However, it is not as liberal a role as would have been found in contemporaneous Greek society. Whereas Socrates's contemporaries would have permitted any of the writings of Homer or Hesiod to enter the curriculum, Socrates is far more discriminating. He believes that many of the texts to which children were traditionally and thoughtlessly exposed were actually pernicious. Thus, Socrates begins by discussing which kinds of texts are appropriate to the curriculum of the rulers-to-be and, more importantly, which are not.

However, before you jump to the conclusion that Socrates and Plato are obviously wrong in their desire to police poetry, recall that they are speaking—first and foremost in Books 2 and 3—about children and about what children should be exposed to. Many of the things that Socrates/Plato would prohibit in the classroom are probably the sorts of things that even modern liberals would also keep out of their children's schools. For example, here is one of the items that Socrates says would be kept from children in the ideal Republic. It is a legend recounted in Hesiod's *Theogony* (lines 176–82). It reads:

> Great Ouranos came, bringing on night and upon Gaia he lay, wanting love and fully extended: his son [Cronos], from ambush, reached out with his left hand and with his right hand took the huge sickle, long with jagged teeth, and quickly severed his father's genitals, and threw them to fall behind.

I suspect that even liberal parents today might have some reservations about this story being told in their children's grammar school.

In the schools of Plato's ideal Republic, poems that portray gods and heroes as immoral and dishonest should be withheld from the rulers-to-be since gods and heroes are paradigms of human behavior, and it is inadvisable to present as paradigms to children those who are immoral and dishonest. Tales of gods mutilating each other, including their parents, as in the preceding myth from Hesiod's *Theogony*, are also of dubious moral value since, among other things, they might prompt children, impressed by the precedents portrayed by the poet, to claim justification for behaving likewise when they become adults.

Plato did not want the young guardians- and auxiliaries-to-be exposed to stories of wars and coups between the gods, lest it suggest that civil war and rebellion among the guardians is acceptable behavior. Plato forbade the gods being shown acting tyrannically—for example, by dispatching children—because he did not wish his guardians and auxiliaries to think that tyranny, including the inclination to act immorally to defend one's dominion, was justified.

Oddly, stories of the gods as shape-shifters are also regarded by Plato as out-of-bounds and even dangerous as well since such stories might be read as endorsing changing the kind of thing one is by nature—that is, as smiling on transgressions of the natural order of the social division of labor. Plato would not grant that this might be alright on the grounds that these myths were really allegories, because Plato thought that the young—including young guardians and auxiliaries—were incapable of understanding allegories (378d).

Similarly, since poetic representation may induce emulation, vice in ordinary humans, demigods, and heroes should not be depicted. Pity, including self-pity, and fear of death should not be illustrated, since these would be dysfunctional attributes in the warriors of the auxiliary class and their commanders in the guardian class. Could someone prone to pity himself or, for that matter, the enemy, or someone terrified of death charge into battle with utter conviction?

For the same reason, the afterlife should not be poetically pictured as horrific, since that would only incite fear of death in impressionable students, such as aspiring auxiliaries, who, in consequence, might grow up cowardly. For this reason, Plato would want to censor the scene in Homer's *Odyssey* of Achilles bemoaning his plight because of its negative representation of death. Indeed, one suspects that Plato ends the *Republic* with the Myth of Er in order to exemplify what he has in mind as a non-fearful rendition of the afterlife with the added guarantee of reincarnation — just the sort of perspective the guardian needs in order to carry on courageously. Nor should the rulers-to-be be exposed to buffoonery because if they develop too avid a taste for laughter, they will lack the sobriety their calling requires.

Two themes thread their way through these arguments. One is that much poetry needs to be censored because it is false. It misrepresents the *true* nature of things, such as the gods. If the gods are represented as immoral and dishonest, then the faith of the guardians in them will be undermined, and the impressionable students may be tempted to emulate the misbehaving gods. Likewise, poets should not represent the unjust as thriving and the just as suffering because that is not the true nature of reality. It is not the *true* nature of reality, even if history records examples like this, because it is not the way *things should be*. For Plato, ultimate reality is not the way things are or *appear* to be, but the way they ought to be—that is, "reality" is ultimately a normative concept.[9] Plato draws a distinction between what is normatively true versus what is apparently true and maintains that it is the former that is really real.

Guardians must be inculcated with a commitment to what ought to be. Poetry that appears to portray as acceptable anything less than what ought to be should be withheld from inquisitive students (and, at points, Plato suggests, from most adults as well) because it will confuse them about what is right and wrong.

But the problem with such poetry is not simply that it confuses prospective rulers intellectually about the principles that govern right and wrong. There is also a second problem, namely, that such poetry will encourage emulation. Put in modern jargon, Socrates is afraid that portraying the gods as immoral and dishonest, and heroes as self-pitying and afraid of death, will seduce students into *emulating bad role models*. Seeing gods and heroes behave badly, students may imitate them.

Plato reasons that no one will find his own badness reprehensible, once he's persuaded those comparable disreputable things are and have always been done by the descendants of the gods (391c). When they see the gods and demigods behaving

---

9. As we will see later in this chapter, this normative conception of ultimate reality is tied to Plato's theory of Forms.

immorally, Plato surmises, the young are apt to presume that such doings are permissible and, in consequence, indulge in them.

Thus, many depictions of gods, heroes, and ordinary people that we find in Homer must be excluded from the curriculum because they foster false principles of action, which may issue in evil deeds, and false models of behavior that, if imitated or identified with, will also result in immoral behavior. Because Socrates is concerned with the education of young people, the censorship he advocates here is perhaps understandable; however, every once and a while, he also intimates that this sort of censorship should probably also extend to most adults (save perhaps some guardians whose wisdom might enable them to read the offending texts allegorically).

Of course, this is not a blanket condemnation of poetry, since at this point in his *Republic*, Plato is willing to countenance poems and stories that exhibit socially beneficial behavior.[10]

Plato's anxieties over bad role models should remind us of the contemporary rhetoric of censorship. The idea that audiences will take up the questionable conduct of the characters in stories and songs—not to mention the lifestyles of the performers who portray them—is as self-evident to current-day moralists as it was to Plato. The only differences between our would-be censors and Plato concerns what they wish to suppress. Nowadays, our moral gatekeepers worry about the representation of graphic violence, which they fear will lead to crime, and graphic sexuality, which they believe will provoke rampant promiscuity, leading to STDs and teen pregnancy. Plato, on the other hand, wants to censor pity, including self-pity, and fear, including fear of death, because he maintains that these emotions will impede the performance of their duties by the guardians and the auxiliaries. Contemporary moralists want to censor aggressiveness; Plato wants to censor that which might compromise martial aggressiveness.

Up until the middle of 392c, Plato's arguments primarily dwell on the kinds of bad role models that need to be censored (with some remarks about the good role models which should be fostered). Basically, he argues that if young guardians and auxiliaries are told that gods, demigods, and heroes behave nastily, these impressionable youths will take this as endorsing nasty and/or cowardly behavior. But why think that? Is this a plausible psychological view? At 392c, Plato shifts to a discussion of the formal device that triggers a psychological mechanism that he believes does the work of securing identification with bad role models.

---

10. Plato also reviews the sorts of music to which the guardian/auxiliary class should be exposed. Certain modes are preferred since they will contribute to the kind of character to which these future rulers should aspire. Other modes should be eschewed because of their putatively deleterious effects. Like Confucius, Plato believes music has the capacity to mold character. One suspects that Plato would not have smiled on rock 'n' roll or hip-hop.

If the bad role models and their unworthy behaviors are the content of the offensive poems, this content must also be served up formally in a way that abets emulation/identification. And this formal mechanism—the mechanism that invites identification—is suspicious in its own right. At 392c, Plato starts to focus in on the mechanism that he believes secures audience identification with dubious role models.

Plato's suspicion of the capacity of poetic texts to elicit identification with bad role models derives from his understanding of the nature of poetic genres and their formal structures. He categorizes poetic genres according to a tripartite scheme. Some texts, such as dramatic presentations, are all dialogue. These can be called examples of *mimesis*—the form in which stories are told not through the voice of the author directly but through the voices of the characters.

A second form of poetic narration is *diegesis*, where the poet speaks directly in his own voice. "Mary went to the store for candy" is diegesis or pure narrative. Telling the same story through dialogue—Mary: "Mom, I'm going to the store now to get candy"—is mimesis or representational narrative. Lyric poetry is diegetic. Furthermore, some forms, like the typical novel, mix diegesis and mimesis, thereby constituting a third category. Comedies and tragedies exemplify mimesis; epic poetry mixes both diegesis and mimesis, where the mixture of mimesis and diegesis is the third member of Plato's tripartite scheme.

But what exactly does this formal analysis of poetry have to do with identifying with bad role models? As noted earlier, much Greek education and, in fact, much Greek entertainment involved people reading poetry aloud to each other. Indeed, in the ancient world, reading aloud seems to have been the norm. Supposedly, we find no explicit mention of silent reading until Augustine of Hippo mentions it in his *Confessions*. So, Plato is worried that when people read, they literally speak, and even declaim, the lines of the characters in the relevant texts.

Where the poetry was mimetic or a mixture of mimesis and diegesis, then, people would enact the words of characters when it was their turn to read. Thus, where the character in question is a bad role model, Plato feared that the reader would take on the attributes of that character. Think of this as evil by osmosis. Plato notes that we acquire personal attributes by habituation. Thus, the anxiety is that in speaking the lines of bad role models, such as dishonest or immoral heroes, the young guardian would begin to habituate herself to vice at an early age. And this is especially troubling for Plato since he believes that one's character is shaped by habituation at the impressionable stages of one's development.

Moreover, in the *Ion*, Socrates claimed that the attitudes of the poet moved through speakers of the poetry, such as the rhapsode, like a magnetic force, taking possession of the soul of the speaker. Therefore, Socrates fears that the common practice of reciting poetry aloud, where the words are those of a bad role model, would cause the speaker to identify by assimilation with the attributes of evil characters. For this reason, in the *Republic*, Socrates recommended that the only poetry that the rulers-to-be (and others) be exposed to should be that in which the roles readers assumed be good ones, ones underwritten with true principles—principles that reflect the way things ought to be—and exemplary behavior. All other roles should be censored. Likewise, guardians should not sing drinking songs or dirges, but only songs which imitated the verbal cadences of virtuous men.

In addition to these anxieties, Socrates airs another. So far, the only poetry to be restricted is that which calls on the reader to speak the dialogues or enact the parts of bad role models. There is no prohibition against mimesis or mixtures of mimesis and diegesis across the board. However, Socrates's analysis of the forms of poetry leads him to voice a further, deeper problem with mimesis.

When actors speak the parts of others—say those of kings or generals—they take on roles other than their own. For, they are actors, not kings or generals. On account of this reason, Socrates is wary of the activity of acting as such and he fears that acting—including the amateur acting of ordinary readers—by its very nature destabilizes the order of the best state. He believes the stability of the best state depends on rigorously upholding the social division of labor. People should keep to the role that naturally suits them and not experiment with roles for which they are not naturally suited. Merchants should not aspire to be generals, farmers should not pretend to the role of auxiliaries, nor should auxiliaries usurp the role of guardians. Social chaos, Socrates feels, would be the result.

But acting, in principle, is a violation of the social division of labor. Acting demands of the performer that he become something he is not. This is why professional actors are such objects of distrust for Socrates. They, like the shape-shifting gods, behave as though it is acceptable to take on identities at variance with one's own nature. And this threat to the stability of the social division of labor is also risked when nonprofessionals, such as student guardians, act out a series of roles which, even if benign, nevertheless do not belong to them. For it is the very practice of acting—whether professionally or nonprofessionally—that offends the division of labor (which is what finally makes justice in the best society possible). Thus, in addition to prohibiting poetry that engenders the emulation of bad role models from the curriculum of the guardians (and perhaps from many others as well), Socrates has also discovered grounds for censoring almost all poetry that involves speaking the parts of others, including mimesis and mixtures of mimesis and diegesis. That is, since Socrates's censorship of poetry is based not only on considerations of content but of form too, the censorship enjoined by Books 2 and 3 of Plato's *Republic* may be much broader than it appears at first.

The actor is like the shape-shifting sea-god Proteus, who could take on any semblance. But that signals a certain instability regarding one's own nature. One's nature—acting seems to imply—is fungible. But such an opinion is at odds with the rigid social division of labor—putatively rooted in each person's essential nature—that underwrites Plato's ideal Republic. Plato distrusts acting as such, presupposing that it is a denial of one's nature. In this regard, he sets in motion an anti-theatrical prejudice that reverberates antiphonally throughout the history of Western culture, but which begins with the notion that acting is fundamentally a gesture of ontological dishonesty. Moreover, the Greek practice of reading the poets, notably Homer, aloud, implicated, for Plato, the entire culture in this transgression.

Thus, if mimesis is the craft of poetry, a possibility that *Ion* left unresolved, Plato has now offered reasons to believe that it is at best a suspect craft, exactly because it encourages the subversion of the division of labor.

At this point, you may feel that Plato has painted himself into a corner. For is not the Socratic dialogue itself an instance of mimesis? If Plato intends his arguments to be general, then should not they apply to his work as well as to the work of the tragedians? Should not Plato's arguments be reflexive—should not his conclusions lead us to argue that his *Republic* should be censored too, if, given his analysis of mimesis, Aristophanes's *Clouds* is prohibited?

But perhaps Plato has not shot himself in the foot. His *Republic* is a case of mimesis, but the lines one should speak aloud in reading it are primarily Socrates's, an eminently virtuous man and a stainless role model. Socrates is the very sort of person with whom the guardians and the auxiliaries should identify. Also, since Socrates is committed to saying how things should be, students will not assimilate false principles from his speeches. Moreover, in reciting these lines, the student guardians are not taking on a role alien to their nature, since they are being trained to be philosophical. That is, by reading Socratic dialogues aloud, the guardians are being tutored in a specialty that belongs to them by nature. Thus, it is fitting that they should be habituated to the words of wisdom of such a mentor and to Socratic dialectical thinking early on.

Furthermore, even those of us who are not prospective guardians can recite the words of Socrates without violating the strictures of the social division of labor, since philosophizing itself may not be a defined social role, but an activity open to any reflective person, her social station notwithstanding.

However, even if Plato can be saved from charges of compromising his own practice, there may still be serious problems with the position he advances in Books 2 and 3. Since Plato's worries concern the audience's putative identification with characters, we can call this argument the identification argument (which, it seems, makes its first appearance in history in Plato's *Republic*). We can interpretively summarize at least one line of the identification argument in this way:

(1) If any educational practice produces immoral and/or antisocial behavior (such as transgressing the social division of labor) in a regular, predictable, systematic way, then that practice should be censored or, at least, regulated.

(2) The poetic practice (mimesis) of representing immoral and/or antisocial behavior to children at an impressionable age standardly disposes them

to identify with the relevant characters and to emulate their behavior. (That is, identification is the psychological mechanism that leads to or induces emulation.)

(3) If, as children, we are standardly disposed to identify with the relevant characters and to emulate immoral and/or antisocial behavior, then as adults, we will produce immoral and/or antisocial behavior in a regular, predictable, systematic way.

(4) Therefore, the poetic practice of representing immoral and/or antisocial behavior produces such behavior in a regular, predictable, systematic way.

(5) Therefore, the educational practice of the aforesaid type of poetic representation should be censored or, at least, regulated.

This argument is probably the first known attempt to use the phenomenon of so-called identification as grounds for censorship. And although Plato's argument is geared toward ancient poetry—understood as encompassing tragedies, comedies, and epics, as well as songs—we are, of course, familiar with similar modern arguments, aimed at contemporary mass media, with respect, for example, to violent behavior. Undoubtedly, the reason for this is historical; contemporary arguments against the mass media are descended from Plato's arguments against the most popular arts of his own day, such as tragedy and comedy.

The first premise of this argument seems unobjectionable. If we could *really* show that some educational practice—specifically some type of representation (either in terms of content, form, or both)—produced in a regular, predictable, and systematic way immoral and/or antisocial behavior (such as, in our own day, violent behavior), then probably most would agree that it should be controlled. We would be especially loath to expose children to it, whether prospective guardians or anyone else. Indeed, even in a liberal society such as our own, we restrict certain types of mass media presentations to adults. And if we were *sure*—really absolutely certain—that the relevant kinds of representation caused immoral and/or antisocial behavior of a harmful variety in significant numbers of adults, we might even be tempted to advocate that it be controlled and possibly censored.

However, the important point to make nowadays is that we are not certain that any form of representation can be said to produce such behavior in a regular, predictable, and systematic way. Thus, the burden of proof for arguments like Plato's is to establish empirically reliable linkage between exposure to the representation under examination and the questionable behavior—something that arguably has never been done in the course of debates like this. Of course, needless to say, Plato's own claims are based completely on armchair psychology, not empirical psychology.

Nevertheless, the second premise of the argument tries to do just this by specifying the mechanisms—identification (imitation of the words of the characters) and emulation (imitation of the actions of the characters)—which regularly dispose children to immoral and/or antisocial behavior. Plato thinks that identification obtains through the recitation of the lines of morally dubious characters. In speaking their words, children take on their attributes, just like actors striving to "get into a role" do. But this seems questionable for two reasons.

First, actors need not and probably rarely ever do fully identify with their characters. As pointed out by Denis Diderot in his *The Paradox of Acting*, actors cannot fully identify with their characters because if they ever forgot that they were actors and "became" their characters, they would not be able to carry on effectively. How could one continue declaiming complicated poetry if one really believed that he had just learned that he had killed his father and slept with his mother—that is, if one fully identified with Oedipus? How could one remember his lines if he were in such a state of pain and remorse?

In order to exert the necessary control over their performance, actors, as Ion observed, must stay aware that they are playing a role and not merge entirely with their character. They must stand outside their characters, observing the effects of their line readings on the audience, in order to modulate and adjust their performances. For this reason, if for no other, actors cannot fully identify with their character. Playing a character is not the same thing as becoming the character, even if actors often speak hyperbolically in this way.

Similarly, the student guardians who recite their lines must not and do not forget themselves; they do not become possessed by the evil characters they portray for the same reason that professional actors do not. Plato exaggerates the degree to which readers are likely to identify with fictional characters and, therefore, exaggerates the degree to which reading poetry—even mimetic poetry of a morally disreputable sort—is likely to dispose anyone toward evil behavior.

And apart from the practical requirements of performance, there is also a wall between the moral self of the reader and the evil characters he might portray that insulates us from, so to say, moral contamination and antisocial identification. If this were not so, the actual onstage death rate of actresses playing Desdemona would be astronomical.

Likewise, certain actors, like Boris Karloff, Vincent Price, and Christopher Lee, specialized in playing villains and monsters. They spoke the lines of evildoers for decades. But there is no evidence that they were either immoral or antisocial people. When I was a child, I met Boris Karloff; he was a very nice man. Playing the role of evil characters does not transform the actors in these roles into morally disreputable agents. Thus, Plato has scant reason to suppose that in declaiming the words of reprobates, the student guardians will become ethically degraded.[11]

---

11. Though the aforesaid examples pertain to adult actors, the same observation can be made with respect to child actors. Patty McCormack, who played the Bad Seed in the play and film of the same name, has never murdered anyone (at least to our knowledge).

Nor is it the case that audiences identify with the characters that they see others portray in tragedies and comedies, whether in ancient Greece or contemporary America. Rather, our relation to such characters is that of outside observers, often observers who typically judge the pertinent characters for their moral shortcomings. We do not identify with Creon or Richard III or Macbeth or Darth Vader due to magnetic acting that supposedly makes us one with these characters, but rather we are typically appalled by their deeds. In most cases, immoral and/or antisocial behavior is portrayed artistically for the purpose of condemning it. Most normal audiences understand this. Most normal audiences do not leave the theater wishing they were Iago. And this supplies us with another reason to disbelieve that typically the poetic representation of evil predisposes everyone, including children, toward identification with evil characters.

It is true that Jeffrey Dahmer claimed that his cannibalism was inspired by watching the third installment of the *Exorcist* series. But this hardly proves that normal spectators are so influenced by representations. For there are no other cases where anyone else was so affected thusly by the movie, although millions saw it. Therefore, the Dahmer case really illustrates how extraordinary the kind of influence is that Plato attributes to all mimetic representations.

Were we to take Plato at his word, the representation of any evil characters should be censorable, but this, among other things, would, of course, preclude the possibility of representing evil characters in order to criticize them. And this would hardly be advantageous from the perspective of moral education.

Plato speaks not only of something like identification, but of emulation and imitation. If children are exposed to evil characters, they will be disposed to imitate them. But again, this overlooks the fact that evil and antisocial characters are most often represented in order to chastise them, and even children can be made aware of this by the discourse of the play, notably, in Greek times, by the chorus (whose lines the guardians-to-be will also read aloud). Consider the ways in which the chorus abjures Creon to bend in *Antigone*. In such cases, the children are unlikely to emulate the characters whom they are being expressly told are morally vicious or misguided and whose behavior is explicitly signaled to be undesirable.

Undoubtedly it may be said that there is a trivial sense in which children imitate the evil characters whose lines they speak, just because reading these lines in character is a form of imitation. However, the question is whether merely reading the lines has any enduring tendency to encourage continued emulation in action of said characters in everyday life. But this seems unlikely, especially where the text in question calls attention to the morally repulsive or mistaken nature of the relevant characters' actions. If it happens at all, it is not the standard case and, therefore, not predictable.

There are, of course, cases where morally reprehensible behavior is marked as acceptable in a play. Here is one place that the probability that children might emulate the character seems more likely. But how likely emulation is, is a genuine question for several reasons. First, given the extraordinary circumstances of most plays, when would one have to opportunity to emulate the relevant characters in daily life? How often do sons have mothers who have killed their fathers because their fathers have sacrificed their sisters to the gods? The case of Orestes, for example, is virtually singular.

Second, before one imitated the behavior of evil or misguided stage characters in everyday life, as opposed to pretending to be them during a play reading, one would have to overcome one's antecedent moral training. But instead, one's own moral character serves as a brake on future emulation here; indeed, it is a sufficient brake in most people to cut short the likelihood of antisocial behavior. If and when we are inclined to emulate fictional characters, I suspect, hinges on whether the behavior of those characters is consistent with our antecedent moral tendencies as those have been inculcated by our caregivers and peers.

And lastly, even where a representation of immorality does not, as most do, unmask the undesirability of the relevant characters, it may still be useful for teachers to expose children to it in order to call their attention to the subtle ways in which evil may insinuate itself, thereby providing an object lesson in moral discrimination. Thus, for all these reasons, we may question Plato's confident presumption that the poetic practice of representing immoral and/or antisocial behavior to children disposes them to identify with evil characters and to imitate their behavior.

Of course, if we deny the efficacy of the mechanisms of identification and imitation that Plato, in premise (2), alleges operate on the dispositions of children, then he cannot reliably predict the adult behavior he correlates with such poetry in premise (3). But suppose that premise (3) does not require the doubtful processes of identification and emulation as its antecedent condition. Suppose that Plato admits that he does not understand the relevant mechanisms here, but only that he knows that exposing children to representations of immoral and/or antisocial behavior leads adults to produce immoral and/or antisocial behavior in a regular, predictable, and systematic way.

Here we can only be skeptical. In our own society, a great many people are exposed to representations of antisocial behavior, such as the use of violence to solve problems and vigilante justice, but most citizens do not indulge in these behaviors. Presumably, most Greeks did not embrace matricide, though they recited poetry in which it figured. Thus, it does not seem credible that exposure to such representations creates the clear and present danger of antisocial behavior. Certainly, this sort of evidence undercuts any claim of a regular, predictable, and systematic connection between the relevant sort of poetry and antisocial behavior. Were it so systematic, why does it occur so infrequently and so unpredictably?

Of course, we have written this argument in terms of a correlation between poetic or artistic representation of evil, and overt, antisocial behavior. Perhaps Plato might argue that this is not fair to his intentions, since he is only talking about a correlation with the production of an impoverished moral character, which depravity might not manifest itself in overt antisocial behavior. But this correlation will be even harder to motivate than the previous one, if only because what need not manifest itself overtly is exceedingly difficult to substantiate. And if a correlation eludes us here, all talk of regular, predictable, and systematic consequences becomes just so much arm waving.

If the preceding identification/emulation argument strikes a resonant chord with contemporary ways of defending censorship, Plato's other major line of argumentation is resolutely premodern. Recall that Plato not only advocates the censorship of poetry that involves mimesis in the portrayal of unwholesome characters, he also opposes most mimesis (save perhaps his own dialogues) on the grounds that it violates, at least in principle, the notion of a strict division of labor. Each person in Plato's Republic has his or her place and should not wander from that naturally preordained station in the social order. Inasmuch as role playing offends, at least symbolically, the division of labor, acting, even in the context of domestic recitation, is abhorrent.

Of course, this sentiment is exactly opposed to the principle that underpins liberal education in modern societies. We think that it is a beneficial feature of literature that it enables us to explore lives and roles other than our own. Through literature, it is said, we can empathize with points of view different from the one that we inhabit. If nothing else, this is thought to promote tolerance and social understanding. Plato, on the other hand, is in the business of designing a highly regimented society, one that precludes not only social mobility as we know it but also alternative conceptions of the good as enshrined in the political philosophy of John Rawls. Although it is a meritocracy of sorts, Plato's Republic is unflinchingly hierarchical in structure and monolithic in terms of its values. Thus, it should come as no surprise that we—who do not believe that people are naturally suited to only one role, and therefore, who believe that they should experiment with several roles, and who also concede the possibility of alternative political conceptions of the good—should not only be put off by Plato's overall conception of utopia, but also by the ways in which literary education is to be blinkered, by Plato's constraints, in its service.

But, needless to say, the fact that we would disapprove of Socrates's educational recommendations will cut no ice with Plato. He would probably have less sympathy for our kind of culture than we have for his. However, our distance from Plato's way of thinking may alert us to a shortcoming in his argument that even an insider might appreciate.

Plato's attack on mimesis so far is based on the assumption that professional and nonprofessional acting—the very recitation of lines suited to characters not of our class—constitutes a transgression of the principle of the division of labor. This is also the worry he has about the representation of shape-shifting gods. But, even granting a Platonic viewpoint, is there really any cause for anxiety in either of these cases?

How likely is anyone, even a very bright prospective guardian, to recognize in the notion of shape-shifting gods a license to change social class? Who would infer from the story of Zeus turning into a bull or a swan an implicit recommendation that a natural-born merchant might be a general or a lawgiver? Similarly, how probable is it that a guardian-in-training will be deterred from her commitment by playing a soothsayer today and seafarer tomorrow in her recitation classes? It seems so psychologically implausible. Moreover, as noted earlier, Plato himself maintains that children will not understand allegories. But isn't the correlation between acting and shape-shifting gods and the license to jump one's place in the division of labor allegorical?

Furthermore, even guardians will have to be adept at some degree of role playing. It is certainly alarmist to worry that any kind of role playing will unravel the division of labor called for by Plato. Plato's argument against mimesis thus far seems to presume that human psychology is far more potentially fragile than is reasonable. Indeed, there is something close to an incoherency in Plato's exposition here. On the one hand, he contends that we are born with a rigidly fixed nature—a destiny, so to speak. But, on the other hand, we can be knocked off course by reading some lines in a poem. For example, we are a born leader—a guardian—and yet when we read the lines of a slave, we risk becoming servile. This is certainly a bizarre combination of dispositions—to be fixed in our natures, but also so plastic at the same time.

And, as noted previously, it requires a highly recondite interpretation of the *symbolism* of acting in order to "read" it as an affront to the division of labor. How probable is it that many, including fledgling guardians, will come to such an obscure, almost arbitrary interpretation of the social meaning of the practice of acting? Yet, if few are likely to reach such a symbolical conclusion, how real a danger has Plato identified?

Thus, Plato's arguments in Books 2 and 3 against certain forms of poetic imitation appear unsuccessful. Does he have more powerful arguments at his disposal to dispute the role of literature in the education of the Greeks?

Republic, Book 10

In Books 2 and 3, Plato provisionally accepts the notion that poetry is the craft of imitation, only to place strict boundaries on the way in which such a craft might contribute to education. In Book 10, Plato returns to the charge that the poets have no genuine knowledge and, therefore, have no claim to the title of educators of the Greeks. Whereas in *Ion*, Plato had not yet confronted the possibility that poetry might be the craft of imitation, in Book 10, Plato, for the purposes of the argument, seems to entertain provisionally this characterization of poetry—and of painting—only to contend that if this is the case, then artists are not fit teachers, since imitation is not a source of knowledge. But indeed, the situation is worse than this, for not only are artists ill suited for teaching; they are downright dangerous to the well-being of society and, for that reason, they, or, at least, many of them, should be banished from the ideal state.

The scope of Book 10 is broader than what we find in earlier dialogues since Plato's findings here pertain to *all* art and not just poetry. And his findings appear to pertain not only to the education of children, but to adults as well, since now Plato is dealing with the governance of the entire republic. Moreover, his conclusions appear harsher: that all artists proceed without knowledge and are dangerous for the ways in which they subvert reason; thus, their productions must not merely be carefully monitored, as Books 2 and 3 suggest; rather, the poets—or at least those who traffic in pleasure first and foremost—should be cast out of the good city altogether.

One reason that these powerful arguments do not appear until Book 10 is that in order to make them, Plato needs to establish his theory of the Forms and of the tripartite soul, and these are only put in place after Book 3. Thus, it is not until Book 10 that Plato has in hand the premises he needs to launch his strongest arguments against poetry. And what appears in Book 10 makes the discussion in Books 2 and 3 seem almost tame.

In order to address the first argument in Book 10, it is necessary to say something about the theory of Forms. Rather than expound the view at length, it is perhaps more convenient to briefly rehearse the kind of considerations that a Platonist might invoke on its behalf.

Plato believes that there are Forms or Ideas. What are Forms and why does he believe that such things exist? Consider some sentences: x is a *general*; x is a *doctor*; x is a *tiger*; x is a *bed*. In asserting these sentences, we predicate *generalhood, doctorhood, tigerhood*, and *bedness* to certain things. But in virtue of what do we apply these predicates? In virtue respectively of the idea of generalhood, doctorhood, tigerhood, and bedness. Now what is the *nature* of these Ideas? They would appear to exist, *in some sense*, in order for us to apply them. How could they fail to exist, in some sense, if we apply them?

But in what sense do they exist? Consider the idea of tiger or tigerness or tigerhood. They cannot merely exist in people's heads, since when we refer to a tiger, we are not referring to mental images that exist in people's heads—including our own heads. Why can't I be referring to an idea in my own head? Because I can talk about the idea of tigerhood—I can refer to tigers—even if my idea of a tiger is mistaken (even if I associate it with a mental image of a leopard). And for similar reasons, we cannot say that the idea of tigerhood exists in the form of a consensus between members in a given society; for this societal consensus could be mistaken about the nature of some general idea. For example, Socrates thought that the consensus in Greek society about the nature of justice was mistaken.

Moreover, another reason that these general ideas cannot exist as a function of social consensus is that we have to discover what it is to be a tiger. Likewise, we have to discover what constitutes justice. If these concepts were simply a matter of social consensus, then we would not have to discover anything about them. The nature of tigerhood or of justice would simply be a matter of social convention or fiat—not a matter of discovery. But we do have to discover the nature of these things.

So, these ideas—like justice—cannot exist as ideas in people's heads or as social constructions. How do they exist? The only alternative seems to be that they exist independently—independently of our individual thoughts and social conventions.

That is,

(1) Since we are able to refer to them, general ideas exist in some sense.
(2) If general ideas exist, they must exist either as mental contents in the heads of individuals or as social constructions or as independent entities.
(3) They cannot exist as mental contents or social constructions.
(4) Therefore, they exist as independent entities.

These independent entities are the Forms—the Platonic Ideas. They are ideas or paradigms or ideal types in virtue of which we think and talk about things. If I say that Tony is a tiger, I must be employing some idea—some list of properties—which define the nature of a tiger. That is, I must have a paradigm or a concept or a model of what a tiger is. That paradigm or concept is a Form, an ontologically independently existing entity. Forms are abstract entities, like numbers.

Not only does Plato believe in the existence of Forms. He also draws a distinction between appearance and reality. The world as we experience it is ever-changing and variable. The tigers we experience are always particular, and there is a great deal of variation from one tiger to the next. We never experience a generic tiger, but only particular tigers. And yet there must be some general idea of a tiger, if we are consistently able to call particular creatures tigers.

The general idea, or Form, of tiger must be stable and invariant—providing us with a constant and unchanging standard of tigerness. If the idea of doctor were not constant, we would be never sure that we are talking about the same thing when we call this or that person a doctor. So, the general standards are stable and invariant, whereas the things we apply them to—the doctors of our everyday experience—are constantly undergoing change and are widely variant.

The realm of change and variation is, for Plato, the realm of appearances; the realm of stability and invariance—the world of the Forms—is the realm of reality, or ultimate reality, if you like that phrase. The realm of the Forms represents the Truth, and the Truth is eternally true, true for all time, and this is the sort of object that knowledge, properly so called, requires. Moreover, this level of reality is normative since the Forms are standards of what the particulars subsumed under them ought ideally to realize.

The realm of appearances is that of particulars which are transient and variable. This is the world as we encounter it in everyday life. The realm of Forms or general Ideas is permanent, unchanging, and imperishable. The Forms are the bedrock of reality where reality is understood in terms of what is ideal or paradigmatic.

In the realm of appearances, we meet particular things like beds—your bed, my bed, and all those beds that George Washington slept in. These beds are only *instances* or copies of a more abstract idea of a bed—call it the Form or Idea of bedness—the prototype or paradigm of all the beds encountered in our ordinary experience in the realm of appearances. These Forms or Ideas are the objects of knowledge. To count as knowledge, something must be true, and the truth is unchanging. Truth is eternal. Forms meet this criterion. Particular objects are merely copies of Forms—reflections at one remove. This is why they are called appearances.

Those who have the closest and keenest knowledge of beds are those who deal most intimately with the function of beds, namely the craftspeople who make beds and those who use them. Why should this be so? The Forms are normative concepts—they embody the ideal. They are paradigmatic types. They not only define the class of things that we call beds, but they classify them functionally in terms of what they are ideally designed to do. And who would be in the best position to have an approximate idea of the ideal function of something like a bed? Someone in the practice of making and/or using the very beds that approach the realization of that function.

This is not to say that the craftsperson ever produces a perfect replica of the Form of bedness, but only to say that insofar as her practice is intimately involved with producing well-functioning beds, her understanding of what paradigmatic bedness comprises is closer than that of others. Similarly, when it comes to generalship—to the Idea of a general—it is the military man who has access through his practice of the craft of war to the closest approximation of the relevant Form.

But what does all this have to do with poetry and art?

There are Forms and appearances. The generals and beds that we encounter in everyday experience are copies of the ideal bed and the ideal general, at best approximations of the eternal standards or paradigms of bedness and generalship. These particular generals and beds are variable in their variety; they are approximations of the pertinent forms—serviceable, but at best still only copies, at one remove, from the abstract ideas of bedness and generalship.

By imitation, painters represent particular beds, and poets represent particular generals and warriors. When they do so, they do it on the basis of beds and generals that exist in the world of particulars. In this sense, they are copying everyday approximations of the paradigms. In effect, they are copying copies. Pictures of beds are copies of everyday furniture, which furniture is already a copy of the idea of bedness. So, pictures of beds are copies of copies. They are at a third remove from the Forms that are the objects of knowledge proper.

Furthermore, and this is the crucial move in Plato's argument, in order to make the kinds of copies that painters and poets produce, one need not have knowledge of the Forms. Representation is—as Hamlet echoing Plato says—like holding a mirror up to nature. And to imitate in this way—to point a mirror at something—requires no knowledge of the thing in question in order to capture the appearance of things. A self-adjusting, automatic video surveillance camera can obviously produce a recognizable representation of a terrorist assault without knowing or understanding what is happening. That is, for Plato, one can imitate appearances successfully without knowing about or understanding the nature of what one is imitating. And that is the way in which he characterizes the imitative practices of painters and poets. They trade in appearances where such commerce may transpire sans knowledge, properly so called.

Note that this argument is not essentially about attacking the relevant art objects—namely, the paintings. It is designed to undermine the epistemic authority of the person making the object—in this case, the painter. Specifically, Plato wants to convince us that said artists know nothing about the things they represent in order to represent them—or, at least, it is not necessary to know anything about what they represent in order to be bona fide painters.

Consider these analogies. The actor playing a doctor does not really have to know anything about medicine. The actor playing Bones on *Star Trek* couldn't know anything about the medicine he practices, since it doesn't exist. Likewise, the TV writers who authored the role of Bones didn't know anything about the relevant medical procedures for the same reason. Thus, one need not know anything about futuristic medicine—or even contemporary medicine—in order to build a character in such a way that the character gives the appearance of being a doctor. Is Hugh Laurie, the actor who played Dr. House, an expert diagnostician? Hardly, though he may look and sound like one.

The alleged craft of mirroring appearances—the craft of mimesis—if it is even a craft at all, is not a craft that delivers genuine knowledge of what it represents.[12] Thus, in accordance with Plato's master argument concerning the question of who should educate the Greeks, mimetic artists, even if they have a craft, know nothing and, therefore, are disqualified as teachers.

The painter of beds—like the photographer of beds who uses a self-adjusting camera—need not have any knowledge or understanding of beds, that is, an idea of what makes a good or well-functioning bed. Just as you can take a recognizable Polaroid of a piece of scientific machinery without understanding what it is, what it can do, or why, similarly the painter of beds need have little or no understanding of what he is imitating. All such a painter needs to know is the way in which the particular bed he is painting looks. He must "mirror" the appearances of the bed,

---

12. Mirroring would not count as a craft at all if a craft, properly so called, requires craft knowledge.

but just as a mirror can do this without making any cognitive contribution to our understanding of beds, so the painter can replicate the look of a particular bed, in a manner of speaking, mindlessly, that is, with no conception of what constitutes a well-functioning bed.

Indeed, from the standpoint of the painter, it makes no difference whether the particular bed in question is a good bed or a faulty one. For, painting is only concerned with the *look* of the particular, which it attempts to mirror with high fidelity. But high fidelity in the appearances of particulars is not knowledge, properly so called. Thus, painting, construed as a matter of mirror imitation, is not a genuine craft, since, echoing the debate with Ion, it is not connected with knowledge, and, for the same reason, it cannot teach anyone about the nature of the things it depicts.

Likewise, poets represent generals and warriors. But since poets are not themselves generals, they merely describe how generals *appear* to them. Since they have no grasp of the essentials of military command, what is most often likely to strike them about generals are their accidental rather than their essential features. So, they tend to emphasize flashy, eye-catching aspects of generals—like Patton's pearl-handled pistols and his shiny silver helmet or Custer's flowing blonde hair—rather than the way in which these generals do or do not approximate the norm of ideal generalship. That is, painters and poets will be drawn to portray *what looks good* rather than what is good. In this way, what they produce is unlikely to be authentically instructive.

Two things follow from the fact that the artist's job is that of a mere transcriber (a mirror) of appearances (i.e., a role that requires no real knowledge of the object or activity represented). First, the work of the artist is a second-rate or, probably more accurately, an ersatz craft—a matter of copying copies mechanically rather than knowingly. Art, construed on the model of the imitation of appearances, is essentially a *mindless* craft, if it is a craft at all, since for Plato, a mindless craft is virtually a contradiction in terms. Second, there is no guarantee that poets or painters can be regarded as reliable sources of knowledge (knowledge of the Forms), and, therefore, their eligibility for the role of teachers is highly dubitable.

Indeed, the situation is worse than this. Since it is the practitioners who are engaged with the objects and activities in question who have the keenest knowledge of the Forms, and since poets are not practitioners, poets are a highly unlikely source of knowledge about the objects and activities they represent. Their skill is with transcribing appearances (after the fashion of a mindless mirror) and, since they are ignorant in crucial ways of the essence of what they represent, there is every reason to regard their productions with circumspection. They are not simply at a second remove from the Forms; since their expertise is inextricably tied to appearances, they have no access to the Forms whatever. It is a palpable understatement to say they cannot guarantee knowledge about the objects and activities they mechanically transcribe. Rather, it is vastly improbable that they could provide genuine knowledge, save by a freakish accident.

Moreover, even if some artist did possess the relevant craft knowledge—as the amateur painter Winston Churchill possessed knowledge of statecraft—it would merely be coincidence. There would be no essential connection between Churchill the painter and Churchill the statesman. Were Churchill to paint a portrait of Roosevelt, his understanding of how to paint Roosevelt would not flow from his knowledge of statecraft. It is merely an accident that Churchill's two abilities developed in one person, just as it would be a coincidence if a pastry chef were also a champion wrestler. Artists *qua* artists do not have knowledge of that which they represent, and, for that reason, they are unfit to be the educators of the Greeks.

Thus in Book 10, Plato reaches pretty much the same conclusion advanced in *Ion*—that the poets know nothing. However, this time around, Plato has dealt with the possibility that poetry might be conceptualized as the practice of imitation. But by means of the distinction between the world of Forms and the world of appearances, Plato is now in a position to say that even if poetry is conceived of as imitation, it has no purchase on genuine knowledge, given the nature of imitation. And he is also, once again, free to insinuate that poets have no claim to being the educators of the Greeks, since they have no knowledge, even *qua* imitators, since imitators need not know anything and, in fact, are extremely unlikely to know anything, even about that which they represent.

Although Plato has couched his argument in the language of Forms, it can be stated without reference to them. That is, the argument can be made without Plato's somewhat extravagant metaphysical commitments. One simply begins by supposing that all art is imitation, where imitation is understood on the model of pointing a mirror or a self-adjusting video camera toward something. It is incontrovertible that either procedure can yield a recognizable representation of whatever stands before the mirror or the camera—that is, an image that matches the appearance of the original. Furthermore, it is equally noncontroversial that one can perform such a procedure successfully—in terms of rendering congruent appearances—without knowing anything about what one is mirroring or videoing. So, one can practice this kind of imitation without knowledge of the object of one's representation. Thus, if art in general and poetry in particular are really a matter of imitation of this sort, then they have nothing, in principle, to do with knowledge, nor is a practice with this kind of relation to what it represents suited to teach people about the objects it has represented.

Summarizing Plato's argument then:

(1) Art (poetry and painting) is imitation.
(2) If art is fundamentally imitation, then art simply transcribes or mirrors appearances.

(3) If art simply transcribes or mirrors appearances, then it need not and almost never does, save by a quirk of chance, involve genuine knowledge.

(4) Therefore, art need not and almost never does, save by a quirk of chance, involve genuine knowledge.

That is, if art is construed as imitation, as perhaps Ion had suggested, then art has an all but adventitious and thoroughly unreliable relation to knowledge. Even if poetry is the art of imitation, the poet has nothing to teach—has no knowledge properly so called. On the other hand, the philosopher, whose specialty is studying the essential Forms, and who thereby transcends mere appearances, is far better suited to serve as the educator of the Greeks.

Of course, the friend of poetry need not take this argument lying down. She may deny either of the first two premises: either that art is imitation or that imitation is simply a matter of transcribing appearances in the manner of a mirror or a self-adjusting video camera. That art is not necessarily imitation is probably fairly obvious to anyone who considers the permutations in artistic practice since the eighteenth century. Consider, for example, abstract art and surrealism. However, if one is arguing with Plato, one perhaps should focus on the kind of art that flourished in his world. And that art, or at least the most significant part of it, probably could be assimilated to the notion of imitation.

However, even granting Plato his first premise, for the sake of argument, we need not accept his conclusions. For even in his own times, his second premise—that imitation is roughly equivalent to the mechanical transcription of appearances—was arguably objectionable. Although there may be the kind of mechanical transcription or reproduction that Plato alludes to, it is not typical of what we esteem as the art of painting, nor is its analogue easily identified in poetry. Most of what we call art involves much more than mechanical transcription or reproduction. It involves selection and emphasis, shaping and salience, interpretations, and points of view in regard to the objects of representation. Art characteristically aspires not simply to the presentation of an object or activity for the purpose of our recognizing what is being represented. It also typically makes some comment on or offers some insight into that which it represents. The visual artist uses framing and angles, among other things, to present a conception of whatever she represents, while a poet presents actions and events in the hope of elucidating them. Both depict or describe appearances, but they do more than that, or at least they are expected to do so.

Thus, one way of opposing Plato's juggernaut is to reject his characterization of artistic imitation as inadequate and to note that artistic imitation aims at interpreting, not merely mechanically transcribing, the objects and activities to which it attends, where such interpretation mandates an attempt to get beyond the level of appearances and at the essence of whatever is being represented. This both presupposes knowledge and understanding on the part of the artist or poet, and it also affords knowledge and understanding to the audience. Therefore, if one construes imitation as involving interpretation, one can reinstate poets in the knowledge game and, in consequence, in the education game.[13]

Plato's next two arguments against poetry raise the stakes in the rivalry between poetry and philosophy. For at this point in the discussion, Plato is not only prepared to disenfranchise the poet from his role as educator; now Plato is also contemplating urging that certain poets, and not a few, be banished altogether from the Republic. In order to make his first argument to this conclusion, Plato not only relies on the distinction between reality and appearance, but also on the notion of the tripartite soul.

For Plato, the soul is divided into three parts: a rational part, a spirited part (whose primary passions are courage, endurance, discipline, loyalty, an appropriate level of pride, and a sense of duty), and the appetitive part (the remaining emotions and desires). Obviously, these parts of the soul also correspond to the major class divisions in the best city: the guardian class is the reasoning part of the city; the auxiliaries correspond to the spirited part of the soul; and the rest of us correlate to the emotions and desires that must be guided by reason and kept in their place by discipline.

Plato grounds this division of the soul on the observation that we readily discern conflicts within our own breasts. Sometimes I want to gorge myself on pizza, but reason tells me to do otherwise. Sometimes I may be afraid to speak out against some injustice, but my sense of duty impels me in the opposite direction. Plato's own example in his *Republic* is the case of Leontius, a man who feels compelled to look at dead bodies but who suffers shame for doing so (439e–440a).

For Plato, that there can be conflicts within one of this sort indicates that our selves are divided into various parts that can point one toward different lines of action. If the soul is not divided, Plato would ask, what else could account for this internal conflict?

In order to deal with this conflict, Plato hypothesizes that the soul must be ordered in a specific way. Reason must rule or govern the soul, and the spirited part must contribute its powers to implementing the dictates of reason by disciplining the inclinations of our desires and appetitive emotions. Similarly, in the best city, reason reigns and is served by the auxiliaries who use their martial prowess to keep the rest of us in line. If the order of the soul is unstable, the individual will be unstable. If the relation between the guardians, the auxiliaries, and the rest is undermined, the order of the Republic will be undermined and the common good

---

13. Plato would undoubtedly respond that these so-called interpretations are really, almost necessarily, all misinterpretations for reasons we will soon see. However, there are certainly an estimable number of counterexamples to Plato's assertion from the histories of literature, theater, and cinema.

imperiled. Moreover, there is a connection between order in the soul of individuals and the order of the state: namely, if the individual souls of the citizens are disordered, the Republic will be disordered.

For example, if merchants, driven by their overweening and uncontrolled desires, install themselves as rulers, the common good will be swept aside for the sake of personal, financial advantage that, in the long run, will produce social disorder.

Plato believes that anything that leads to the disorder of the souls of the citizens—anything that loosens the grip of reason on their soul—poses the gravest threat to the state and, for that reason, must be expelled. Poetry, Plato argues, is just such a danger. Therefore, poets should be banished from the Republic.

But why does Plato think that poetry disturbs the rule of reason and the proper balance between the parts of the soul?

Plato begins his first argument for the banishment of poets with an analogy. He observes that when we see a bent stick in water, it *appears* bent to us, but we *know* that it is straight. That is, though the stick seems bent to our visual senses, the rational part of our mind corrects this distortion. But the appearance of bentness appeals to some part of our psychology other than the rational part. The faculty of reason in us—which deals with issues like measuring and whose objective is knowledge—is not deceived by the appearance of the stick. Nevertheless, we do see the stick as bent; so, this appearance must be appealing to some part of the soul other than reason.

On the basis of this analogy, Plato hypothesizes that appearances in general appeal to some non-reasoning part of the soul—to some nonrational or irrational element in us. Furthermore, imitation, insofar as it trades in appearances, appeals to the same unreasoning part of the soul—specifically to the part of the mind wherein the unruly emotions and appetites reside. Imitation addresses the destabilizing emotions or activates them in such a way that they are unconstrained by reason—in a way that sends reason on a holiday. And in this sense, imitation, as such, disrupts the balance of the well-ordered soul.

Plato supposes that imitation trades in illusion—like the appearance of bent sticks in water—and since being captivated by an illusion means to be convinced of something that is false, illusion undermines the part of the soul dedicated to knowledge and truth, that is, reason. Any illusion addresses the nonrational part of the soul and empowers it, thereby overturning the rule of reason. How exactly does this rather abstract argument apply to poetry?

Consider the cases of tragedy and comedy. It is commonplace to refer to theater as an illusion; Plato exploits this commonplace to the hilt. Insofar as theater is an illusion, it appeals to the unreasoning part of us, encouraging the audience to abandon the rule of reason. In particular, it addresses the *emotions*. It makes us laugh and cry, makes our hair stand on end, induces pity, fear, joy, and mourning. It seems undeniable that a large part of what theater does is to arouse the emotions.

According to Plato, it is able to do this just because theater traffics in illusions. Its arena of operation is the senses—the eyes and the ears—and not the higher reaches of our psychology where reason dwells.

Theater's currency is appearance, not knowledge, for, as the first argument in Book 10 established, artists have no knowledge to impart since artists are merely copiers of the copies of the Forms which populate the realm of appearance. What Plato now adds to that conclusion is that a diet of such second-order appearances, such as theater affords, is bound to unhinge the citizenry by stoking their emotions, not only pity and fear, but "sex, anger, and all the feelings of pleasure and distress" including comic amusement (606 c–d). Theater—poetry and art in general—encourage the audience to vent their emotions freely, to weep, to laugh, and to shout, without discretion. The spectacle of Oedipus arouses pity and fear and relieves us of any feelings of self-recrimination for exhibiting these feelings in public. Not only is this behavior unbecoming of a guardian or an auxiliary, in any citizen, this inverts the justifiable dominance of rationality over irrationality in the soul, which, in turn, foreshadows social disorder. For this reason, not only should tragedians *not* be the educators of the Greeks; exiling them should be considered.

Summarizing then: dramatic poets especially—those who specialize in mimesis—but all artists, inasmuch as they trade in illusory appearances, incite the lower or unreasoning parts of the soul. The way in which they design these illusions appeals to the visceral and suspect emotional elements in audiences, putting the influence of reason on hold, while irrationality is given free rein. This disrupts the proper balance of the soul, for a properly balanced soul is one in which the unruly passions are always governed by reason. By upsetting the balance of the soul, the character of the citizenry is undermined in untoward directions that find their way into social life. This constitutes a threat to the order and well-being of the commonwealth. Thus, art—particularly mimesis—should be expelled from the Republic.

That is,

(1) If something threatens the well-being of the commonwealth, it should be banished.

(2) If something disrupts the balance of the souls of the citizens (i.e., corrupts the character of the people), then it threatens well-being of the commonwealth.

(3) If something undermines the rule of reason in the soul, then it disrupts the balance in the souls of the citizens.

(4) If something trades in illusions (appearances), then it stirs the unreasoning, irrational, and unsavory emotional parts of the soul.

(5) If something stirs the lower, unreasoning, irrational, and unsavory emotional parts of the soul, then it undermines the rule of reason in the soul.

(6) Art, poetry, and drama trade in illusion (appearances).

(7) Therefore, art, poetry, and drama stir the lower, unreasoning, irrational, and unsavory emotional parts of the soul.

(8) Therefore, art, poetry, and drama undermine the rule of reason in the soul.

(9) Therefore, art, poetry, and drama disrupt the balance of the citizen's soul.

(10) Therefore, art, poetry, and drama threaten the well-being of the commonwealth.

(11) Therefore, art, poetry, and drama should be banished.[14]

One of the critical presuppositions of this argument is that art, drama, and poetry trade in illusions, where illusions are understood as a form of deception on the model of the false appearances that fool us into believing that submerged sticks in water are bent. The Greeks enjoyed telling stories about visual artists whose pictures of grapes and curtains were so arresting that, respectively, birds tried to eat them, and even other artists attempted to open them. Likewise, even today, people report that this or that movie appeared "so real" that "they felt like they were there" (wherever "there" is: the steamship Titanic, Casablanca, Oz, Middle Earth, Transylvania, etc.). Plato is exploiting such talk in order to mount his argument.

But there is a genuine question about whether such talk is really plausible. Although in praising a picture or a drama, people may say these things, their behavior suggests that they are never, so to speak, really taken in by appearances. When I appreciate the realism of a picture of a table laden with fruit, I do not believe that there is actually fruit before me. For if I did, it would be unlikely for me to commend it for its *realism*. I don't go around applauding real fruit for its fruity appearance. It is only because it is a picture of fruit and because I know that it is a picture of fruit that it makes sense to commend its realism.

Pictorial appreciation, in general, requires that we realize we are dealing with pictures, but this would not be the case if we were gulled into taking pictures of things for the real things themselves. That we do appreciate pictures as pictures shows that we are not victims of illusions. If people sometimes say the picture seemed so real that they believed that they could touch the fruit in it, that is just a *façon de parler* intended to flatter the painter. It is not evidence that reason has been sent on a vacation.

---

14. Plato's conclusion may be somewhat weaker than this since despite his overt condemnation of tragedy, comedy, epic, poetry, and the lyric, at one point, he appears to allow hymns to the gods and eulogies to virtuous men to be sung in his Republic (607a). This would appear to put the conclusion of Book 10 closer to that of Book 3 (and to the position on the arts in Plato's *Laws*) than indicated above, although one wonders whether Plato is consistent here, since hymns and eulogies will also, to use his metaphor, "irrigate" the passions.

Likewise, when viewing dramas, people do not act as though they believe they are witnessing real events. If they did, the characters playing the villains would be throttled on a nightly basis; viewers watching *Dial M for Murder* would call the police; audiences viewing *Titanic* would start looking for lifeboats by the fifth reel of the film; and so on. That is, viewers of drama do not behave as if they are in some state of illusion. They stay in their seats because they know the status of what they are watching. Reason has not been retired. People who say the movie made them feel "that they were there" are speaking figuratively. They are not providing support for Plato's sixth premise, which if we read it as Plato appears to intend it, seems false.

Of course, someone attracted to the drift of this argument might drop premise (6) and simply assert that no one can deny that dramas arouse emotions (though this would make the analogy with bent sticks in water beside the point). And they might further assert that since the emotions always undermine reason, the rest of Plato's argument is still available.

However, it is highly questionable whether the emotions are always irrational in the way depicted by Plato's account of the soul. Emotions, like fear, are adaptive mechanisms that very often enable us to scope out situations quickly and accurately without engaging in lengthy deliberations where time is at a premium. Fear motivates us to step out of the way of oncoming traffic where pausing to think about what to do might be fatal.

So, the emotions need not be cast in the negative light Plato proposes; they need not always be regarded as irrational. If drama trades in emotion, we need not regard it as at odds with reason. Many emotions are rationally appropriate. It all depends on the situation—on the emotion in question and its object. Therefore, a drama may elicit an emotional response that is rationally appropriate. Isn't it rationally appropriate for us to respond to Richard III with fear and indignation? Thus, simply noting that art, poetry, and drama arouse emotions, such as fear, leads to no general conclusions about such emotions being antithetical to reason or their destabilizing the rational element in the psyche as evidenced by the service the spirited part of the soul performs for the reasoning part.

Many would also criticize the fifth premise in Plato's argument from a somewhat different direction. Plato presumes that if something stirs the emotional and/or irrational part of the psyche, then that undermines the rule of reason. But some argue that actually stirring up the emotions every once in a while is good for us since it relieves pent-up emotion. This is how many interpret Aristotle's notion of *catharsis*. Whether this interpretation is accurate is something we'll discuss in the next chapter. Yet if there is something to the idea that venting or purging built-up emotions serves mental equilibrium—that, for example, watching violent TV shows enables viewers to spend their accumulated aggressive feelings and work them out of their systems—then stirring up such emotions might be seen in the long-run interests of reason's governance of the soul. That is, reason itself would, on this view, have a stake in the kinds of emotional stirring-up that art affords, since that is a way of flushing toxic substances out of the psyche.

And, for similar reasons, such commentators might also challenge Plato's second premise by arguing that the occasional and controlled disruptions of the soul that theater provokes actually sustain the ongoing balance of the soul and, therefore, do not threaten the well-being of the commonwealth, but protect it. The citizenry needs to be emotionally shaken up intermittently. Thus, the artists who do this should not be banished, but honored and esteemed in the way we honor and esteem physicians.

The next argument that Plato brings forward in order to argue that artists be banished relies on combining certain observations about the nature of the art market with premises advanced in earlier arguments. Plato—by means of the Form/appearance distinction and his presuppositions about the relation of genuine knowledge to the practice of established crafts—has already argued that artists have no knowledge to impart. In addition, he has identified the business of art with the arousal of emotion. These ideas are, of course, connected: it is because the artist knows nothing that he must fall back on arousing emotions. It is because the artist knows nothing about warfare that he spends all his energy representing fancy uniforms and martial histrionics of a Patton or a Custer. These are the sort of superficial appearances that catch his uninformed eye and engage his emotions.[15] Since the artist doesn't know anything about warfare, his representations perforce stay on the surface.

Likewise, TV shows about the law, like *LA Law* and *Boston Legal*, spend most of their time narrating interoffice rivalries and romances because their creators do not know anything about the law and have nothing deep to say about it. Lacking legal knowledge, they go for emotionally alluring stuff like love affairs and competition. If they really were committed to showing viewers how the law works, the camera would be set up in the law library for hours on end. But the creators of such programs don't show us how the law works because, as non-practitioners of the law, they are in no position to inform viewers about it; instead, they go for the emotional stuff—the drama of love affairs and office conflicts. Moreover, this situation cannot be remedied, and the reason has to do, to an important degree, with the nature of the market for art.

The poet knows nothing about the practices he depicts. So, what then will guide his representation of them? Clearly, whatever succeeds with audiences. But the general audience, as we saw earlier, also lacks knowledge of the relevant practices. The only resources they have to respond to poetic representations are their emotions. For dramas to succeed, spectators must be able to connect with them

---

15. Note how nicely this view fits with the notion that mimesis is a matter of mirroring. Such superficialities are exactly the sort of eye-catching eye candy that shows up in a mirror.

emotionally. If they cannot respond to them emotionally, then dramatists will be out of business.

Thus, financial considerations impel the poet to keep his portrayals at the superficial level of emotional involvement. If he attempts to get at anything deeper—if he attempts to communicate genuine knowledge of the practices he depicts—he will lose his ignorant audience and his career will founder. So even if the poet could convey genuine knowledge (a proposition Plato probably finds doubtful), the structure of the marketplace would not permit him to do so. As contemporary TV producers perhaps disingenuously lament, they serve up emotional pap because that is what the audience wants.

Thus, in his *Republic*, Plato advances the first economic analysis of artistic production. It is an argument that has been constantly repeated in our own time—often directed at mass culture. Insofar as the artist depends on audiences for his livelihood, he will appeal to the lowest common denominator since that will ensure the largest audience. For Plato, the lowest common denominator comprises the baser emotions, the lowest part of the psyche. The artist will use his own emotions, rather than knowledge, in order to locate what will arouse the audience. It will be a case of the blind leading the blind, driven by an unbreakable feedback loop of emotional sloth and ignorance. In this way, the relevant poets will draw the citizenry into further and further degradation. And for this reason, they should be banished.

(1) If the artist lacks knowledge, he must depend on the audience's response as the only guide for constructing his work.

(2) If the audience lacks knowledge, its response can only be emotional.

(3) If the audience's response can only be emotional, then arousing their emotions is the only guide the artist has for constructing his work.

(4) If the arousal of emotion is the only guide the artist has for constructing his work, then his work abets the degradation of the citizenry (by undermining the rule of reason).

(5) If the artist's work abets the degradation of the citizenry, then it threatens the well-being of the commonwealth.

(6) If anyone threatens the well-being of the commonwealth, then he should be banished.

(7) The artist lacks knowledge.

(8) Therefore, the artist depends on the audience's response as the only guide for constructing his work.

(9) The audience lacks knowledge.

(10) Therefore, the audience's response can only be emotional.

(11) Therefore, arousing the audience's emotions is the only guide the artist has for constructing his work.

(12) Therefore, the artist's work abets the degradation of the citizenry (by undermining the rule of reason).

(13) Therefore, the artist's work threatens the well-being of the commonwealth.

(14) Therefore, the artist should be banished.

Here, as before, Plato is assuming that the arousal of the emotions degrades the citizenry because it unhorses the rule of reason in the soul. However, if we challenge that presumption, as we did earlier, it is not evident that we should endorse the fourth premise in this argument. For, even if the arousal of emotion is all that the artist does, it would not be obvious that this necessarily contributes to the degradation of the citizenry. Moreover, it is assumed in this argument that the emotions in question are the baser emotions. But there is no reason to presume this. Might they not be the emotions of the spirited part of the soul, such as loyalty, courage, patriotism, a sense of duty, or self-discipline? And should Plato be so quick to banish those who promote the exercise of those emotions?

Furthermore, the argument rests on characterizing the relation of the artwork to the audience's emotions in terms of simple arousal. But may not the artwork also educate the audience's emotions? Emotions like fear and anger may be rational in context and, therefore, it may be the case that some artworks serve to enable the audience to cultivate them in the right way: to learn to identify the appropriate objects of the relevant emotions and to acquire the ability to express them with the right level of intensity and for the right reasons. This would hardly abet the degradation of the audience but might improve them. If some art could be shown to improve the citizenry, it would scarcely seem advisable to banish all art from the commonwealth.

Book 10 of Plato's *Republic* appears to roundly condemn mimesis/imitation in all of its manifestations. Mimesis, as such, is characterized as dangerous and not just regarding children. Mimesis can erode the psyche of adults as well. Thus, since Plato equates art with imitation, he recommends that artists be cast out of the ideal republic.

Yet this, once again, raises the question of self-refutation. Isn't Plato's *Republic* an example of mimesis? And if it is, then it shares all of the liabilities that Plato attributes to the works of writers like Aristophanes. So, if Aristophanes must go, shouldn't Plato follow him into exile?

However, it is not clear that from Plato's perspective his *Republic* suffers the same systematic defects that plays and other typical artistic representations do. Artistic representations are copies of copies—copies of existing particulars that are copies of the Forms. It is for this reason that they are remote from knowledge which predisposes them to address the unruly emotions.

However, Plato's *Republic* is not a copy of anything that exists. His Republic is a utopia. It does not exist. So, it is not a copy of a copy. It does not belong to the world of appearances. It presents an ideally just state. It advocates what ought to be rather than imitates what is. Thus, it is more nearly of the nature of the realm of Forms than it is of the realm of appearances, inasmuch as it articulates a standard of what should be obtained or realized by way of justice. What is ultimately true for Plato is what is normatively correct. Plato's *Republic* outlines the normatively correct ideal of the state. In that regard, Plato's *Republic* is on the side of truth and knowledge and not on the side of appearances and the baser emotions. Consequently, it is not subject to Plato's verdict regarding the other practitioners of mimesis—the poets, painters, and the other artists.

Moreover, the ostracism that Plato imposes on the poets and the artists is not implacable. For certain artists and under certain circumstances, Plato is ready to withdraw his decree of exile. He says: "And I suppose we'd also allow people who champion poetry because they like it, even though they can't compose it, to speak on its behalf in prose, and to try to prove that there's more to poetry than mere pleasure—that it also has a beneficial effect on society and human life in general. And we won't listen in a hostile frame of mind because we'll be the winners if poetry turns out to be beneficial as well as enjoyable" (607d–607e).

Here Plato returns to the notion of beneficial pleasure, which is how he defined *kalon* at the end of the *Hippias Major*. Perhaps, if his book *Republic* were attacked, he could defend it by adverting to the fact that it is not only enjoyable but beneficial too, in that it clarifies the ideal or Form of justice.

But, in any event, this challenge—to show that poetry is both pleasurable and beneficial in prose language—is precisely the line of argumentation that Aristotle, the student of Plato, embraces in his defense of mimesis in his *Poetics*.[16]

Bibliography

The translations of Plato employed in this chapter were *Two Comic Dialogues: Ion and Hippias Major*, translated by Paul Woodruff (Hackett, 1983) and Plato's *Republic*, translated by Robin Waterfield (Oxford University Press, 1963).

Annas, Julia. *An Introduction to Plato's Republic*. Oxford: Oxford University Press, 1981.
Battin, Margaret Pabst. "Plato on Truth and Truthlessness in Poetry." *Journal of Aesthetics and Art Criticism* 36 (1976): 163–74.
Destrée, Pierre, and Fritz-Gregor Herrmann, eds. *Plato and the Poets*. Leiden: Brill, 2011.
Dorter, Kenneth. "The *Ion*: Plato's Characterization of the Arts." *Journal of Aesthetics and Art Criticism* 33 (1973): 65–68.
Janaway, Christopher. *Images of Excellence: Plato's Critique of the Arts*. Oxford: Clarendon, 1995.

---

16. Aristotle does not say that he is specifically responding to Plato's challenge in his *Poetics*, although it seems reasonable to hypothesize that that is what he is doing.

Moravcsik, Julius, and Philip Temko, eds. *Plato on Beauty, Wisdom, and the Arts.* Totowa, NJ: Rowman and Littlefield, 1982.

Murray, Penelope. "Inspiration in Early Greece." *Journal of Hellenic Studies* 101 (1981): 87–100.

Pappas, Nickolas. "Plato: Aesthetics." In *Stanford Encyclopedia of Philosophy.* Stanford University, 1997–. Published June 27, 2008; last modified June 22, 2020. https://plato.stanford.edu/entries/plato-aesthetics/.

———. *Plato and the Republic.* London: Routledge, 1995.

———. "Plato's *Ion*: The Problem of the Author." *Philosophy* 64 (1989): 381–89.

———. "Plato on Poetry: Imitation or Inspiration." *Philosophical Compass* 7 (2012): 669–78.

Sachs, David. "A Fallacy in Plato's *Republic.*" *Philosophical Review* 72 (1963): 141–58.

———. "Plato's Early Aesthetics: *Hippias Major.*" *Journal of Aesthetics and Art Criticism* 35 (1977): 465–70.

Stern-Gillet, Suzanne. "On (Mis)interpreting Plato's *Ion.*" *Phronesis* 49 (2004): 169–201.

White, Nicholas P. *A Companion to Plato's Republic.* Indianapolis: Hackett, 1979.

Chapter 2

Aristotle's *Poetics*

Aristotle lived in Greece in the fourth century BCE. He was reputedly the teacher of Alexander the Great, a fellow Macedonian. Aristotle studied philosophy in Athens and is the best-known product of Plato's Academy. That he studied with Plato is one key to understanding *Poetics*.

Just as Plato's texts on art stage a running debate with the poets, especially Homer, so there is a running debate in Aristotle's *Poetics*—a running debate with Plato, although Plato is never mentioned explicitly.[1] You'll recall that around 607d–607e of his *Republic*, Plato's interlocutors ask—after Socrates has fictionally banished poets from his good city—whether there are any conditions which would lead him to reconsider allowing poets back into the city. Socrates replies:

> And I suppose we'd also allow people who champion poetry because they like it, even though they can't compose it, to speak on its behalf in prose, and to try to prove that there's more to poetry than mere pleasure—that it also has a beneficial effect on society and on human life in general. And we won't listen in a hostile frame of mind because we'll be the winners if poetry turns out to be beneficial as well as enjoyable.[2]

Thus, Plato explicitly introduces a challenge for his audience through the voice of Socrates—to defend poetry in prose (prose perhaps since then it will not have the advantage of poetry's seductive powers and its charm).

One way of reading Aristotle's *Poetics* is as an attempt to meet that challenge and to refute Socrates's objections with regard to poetry—tragic poetry (mimesis in the narrow sense)—as well as art (mimesis as imitation) in general. Accordingly, in the *Poetics*, we find a series of rebuttals of the Platonic position, written in prose.

---

1. For that reason, readers should be warned that the notion of a debate here is somewhat conjectural.

2. The requirement that it be demonstrated that poetry is beneficial *and* enjoyable recalls Socrates's definition in the *Hippias Major* of *kalon* as beneficial pleasure. In effect, Socrates wants the party of poetry to prove that poetry is *kalon*—a challenge that I believe Aristotle takes on implicitly. Moreover, insofar as something is intrinsically valuable and instrumentally valuable, Socrates believes that it falls into the category of the best things (*Republic*, 358a). Thus, Socrates wants the friend of poetry to show that it is among the best things, something Aristotle shows by arguing that it has not only good consequences but is also naturally pleasurable as a species of learning, where pleasure, in turn, is putatively something valuable for its own sake.

Where Plato maintains that art (imitation) is inimical to reason, Aristotle believes that art (imitation) is not inimical to reason since imitation is a condition for learning. Plato argues that art is an illusion, but Aristotle rejects this claim. Art is not an illusion. Instead, it reframes reality. For Plato, art merely mirrors nature, but for Aristotle, art abstracts (in the sense of distills) from nature—in particular, tragedy abstracts general features of human life and refocuses and exhibits them in telling ways. Plato believes that art has nothing to teach, but Aristotle instead shows that art indeed has something to teach about general patterns of human behavior and, arguably, about the emotions.

Plato claims that dramatic poetry only arouses unsavory emotions, unbalances the soul, and thus endangers the society. Aristotle shows instead that dramatic poetry purges (or purifies or clarifies) unsavory emotions in ways that are conducive to the well-being of society. Where Plato believes that art causes imitation of lamentable emotions through identification, Aristotle maintains that art causes the catharsis rather than the imitation of the emotions in question. Plato argues that dramatic poetry is either a second-rate craft or not a craft at all, but Aristotle shows that dramatic poetry is indeed a craft—the craft of making an imitative structure that will elicit catharsis. A tragedy is in this sense a carefully calibrated and crafted machine, an emotion machine, if you will.

Some of the differences between Plato's and Aristotle's theories of art stem from greater theoretical differences. For instance, Plato's official view of the emotions in his *Republic* is ostensibly negative, whereas Aristotle sees them as connected to understanding and, for that reason, as beneficial.

Although Aristotle opposes many of Plato's conclusions, one should not imagine that Aristotle rejects everything that Plato has to say. Aristotle was Plato's student and in many ways, he accepts fundamental elements of Plato's framework. Plato and Aristotle agree that art, in the broadest sense, is imitation. Aristotle, in addition, agrees with Plato that dramatic poetry trades in emotion.

Aristotle also accepts Plato's requirement that if art in general and dramatic poetry in particular are to be countenanced within the walls of the good city, then they will have to be shown to afford social benefits. These benefits are the kinds of benefits that Plato expects—that art will have to contribute to knowledge and will have to contribute to the education of the citizenry by promoting virtue, where an important function of virtue is the ability to discipline socially disruptive emotions—that is, to put a brake on excessiveness.

In deference to his teacher, at the very least, Aristotle must reassure people that the arts, especially tragedy, do not feed or irrigate the emotions—inflame them so that they have socially destructive repercussions.

Interestingly, you will probably notice that Aristotle is especially concerned with the emotions of *pity* and *fear*, the very emotions that crucially concerned Plato. To answer Plato, Aristotle is at pains to show that even though tragedy traffics in pity and fear, it does so in a way that is beneficial to society. Thus, though Aristotle rejects many of Plato's particular conclusions, he operates in a Platonic framework—that is, he accepts the burden of proof that Plato lays down before lovers of poetry. He agrees with Plato about what must be shown in order to defend poetry. And that is an agreement at the fundamental philosophical level. In this way, Aristotle, despite his numerous differences with Plato, nevertheless, with regard to poetry, still belongs to the school of Plato.

In keeping with Plato's brief for those who would argue in favor of poetry, Aristotle does conduct his defense in prose, thereby eschewing the seductive allures of poetry. This is unfortunately a downside for readers, as the *Poetics* is a less exciting text to read than a dialogue would be. The style of the text is dry and prosaic. In fact, Aristotle has been said to be the world's first graduate student since the text of his *Poetics* that has come down to us is composed of the notes his students took while listening to his lectures. This also accounts for the fragmentary nature of the text. Parts, such as Aristotle's discussion of comedy, have been lost. Indeed, it is remarkable that the text flows as smoothly as it does, given the patched-together origin of the text.

Aristotle's Project in His *Poetics*

With this general orientation to the *Poetics* in mind, we are now prepared to turn to the text itself. Aristotle is explicit about what he intends to do in the text. He opens by saying:

> Let us discuss the art of poetry in general and its species—the effect which each species of poetry has and the correct way to construct plots if the composition is to be of high quality, as well as the number and nature of its component parts, and any other questions that arise within the same field of enquiry. (47a)[3]

That is, Aristotle promises to provide a map of poetry in its various forms—to say what poetry in general is and to say what each of its forms (species, or, as we would say, genres) amounts to. These forms include tragedy, epic, and comedy. However, as we mentioned above, the extant text is incomplete and is really only primarily concerned with tragedy rather than poetics across the board. But that is especially important since it is tragedy—the leading form of mimesis in the narrow sense—which Plato found to be the most dangerous of poetic forms.

So, Aristotle is going to tell us about poetry in general and its species. This means that one part of his task is definitional. He is going to provide us with a number of definitions that answer questions such as What is poetry in general? and What is tragic poetry? Moreover, he tells us the kind of definitions he's going

---

3. Throughout this chapter, the line identifications refer specifically to the *Poetics*.

to offer—*functional definitions*. In other words, he will tell us about the nature of a poetic species, such as tragedy, by telling us what *effect* the relevant kind of poetry is designed to bring about. For example, tragedy is defined in terms of its function to bring about the effect of the catharsis of pity and fear in audiences. That is, things are going to be defined in terms of the *effects* it is their *function* to promote—hence the term "functional definition." Aristotle is going to identify the emotional effect the function of tragedy is meant to elicit, as we might today define genres like horror, mystery, suspense, or tearjerkers in terms of the specific emotions they are designed to provoke in audiences.

But he is not just going to define these species—or what we might call genres. He is also going to examine the *correct* way to construct them. In other words, he is going to *explain* how to make works of the relevant sort, such as tragedies, correctly—that is, in such a way that they perform the function that is pertinent to the genre in question. For example, he will *explain* how the plot and the other component parts of tragedy—like character—have to be designed in order to discharge the function that defines the genre of tragedy. And, in addition, he will take up and attempt to answer any other questions that arise about the genre in question—such as What is the source of the pleasure that we derive from tragedy?

So, in 47a, Aristotle alerts us to his two major orders of business: first, the definition of poetry in general and of particular genres in poetry, notably tragedy; and second, an explanation of how poetry works—particularly how tragedy works—in terms of delivering the effects that define the genre. And he will also try to account for or explain other questions and paradoxes that we may pose about tragic poetry, such as how we can derive pleasure from the terrifying events tragedies portray.

The notion of poetics, from which Aristotle takes his title, comes from the Greek concept of *poesis*, which is connected to the idea of making. In this regard, Aristotle's philosophy of art is primarily concerned with the construction side of things—with what goes into a tragedy in order to secure its intended effect. Thus, one might think of Aristotle's *Poetics* as directed primarily to the playwright.

But as we will see in the next chapter, this emphasis on the construction side of things contrasts with the tendency of many modern philosophies of art to be preoccupied with the reception side of things, a tendency signaled by the concept of aesthetics, which, rooted in the Greek word *aisthestis* (sensation), comes to be associated with the perception of artworks. Of course, Aristotle is not oblivious to the reception of artworks; his account involves what tragedies *do* to audiences. And the moderns are not unaware that the aesthetic response involves a stimulus. Yet, as a generalization, Aristotle's emphasis is on the artistic construction of the works in question, whereas the moderns are frequently more interested in limning the experience—often called the "aesthetic experience"—that the audience undergoes.

Defining Poetry

Aristotle's first order of business is definition. This is fairly commonsensical—before you go about explaining how something works, you have to be able to say what it is you're talking about. That is, you need a way of picking out or identifying whatever it is you're going to explain. If you're going to explain how chain saws work, you need a way to pick out chain saws from other machines. You don't want to mix together chain saws and other machines, like bread makers. If you do, you'll only be confused about the way in which all of these machines can be covered by the same explanatory principles. You have to know what you're talking about and be talking about a unified class of things. Hence, definition comes first.

Moreover, Aristotle tells us that these definitions will come in a certain order. He will first define poetry in general and then define its various species, like tragedy.

Aristotle defines poetry in general as imitation (as imitation in the broad sense), just as Plato did in Book 10 of his *Republic*. Tragedy, comedy, all sorts of poetry and music, are all considered to be kinds of imitations. Aristotle says: "Epic poetry and the composition of tragedy, as well as comedy and the arts of dithyrambic poetry and (for the most part) of music for pipe or lyre, are all (taken together) imitations" (47a). Music is included under the rubric of imitation not only because it generally accompanies songs, which are representational, but also because, like dance, it was typically integrated into dramatic productions like tragedies. And two sentences later in the discussion of medium, we see that Aristotle also counts painting and sculpture under the concept of imitation.

In other words, Aristotle is basically saying that all the things we count as arts are matters of imitation. Imitation, that is, is a necessary condition for what he calls poetry, but which we would call art. So, what is being claimed by Aristotle here is that all poets—all of those whom we would call artists—are makers of imitations, a claim implausible for us but which perhaps came much closer to the mark in Aristotle's day.

Thus, Aristotle begins with a broad generalization: all poetry or art is imitation. What marks poetry is not that it is in verse or dramatic form. It is imitation that warrants calling something poetry. Rewriting a math textbook or a cookbook in rhyme would not make them poetry. Imitation is the hallmark, a necessary condition for poetry. And the pertinent artists are the makers of imitations.

But supposing this tells us in a general way what poetry is, nevertheless, how are we to discriminate and define the various *kinds* of poetry—how are we to tell them apart? Aristotle says that there are at least three ways to tell certain kinds of poetry from other kinds—three differences to look for in order to differentiate one kind of poetry from another. These are

(1) Differences in media (47a–b). For instance, painting uses color and shape as its medium—its material—whereas song uses the human voice.

Consequently, where the painting is an imitation and so is the song, we can differentiate these as two different kinds of art in virtue of their medium: paintings are imitations in the medium of color and shape, whereas songs are imitations in the medium of the human voice. But not all kinds of poetry can be differentiated in this way. Some forms of poetry share a medium, for example, comedy and tragedy. So how do you tell these kinds apart?

In this case, we look to the second way in which to differentiate imitative art forms, namely in terms of:

(2) Different objects (48a). The objects of comedy—what comedy is about—are people who are inferior to us. In contrast, what tragedy is about is admirable people—not perfect people, but nevertheless commanding folk like King Oedipus. But still, this won't differentiate every kind of poetry from every other, since certain forms of poetry share the same medium and the same objects. For example, both tragedies and epics proceed in the medium of words and are about admirable or commanding figures—heroes. So, what differentiates these genres?

In such cases, Aristotle recommends that we attend to

(3) Differences in mode (48a–b). Remember that in his *Republic*, Plato drew distinctions between three different modes of narration: mimesis, diegesis, and the mixture of mimesis and diegesis. These are the differences between modes that Aristotle has in mind in this section of his *Poetics*. On the basis of this distinction, tragedy can be differentiated from epic on the grounds that tragedy is narrated by means of the mode of mimesis in the narrow sense—by characters speaking lines—whereas epic is narrated by a mixture of mimesis and diegesis—a mixture of the voices of the characters and the voice of the author.

So, according to Aristotle, everything that falls into the catchall category of poetry—or the arts, as we would say—is some kind of imitation *and* to figure out which kind, scrutinize the work in terms of its medium, object, and/or mode.

Having posited that imitation is the class that the arts belong to, Aristotle stands back and tries to explain why the arts exist. He says that

> imitation comes naturally to human beings from childhood (and in this they differ from other animals, i.e., in having a strong propensity to imitation and in learning their earliest lessons through imitation); so does the universal pleasure in imitations. What happens in practice is evidence of this: we take delight in viewing the most accurate possible images of objects which in themselves cause

distress when we see them (e.g., the shapes of the lowest species of animal, and corpses). The reason for this is that understanding is extremely pleasant, not just for philosophers but for others, too, in the same way, despite their limited capacity for it. This is the reason why people take delight in seeing images; what happens is that as they view them they come to understand and work out what each thing is (e.g., "This is so-and-so"). If one happens not to have seen the thing before, it will not give pleasure as an imitation, but because of its execution or colour, or for some other reason.

Given, then, that imitation is natural to us, and also melody and rhythm (it being obvious that verse-forms are segments of rhythm), from the beginning those who had the strongest natural inclination towards these things generated poetry out of improvised activities by a process of gradual innovation. (48b)

To summarize: the arts exist primarily because they involve imitation, and imitation is a source of natural pleasure primarily because it affords knowledge and understanding.[4] Here, the case that Aristotle adduces may seem perhaps a bit strained: Is it really learning that is involved when we recognize a picture to be a representation of a horse? Nevertheless, later, when Aristotle applies the principle that imitation-yields-the-pleasure-of-learning to the case of tragedy—where what we are said to recognize and to learn from the plot of the play are *general patterns of human existence*—Aristotle's point makes more sense. Moreover, Aristotle in this passage is certainly right in pointing out that imitation and emulation are integral to human learning—as evidenced already in children. That is, Aristotle is correct to note that there is a connection between imitation, on the one hand, and understanding, knowledge, and education on the other. For, without imitation, there is no learning among humans. And that which Aristotle observed informally has been abundantly verified by some contemporary developmental psychology.

The importance of this claim about the connection between poetry and learning becomes apparent when we recall Aristotle's apparent debate with Plato, for we now see that, contra Plato, knowledge is not at odds with imitation. Imitation is intimately connected to the acquisition of knowledge and, therefore, education. Indeed, surely Plato must have known this. Doesn't he acknowledge it in the educational plan that he sketches for the guardians? So, Plato's attacks on poetry and drama *tout court* in Book 10 must, Aristotle implies, be either modified or abandoned.

Aristotle's discussion of poetry as imitation further challenges Plato's claims in Book 10 by showing that images are not illusions. The pleasure we take from

---

4. Or, as we might say today, the evolutionary process has naturally selected for humans who take pleasure from imitation. This pleasure in imitation, then, abets learning through imitation which is adaptive for creatures like us who must *acquire* the skills and knowledge to survive rather than coming by them, in the main, instinctually.

images depends on our realizing they are images/representations, not the things themselves. As Aristotle notes, we take pleasure from images of things whose originals we do not enjoy seeing—such as corpses. The origin of this pleasure, according to Aristotle, is the understanding the images impart. We take pleasure from images exactly because they afford understanding of things (through distancing, framing, reframing, and focus). Yet if we are to derive understanding—and the pleasure of learning—from images and if we realize that we often do not derive pleasure and understanding from the things themselves (such as corpses), then we must know the images are not illusions. Hence, we are not deceived by them.

Thus, Plato's analogy between imitations and illusions is wrong. Therefore, imitations need not be construed as addressing the lower part of the soul. Indeed, they address the understanding which one supposes is part of reason. So inasmuch as imitations are not emotion-roiling illusions and instead address the rational understanding, they do not, as Plato asserted, threaten to disrupt the souls of the citizens of the state.[5]

Aristotle follows this account of the pleasures of imitation with some general remarks about the history of tragedy, comedy, and epic. These are the three genres he intends to analyze most extensively, so he wants to give us sufficient background information to make his analyses intelligible.

The Definition of Tragedy

The first genre and, in the extant manuscript of Aristotle's *Poetics*, the only genre to be extensively analyzed—defined and explained—is tragedy.

The kind of definition Aristotle offers us is in terms of species and their differentiae. For instance, in Aristotle's well-known definition, "a human being is a rational animal," the species under consideration is "animal." Which animals are the human ones? The rational ones. Here, "rational" is the differentia (the contrast class). It tells us that which differentiates members of the species of human animals from the members of other species.

---

5. The pleasure of learning is the first cause of poetry. But there is also a second cause—form, rhythm, and the natural pleasure we take from them. This is the sort of aesthetic pleasure that Plato acknowledges in Book 10 of his *Republic* and elsewhere. It is also the sort of aesthetic pleasure that preoccupies many modern philosophers of art. But Aristotle says little about it in his *Poetics*, except to recognize its existence. Aristotle's allusion to the pleasure taken from an imitation of a corpse in contrast to a corpse in nature, moreover, is his evidence for the claim that we take pleasure in the craft of imitation, notably in terms of its service to learning.

It is also interesting that one of Aristotle's examples here is a corpse; recall the case of Leontius, whom Plato invoked to advance the idea of the tripartite soul whose lower part *mimesis* allegedly irrigates.

Aristotle's "species and differentia" definition of tragedy is the following:

> x is a tragedy if and only if (1) x is an imitation of (2) an action that is (3) important, (4) entire (complete), and (5) has magnitude and (6) which is embellished by pleasurable language (7) which is mimetic (8) where such imitations evoke pity and fear (9) for the purpose of the catharsis (the purgation, purification, or clarification) of such emotions. (49b)

The species to which tragedy belongs is imitation or representation, broadly construed. The rest of the preceding conditions are the differentiae that demarcate that which sets tragedy off from other sorts of imitations.

The second condition asserts that tragedy is not simply the imitation of just anything, but specifically that it is the imitation of an action. In this respect, tragedy is distinct from the practice of drawing still lifes since such pictures imitate objects, not actions. Also, tragedies are different from portraits, like those painted by Theophrastus, which, although they contain persons, contain persons in repose and not in action. Ditto sculptures of people posing.

However, tragedies also differ from paintings and sculptures of people in action in terms of their medium since tragedies are composed by actors speaking (condition 7), rather than of pigment or stone.

It may seem strange to you that Aristotle links tragedy with action, but it shouldn't. Our own word "drama"—which names the category to which tragedy belongs—is descended from the Greek word for doing (*draō*, which signifies "I do"). Indeed, the Greek word that drama comes from is *dran*, meaning roughly "to do." Aristotle, himself, notes this association. And, of course, there is a direct relation between "doing" and action since what is it that we do or have done, but an action?

Another reason, I think, that Aristotle articulates the definition in terms of an action is that he believes that the function of tragedy is to evoke pity and fear—to throw us into that state—and he conjectures that the way to provoke an emotional state is through some kind of *change*—something has to happen, something has to *be done* to get us into an emotional state. That is, we will only be brought into such a mental state by an action—some change, usually initiated by a human being. Furthermore, the notion of an imitation of an action draws a contrast with comedy in terms of the contrasting objects of comedy and tragedy since comedy, although it possesses plots, is *primarily* about characters (not actions), specifically characters of inferior people.[6]

---

6. By emphasizing that the object of tragedy is an action, rather than a character, Aristotle also, in effect, draws a distinction between tragedy and modern dramas that specialize in character studies, not to mention modernist dramas, like Beckett's *Waiting for Godot*, in which nothing happens—in which nothing is done.

In order to distinguish tragedy from adjacent genres, Aristotle continues to add further differentiating conditions. The third condition of this sort requires that the action imitated be *important*. This draws a further contrast with comedy since comedy imitates actions that are ridiculous. Aristotle's fourth condition demands that the action imitated be complete or entire. Here, Aristotle is focusing on the kind of plot structure that is appropriate to tragedy. The tragic plot should not be episodic, made up of lots of different stories in the way a TV dramatic series like *ER* is. *ER* is an imitation of a series of actions that are serious, but in each episode, there is a different story, which is not necessarily tied tightly to previous episodes.

In the ancient world, this kind of episodic plot structure was associated with epics, like Homer's *Odyssey*, where the episode with the Cyclops is not tied by a direct line of causes to the episode with Circe. In most cases, episodes in Homer's *Odyssey* are discrete stories, in principle detachable from the rest. Likewise, in epics about the adventures of Hercules, the stories that constitute the whole are separable. Tragedies, on the other hand, comprise a single complete story whose component events are linked causally from beginning to end. Thus, the requirement—that tragedies must be entire or complete—hives tragedies off from the related genre of the epic.

Aristotle's fifth condition for tragedy is that the imitated action be of a certain magnitude. What Aristotle has in mind here is that that the story be of such a scale that it can be readily held in the spectator's mind.[7] A tragedy should be taken in in one sitting. It is hard, if not well nigh impossible, to keep five seasons of *The Sopranos* or over twenty seasons of *The Simpsons* in one's mind's eye. There is just too much to process. But a tragedy, on the Aristotelian view, is more like a movie than a soap opera in this regard.

In terms of Aristotle's own time, the pertinent contrast would be with some epics—for example, epics about heroes like Hercules—that just throw together

---

7. The notion that the tragedy be of a certain magnitude, namely, one such that the audience can easily keep the action in its entirety before the mind is connected to the notion that plays should respect a unity of space and time. That is, the play, it has been stipulated, should occur in one place in such a way that the duration of the action represented in the play coincides with the duration of the performance of the play. Aristotle is often criticized for laying down these "unities" as rules—rules defied by the likes of Shakespeare. However, Aristotle's concern here is not with adhering to a set of rules but with trying to figure out what would be the ideal structures for the facilitation of the purpose of tragedy which is to evoke a strong emotional response. If Aristotle suggests a limitation of the temporal and spatial scope of the best tragedies, that is more of the nature of an empirically motivated, psychological hypothesis about the structural choices most likely to focus the audience member's mind in the right way. The transformation of the so-called unities into irrevocable rules was the work of Renaissance theorists and the French classicists. The latter especially had a problem with Shakespeare, but I suspect that Aristotle would not have shared their reservations.

a rambling string of adventures unconnected by little more than a recurring character.

Furthermore, one suspects that Aristotle's reason for recommending that tragedies be of a cognitively manageable scale is connected to the emotional impact which he believes it is the function of tragedy to engineer. For in order to bring about a focused emotional reaction—such as pity and fear and the catharsis thereof—it is reasonable to presume that the object of that emotional state itself be focused on perspicuously. It should not be disparate or shambling. It should be compact enough that the minds of the audience can wrap themselves around it.

In this way, the expectation that the tragedy be of a magnitude that it can be assimilated in a sitting is not unrelated to the demand that tragedy be complete—that is, single, unified narratives. In both cases, Aristotle's idea is that tragedies maintain a lock on the audience's attention with no loose ends to distract spectators and with no digressions of the type in which the viewers' focus might founder. For in either of the preceding cases, the audience's emotional response is apt to be diminished, if not lost altogether.

Tragedy is also marked by its use of language that has been made pleasurable by means of the devices of versification, such as meter, rhythm, rhyme, and tropes. The language of tragedy is embellished. In this regard, tragedy is opposed to the language of the Socratic dialogues, which, although mimetic, does not benefit from prosody. Thus, tragedy differs from the Socratic dialogue by medium as well as by object (insofar as the Socratic dialogue has thought rather than action as its object).

In addition, tragedy differs from many of its near neighbors by mode. It is mimetic in the narrow sense in that it narrates by way of the dialogue of characters. This separates tragedy from epic, which mixes mimesis and diegesis, and from dithyrambs—lyric poems with an impassioned or exalted theme and/or irregular form, such as Sappho's "The Beat Goes On" (frag. 58). For, dithyrambs are spoken in the character of the poet and not the voices of characters other than the author. Tragedies, epics, and dithyrambs are all crafted by means of elevated language, but they can be distinguished by the modes they mobilize.

The eighth condition of Aristotle's definition of tragedy begins to identify the output or effect the genre is designed to secure. The imitated action is intended, in the first instance, to evoke pity and fear. This stands in contrast to comedy, which evokes laughter (which itself is inimical to pity and fear). But these emotions are not precipitated for their own sake. Tragedy is supposed to make something happen with regard to these mental states; namely, tragedy is to operate somehow upon these emotions in a way that leads to catharsis. Thus, the ninth condition of Aristotle's definition of tragedy is that tragedy provokes pity and fear *for the purpose of the catharsis thereof*. That is, the function of tragedy is to purify, purge, and/or clarify the emotions, notably pity and fear. In this respect, tragedy is the antipode of marches and anthems, which are intended to arouse *and* intensify the relevant emotions, rather than to do something else with them or to somehow transform them. What precisely that something is—what *catharsis* is—is a topic for future discussion in this chapter. But for now, it suffices to observe that tragedy operates on the emotions it arouses, whereas marches and anthems simply arouse certain emotions.

This definition, then, specifies the nature of the thing Aristotle intends to explain. It places tragedy in the broad field of imitation and then isolates tragedy from a range of similar kinds of things—comedies, epics, dithyrambs, pictures, statues, dialogues, marches, anthems, and so on. In sum, tragedy is different from other imitations in terms of action versus states of affairs (still lives and portraits); important or admirable objects versus low ones (comedy); complete versus episodic stories (epics); cognitively manageable scale versus sprawl (epics); prosody versus ordinary language (dialogue); mimesis versus diegesis (dithyramb) and mixtures of mimesis and diegesis (epic); the arousal of pity and fear versus the arousal of something else, like laughter (comedy); and the catharsis of emotion versus its mere intensification (marches and anthems).

Once we know what we are talking about, Aristotle is ready to explain how tragedy works. As indicated, his approach to explanation is functional. That is, he intends to explain how the component parts of a tragedy function in concert to bring about a specific effect, notably the one singled out in the definition of tragedy—the arousal of pity and fear for the sake of catharsis.

Explaining Tragedy: The Function of Its Component Parts

Before Aristotle can explain how the component parts of tragedy work in concert, he must tell us what the component parts are. He begins his explanation of tragedy by first laying out the components of tragedy that will figure in his account of its function (50a).

For Aristotle, the components of tragedy are *plot, characters, diction,* and *spectacle*. Briefly, the plot is the imitation of an action, or an arrangement of events. Characters are, of course, the agents who perform the action. Action involves making choices, and characters are responsible for the choosing. In order to choose, the characters must reason about what they should do and why. That reasoning must be made manifest to the audience through speeches in which they argue for one choice rather than another and advance their opinions. The reasoning in speeches of the characters gives us the agents' interpretations of their situations, and, since they are speeches, diction is also a component of tragedy. Finally, the tragedy has a component of spectacle. The importance of spectacle is not surprising considering that the English word "theater" comes from the Greek *theasthai,* meaning "to behold."

Aristotle sees these four components as functioning together in concert. But these components have to be organized in a certain way in order to achieve the ideal effect of tragedy. Some of these components must be subservient to others if tragedy is to function properly. That is, if the effect of tragedy is to be realized, the ordering of the parts of tragedy must abide by a definite hierarchical patterning of its components or elements.

Central to Aristotle's conception of the proper arrangement of the components of tragedy is the idea that the plot is the primary component or element of tragedy (50a–b). For Aristotle, plot is the lead element because he believes that the defining function of tragedy is to arouse pity and fear, and he believes that the plot is the element through which this effect is primarily secured.

What causes pity and fear—what happens to people as a result of the characters' choices and actions—is a consequence of what they do and how they choose. The provocation of emotion in spectators depends on there being some *change* in the character's situation, and so plot—the imitation of action—is the central element of tragedy. Every other component needs to be subordinated to the plot, and so the tragedy should be designed in such a way that each component enables the plot to secure its desired effects.

One might think that this concern with arousing pity and fear would lead Aristotle to argue that character is at least as important an element as plot, but he says that plot is primary. This is because something has to happen to someone—something has to befall them—for an occurrent emotion to be aroused in the audience. There must be a change in the situation that causes an emotional change in us. Moreover, that which befalls the characters must be the result of their choices. So, for these reasons, Aristotle thinks that actions are what elicit pity and fear, not character studies.

Tragedies on the Aristotelian model contrast to plays that mostly develop character, such as those by Chekhov (e.g., *The Cherry Orchard*), which are not likely to elicit such powerful emotions. Strong emotions tend to be elicited by *abrupt* changes in states of affairs to which we react to clearly and vigorously. Character studies may be absorbing, but they don't elicit extreme emotional responses unless the characters are doing something that eventuates in an arresting turn or change of fortune.

Not only are characters not central to tragedy, but also the characters need only be sketched to the extent required in order to make a plot work. This is analogous to the case of characters in many classic detective stories, such as those of Agatha Christie. Characters need not be deeply developed psychologically in order to afford an emotionally gripping story. Thus, in the hierarchy of the components of tragedy, Aristotle rates plot development over character development.

Indeed, there can be a tragedy with very little character development. For example, say a stranger about whom you know little more than that she is a human being gets hit by a train; this story, this plot, can elicit a strong emotional response even though you barely know who the character is. In this sense, Aristotle argues that an effective tragedy without character—that is, a tragedy with almost no character development—is imaginable, though a tragedy without a plot is not.[8] Hence, plot is a more important element when it comes to tragedy, even though it might not be with respect to other genres.

Because plot is, hierarchically speaking, the leading element in tragedy, other elements, like character, must be designed with the aim of facilitating the plot—the structures of the tragic plot cannot be compromised for the sake of character interest. Character, like all the other elements of tragedy, must be subservient to the plot—must contribute to whatever makes the plot an effective instrument for evoking pity and fear. Ambiguous, complex, or psychologically dense characters, for example, risk muddying the clarity of the arc of the action in the narrative.

Characters in tragedies need be specified only in terms of the attributes requisite to make the plot move expeditiously. Oedipus need only be sketched in terms of his pride, since that is what drives him onward in his pursuit of the investigation, which, in turn, leads to the disaster that raises pity and fear in us. Ditto Pentheus in Euripides's *Bacchae*. Tragic characters do not have to be richly imagined. In fact, it is generally better that they are not, since that might slow down, diffuse, or clutter the plot momentum needed for tragedy.

Since plot is the key element in tragedy, Aristotle spends a great deal of energy analyzing it, and in doing so, he makes a great contribution to narrative theory. In his definition of tragedy, Aristotle says that the imitation of action in tragedy must be entire. Unlike some epics and all soap operas, a tragedy cannot be a desultory string of episodic events. The incidents that comprise a narrative must be unified so that they flow into each other seamlessly, giving the appearance of one continuous event. Everything in a tragic plot must be there for a reason, and when the play is over, there should be no loose ends. Tragic plots should be complete or whole in themselves. For Aristotle, this is a structural consideration.

Aristotle, furthermore, delineates what kind of structure he believes will yield the impression that the tragic narrative is complete unto itself. What is it for a plot to be whole? Aristotle says, "A whole is that which has a beginning, middle, and end" (50b). This proposal may sound pretty vacuous to you since, of course, everything that is measurable has a beginning, middle, and end. For instance, the frankfurter lying before you on your dinner plate has a beginning, middle, and end. Consequently, it may strike one as stupendously uninformative that this is what Aristotle has to say about tragic plots.

---

8. Perhaps an example of this possibility is the use of the mass hero in Soviet constructivist films like *Battleship Potemkin*. Here there is no central character—no single focus of attention from one end of the story to the other. Instead, different characters—often more than one—come to the fore in each scene. Interestingly, the director of this film, Sergei Eisenstein, thought of *Battleship Potemkin* as a tragedy.

However, Aristotle's observations are not empty because he is using these terms as *technical categories*; he is not using them in their ordinary sense of quantitative measurement, where everything has a starting point and an end and where everything between these two is the middle. For Aristotle, the beginning, the middle, and the end of a tragedy are structural components designed to discharge determinate functions.

On Aristotle's account, the end is that which follows something else as a necessary or usual or probable consequence, but which is not itself followed by anything else. Taken as a metaphysical statement, this appears absurd; every event is followed by another. But Aristotle's terminology in this instance is not metaphysical but literary. He uses the word *end* here the way in which contemporary literary theorists use the word *closure*.

Closure refers to the sense we have that when a story concludes, it does so at exactly the appropriate place. Nothing, it seems, needs to be added or subtracted. It is a feeling like the one that accompanies the ending of a piece of music—that all its themes have been wrapped up; that it ends on precisely the right note. Had it ended earlier, it would have been jarring or abrupt; had it gone on, it would seem aimless or monotonous. Because tragedies evoke this sense of closure or finality, they have an aura of necessity.

One way of explicating this idea of closure is to notice that an unfolding fictional narrative raises certain questions about its fictional world. Will the girl marry the boy next door, or will she run off with the shallow rock star? When all the relevant questions that the story has saliently posed are answered, the story is over. Moreover, the audience wants to know such and such has transpired because the narrative has posed certain questions before them as highly salient.

For example, *Oedipus Rex* begins with the plague. This raises the question of whether it can be ended. This is partially answered when we learn that it can be if the murderer of Laius can be identified and punished. This, then, introduces the question of who killed Laius? And pursuing this line of inquiry soon leads to the question, Who is Oedipus? As these questions are answered and we discover that Oedipus killed Laius and that, in consequence, Oedipus has punished himself for this action by blinding himself, the conditions for lifting the plague are in place, thereby answering the question that initiated the play.

Closure obtains when we learn everything we wanted to know—or were prompted to desire to know—as the play evolves. When all our questions are answered, in other words, closure results. The play ends at exactly the perfect moment. It has not ended before its time, as it would if it left loose ends dangling (i.e., left us with pressing questions on our mind). It does not overstay its welcome by telling us about irrelevant issues the story never posed—such as after the boy next door won the love of the girl, he bought a Hummer. That is, in terms of what the audience wants to know, the end of the play ideally coincides with an end to the questions that have engaged and governed their attention. As far as the audience is concerned, from their perspective, the end of the play need not be followed by anything else. There is no more relevant information they crave. From an information standpoint, it is extraneous to follow the end with anything more. Nothing need follow the end in an *epistemic* rather than a metaphysical sense. There is nothing left to learn.

Similarly, when Aristotle says that "a beginning is that which itself does not follow from anything else, but some second thing naturally exists or occurs after it" (50b), he is not speaking metaphysically. It would be absurd to read this assertion metaphysically since it would mean that something comes from nothing. Rather, Aristotle is speaking again from an epistemic viewpoint in terms of what an audience knows or needs to know. That is, Aristotle is discussing the control of the flow of knowledge or information to the audience. In this case, Aristotle is treating the beginning of the tragedy as a *narrational unit*, not as a real event. Every real event occurs as a consequence of some earlier events. However, the beginning of a tragedy need not elucidate all of the causal conditions of the event depicted in order to get the story rolling for the audience.

A story starts out usually by describing the time and place of the action and by introducing the central characters—and then sooner or later introducing some problem or question. *Oedipus Rex* begins by informing the audience that there is a plague, and that Oedipus is the kind of person who is extremely determined and accustomed to succeeding at whatever he sets out to accomplish. This *establishes*, as we say today, the action. In other words, it gives us that which we need to know so that the play will be intelligible when further details begin to pile up.

The beginning of the tragedy is a packet of information that contains just the knowledge (including who, what, when, where, and why) we need in order to follow the evolving action—to be able to generate the kind of questions whose answers will be delivered by the end of the story.

In order to follow the play and to generate these questions, it is not necessary that one needs to know everything about Oedipus or everything about the history of Thebes. The beginning of a story need only lay out or establish the basic facts that are required to make what follows intelligible. So, when Aristotle says that the beginning does not necessarily come from anything else, he is not saying that it is an event that metaphysically comes from nowhere;[9] rather, he is speaking from the perspective of *the narrative control of information*.

The beginning comprises just the information that is sufficient to follow what comes next. It does not come after anything else in the special sense that it is not necessary for the spectator to *know* anything more than what the beginning establishes in order to follow the work. Tragedy begins on a *need-to-know basis*. With respect to narration, a beginning x is comprised of events and states of affairs such

---

9. Just as when he talks about *the end*, he is not literally, metaphysically talking about an event that goes nowhere.

that no knowledge of unmentioned states of events prior to x—such as x - 1—is necessary in order to follow either x or the events that follow x—that is, x + 1.

The middle of the tragedy is, of course, that which falls between the beginning and the end. If the beginning introduces certain questions in the spectator's mind which she expects will be answered by the end, it falls to the middle of the story to draw these questions out and to pose them, eventually refining and complicating them, perhaps by partially answering them or by replacing them with other questions. In the language of the modern stage, the middle *complicates* the action. In *Oedipus*, the complication involves refocusing the question about the identity of the killer as a question about the identity of Oedipus.

Or, for an extremely simplified version, drawn from old-time movies: boy loves girl (beginning); boy loses girl (middle); boy gets girl (end). Of course, this is not a tragedy since it ends well. But it does illustrate the relationships between the beginning, the middle, and the end that Aristotle has in mind. As such, it is a complete, or whole, narrative.

For Aristotle, the beginning, middle, and end are the names of interrelated functional states of narration. The beginning sets out the information we need to follow what happens next and orients us to the further accumulation of detail by inducing us to ask various predetermined questions about it. The middle refines and complicates these questions by adding additional facts to the story, and it also typically raises new questions. The function of the end is to answer all of the pressing questions the story evolves. Because these functions are linked, the beginning/middle/end structure, in Aristotle's sense, gives the tragedy *a very tight sense of unity*. It does not ramble, as some epics or novels might, by confronting us with digressions. Everything neatly fits into the overarching structure, engendering a sense of necessity. There are few if any extraneous details. Everything feels locked in place, inexorably.

This unity, moreover, is such that it is easy for the spectator to hold the story before her in her mind. Thus, the beginning/middle/end structure ensures that the tragedy *will have the right magnitude*; that is, it will not overwhelm the spectator with so much information that she will lose track of it. For if she loses track of it, the story will not support *a focused, unified, emotional response* of the sort to which tragedy aspires. If the tragedy is to elicit or arouse a powerful emotional response, it must fix all the information relevant to that response in the spectator's mind and drive toward closure. The beginning/middle/end structure facilitates this by organizing the relevant information—by unifying it—into one tidy, internally coherent package of readily comprehended details.

A Brief Digression: On the Importance of Tragedy

The organization of the tragedy in terms of a tightly interwoven beginning, middle, and end serves the aim or goal of tragedy by functioning to make a strong, focused, emotional response likely. Of course, we do not yet know *why* that emotional response takes the form of pity and fear and the catharsis thereof. We will not understand that until Aristotle discusses other features of the tragic plot, namely, reversal, recognition, and calamity. However, before doing that, Aristotle pauses in his discussion of narrative structure in order to locate the position and importance of tragedy—or poetry in general—with respect to other neighboring discursive genres such as history and philosophy.

In addition to the beginning/middle/end structure, the tragedy is rendered readily accessible to the mind of the viewer because in tragedy, the poet says not "what has happened but . . . the kind of thing that *would* happen, i.e., what is possible in accordance with probability or necessity" (51.a.9). That is, there is something lawlike or patterned that connects the events in a tragedy. The tragedy is easier to track just because it is underwritten by patterns. What patterns? Patterns or regularities of human behavior.

The tragedian, in other words, presents us with representations of how human events are likely to go. What will probably happen if one puts two strong-willed people with fundamentally different aims—such as Creon and Antigone—on a collision course? Will either relent? Not likely. For Aristotle, it is the task of the poet to reveal these kinds of patterns in human life to audiences—to disclose how things are apt to go when certain personalities are put in play in the same place and time. In the film *House of Sand and Fog*, we see how two personalities convinced of their own rectitude can engender a spiral of destruction.

The tragedian is a chemist of human inclinations, juxtaposing them in different combinations and then charting the scenario that is likely to result. In this way, *pace* Plato, the poet gives us knowledge of human nature, specifically as Ion suggested, in terms of what people are likely to do or to say in certain generically recurring situations of human life, especially those involving human interactions. At the same time, since the poet works with patterns of human life—patterns of probability—the tragedy is organized in a way that the spectator can keep its relevant details readily before the mind, thereby satisfying the conditions for eliciting the focused emotional response that it is the aim of tragedy to elicit.

At 51a9, Aristotle makes this point by saying that "the function of the poet is not to say what *has* happened, but to say the kind of thing that *would* happen, i.e., what is possible in accordance with probability or necessity. The historian and the poet are not distinguished by their use of verse or prose; it would be possible to turn the works of Herodotus into verse, and it would be history in verse as much as prose; the distinction is this: the one says what has happened, the other the kind of thing that would happen."

For this reason, poetry is more philosophical and more serious than history. Poetry tends to express universals, history particulars. History, cluttered with facts, obscures the universal. The universal is the kind of pattern of speech or action that is consonant with the behavior of a person of a given kind in accordance with probability or necessity. And displaying this pattern is what poetry aims at, even though it trades in individual names. Characters in tragedy are sensuous universals, as Hegel might have it—concrete representations of ideal types or ideas. For example, in *Antigone*, Creon stands for the claims of the state, while his niece Antigone is a cipher for familial or tribal obligations.

Tragedy explores recurring situations in human life, including family conflict and political obligation and betrayal, love and loss, death, and so on. *Medea*, for example, recounts the scenario of a woman scorned, vividly annotating the rage that can ensue. Medea, here, is the locus of a universal, which, for Aristotle, is "the kind of speech or action which is consonant with a person of a given kind in accordance with probability or necessity" (51b).

This passage in Aristotle on the relationship between poetry and philosophy is very important. It packs a lot into a short space. First of all, it answers several of Plato's charges against poetry, though it does not name him outright. Recall that Plato charged that poetry merely holds a mirror up to things, capturing the appearances of particulars. Here Aristotle suggests that that is a far better description of history than of poetry. Poetry is more abstract. It has a universal or general dimension. It illuminates abstract scenarios of how human events are likely to unfold. It depicts how people are likely to speak and likely to act in certain recurring situations.

Also, remember that Ion said that what the poet knows is what it is fitting for people to say and to do. Aristotle apparently concurs. He thinks, against Plato, that the poet *does* know something, namely, how certain kinds of people are likely to behave in certain kinds of situations—how people as stubborn as Creon and Antigone are likely to behave once set at odds. Neither will flinch, neither will blink, and once their deadly opposition is set in motion, the outcome is apt to be disaster. Therefore, contra Plato, the poet knows something and has something to teach, something about human existence, namely about the way in which the tendencies of actions and events, once certain personalities and the forces and emotions they incarnate are set in motion, are likely to trend.

This is usually only a matter of probabilities. The poet outlines the natural tendencies of events. Sometimes these probabilities don't pan out in particular situations. They are abstract scenarios with a high probability of unfolding in the manner the poet predicts. The requirement of probability indicates that these stories are generalizable. "Probability" here is not about what an audience can or will accept (as contemporaries understand it) but is epistemically significant in terms of how things are likely to work themselves out.

The historian tells us what happened in particular cases, which may or may not coincide with what antecedently was likely to have happened. The poet gives us deeper or more abstract insight into the natural vectors or tendencies of events. The poet teaches about certain regularities in human experience. The poet gives us a blueprint for human action, not the buildings constructed from those blueprints, which, of course, may deviate from the blueprint.

Nevertheless, the blueprint still gives us a picture of the structure of appearances rather than actual appearances. The blueprint of a landscape, for example, enables us to tell the forest from the trees. Thus, we can learn from the blueprint. We can learn from the tragedy, despite Plato's denial of this possibility. This also accounts for why we take pleasure from tragedy, whereas we wouldn't take pleasure from actual tragic events. Tragedies are constructed so that the events they depict are perspicuous and the pleasure we derive from tragedy is, in large measure, the pleasure of learning, a pleasure that, therefore, again despite Plato, is not inimical to reason, but indispensable to it.

As you may recall, earlier Aristotle maintained that we take a natural pleasure from mimesis or imitation. Tragedy is the mimesis or imitation of an action. Furthermore, the pleasure that mimesis bestows is primarily a matter of learning. The tragedy teaches about human action. What does it teach us about human action? It teaches us about how certain human events are likely or necessarily to go once certain kinds of persons and forces make contact.

Since what we learn from tragedy are probabilities and necessities, this knowledge is obviously general and more akin to philosophy than history. Because the pleasure in mimesis here is conducive to the acquisition of philosophy-like knowledge, it does not threaten reason but buttresses it. Moreover, this knowledge is beneficial to the ruler and citizen alike. So, from the viewpoint of the commonwealth, it is *beneficial pleasure*. Thereby, Aristotle rises to the challenge that Socrates issued to the advocates of poetry at the end of the *Republic*.

Furthermore, this knowledge is available to us predominantly through the plot—the sequence of probable actions. This is why Aristotle is so disparaging about the importance of the spectacle element in tragedy. Note that for Aristotle, tragedy and the pleasures thereof are a function of what one learns from mimesis. Thus, if it is the case that what we learn from tragedy/poetry is how human affairs—actions and events—are likely to go, then we can learn this simply by reading the play. We don't have to see it represented through spectacle. What there is to be learned from the play is already on the page. This implies for Aristotle that in point of fact, spectacle is less important than plot since everything there is to know with respect to a play can be derived by following the plot. For this reason, plot is more important than spectacle.

There is a corollary to this. Since plot is more important than spectacle, then if a play is mounted, the spectacle elements should not interfere with the knowledge available from the plot. The spectacle, so to speak, should never upstage the plot. It must be subservient to the plot, at all times contributing to making the knowledge embodied by the plot clear and accessible.[10] Moreover, since tragedy is not

---

10. In the twentieth century, the bias toward plot over spectacle called forth a predictable reaction which contends that it is spectacle, in contrast to literary artifacts like plot, that constitutes the essence of theater, such that all genuine practitioners of drama stress spectacle over story. Hence, the aesthetics of Antoine Artaud and then of Richard Foreman and Robert Wilson.

literally tied essentially to visual appearances, Plato's analogy to optical illusions and paintings is thereby undercut.

This brief passage also makes clear what Aristotle believes to be a primary source of pleasure with respect to poetry. Earlier he maintained the pleasure to be had from imitation in general is connected to learning. He said that the pleasure we derive from pictures is connected to recognizing what pictures are of. I said that this didn't seem to be a particularly persuasive way to describe the pleasure we derive from pictures. However, when we connect what he said about the pleasure in learning to be had from mimesis in general to this passage on poetry, the account makes more sense. For what we recognize in a plot is the probable tendencies of human events, something that would be unavailable to us without the poet's distillation of the relevant human forces in juxtaposition.

That is, the semiabstract depiction of human affairs enables us to see or to recognize how human chemistries work, and also the ways in which the events in which they figure are likely to turn out. This affords us an opportunity to come to some genuine discoveries about human existence.

A feminist novel, for example, can highlight certain likely forces, personality types, and practices in such a way that they stand out and can be recognized, whereas in the flow of everyday life, they might otherwise be obscured. Because the poet shows likely patterns in human affairs, she has, despite Plato's claims to the contrary, something to teach, and this is because she knows something about people's tendencies to behave in certain ways. Moreover, the sort of pleasure we derive from this is cognitive. It does not just appeal to the lower parts of the soul. The kind of knowledge the poet trades in is closer to philosophy. Also, this kind of knowledge is not necessarily tied to particular practices or skills like medicine or generalship. It is general human knowledge available to any astute observer, including poets. So, the fact that the poet is not a practitioner of any other craft is beside the point. The poet's craft is the craft of imitating actions, which, in large measure, is the craft of exhibiting probable tendencies in human affairs.

Of course, it is only closer to philosophy. It is not identical with what philosophy has to offer. For philosophy yields knowledge of what is necessarily the case, whereas poetry usually trades in something less certain than this. Typically, it merely trades in what is probably the case, that is, how things are likely to go. But this does not entail that the poet has nothing to teach, but only that it is not the highest sort of knowledge.

Aristotle in his *Nicomachean Ethics* (1177a15–20) announces that the best sort of life involves theoretical contemplation, contemplation of eternal verities, like the truths of mathematics. Poetry does not afford precisely this type of contemplation. However, it does afford a related kind of contemplation of generalities, namely, the contemplation with understanding of certain of the deep regularities of human life. This not only connects poetry with cognitive pleasure but also suggests that poetry, by encouraging the contemplation of truths, may make some contribution to the very best life, not by presenting us with eternal, unchanging verities for contemplation, but with something closer to them than what we ordinarily encounter in the flow of daily life. So again, *pace* Plato, Aristotle seems to find a place for poetry in the creation of virtuous living, in the education of our cognitive powers, rather than simply consigning poetry to the realms of irrationality. That is, Aristotle finds a role for poetry in the good city, the city of virtuous citizens.

Back to the Components of Tragedy

After discussing the importance of the plot dimension of poetry for exhibiting generalizations about human existence, Aristotle returns to his analysis of plot structure in terms of the ways in which it functions to elicit pity and fear—culminating in astonishment—from audiences.

Aristotle has told us that tragic plots should be unified; they should possess beginnings, middles, and ends, in his special sense of those terms. This, putatively, is necessary in order to elicit a strong, focused emotional response from readers, viewers, and listeners. But why should these strong emotional responses be a matter of pity and fear? In order to explain this, Aristotle offers us a more detailed account of the functional ingredients that go into making a complete tragic plot. That is, Aristotle next isolates the ingredients that go into causing *precisely* pity and fear in the spectator.

All tragic plots have beginnings, middles, and ends. But Aristotle also distinguishes between two sorts of tragic plots: simple plots—which have a beginning, middle, and then an end in which calamity or suffering befalls the protagonist—and complex plots. Moreover, complex plots are best suited to arousing pity and fear.

In complex plots, the ingredients responsible for the elicitation of pity and fear involve reversal, recognition, and calamity (or suffering). Reversal and recognition occur during the middle of the tragedy and are the plot complications. What is reversal, what is recognition, and how do they contribute to causing pity and fear?

With respect to reversal, Aristotle says, "A reversal is a change to the opposite in the actions being performed as stated—and this, as we have been saying, in accordance with probability and necessity" (52a11). A reversal is a plot turn—called a *peripeteia*. Specifically, peripeties are plot turns where things suddenly start heading in the opposite direction with respect to the plight of the protagonist—that is, where actions begin to take on significance opposite from the protagonist's original purpose. Very often this opposition is a matter of a reversal of the original intention of the agent. For example, Oedipus initiates the investigation of the plague in order to establish further his leadership of Thebes but his efforts boomerang and lead to his own banishment. This is the idea, enshrined in ordinary language, in the well-known idiom of a *reversal of fortune*.

The reversal is an element of a complex tragedy. But remember that Aristotle is analyzing plot structures functionally. So how do reversals contribute to the effect of tragedy—the raising of pity and fear? On Aristotle's view, reversal is the cause of fear. The reversal reminds the spectator that things can swing out of control. Tragedy emphasizes the theme that bad luck can ruin our lives at any moment, a theme that Martha Nussbaum insightfully calls the "fragility of goodness."

Tragedy invites the recognition that bad things can happen to good people—that being virtuous does not guarantee happiness. One may act in accordance with what one believes is right but nevertheless suffer calamity—that is, a reversal of fortune.

For example, Oedipus left Corinth and traveled to Thebes in order to evade the prophecy that he would kill his father and consummate incest with his mother. Little did he realize that in coming to Thebes, he was actually fulfilling his destiny since the king and queen of Corinth were not his birth parents, but only his adoptive parents. In fact, the king and queen of Thebes were Oedipus's natural father and mother. Oedipus left Corinth with the best intentions, and yet the outcomes of his choices were precisely the opposite of that which he meant to do. The results were horrendous, tragic.

The realization that good people with the best intentions can be struck down at any moment was a terrifying prospect for the Greeks. Therefore, this particular plot turn—the reversal of fortune—functioned to strike fear in the hearts of ancient audiences because it reminded spectators of their own inescapable vulnerability.

The last line of *Oedipus Rex* is "Call no man happy until he is dead." By this aphorism, the ancient Greeks signaled that one can never assess a person's life until he or she has passed, because it is only in death that one is finally placed out of the reach of ill fortune. Only after the last breath is exhaled can we be in a position to say with utter confidence that a person's life had been a good one. That the fortune of even the virtuous person is so precarious—such a hostage to fate—is the bleak lesson of tragedy: its deepest insight into the verities of human existence. Tragedy makes this necessary feature of human life graphically manifest. And this is what makes the audience's emotional response to the tragic reversal one of fear—fear for oneself, fear for one's own prospects of continued flourishing.

Tragedy reminds spectators that no matter how powerful or virtuous, our best intentions can have the worst consequences. The reversal component of tragedy stresses that the stories we plan to tell for ourselves are not guaranteed to be the story that gets told when all is said and done. It makes us realize the contingency of human life—including our own lives—and this causes fear in us.

In the complex plot, reversal may be followed by recognition or discovery. This plot movement is connected especially to prompting pity. It instills pathos with regard to the reversed situation of the protagonist. Recognition comes about particularly when characters realize that they have been, through errors that are no fault of their own, the agents of their own destruction.

Aristotle defines recognition as a change from ignorance to knowledge as when Oedipus realizes that he is the murderer of Laius. We pity him all the more because we understand that he recognizes that he has brought about his own suffering, just as Creon recognizes that through his own action in executing Antigone, he has caused the suicides of his son Haemon and his wife Eurydice. He sees that this disaster is his own fault due to his error in judgment.

Why does this sort of plot lead to pity? Well, it is bad enough that terrible things happen to someone, it is worse when you've brought it on yourself and you know it. Your plight is all the more pitiable since, added to the pain of what has happened, there is the added psychological pain that comes with your awareness that you've done it to yourself.

Watching a character exhibiting this sort of self-conscious pain accentuates the pity we already feel for a character who has been lowered by fortune. A self-initiated misfortune is compounded by remorse borne of the recognition that you yourself could have averted disaster. The victim here suffers the familiar "if only I'd done otherwise" experience as in the case of the parent who, after a swimming accident, says, "If only I'd made Johnny stay home and do his schoolwork." And, again, since the distress of such characters reminds us that the same thing could befall us, we once again feel fear for ourselves.

The last plot movement in this triad of factors in the complex plot is calamity or suffering. The name of this plot development is self-explanatory. The calamity involves destruction or pain—deaths in full view, extreme agony, and so on. And this makes us pity the victim of fate.

The reversal in the play brings suffering in its wake. In *Oedipus Rex*, the reversal occurs when it is revealed that Oedipus is the murderer and the son of Laius rather than his avenger, which, of course, causes the suicide of Jocasta, his self-blinding, his banishment, and anguish. This heightens our sense of both pity and fear. Fear arises in the audience because we realize that such calamities could issue as the unintended consequences of our own actions. Pity for the character is provoked as the misery heaps up upon him. Moreover, there may also be a dimension of pity for ourselves because we recognize that as fellow human beings, we are liable to the same contingencies of human life (a.k.a. bad luck).

In sum, the component parts of the complex, tragic plot function to engender the intended response of tragedy in the following way. The beginning/middle/end structure guarantees a strong, focused emotional response to the drama. The reversal component refines that emotional response primarily as one of fear. The recognition component when connected to the reversal functions to arouse pity. And, of course, the calamity will stoke both pity and fear.

In the simple, tragic plot, the calamity does all the work of eliciting pity and fear. Complex plots are better because they are more fully articulated in a way that is predicated on ensuring the output of pity and fear. They are more intricately calibrated to get the job done. Moreover, this account is obviously a functional one because the form of the tragedy—the form of the plot—has been broken down by Aristotle in terms of the way the parts function to bring about or realize the goal of tragedy—the production of pity and fear.

Character

For Aristotle, after the plot, the construction of the characters is the most important element in tragedy. And just as Aristotle analyzes plotting with an eye to what is most conducive functionally to bringing about the effects of tragedy, so his examination of the construction of characters is carried out in terms of what will be most effective for raising pity and fear in the audience.

Of first importance in this regard is obviously the construction of the major character—the character whom tragedy befalls. This character has to be molded in such a way that he/she best serves the tragic plot, which in turn, best serves the promotion of the tragic emotion. Of this character, Aristotle says,

> It is clear first of all that decent men should not be seen undergoing a change from good fortune to bad fortune—this does not evoke fear or pity, but disgust. Nor should depraved people be seen undergoing a change from bad fortune to good fortune—this is the least tragic of all: it has none of the right effects, since it is neither agreeable, nor does it evoke pity or fear. Nor again should a very wicked person fall from good fortune to bad fortune—that kind of structure would be agreeable, but would not excite pity or fear, since the one has to do with someone who is suffering undeservedly, the other with someone who is like ourselves (I mean, pity has to do with the undeserving sufferer, fear with the person like us); so what happens will evoke neither pity nor fear.
>
> We are left, therefore, with the person intermediate between these. This is the sort of person who is not outstanding in moral excellence or justice; on the other hand, the change to bad fortune which he undergoes is not due to any moral defect or depravity, but to an error of some kind. He is one of those people who are held in great esteem and enjoy great good fortune, like Oedipus, Thyestes, and distinguished men from that kind of family. (52.6.15)

Note the requirement that the character be mixed. Furthermore, the reasons for this are all connected to what it would take to move us precisely into the state of pity and fear. Destroying an altogether good person would disgust us. Lynching a Mother Teresa would provoke indignation, not pity and fear. Moreover, it is clear that something like what some nowadays call identification or, perhaps better, should call solidarity or allegiance or alignment, with the tragic character plays an important role in Aristotle's theory.

The characters are elevated or heroic in order to remind us that no matter how great, everyone may become a victim of fortune. And since the great ones are, like us, not perfect, we feel pity rather than outrage when they are destroyed. Indeed, since they are like us in this respect, their destruction recalls to mind the contingency of our own well-being.

That is, we are moved to fear especially because we can see that the character is enough like ourselves that similar disasters could befall us. We recognize the protagonists as our allies in the sorts of vulnerabilities that flesh is heir to. This means that the character, although of impressive stature, has also to be like the average viewer at least in some respects. The character cannot be too good, but neither can the character be worthless. Why? Because misery befalling a worthless person, although it might evoke feelings of sympathy, won't evoke fear, since the fear in question is supposed to be fear for ourselves, for people like us, the average viewer, a person of average virtue. And putatively the average viewer, who is neither perfectly good nor utterly worthless, cannot relate the miseries of a worthless person to his/her own life prospects.

Similarly, the tragic protagonist should not be consummately evil, since in that case the calamity he suffers will be greeted by spectators as his just deserts. That is, *The Tragedy of Heinrich Himmler* is an inadvisable theatrical venture since his demise, rather than provoking pity and fear, is more likely to invigorate our sense of justice.

Also, in line with this requirement of solidarity with the character is the notion that the character be a mean between conspicuous goodness and depravity. For example, the mistake that sends the character hurtling toward disaster should be a matter of error, not depravity. In the ideal case, Aristotle recommends that it should be an innocent error rather than a vicious one, as is Oedipus's flight from Corinth. For, again, the protagonist should be, like the viewer, of average virtue and not a villain. His downfall issues from no moral fault of his own, for he should not deserve the calamity that befalls him.

The tragic hero should be someone akin to the normal viewer, inasmuch as she is a generally good person brought low. In this respect, even the language of the character should be subordinated to the end or purpose of tragedy. For this reason, Aristotle recommends iambic trimeter on the grounds that this is the meter that most closely approximates ordinary dialogue rather than, for instance, song. By making the protagonist sound more like us, perhaps Aristotle thinks we will be more likely to see ourselves in the character and, thereby, more susceptible to fearing that a reversal of fortune such as the one that besets the protagonist could strike us down as well.

The aforesaid type of character, housed in this kind of plot, culminating in misfortune, will cause pity and fear in us. Similarly, speech contributes to raising pity and fear in the audience since misfortune comes as the result of a mistake that has been chosen, albeit innocently, while the spectacle incites these emotions by graphically presenting the calamity. Presumably, these factors will cause so much pity and fear in us that by the end of the play, we will be emotionally exhausted; we will be emptied of pity and fear. Tension will be raised in us and then resolved so that all the emotions embroiled by the plot are spent.

Thus, rather than exciting the relevant emotions to the point where they are out of control (to the detriment of the rule of reason in the soul), tragedy, on Aristotle's account, may quell pity and fear. In this way, Aristotle may be in the business of derailing Plato's most severe criticisms of tragedy.

Catharsis

As we have seen, Aristotle's analysis of the components of tragedy has been dedicated to showing how the parts of tragedy arouse pity and fear in spectators. But pity and fear, especially fear for our own fate, cannot be a pleasant state in which to be. So, why do we consume tragedies if that results in unpleasant or negative mental states, such as pity and fear? This may be where the notion of catharsis enters the picture. But what is catharsis?

So far, Aristotle's analysis of tragedy has been proceeding by explicating the ways in which tragedy performs the function of raising pity and fear. This procedure makes sense since, given Aristotle's definition of tragedy, arousing these emotions is necessary for the imitation of an action to count as tragedy. However, tragedy is also supposed to precipitate the *catharsis* of pity and fear. So, we won't have a complete understanding of Aristotle's view until we have some idea of what it is for pity and fear to undergo catharsis. And, as indicated above, this may help us, in addition, with answering the question of why we submit ourselves to undergoing the negative emotions of pity and fear—a question about tragedy which Hume will subsequently christen as the "paradox of tragedy."[11]

Although a grasp of Aristotle's conception of catharsis would appear integral to his theory of tragedy, it is a task whose completion is called for rather than done since Aristotle is never very forthcoming about what he means by *catharsis*. He doesn't define it in his *Poetics* or elsewhere, despite the fact that he has said that he had done so in his *Politics*.[12] Moreover, Aristotle only uses the phrase a couple of times in his *Poetics*, which doesn't give us a great many contextual clues to go on. Thus, what Aristotle means by catharsis is wide open to conjecture. Many commentators have offered alternative interpretations of catharsis over the years. In what follows, I will review some of the strengths and weaknesses of the leading interpretations of catharsis.

---

11. In his statement of purpose, Aristotle promised not only to define and to explain poetry but also to deal with whatever special problems the various poetic genres raise. Perhaps, the introduction of catharsis into the discussion of tragedy is meant to deal with the problem Hume called the "paradox of tragedy."

12. Of course, since we only have a fragment of his *Poetics*, it might be the case that Aristotle defined catharsis in one of the missing segments.

Aristotle's Poetics

Some common meanings of *catharsis* include purgation, purification, and clarification, but there are questions about which one of these to use with regard to Aristotle's *Poetics* as well as how to apply the chosen one. Does catharsis pertain to the emotions of the audience members, or to the emotions of the characters, or does it have something to do with the plot?

In order to get a handle on the concept of catharsis, the first question to answer concerns its object. Catharsis appears to be a process—a process involving pity and fear. But who or what undergoes the process of catharsis? There are three alternatives: the characters of the tragedy, the spectators, or the narrative itself.[13]

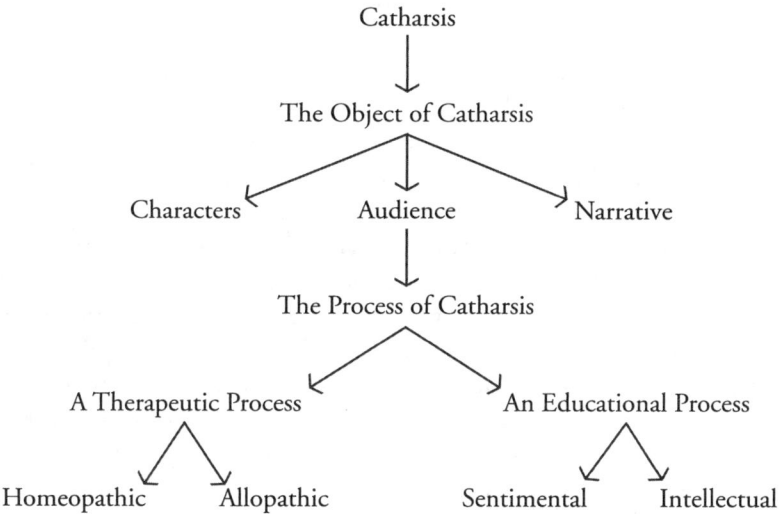

Goethe proposed that the objects of catharsis were the emotions of the characters. But this does not seem very convincing. Let us suppose that catharsis means "purged." Yet many of the protagonists at the end of tragedies do not seem as though they have had their emotions purged by the end of the play. Oedipus is still in agony at the end of *Oedipus Rex*, as is Creon at the end of *Antigone* and Agave at the end of *Bacchae*. Nor has Medea's rage abated at the end of the play that bears her name. Perhaps by the conclusion of *Oedipus at Colonus*, Oedipus appears purged and purified, or at least reconciled, but this play is the exception, not the rule. Moreover, the emotions that grip most tragic characters are not pity and fear, but anguish and/or remorse or, in the case of Medea, rage. Consequently, even if

---

13. Jason Cutmore suggested to me that there should be another alternative here, namely that the object of catharsis might be the artist. I think that this would have been unlikely since Greek tragedies were civic and religious rituals. The view that it is the catharsis of the artist that tragedy aims at provoking seems unlikely in this context. It would appear to require faith in some sort of post-Romantic individualism.

the pertinent characters are said to experience catharsis, it is not the catharsis of pity and fear. Therefore, since this account of catharsis fits the facts so badly, it is implausible to endorse it.[14]

A second alternative interpretation of the object of catharsis is that the object catharsis operates on is the plot. Here the relevant sense of catharsis is *clarification*. Catharsis, on this view, clarifies the plot tendencies by bringing them to resolution. What gets clarified, in other words, is the development of the plot. Where events are headed is clarified by carrying things to their natural conclusion, inasmuch as the conclusion clarifies the significance of the earlier events in the plot.

One shortcoming of this view is that plots don't have emotions like pity and fear to be clarified. Instead, on this interpretation, the only thing that happens to the emotions is that pity and fear are aroused. The catharsis/clarification of plot lines is just what causes pity and fear. Catharsis is not some extra process that operates on pity and fear. Catharsis is simply what arouses pity and fear. But if catharsis is just what arouses pity and fear, then it does not, appearances notwithstanding, add anything to Aristotle's definition of tragedy. And a further downside to this approach is that it fails to provide a response to Plato's objections to poetry. It is as if Aristotle writes his definition of tragedy in ignorance of Plato's criticisms, which seems at least improbable.

The third candidate for the object of catharsis is the emotions of the audience, notably pity and fear. Somehow it engages these emotions and transforms them. But how?

One place where Aristotle mentions *catharsis* is in chapter 7 of Book 8 of his *Politics*. There he says that he won't speak at length about catharsis, because he says he will discuss it at length in his *Poetics*, although, of course, we know that this doesn't happen in the fragments of that text which have come down to us. Nevertheless, Aristotle does suggest something that he might have in mind by catharsis, at least with respect to that which he is discussing at that point in his *Politics*.

At the juncture at which he is commenting on various religious rituals, notably the rites of Dionysius, Aristotle uses *catharsis* in a way that suggests the purgation or lightening up of strong feelings, such as pity and fear. Aristotle appears to regard these cases as instances of healing. So, if the catharsis of pity and fear in tragedy is analogous to the catharsis obtained in religious festivals, then it may be that Aristotle believes that catharsis in tragedy is somehow therapeutic.

---

14. It has been hypothesized that there may be a political motivation lurking behind the suggestion that it is the emotions of the characters that serve as the objects of catharsis. Specifically, it is conjectured that this is a gambit designed to elude censorship. The idea is that by denying that tragedy has the power to arouse the emotions of the audience—by, in effect, relocating the emotions at issue in the characters—the friend of tragedy can assert, "There is no reason to censor tragedy, since it lacks the causal efficacy to influence the audience emotionally." Nietzsche attributes a comparable emotion to the slogan "art for art's sake" in "Raids of an Untimely Man," in *Twilight of the Idols* (section 24).

In Greek culture, there were at least two conceptions of catharsis as therapy. Thus, if Aristotle, the son of a doctor, thinks of tragic catharsis as therapeutic, it is likely that he had one of these two conceptions in mind. The pertinent conceptions of catharsis as therapy are the homeopathic model and the allopathic model.

According to the homeopathic model, a treatment or therapy is homeopathic if it combats an illness with more of the same. For example, piling on more blankets to deal with a fever is a homeopathic cure. The idea here is to fight fire with fire.

One problem, however, with attributing this understanding of catharsis as therapy to Aristotle is that the homeopathic model of medical treatment was rare among the Greeks, so it may be improbable that Aristotle is presupposing it in both his *Poetics* and *Politics*. The allopathic approach to catharsis—the notion of confronting an affliction with its opposite (as in applying cold compresses to a fever)—was far more popular.

Furthermore, there is an even deeper reason to suspect that Aristotle is not thinking of tragic catharsis as a form of homeopathic treatment. At the conclusion of his *Poetics*, Aristotle is at pains to show that tragedy is not inferior to epic poetry—that, like epic poetry, tragedy is addressed to decent audiences, not to vulgar, inferior, or second-rate audiences (62a). That is, Aristotle wants to prove that tragedy is appropriate for consumption by decent, first-rate audiences.

But this calls into question the homeopathic healing model. Why? Well, if what tragedy does is heal people, then its audiences must be in some way deficient. According to the homeopathic therapeutic model, they are stricken with an excessive amount of pity and fear that must be flushed from their system through a surfeit of stimulation. But this suggests that they are emotionally unbalanced or defective to begin with. Tragedy cures them. But if they need to be cured, then they were ill. So, the natural audience for tragedy, on this model, are people who are in some sense defective. That would appear to suggest that emotionally balanced people, virtuous people—or decent people—would not comprise the kind of audience at which tragedy is aimed. That would follow from the homeopathic healing model of tragedy. Yet that can't be Aristotle's view. For Aristotle asserts that decent, indeed, superior people are also the appropriate audience for tragedy. That is,

(1) If the homeopathic healing model of catharsis is what Aristotle has in mind, then decent folk (persons with well-balanced emotional profiles) would not find value in tragedy.

(2) But decent folk can find value in tragedy.

(3) Therefore, it is not the case that the homeopathic healing model of catharsis is what Aristotle had in mind.[15]

---

15. Perhaps it might be suggested that decent people are not unbalanced when they enter the theater but are imbalanced emotionally by what they see and then relieved by the play itself. Yet, isn't this an absurd hypothesis? It is as if I put my hand in a vice to feel the pleasure of release. Why not just refrain from hurting myself from the start?

So far, we have been exploring the homeopathic model of catharsis. This is a healing model—the idea is that one drives away noxious afflictions or purges them by applying more of the same substance to the subject. But there is also the allopathic model of catharsis as therapy.

Allopathic therapy is treatment by way of opposites. On this model, pity and fear would be raised in spectators in order to *purge* the opposite emotions from them. Pity and fear are aroused in spectators in order for audiences to master and purge certain other emotional tendencies that are unsavory and unwanted, and that pity and fear are mobilized to counteract. However, to even begin to find this suggestion plausible, obviously we would need some conception of the state that pity and fear is meant to drive away.

One suggestion is that the state that tragic catharsis is designed to dispel involves a kind of arrogance or complacency. The fear engendered by tragedy is the emotional realization that we are vulnerable. Through tragedy, we recognize that our actions may bring with them unintended consequences of the sort that can bring down low commanding personages like Oedipus and Creon and Pentheus. Thus we, who are so much less powerful, become apprised of our vulnerability upon exposure to tragedy. In contrast, in the daily course of affairs, it is easy to forget how precarious human existence really is. It is easy to become brash, incautious, and overconfident. We plunge ahead with our projects, scarcely cognizant of the possibility of a reversal of fortune.

Furthermore, this kind of arrogance or complacency can become a liability in the citizen. Why? Because a populace of brash risk-takers—who have forgotten how readily the best of plans can go awry—will be prepared to take chances that can eventuate in disaster (such as embarking on imperial wars, as Athens did). One wants a prudent citizenry, one that is sufficiently risk averse. Instead of reckless citizens, one prefers careful and reflective ones. Tragedy, it may be claimed, encourages prudence, inasmuch as it instills fear in spectators by apprising or reminding them of the possibility that undesirable and unintended contingencies may wreck their best designs due to the fickleness of fortune.

Through raising the tragic emotions of pity and fear in us, tragedy, *ex hypothesi*, compels us to reflect on the likely dangers that can ensue as the unintended consequences of our actions. Tragedy cultivates a sober cast of mind. With tragic outcomes vividly embedded in our memories, it is impossible to sustain an arrogant and brash faith in our own invulnerability. Tragic pity and fear are incompatible with the kinds of mental states—such as a belief in one's invulnerability—that invite arrogance and complacency.

That is, Aristotle may be concerned that in peacetime, especially, people can become contemptuous and intemperately bold when fear is not near at hand. A kind of pride or hubris is apt to emerge. Provoking fear of fortune's wiles in such people is a tonic. It is the role of tragedy to function as an antidote that stifles that sort of hubris—an antidote to pride and overconfidence.

This interpretation of catharsis, moreover, gives Aristotle a way of answering Plato by spelling out the social benefit to be derived from the pity and fear that tragedy engenders. And further support for the allopathic interpretation of catharsis might be that the sort of pride and overweeningly confident enthusiasm that tragedy curbs in the spectator is also addressed within the plays, since many tragic characters themselves are noteworthy for being prideful and overconfident.

However, there are several problems with the view of catharsis as allopathic therapy. First, it is surprising that if Aristotle thought that tragedy is the antidote of pride, he never specified so important a part of this theory.[16]

Second, the allopathic theory of catharsis faces the same problem which we identified with respect to the homeopathic theory, namely, that tragedy would only appear to perform a service for people who are not completely decent. Decent people, one supposes, are already prudent. Only vulgar and inferior people are afflicted with the sort of imprudence that our version of the allopathic theory maintains that tragedy cures. But as Aristotle appears to believe that tragedy is appropriate for decent people, he cannot hold the view that the point of tragedy is essentially therapeutic, even allopathically.

For if audiences require an antidote, then there is something wrong with them. One can concede that Aristotle might think that the vulgar could profit from some therapy. But he also thinks that tragedy is suitable for decent people. Yet, since they are not afflicted, one imagines that they are not in need of an antidote. However, Aristotle thinks they can benefit from tragedy. So, he must think that the benefits of tragedy lie in something other than being an antidote.

Even supposing that the allopathic theory were the right account of catharsis and that what tragedy is about is sobering brash and bold tendencies by instilling an awareness of our vulnerability in spectators, that would still leave us with a question—What is the connection between being brought into that state and pleasure? Presumably catharsis is connected with pleasure. The homeopathic model accommodates this by proposing that tragedy removes or evacuates negative or painful emotions such as pity and fear. Removing pain is an obvious source of pleasure. But how does administering dosages of painful emotion and making us more wary amount to any sort of pleasure? Being shocked by electricity makes a rat increasingly wary, but where's the pleasure for the rat in that? And, in any event, wariness itself is an unpleasant state to be in. But if the allopathic model of catharsis makes no connection with pleasure, then it appears to be an unpromising account of tragic catharsis.

If catharsis is connected with pleasure, then we must ask ourselves what the source of pleasure might be. In his *Poetics*, Aristotle is quite explicit about what he takes to be the primary source of pleasure in tragedy. The source of pleasure

---

16. Of course, this is not a decisive objection. Since our version of the *Poetics* is incomplete, for all we know, he may have outlined this possibility.

in tragedy is learning; the source of pleasure is educational. So, if catharsis is connected to pleasure, perhaps it secures that link by teaching us something. Thus, it seems reasonable to explore some educative interpretations of catharsis.

There are at least two ways in which catharsis may play a role in the education of spectators. It could contribute to either their sentimental education or to the intellectual education of the audience. Let's take sentimental education first. What does this mean? That tragedy might educate our emotions—train our emotions—just as a dancer trains her muscles so that she can execute certain movements precisely and correctly. Likewise, it may be supposed that one can train one's emotional responses so that they are accurate and appropriate. Our sentiments can be educated—a process, which for obvious reasons, we may call a sentimental education. In this regard catharsis might be seen as the process of educating our sentiments by purifying our emotions in the sense of getting them into perfect working order.

Emotions in everyday life can be advantages or impediments. They are impediments when we mobilize them with the wrong intensity or for the wrong reasons, in the wrong situations, or when we direct them at the wrong objects at the wrong time. For example, our emotions are pitched at the wrong intensity when we are too angry or not angry enough—when we scream at the top of our lungs calling for the beheading of the waiter because he brought us sugar rather than sugar substitute (a case of being too angry), or when we fail to be indignant at the torture of prisoners of war (a case of not being angry enough). We may level our emotions at the wrong object when we vent our anger on our lovers rather than our bosses who have canceled our Christmas bonuses. Or our emotion may be empowered by the wrong reason, as when we rev up hatred for the other team in order to "psych" ourselves to win the game.

These are some of the ways that the emotions can misfire. Building a virtuous character involves educating the emotions through habituation so that they don't go wrong in these ways. The virtuous person keeps the emotions in check insofar as the virtues are dispositions that we develop in order to put brakes on excessive or otherwise inappropriate emotions.

According to Aristotle in his *Nicomachean Ethics*, the virtuous person aspires to have the appropriate emotions in the appropriate way—that is, she aspires to direct the right emotion to the right objects with the right intensity at the right time for the right reason. For example, I *fear* (right emotion) the snake (right object) because it is two inches away from me (right time) and because it is harmful (right reason), while, simultaneously, my fear is of the order of a red alert (the right intensity).

Educating the emotions, then, is a matter of acquiring the habit of mobilizing the right emotions, directing them at the right objects for the right reasons at the right time and at the right level of intensity. That is, we learn to calibrate the emotions by proper exercise. Thus, one way of reading Aristotle's definition of tragedy is to understand him to be claiming that tragedy educates the emotions by training the audience to bring pity and fear to the right emotional objects at the right level of intensity, for the right reasons and so forth. *Catharsis* is just this process or calibrating or recalibrating the relevant emotions.

Moreover, the definition of tragedy suggests that it may be more than the emotions of pity and fear that are educated since the definition speaks of "pity and fear . . . [and] such emotions." Which emotions? Perhaps, the gamut of negative emotions including anger, indignation, and the like. On the sentimental-education view, tragedy purifies the emotions—places the audience in a position to undergo the emotion with perfect focus—with all defects removed. *Catharsis*, that is, is the name of this process of clarification.

For Aristotle, virtue is acquired through habituation. Virtuous habits are instilled by constant exercise. We learn virtue as we learn to ride a bicycle—by practice. In this respect, exposure to tragedies may be part of the relevant process of habituation. Tragedy enables one to find the mean with respect to virtue—the appropriate emotion and level of affect—automatically. For example, watching *Oedipus Rex* may help a timorous man recognize that his own fears are exaggerated, while helping a brash man to see that his assumption of invulnerability is reckless or, at least, complacent. Tragedy, in other words, may enable us to recalibrate our emotions—to get them in synch with the right objects, at the appropriate level of intensity, and so forth. And viewers also learn from tragedy to respond with the most intense form of pity to the decent man whose actions have the unintended consequence of raining disaster down upon himself and his household.

Tragedy educates the emotions and, in the process, they cultivate virtue. The brash learn to temper their arrogance and rein in their recklessness by coming to view their own projects as highly contingent and prey to upset. They learn to curb their enthusiasm.

Moreover, in terms of educating the sentiments, the friend of tragedy has a way of answering Plato: tragedy, it may be argued, provides a service to the commonwealth by being a civilizing force for the cultivation of virtue by perfecting emotions like pity and fear so that we can automatically select the right targets and respond to them in the appropriate manner.

But what about pleasure? How is getting the emotions in working order connected to the pleasure tragedy offers? Here, Aristotle, like others such as Thomas Aquinas, maintains that there is pleasure to be had in faculties operating as they should, as in the case of the pleasure of one's muscles burning after rigorous exercise. Similarly, the pleasure to be derived from the sentimental education through tragedy might be the pleasure sensed when the emotions are functioning as they should be. Moreover, most emotions can be pleasurable so long as you don't have to pay the price they typically exact. For instance, sadness can be savored if you do not have to suffer the actual loss it generally incurs.

One problem with the sentimental education conception of catharsis is that it presupposes that there is some possibility of a transfer of the emotions raised by tragedy and those of ordinary life. Like Plato, only with reference to positive or virtuous emotions rather than to negatively valued ones, the sentimental education hypothesis presumes that the emotions enlisted in response to tragedy will spill into life in some regular, predictable way. But do we have any more grounds to be confident that emotional exercise of the virtuous sort is any more likely than that of the vicious sort to take hold in any systematic and predictable way?

Moreover, it is unlikely that viewers will encounter with any frequency occasions to enlist the emotions they undergo while witnessing tragedies in response to occasions encountered every day. How many sons are going to discover suddenly that they've killed their fathers and slept with their mothers? Tragedy, it may be argued, is hardly a template for the emotions of life outside the theater.

Furthermore, the sentimental education model is open to the same objection that felled the therapeutic or healing models of catharsis; namely, that Aristotle believes that tragedy is addressed appropriately to decent people, not inferior people. But decent people, one supposes, are virtuous people, and virtuous people by definition don't need their emotions educated. They have already been habituated to recruiting the right level of affect in response to the right objects for the right reasons, and so on. Consequently, if the sentimental education that tragedy has to offer involves calibrating or recalibrating the emotions in this way, then decent folk have nothing to get from tragedy.

However, Aristotle maintains that they are part of the audience for tragedy and, by extension, the process of catharsis it involves. Therefore, Aristotle would not appear to accept the view of catharsis as a matter of sentimental education.

But perhaps the kind of education that catharsis has to offer is not just a sentimental education but an intellectual one. That is, we not only are encouraged to respond to the tragic events in drama with the right emotions but, because we are not agents in the fictional world that we behold, we need not act on those responses but instead find ourselves in a position to scrutinize them. In other words, tragedy affords us the opportunity to reflect on the nature of the appropriate objects of the relevant emotions—to contemplate, for example, the true nature of fear, or at least a certain kind of fear which we might call tragic fear.

The proper object of such fear is human life as it is perennially vulnerable to the vicissitudes of fortune and especially to bad luck. Tragedy reveals this as the proper object of such fear and enables us to recognize it in clearly refined and extremely legible fashion, thereby facilitating our conception of this emotion. The intellectual education that tragedy advances is the clarification of certain of our emotional concepts, such as pity, fear, and perhaps other negative emotions.

As noted previously, the emotions have proper objects, appropriate levels of intensity, motivating reasons, and so forth. On the conception of tragic catharsis as a matter of intellectual education, what tragedy invites is the clarification of our concepts of the pertinent emotions with respect to the factors that make for the appropriate exercise of the emotions in question.

Earlier we learned that for Aristotle, a primary source of pleasure with regard to tragedy was the pleasure of learning. Aristotle maintained that we can learn something universal from tragedy. The suggestion under consideration at present is that we may not only learn probabilistic behavioral patterns from tragedy but also something about the relation of certain emotional states to their conditions of appropriateness. That is, through tragedy, we are given a vantage point from which to contemplate a verity of human life—the structure of certain emotions.

Admittedly, this is a verity which possesses less necessity than a mathematical truth. Nevertheless, it is worthy of recognition by the decent or virtuous man not only because it is apt to encourage virtue—a cautious moderation in our activity as a way of not courting disaster—but because it reveals a nearly constant truth of human life: that luck, good or bad, is an ineliminable feature of life and that bad luck is the appropriate object of the deepest variety of fear.

Usually when we have emotions, they are prods to action. Artworks, like tragedy, provide contexts in which we are able to have certain emotional responses without having to act on them immediately. Call this detachment. Because we have these emotions in a detached way, we have the opportunity to examine closely and to reflect on these emotions and the conditions that give rise to them. We have the opportunity to inspect, study, and analyze our emotions. Perhaps what tragedy does in this regard is to provide us with the opportunity to discover the normatively correct conditions that govern having certain emotions like pity, fear, and other such negative emotions. Thus, the pleasure to be had from tragedy is educational—the intellectual pleasure that accompanies the acquisition of knowledge.

This interpretation of catharsis—catharsis as clarification—supplies Aristotle with a further answer to Plato. For in addition to the acquisition of knowledge of recurring patterns of human interactions, tragedy also affords the opportunity to discover something about the nature of the emotions and their conditions of appropriateness.

Against Plato in general, Aristotle can argue that imitation should not be held in low repute, since it is a condition of most if not all learning; but, more specifically, Aristotle can also pinpoint the kind of learning available through tragedy, namely, knowledge of patterns of human behavior as distilled in the plots of tragedy *and* knowledge of certain emotions as a result of the clarification of pity, fear, and comparable emotional states. This sort of knowledge approaches philosophical knowledge and, for that reason, should be congenial to Plato.

Furthermore, this account of catharsis accounts for why tragedy appeals to the decent, superior, or virtuous citizens. For, even if decent people, as a matter of habit, evince the appropriate emotional responses in the right circumstances, they still may stand to benefit from the intellectual clarification of relevant affective states. They will come to understand why what they already do is also the right thing to do.[17]

This is not to say that tragedy may not function to educate the vulgar or, at least, the less superior members of the audience sentimentally. Rather my point is to claim that tragedy *also* has something to offer the superior spectators, namely philosophical insight into the nature of their emotions. That is, this account of the educative interpretation of catharsis is double-barreled. One barrel affords the pleasure derived from their sentimental education to the lesser part of the audience. The other barrel affords the intellectual education to the superior portion of the audience in terms of deepening their conceptual understanding of the nature of certain emotions.

On the account of catharsis as clarification, tragedy arouses pity and fear in superior audiences in order to teach them something of a theoretical nature about the emotions. But how, you might ask, does arousing pity and fear lead to theoretical education, *and* what could we possibly be taught about the emotions in the course of such an education?

In order to answer each of these questions, let us think a bit about the emotions.

Usually when we have an emotion it serves as a prod or an impulse to action—we see something dangerous and we are consumed with fear and our fear prepares us to fight, freeze, or flee. Most emotions *motivate* behavior. Having the emotion readies us for action, typically immediate action, unless the emotion is inhibited.

Tragedy, on the other hand, arouses emotions in a context where we do not have to respond immediately. In fact, direct response is literally impossible with respect to drama. We can't intervene with the killing of Desdemona. It is ontologically impossible, since we are metaphysically barred, so to speak, from the fictional world of *Othello*. We cannot act in that world (since it does not exist). We can stop the performance by rushing onstage, but we cannot save Desdemona. Hence, our emotions—the emotions that the tragedy elicits—are *disengaged* from the possibility of action. Yet we are still in the emotional state.

But since these emotions are detached or disengaged from action, we suddenly have the opportunity to examine them. We cannot act on them; we do not engage in the kind of activities that would otherwise absorb our attention. Instead, we *can* direct or redirect our attention to the emotion itself.

That is, we suddenly have the opportunity to inspect, study, reflect on, and analyze these eruptive mental states. Thus, by removing these emotions from the motivation/action network, tragedy provides an invitation or solicitation to inspect these emotional states as a clinician investigates a specimen. By removing

---

17. Thus, embarking on the contemplation and understanding of the emotion concepts that tragedy proffers may be connected to that which Aristotle considers to be the good life, namely the philosophical life.

the pressure (indeed even the possibility) of acting on these emotions, tragedy makes reflection on them a live option.

Recall how Aristotle said earlier that imitation interests us in a way that the objects imitated themselves might not—for example, dead bodies. Why? Here it is reasonable to suppose that the answer is because of (1) disengagement, which in turn allows (2) focus, which enables us to learn from the imitations—to learn from that on which we focus. Disengagement affords the space and the freedom to reflect. And the focus that issues from disengagement directs our attention to the essential variables of that which is being represented, which, in the case of tragedy, are, among other things, the appropriate conditions for the emotions of pity, fear, and the like.

Tragedy arouses pity, fear, and other such emotions for the purpose of *clarifying* these emotions intellectually or theoretically (at least for the decent or superior members of the audience). Aristotle's name for this process of conceptual clarification is *catharsis*. Tragedy has something to teach us, including the decent people among us, about the nature of these emotions. Part of what makes this teaching possible is the way in which tragedy disengages the emotions from potentiating action, which in turn permits us the space to study these emotions and to learn how they work.

In our discussion of Plato, we have already seen that the emotions are complex phenomena. They are not simply a matter of visceral feelings; they also contain criterially governed, discriminative elements. The emotions are fast deliberative devices that enable us to evaluate situations rapidly relative to our interests and that prepare us to respond in a way that suits our interests immediately. The everyday emotion of fear is activated when I perceive myself to be in danger, and the emotion prepares me to fight, freeze, or flee. The emotions organize our understanding of the situation. This is their cognitive function. The emotions scan the situation, organizing it in a way that subsumes it under the evaluative category of the harmful.

Inasmuch as our emotive appraisals are governed by criteria of application, they possess a certain rationality—the emotions are rational or irrational in accordance with whether they concord with or violate their conditions of applicability. On the catharsis-as-clarification account, the claim is that tragedy invites us to understand and apprehend those universal criteria of appraisal that govern certain types of pity and fear and other such emotions. In that sense, tragedy makes available the clarification of such emotions.

For example, tragedy discloses that the objects worthy of the deepest sort of pity are not merely those who are victims of calamity but those who recognize that they have made the errors that have brought the suffering at hand on themselves. Likewise, tragedy reveals that the deepest object of fear should be the contingency or fragility of goodness—the inescapable possibility that (a) no matter how virtuous, there is no guarantee against a reversal of fortune and (b) no matter how careful, we may be the cause of the untoward, unintended consequences of our own actions which may bring us down or otherwise go awry. The fragility of goodness is the most fearsome aspect of life, perhaps, in part, because we are somehow almost naturally constituted to neglect it, to deny it, or to forget about it.

One advantage of the catharsis-as-clarification view is that it can be connected straightforwardly to that which Aristotle identifies as the primary source of pleasure in tragedy, namely, intellectual learning, particularly in terms of the discovery of human universals. Second, this account can also explain why tragedy makes a legitimate appeal to decent or superior people. For, even if decent or superior people are already virtuous as a matter of habit, they still stand to benefit from the intellectual clarification of the conceptual structure of the relevant emotional states. Their being virtuous is independent of their theoretical knowledge of virtue. Thus, tragedy can put them in possession of theoretical understanding of a practical ability (virtue) which they already have mastered. And for the lesser folk, tragedy helps cultivate their emotional or sentimental intelligence through exercise by targeting them at that to which it is rationally appropriate to react.

Moreover, the catharsis-as-clarification account gives Aristotle more ammunition in his likely debate with Plato, not only in the sense that it supports the contention that tragedy yields something like philosophical knowledge concerning various emotions but also in the sense that the appeal of tragedy is ultimately rational and not to the appetitive parts of the soul. *Pace* Plato, tragedy provides viewers—through disengagement and focus—the opportunity to achieve an intellectual clarification of elements of the pertinent emotional states and thereby to contemplate the structure of the emotions.

On the other hand, one objection to the catharsis-as-clarification view is that it is just too damn intellectual. It doesn't match with our gut-wrenching experience of tragedy. But this interpretation of catharsis does not have to deny that our actual emotional response to tragedy has a visceral component. Indeed, our physical experience of tragedy, it may be urged, is indispensable to our reflection on our overall emotional response. The gut-wrenching experience tragedy provokes is an important part of the data that we need to reflect on in order to analyze the emotion in question.

That is, eliciting a visceral response is part of the process of clarification that tragedy abets. Clarification involves reflecting on what exactly in the work is giving rise to our visceral response. Moreover, we are able to carry this process of reflection off with our responses to tragic emotions in a way that we cannot with everyday emotions because our emotional system is disengaged from the pressure of having to make an immediate response. Thus, we are able to scrutinize our emotional responses as if they were specimens under a microscope. And this provides us with the opportunity to identify clearly the proper objects, intensities, occasions, reasons for, and appropriate kinds of responses that the emotions in question call for. But for this analysis to proceed, the visceral reaction to tragedy is requisite, otherwise the emotion under the microscope would be incomplete. That is, tragic catharsis is primarily a matter of intellectual learning; however, it has a gut reaction as a subroutine since it involves the clarification of the structure of the relevant emotions as a whole.

Another question for the catharsis-as-clarification theory is, If the analysis of these emotions is what is at issue, why do we have to subject ourselves to tragedy again and again? A plausible answer to this complaint might be that the kind of knowledge that tragedy imparts tends to be forgotten in the course of everyday life.

For example, we rarely take heed of the vulnerability of our plans and projects to the whims of fortune. Consequently, the deepest truths of tragedy need to be brought to our attention again and again.

It may also be objected that the postulation of an "ascent" on the part of the audience to a reflective stage during which we analyze the emotions of pity, fear, and such seems to be quite a stretch. What in the play prompts such reflection, and when would we have the opportunity to perform it in the heat of witnessing the disaster and suffering? However, there often is something in the drama that prompts the reflection, namely, the cautions of the chorus, while there is no reason to suppose that the reflection must be completed during the play. It can emerge afterward, often in conversation with other spectators.

Some commentators reject the catharsis-as-clarification interpretation on the grounds that using *catharsis* to mean "clarification" was not common in ancient Greek. Nevertheless, this interpretation does so well in relation to other interpretive requirements that the preceding etymological reservations cannot be taken to be fully decisive.

Returning, then, to Aristotle's definition of tragedy with our interpretation of catharsis as a process of education, we may rewrite it as follows: tragedy is the imitation of an action that is important and complete and possesses magnitude; in language made pleasurable . . . and performed through the words of characters and not by pure narration which arouses pity and fear in order to clarify (sentimentally and conceptually) said emotions.

A final objection to this account may be that it doesn't apply to every tragedy, nor even to every extant ancient Greek tragedy. As mentioned earlier, it ill suits *Oedipus at Colonus*, among others; its plot structure lacks a calamity, a reversal of fortune, and the recognition of an error, nor does it elicit gut-wrenching feelings.

However, this objection overlooks the fact that from the outset, Aristotle's project was never purely descriptive. Instead, he is committed to identifying the *correct* way of constructing tragedies so as to enable them to discharge their proper function—that is, to explaining the ways in which the structures of tragedy must be so in order to function to bring about the catharsis of pity and fear. This may lead one to question how Aristotle knows that this is the proper function of tragedy. But even if it is not, Aristotle may still have succeeded in isolating those structures that facilitate the catharsis of pity and fear in the tragedies that aim at that effect, while, at the same time, exonerating them of the charges Plato leveled against them.

Bibliography

The translation of Aristotle's *Poetics* employed in this chapter is Malcolm Heath's (Penguin, 1996).

Anagnostopoulos, Georges, ed. *A Companion to Aristotle.* Oxford: Blackwell, 2009.
Andersen, Øivind, and Jon Haarberg, eds. *Making Sense of Aristotle: Essays in Poetics.* London: Duckworth, 2001.
Belfiore, Elizabeth S. *Tragic Pleasures.* Princeton, NJ: Princeton University Press, 1992.
Curran, Angela. *Routledge Philosophy Guidebook to Aristotle and the Poetics.* London: Routledge, 2016.
Depew, David J. "Politics, Music, and Contemplation in Aristotle's Ideal State." In *A Companion to Aristotle's Politics*, edited by David Keyt and Fred D. Miller, 346–80. Oxford: Blackwell, 1991.
Halliwell, Stephen. *Aristotle's Poetics.* Chicago: University of Chicago Press, 1998.
Nietzsche, Friedrich. *Twilight of the Idols.* Translated by Richard Polt. Indianapolis: Hackett, 1997.
Pappas, Nickolas. "The *Poetics'* Argument against Plato." *Southern Journal of Philosophy* 39 (1992): 83–103.
Rorty, Amélie Oksenberg, ed. *Essays on Aristotle's Poetics.* Princeton, NJ: Princeton University Press, 1992.

CHAPTER 3

Francis Hutcheson's *An Inquiry Concerning Beauty, Order, Harmony, and Design*

Francis Hutcheson, born in 1694 in Ulster, was educated at the University of Glasgow, where he was subsequently elected to the professorship of moral philosophy. Influenced by the empiricist philosophy of John Locke, he attempted to extend the tenets of that way of thinking to the analysis of our experience of beauty, including not only our experience of beauty in artworks but also the sensations of beauty we get from natural vistas, gardens, mathematical theorems, and, as we shall see, much else.

In shifting our attention from the Greek philosophers of art—Plato and Aristotle—to the Scottish philosopher Hutcheson, we have not only jumped ahead two thousand years, but we have also entered a world preoccupied with concerns different from those of the ancients, as well as with different ways of doing philosophy.

Whereas Plato and Aristotle primarily thought about what we would consider art in terms of whether it benefited society, Hutcheson is primarily interested in analyzing and explaining the experience that art and other beautiful things afford the individual. Where Plato and Aristotle stage their debate over the social and cognitive advantages that art may or may not provide, Hutcheson focuses on the pleasure, apart from the cognitive pleasure, beautiful things occasion. The pursuit of the beautiful in art becomes important as a way of enriching the life of leisure in the eighteenth century rather than as something that is socially useful.

Of course, Plato and Aristotle were not unaware of such pleasure. Indeed, it was this sort of pleasure that Plato distrusted. And Aristotle also acknowledges that in addition to the cognitive pleasures of learning available in mimetic works, the practice of imitation also yields pleasure through features like rhythm and color. But, at the same time, he offers scant analysis of this pleasure. Thus, if you felt that there was something central missing from the discussions of Plato and Aristotle—namely, a sustained account of the pleasures of art which seem independent from questions of cognitive and social advantage—then you are likely to feel more at home with the writings of Hutcheson.

Hutcheson was writing at a time when the production and distribution of art was undergoing a transformation in the West. Previously art was mostly produced under the auspices of official patronage; it was commissioned by the state, by nobles, by the church, or by syndicates or guilds. Such art was commissioned to advance explicit purposes—usually connected to the purposes of the relevant patrons—and it was assessed in terms of the way in which it implemented those purposes, which might have been religious, moral, political, nationalistic, patriotic, and so on.

However, the rise of capitalism and the bourgeoisie class changed this network of production and distribution. The accumulating wealth of the bourgeoisie provided them with more free time, and they sought to enrich their leisure lives with the pursuit of beautiful things—things that would give them pleasure—not only artworks, but also fine homes, gardens, furniture, tableware, clothing, and so on. They aspired to be like aristocrats, although without the martial trappings.

They were less interested in dueling than in cultivating and refining their sensibilities. For the bourgeoisie, the beautiful stimulus became a commodity whose consumption enlivened the increasing amount of leisure time available to them, while their ability to afford the expenditure of such wealth on pleasure was a mark of social capital among the emerging middle class.

The consumption of artworks and other beautiful things became central to the bourgeois pursuit of leisure. And although the bourgeoisie often commissioned artworks, such as portraits, they also began to acquire beautiful things in the way in which they acquired everything else—they bought them. In this way, the artwork became a commodity on the open market. This, in one respect, had a liberating effect on artists; it freed them from patrons who dictated the terms and the purposes their works were required to serve. The artist could create a work for his or her own purpose and put it out on the market like any other commodity where, in the best of cases, it would find a purchaser. Of course, the downside of this is obvious; the work might not find a purchaser. Thus, freedom from one kind of patronage also involved added financial precarity.

Key to this emerging mode of exchange is that the artwork and all other sorts of beautiful things—that have been made without a prior commission—find a buyer whose taste it pleases. For this reason, among others, the question of taste—the question of its nature and its operation—comes to the fore in the eighteenth century. This is not to say that people were unaware of this state of mind, often parsed in terms of beauty, before the eighteenth century. Rather what seems to happen in the eighteenth century (or actually somewhat before then) is that the role of taste in the context of the evolving market style of the production and exchange of artworks (and other objects of beauty) becomes so prominent that a desire for a theory of taste—a theory that explains to the rising middle class what they are doing when they appreciate beauty—becomes pressing.

Without acknowledging the social background for the pressure for such a theory, it is nevertheless such a theory that Francis Hutcheson presents in his 1725 *An Inquiry into the Original of Our Ideas of Beauty and Virtues*, the larger work of which *Concerning Beauty, Order, Harmony, and Design* comprises the first section.[1]

---

1. Hutcheson presents his account of taste before his account of virtue in order to prepare the reader for the idea of a moral sense by first introducing the idea of a sense of beauty.

Eighteenth-century writers, like Joseph Addison and Richard Steele, endeavored to tutor the taste and sensibility of an emerging class of art lovers in, as they called it, the pleasures of the imagination. In turn, Hutcheson wants to provide the philosophical foundations of the reigning idea that comes to be called taste.

Whereas Plato and Aristotle think of art primarily in terms of the social and cognitive costs and benefits, Hutcheson is more concerned with its relevance to the cultivation of pleasure. Hutcheson, of course, is not alone in this. Taste—the name of the distinctive receptivity to the pleasure afforded by beauty—is also a presiding subject for other British writers of the time, like Addison and Steele, as mentioned previously, and other British philosophers, including Hume and Edmund Burke along with many others. Likewise, the French call it "*le goût*," which when it is delighted transmits a feeling describable as *je ne sais quoi*, a certain indefinable pleasure that can only be inexactly labeled "I know not what." And later, the Germans coin the word *aesthetics* in order to label the same domain of discourse—that of the sensuous cognition, frequently with reference to the beautiful.

Aristotle entitled his treatise the *Poetics*. The Greek word *poesis*, as noted in the last chapter, has the connotation of "making." And certainly Aristotle's text can be readily construed as a guide to the making of tragedies, with its emphasis on the production side of things. Undoubtedly Aristotle pays attention to the ways in which poetry affects the audience, but the audience's experience is examined primarily as a guide to the construction of the most effective texts. That is, Aristotle is primarily construction-oriented. The move from poetics to aesthetics signals a shift in emphasis from more production-oriented theorizing to more reception-oriented theorizing, especially in terms of the sort of pleasure that consumers of art and other beautiful things undergo. Though Hutcheson does not use the word *aesthetics*, he, along with the Earl of Shaftesbury, is one of the most important precursors of the aesthetic tradition in the philosophy of art, especially with respect to the concept of "disinterestedness." Indeed, the primary reason that we are examining Hutcheson's theory is because of his highly influential treatment of the concept of "disinterestedness" for, what we can call, the "modern tradition of aesthetics."

This tradition can be differentiated from that of Plato and Aristotle in several ways. Three of these include less emphasis on how art is made in favor of how it is received; less emphasis on the social, cognitive, and moral advantages and disadvantages of art, and instead a preoccupation with the pleasure art and other things afford; and, in a related vein, less concern with the social significance of art and its contribution to the commonwealth and more emphasis on the individual's experience of art and other beautiful things, particularly in terms of pleasure and the personal cultivation and enjoyment of one's own sensibility and powers of discrimination.

Unlike Plato and Aristotle, Hutcheson is an empiricist. That is, he believes that all knowledge derives from experience. From simple sense impressions of colors and shape, the mind assembles more complex ideas of horses, cannons, and castles.

We do not experience objects directly, but only our ideas of things. And from these simple ideas, we derive further, more complex ideas. Similarly, Hutcheson regards beauty as a sensation, felt in us, and not as a property of an object. In this respect, Hutcheson is trying to adapt the state-of-the-art philosophy of his day—Lockean empiricism—to the conceptualization of beauty.

If Locke is the hero who stands behind Hutcheson's project, there is also a villain. As we learn in the second part of his treatise, which is entitled *An Inquiry Concerning the Original of Our Ideas of Virtue or Moral Good*, the villain is Thomas Hobbes, and, to a lesser extent, Bernard de Mandeville. Both of these men are philosophers of egoism who maintain that all human behavior is motivated by self-interest. In contrast, Hutcheson believes that humans are also moved by non-self-interested impulses. Indeed, the idea of beauty is so important for Hutcheson just because he is convinced that beauty is an example of such an interest or motive. For though the sensation of beauty is a pleasure on his account, it is a *disinterested* pleasure, a pleasure not connected to the prospect of personal advantage. That is, certain objects, namely the ones we call "beautiful," please us—we find them to our liking—even though they promise us no further personal benefit. Thus, for Hutcheson, the experience of beauty is a straightforward counterexample to the Hobbesian generalization that all pleasure is ultimately reducible to egoistic interests.

Egoistic interests are self-interested. Our behavior, according to egoism, is always connected to securing our interests. But Hutcheson argues that we also have disinterested interests—that is, non-self-interested interests, such as our interest in experiencing sensations of beauty. Here it is important not to confuse disinterestedness with non-interestedness or with not being interested. We are still interested in the objects that give rise to disinterested pleasure. It is rather that our interest is not rooted in the prospect of personal gain or advantage.

Hutcheson also believes that the perception of virtue also yields disinterested pleasure; he argues for this conclusion in the second part of his *Inquiry*. Thus, both parts of his book are designed to refute egoism by establishing the existence of disinterested pleasure, that is, pleasure not tied to expectations of personal gain. Indeed, the discussion of beauty paves the way for the discussion of virtue by presenting what seems to be a noncontroversial counterexample to egoism.

Hutcheson was not the first philosopher to employ the notion of beauty as a matter of disinterested pleasure. He inherited it from the Earl of Shaftesbury, who also employed the idea as a wedge against Hobbesian egoism. However, the Earl of Shaftesbury was a Platonist, whereas Hutcheson blended the notion of disinterested pleasure with empiricist philosophy, thereby situating beauty as a matter of subjective experience, a move that we shall see has a momentous influence on subsequent philosophers such as Kant, Hume, Schopenhauer, and Bell. However, before discussing Hutcheson's influence on aesthetics, we must first turn to what he said.

Hutcheson's Definition of Beauty

Hutcheson's aim in *Concerning Beauty, Order, Harmony, and Design* is to construct a theory of the beautiful.[2] In this, we are back to the discussion of *kalon* initiated by Plato in his *Hippias Major*. Although Hutcheson intends to explain the occurrence of the beautiful in art, his theory is not specific to art. For, he also wishes to account for the beautiful in nature, in artifacts like carriages, in mathematical theorems, in geometrical figures, and, in fact, in everything that strikes us as beautiful. Thus, the cases he believes his theory applies to include not only pictures and poetic descriptions of things and musical harmonies, but also rolling landscapes, foliage in autumn, sunsets, the plumage of peacocks, gardens, china, uniforms, and geometrical derivations.

According to Hutcheson, these experiences are marked by a feeling of beauty, a pleasure taken in contemplating such objects. When I see a glorious cornfield radiating yellow on a stunning summer day, I immediately take a liking to it. I am favorably disposed toward it. I am drawn to it. The very sight invigorates me. I enjoy allowing my eye to play over the array, not in order to learn something about it, but because it just feels good to do so. I relish the sight of it. I want to keep looking at it. This feeling of pleasure is hard to pinpoint. As already mentioned, the French refer to it by means of the expression *je ne sais quoi*.

The things that we call beautiful correlate with this phenomenon of finding pleasure or delight in the look, the sound, and/or the otherwise perceptible form of things. This feeling is marked by the desire to return to the experience of the things that give rise to it—like a bay sparkling in the moonlight—again and again. This is the phenomenon that Hutcheson intends to analyze. Indeed, it is akin to one of the conceptions of beauty that was examined, though rejected, in Plato's *Hippias Major*—the idea that beauty involves pleasure to sight and audition.

Like Aristotle's theory of tragedy, Hutcheson's theory of beauty falls into two parts: a definitional part and an explanatory part. First Hutcheson seeks to define beauty and, once he has the definition in hand, he goes on to explain the causal factors that give rise to it. Since Hutcheson is an empiricist, he believes that all our ideas arise from experience, where the concept of experience refers narrowly to our perceptions and sensations. This includes our ideas of beauty. For Hutcheson, beauty is an idea raised in or caused in us. It is a sensation, specifically a sensation of pleasure or delight.

Hutcheson takes it as given that there is some connection between beauty and feelings of pleasure or delight. He did not originate this association. It was already widespread in classical, medieval, and Enlightenment writings, not to mention

---

2. Arguably, Hutcheson places his account of beauty before his account of morality in the text in order to pave the way—and perhaps ease the way—for a comparable subjectivist move with respect to virtue.

in non-Western traditions, such as Islamic poetics. However, in general, previous commentators thought of beauty as a property of external objects, which, in turn, causes delight in us.

Hutcheson, in contrast, takes a subjective turn and relocates the property of beauty in us, identifying it with the delight we feel in seeing certain trees, vistas, flowers, and pictures or in hearing various melodies. Just as the pain we feel when stabbed with a knife is in us and not in the knife; just as the pleasure we experience when eating ice cream is in us and not in the ice cream cone; so, Hutcheson argues that beauty, properly so called, is just a sensation of pleasure *in us*. Beauty would not obtain in a world without perceivers, for beauty, literally a sensation of delight, is a property of the perceiver and not of the object perceived. In empiricist jargon, beauty is a sensation or an idea.

Hutcheson writes: "Let it be observed that in the following pages the word *beauty* is taken for *the idea raised in us*, and a *sense* of beauty for *our power of receiving this idea*. *Harmony* also denotes *our pleasant ideas arising from composition of sounds*, and a *good ear* (as it is generally taken) a *power of perceiving this pleasure*" (Article IX, Section I). Two things are being claimed here. First, that beauty is a sensation or idea, and second, that there is a sense—like the sense of hearing—that is the receptor which registers this sensation. Like gustatory taste, there is also a taste receptor with respect to beauty, a power for apprehending the relevant sensations of pleasure. This sense, sometimes called the "seventh sense," is what many would call taste (as in the expression "good taste").

However, you may wonder why Hutcheson thinks that beauty is a sensation. Beauty is said, for example, to denote an idea of pleasure somehow connected to a harmonious arrangement of colors, like a peacock's plumage. Yet this idea of pleasure can only come from within us. It makes no sense to suppose that the pleasure resides in the plumage of the peacock, just as it makes no sense to say that the pain is in the broken glass rather than in the bloodied hand. Colors—not pleasure—are displayed by the peacock. Likewise, when we take pleasure in the order of a colonnade, the colonnade exhibits proportion, not pleasure. That display of proportion causes the idea of pleasure in us. So, if beauty is an idea of pleasure, then it must arise in us. It must be a sensation.

Furthermore, Hutcheson couples the notion that beauty is a sensation with the notion that we have a sense—like the sense of smell—for detecting this sensation. Such a sense is what Hutcheson calls a *power* for receiving the idea of beauty; it is a capacity for having an experience of beauty. It is a faculty—like the faculty of sight—a faculty for detecting sensations of beauty that might also be called the faculty of taste.

Think of what we mean when we say that someone has taste or good taste. That indicates that they are especially sensitive to or appreciative of beautiful things—that they are discriminating when it comes to delicate sights and sounds. In such cases, we say they have taste, which translates for Hutcheson into the notion that they have an especially acute faculty for detecting sensations of beauty, that is, certain vibrations of pleasure.

According to Hutcheson, almost everyone has this faculty, just as normally people are sighted. This allows that some may lack it altogether, just as some people are blind. Similarly, of those who possess this sense of beauty—this seventh sense—some may have it naturally in greater degrees and some in lesser degrees, just as there are people with more or less acute eyesight.

There is an inborn faculty for experiencing beauty—what Hutcheson calls a sense of beauty, and his followers call taste—and this faculty is to be understood on the model of seeing. When we train our attention on an object, say the Taj Mahal, our eyesight takes in the stimulus and then something in that perception, derived from the object, triggers, or activates, our sense of beauty. That is, the sensation switches on the relevant faculty and we feel delight or pleasure.

Later Hutcheson will explain what features of the stimulating object he thinks activate the sense of beauty. But before doing that, he must motivate his claim that beauty is detected by a unique sense, a sense strictly analogous to the senses of seeing and hearing. To this conclusion, he argues that

> this superior power of perception is justly called a *sense* because of its affinity to the other senses in this, that the pleasure does not arise from any *knowledge* of principles, proportions, causes, or of the usefulness of the object, but strikes us first with the idea of beauty. Nor does the most accurate knowledge increase this pleasure or beauty, however it may superadd a distinct rational pleasure from prospects of advantage or the increase of knowledge. And farther, the ideas of beauty and harmony, like sensible ideas, are *necessarily* pleasant to us, as well as immediately so. (Articles XII and XIII, Section I)

That is, the sensations of beauty, like the sensations of color and sound, are *immediate*. They are not inferential; they are not mediated by knowledge. You look at the landscape and it suddenly hits you as pleasing. Pow! You do not apprehend the landscape, gauge that it exhibits certain ideal proportions, and then infer that it is beautiful. It is just like what happens when we perceive redness. For example, when we apprehend that something is red, it is not the case that we possess a definition of redness which we apply to some colored patch and then infer that it is red; we open our eyes, direct our attention, and we just see red. We see the patch as red via the direct acquaintance of our senses with the stimulus.

Moreover, the perceptions delivered to us by the other senses are *cognitively impenetrable*. A patch of color does not strike us as redder as we come to learn more about the physics of light, nor does the explosion alter phenomenologically because we acquire knowledge of sound waves. The senses are resistant, in this way, to knowledge and belief.

Similarly, one might argue that peacock plumage does not appear more delightful to us once we learn that it has a distinctive function in avian mating rituals.

Consequently, since the ideas delivered to us by the other senses are noteworthy for being immediate and cognitively impenetrable, and since our sensations of beauty are also immediate and cognitively impenetrable, then it is reasonable to conjecture that beauty is apprehended by a process just like the one that apprehends redness, namely the operation of a sense which, in this case, is an inner sense.

However, this sense is not precisely like the other senses in every respect. In order to mark the differences, Hutcheson distinguishes between external senses, like sight, and internal senses, such as the faculty that registers the sensation of beauty. Why must the sense of beauty be regarded as an internal sense, in contrast to the external senses, like seeing and hearing? Hutcheson gives two reasons.

The first reason is that the sense of beauty is often concerned with things, like mathematical theorems, that are not necessarily tracked by the external senses. One can entertain a geometrical derivation in the mind's eye and be delighted by its beauty. Yet this is not the sort of thing that can be detected by the external senses that apprehend sights, sounds, smells, tastes, temperatures, and tactile surfaces and resistance. Consequently, it must be a different sort of faculty. Hutcheson calls it an *internal* sense.

Second, it is often the case that people with perfectly functioning external senses fail to notice beauty. Someone can have 20-20 vision but be insensitive to beauty; someone can clearly see every marking on a zebra's hide but feel no delight in consequence. Just as there are some people who are color blind, there can be some people who are beauty blind. And just as there are deaf people, there may be people with acute hearing who find no delight in harmony, no matter how melodious. Since our external senses can be in perfect working order and yet, at the same time, beauty eludes us, this suggests that the sensation of beauty must be something that is superadded to the product of the external senses by some other faculty.

For example, consider two people, both with excellently operating external senses. Both are able to discriminate visual stimuli with exactly the same, extremely high level of precision. It is eminently conceivable that one of them responds with delight to a stimulus—say, Michelangelo's *David*—while the other is unmoved. But this indicates that the one who feels pleasure has something that the other lacks, something that reacts to the visual stimulus, which at the same time remains undetected by the external senses of her peer. What is that something? Hutcheson calls it an internal sense.

The external senses gather impressions from objects and translate these into simple ideas of shape, color, and movement. And then the inner sense finds delight in these. The leading reason for believing that there is such an inner sense is that there are cases where people with excellent external senses are beauty blind. Thus, those who are beauty sensitive have something the others have not got; an inner sense that is responsive in a special way to the deliverances of the external senses.

This sensation or idea of delight is not reducible or decomposable to the congeries of simple ideas presented by external sense, but rather supervenes on them, thus leading some commentators to say the idea of beauty is a simple idea in the Lockean vernacular. However, since it is connected to the simple ideas that issue from external sense, other commentators argue that it is a complex idea of reflection (a proposal that Hutcheson might wish to avoid since it suggests that the idea of beauty might not be cognitively impenetrable). But, in any event, it is clear that Hutcheson believes that our ideas of beauty require the postulation of a separate sense of beauty, as sound requires hearing, albeit a sense that is inner, not outer.

Within the Lockean framework, a distinction is drawn between primary properties and secondary properties. Primary properties are the properties that exist in the objects that stimulate our senses—properties like weight, volume, dimension, and duration (i.e., quantifiable properties). Secondary properties are those that are response dependent—qualitative properties like color, temperature, and sound that arise when the primary properties of objects at a molecular level interact with our human receptors. When ideas of shape are raised in us, we are putatively experiencing qualities that exist in the stimulus object; however, when we register the color blue, it is not the case that this tracks a property of the relevant swarm of atomic particles. Rather, blueness is an effect of said swarm of particles on our sense receptors, although an effect caused by the play of certain primary properties on our sense receptors. So, given this Lockean framework, the question may arise as to whether Hutcheson thinks beauty is a primary or a secondary property.

However, Hutcheson argues explicitly that beauty fits neatly into neither of these categories. On the one hand, since the faculty of taste responds to figure and time, it seems to gravitate toward the registration of primary properties. Yet, on the other hand, since the sensation of beauty is in the subject and not the object, beauty seems more of the order of a secondary property. Nevertheless, Hutcheson does not declare it to be a secondary property outright, but only holds it to be very like a secondary property. Moreover, just as we have a tendency to project secondary properties into the external objects that give rise to them—to imagine that the yellowness is in the banana—so we also have a tendency to speak as though beauty is in objects. We say the palace is beautiful, where, for Hutcheson, it would be more accurate to say that the palace triggers an idea of beauty in us.

So far then, Hutcheson has defined beauty as an idea or sensation of pleasure that is detected by an internal faculty. One way to refine this account further would be to identify the kind of pleasure at issue. Or, to put the matter in Aristotelian language, we know the species that beauty belongs to—namely, pleasure. Can we say anything more to differentiate the kind of pleasure beauty involves from other sorts of pleasure? To this end, Hutcheson says:

> And farther, the ideas of beauty and harmony, like other sensible ideas [ideas derived from the senses], are *necessarily* pleasant to us, as well as immediately so. Neither can

any resolution of our own, nor any prospect of advantage or disadvantage, vary the beauty or deformity of an object. For as in the external sensations, no view of interest will make an object grateful, nor [view of] detriment distinct from immediate pain in the perception make it disagreeable to the sense. So propose the whole world as a reward, or threaten the greatest evil, to make us approve a deformed object, or disapprove a beautiful one: dissimulation may be procured by rewards or threatenings, or we may in external conduct abstain from any pursuit of the beautiful, and pursue the deformed, but our *sentiments* of the forms, and our *perceptions*, would continue invariably the same. (Article XIV, Section I)

Hence it plainly appears that some objects are *immediately* the occasion of this pleasure of beauty, and that we have senses fitted for perceiving it, and that it is distinct from that *joy* which arises upon prospect of advantage. Nay, do not we often see convenience and use neglected to obtain beauty, without any other prospect of advantage in the beautiful form than suggesting the pleasant ideas of beauty? Now this shows us that however we may pursue beautiful objects from self-love, with a view to obtain the pleasures of beauty, as in architecture, gardening, and many other affairs, yet there must be a *sense* of beauty antecedent to prospects [even of] this advantage, without which sense these objects would not be thus advantageous, nor excite in us this pleasure which constitutes them advantageous. Our sense of beauty from objects, by which they are constituted good to us, is very distinct from our desire of them when they are thus constituted. Our desire of beauty may be counter-balanced by rewards or threatenings, but never our *sense* of it, even as fear of death [may make us] desire a bitter potion, or neglect those meats which the sense of taste would recommend as pleasant, [but cannot] make that potion agreeable to *sense*, or meat disagreeable to it, which was not so antecedently to this prospect. [The same holds true] of the sense of beauty and harmony; that the pursuit of such objects is frequently neglected, from prospects of advantage, aversion to labour, or any other motive of [interest] does not prove that we have no *sense* of beauty, but only that our desire of it may be counter-balanced by a stronger desire. [So gold outweighing silver is never adduced as proof that the latter is void of gravity.] (Article XV, Section I)

Had we no such sense of beauty and harmony, houses, gardens, dress, equipage might have been recommended to us as convenient, fruitful, warm, easy, but never as *beautiful*. (Article XVI, Section I)

What Hutcheson is arguing here is that the idea or sensation of beauty is a distinctive type of pleasure. It is a form of *disinterested* pleasure. That is, our feelings of delight are not connected to personal advantage. If we look out over our property, we may feel a certain pleasure of ownership; we delight in the fact that the land is ours. Likewise, if we learn that the property is oil rich, we may register joy in our bosoms at the contemplation of all the profit we may reap from it. Or I may derive a pleasing sense of satisfaction and pride from the fact that my new car raises me in the esteem of others. In all these cases, our pleasure results from our apprehension of the personal advantages that spring from ownership. These feelings of pleasure in each case issue from assessments of self-interest; they are not impartial assessments; each of these things makes me happy as I ponder the practical benefits they afford me. As I have described the cases, it is not the beauty of these objects that makes me happy; it is what these objects can do for me that gives me pleasure.

But there is another kind of pleasure. I can look over the landscape, whether or not it belongs to me, and simply be arrested and pleased by the way it looks—its shape, its colors, and its configuration. Or the car need not be mine, nor need it be something that I desire to own. I can derive pleasure from the sweep of its lines. That is, the pleasure I take from the car is decoupled from the possibility of my personal possession of it, from its being a status symbol, or from the prospect of any gain I hope to derive from it. There is no question of personal interest or advantage here. I say the car is beautiful from an impartial viewpoint, from a viewpoint that is not partial to my personal interests. This way of speaking, of course, involves a projection for Hutcheson since it is not the car that is beautiful, but rather the sensation of pleasure I feel in response to the car. The sensation is not a result of my thought that the car will boost my prestige, my collateral, or my wealth in any way. In this sense, my pleasure is disinterested; all cases of genuine experiences of beauty are likewise disinterested or impartial.

That the pleasure is disinterested does not mean that I have no interest in the car. I am interested in looking at it, but only for the pleasure its appearance and design raises in me. The pleasure is disinterested only in the special, technical sense that it is not pleasing because it serves my self-interested aims and desires. Hutcheson thinks it quite evident that such experiences are possible and even quite frequent. To see why, consider this thought experiment.

Imagine that I offer you one million dollars if you can feel that the local junkyard is beautiful. You may lie to me and say that it is beautiful because you want the million dollars. The junkyard may even engender a feeling of pleasure in you as you dream of how you can spend the money. But that pleasure is simply a function of self-interest. Even the prospect of a million dollars cannot make you really take pleasure in the very look of the junkyard.

The impossibility of simply willing that the junkyard be beautiful—that it raise joy in your heart just by the way it appears—shows that there is a species of pleasure that is distinct from the prospect of personal gain. If gain were the whole story, you should be able to get yourself to derive pleasure from the sight of the junkyard. That you cannot shows that there is a kind of delight that is independent of self-interestedness. There is disinterested pleasure, and this is the category into which sensations of beauty fall.

Sometimes we override our sense of the ugliness of a thing for reasons of personal advantage. We wear braces on our teeth because, for the purpose of health, we realize that we need to straighten our uppers. But though we may be happy that, from a medical point of view, we are doing something that is for our own good, we do not feel that the braces are beautiful. They are good for me, but that does not make their appearance delightful. So once again, it seems obvious that there is a distinction between the pleasure that redounds to things that are personally advantageous versus the joy that derives from things simply because they tickle our sense of beauty. The foliage in autumn does not strike us as more beautiful if we are paid to look at it; nor does a pig's severed, bloody ear become a gorgeous silver purse, though it be filled with money. The pleasure that derives from self-interest is categorically different than disinterested pleasure. Beauty is a sensation of disinterested pleasure. That the experience of beauty is undeniable constitutes, for Hutcheson, a refutation to the Hobbesian conviction that all human gratification is essentially self-promoting.

I can say of my home that it is very convenient because it is very spacious and that I take pleasure from the fact that it serves my interests well. It is big enough to accommodate all my books. But, at the same time, I can readily admit that it is not a beautiful house; in fact, it is very ugly. I can make this distinction because beauty and personal convenience are separate issues. I do not call things that are useful to me beautiful because I recognize the difference between what is pleasurable because it is personally advantageous versus what is pleasurable from a disinterested viewpoint. It is true that some people require beautiful things in order to be admired for what they own. This is a form of social capital. But even in this case, there must be a distinction between disinterested and self-interested pleasure. If there were no such distinction, how would these people know what to acquire in order to be admired?

The pleasure Hutcheson connects with beauty is impartial—impartial in the way we expect judges to be impartial.

For Hutcheson, the pleasure that characterized experiences of beauty is not only divorced from the prospect of personal gain. They are also independent of knowledge, including not only, obviously, the knowledge of whether or not the article in question will be personally profitable, but knowledge in general. In this, Hutcheson diverges from Aristotle for whom the primary pleasure to be gotten from imitation has to do with learning. Contrariwise, Hutcheson does not believe that the acquisition of knowledge increases the peculiar pleasure we call beauty.

Hutcheson supports this conclusion by means of two related considerations: (1) The disinterested pleasure or displeasure we draw from an object neither increases nor decreases as a result of learning more about it. Knowing that a gracefully shaped chromium bar is really part of an engine makes it no more or less attractive visually. (2) Nor does knowing everything there is to know about something alter the full force of the appeal that it makes to our sense of beauty. Even if a course of study in botany may make a rose more interesting to us, such knowledge neither augments nor diminishes the feeling of beauty we take from it. Recall, the sensation of beauty is cognitively impenetrable. Thus, the experience of beauty is independent from issues of self-interest and knowledge. It is disinterested both from the perspectives of profit and learning. We return to the objects that give rise to such sensations of beauty for the pleasure they afford, not for any prospect of gain, either practical or theoretical.

Francis Hutcheson's An Inquiry Concerning Beauty, Order, Harmony, and Design   111

By the end of Section I of *An Inquiry Concerning Beauty, Order, and Harmony*, Hutcheson has completed his definition of beauty. Next, he endeavors to explain the way in which its effects are brought about.

Hutcheson's Explanation of the Cause of Beauty

So far Hutcheson has defined beauty as an idea or sensation of disinterested pleasure that activates an internal sense, one often referred to as taste. Now that he has defined beauty—now that we know what beauty is—Hutcheson is in a position to discover the origin of sensations of beauty—that is, to explain that which causes or triggers the experience of beauty in the human frame.

In order to isolate the causal trigger or structural feature of things that gives rise to the idea or sensation of beauty, Hutcheson contrives to perform what is in effect an enumerative induction. In other words, he proceeds by canvassing a large list of the things that cause the feelings of delight that we identify as beauty with an eye to discovering the common thread that runs through all of them.

Hutcheson proceeds under the assumption that, in the main, we know which things correlate with the relevant feelings of delight. Given this consensus, then we scrutinize this collection of stimuli in order to isolate their common properties. Here the procedure would be analogous to starting with a group of comestibles that people generally find sweet and then asking what are the features they share that could account for the associated sensations of sweetness.

In order to organize this induction, Hutcheson divides the relevant objects into two large classes—Original or Absolute Beauty, on the one hand, and Comparative or Relative Beauty, on the other hand. He then works his way through a large number of cases, looking for the recurring or invariant feature across all of them, presupposing that that must be the origin of their common effect, the engendering of disinterested delight. The reasoning here is underwritten by the presumption: same effect, same cause.

By Absolute or Original Beauty, Hutcheson understands "only that Beauty which we perceive in Objects without Comparison to any thing external, of which the object is suppos'd an Imitation or Picture; such as that Beauty perceiv'd from the works of Nature, artificial Forms, Figures. Comparative or Relative Beauty is that which we perceive in Objects, commonly considered as Imitations or Resemblances of something else" (Article XVII, Section I).

That is, Relative Beauty is the beauty that correlates with imitations or copies, of things like portraits or anything else that Aristotle would have classed as mimesis. All other sorts of beauty—the beauty of an animal, or a geometrical figure, a natural vista, a theorem, and so on—fall into the category of Absolute Beauty. Hutcheson's strategy is to start with cases of Absolute Beauty in order to arrive at an initial approximation of what causes it and then to turn to cases of Relative

Beauty to see if his findings with respect to Absolute Beauty can be generalized so as to apply to all the relevant cases of Relative Beauty.

The first case of Absolute Beauty that Hutcheson considers is that of simple geometrical figures, such as squares and triangles (Article III, Section II). He thinks that the obvious variables governing our delighted responses to these figures are uniformity and variety. He attempts to bolster this conjecture by means of some simple thought experiments. He alleges that we find a square more beautiful than an equilateral triangle. Supposing, as Hutcheson does, that this is true, what, he asks, accounts for it? He hypothesizes that it must be that the square has greater variety—that is, one more equal side—since it is the only difference between the two figures. Therefore, variety is one of the variables that governs experiences of beauty.

Likewise, since an equilateral triangle is putatively felt to be more beautiful than an isosceles triangle (Article III, Section I), Hutcheson hypothesizes that uniformity must be another key variable determining our ideas of beauty, since what the equilateral triangle has in comparison to the isosceles triangle is more uniformity—it has three equal sides as opposed to only two. Therefore, uniformity is also one of the features that governs our ideas of beauty. That is, in at least simple cases, feelings of beauty seem, according to Hutcheson, to be at least a function of uniformity and variety or, as Hutcheson puts it, a function of at least the compound ratio of uniformity amidst variety. Moreover, he goes on to argue that what holds in simple cases can also be found to operate in more complex cases.

The world as a whole is beautiful because it contains many things, hence variety, but it is also organized by laws, hence uniformity (Article V, Section II). Species of plants and animals are beautiful since species have many members (variety) but, in addition, common features (uniformity) (Articles VII–VIII, Section II). The solar system is beautiful since it has many elements, such as planets, but also regular motion (Article V, Section II). Music is beautiful because it is composed of many notes, but also has harmony; indeed, the variety of music is enhanced by employing discords amid concords (Article XIII, Section II).

Furthermore, geometrical theorems are beautiful because they apply to infinite numbers of figures—thereby satisfying the requirement for variety—but in terms of a single principle—thereby securing uniformity (Article II, Section III). And so on. The starlit bay at night has variety—sparkles of light fluttering on and off—but also pattern; foliage in autumn has pattern—gradations of similar and contrasting colors—but an indeterminately large number of leaves. Similarly, works of art have parts and, therefore, variety, but the parts are unified by the artist's intention.

From cases of Absolute Beauty, Hutcheson moves to examples of Relative Beauty, where he finds that the same causal factors obtain—that beauty is a function of a compound ratio of uniformity amidst variety. Cases of Relative Beauty, of course, are matters of imitation. Thus, since in cases of imitation, such as a portrait, there is both the portrait and that whom the portrait is of, imitations have variety. At the same time, they have uniformity, namely, the resemblance relation that exists between the picture and its referent.

Moreover, in keeping with the dominant theory of art of his day—a theory descended from that of Plato and Aristotle—Hutcheson concurs that all art is imitation, specifically the imitation of the beautiful. In Hutcheson's version of this view, imitation is beautiful just because it perforce involves uniformity amidst variety—referents *and* representations yoked together or unified by a relation of similitude. For Hutcheson, all art is imitative and, therefore, beautiful. If painting resembles objects, poetry imitates actions and events, while music, too, is representational—for Hutcheson, music imitates the cadences of the human voice, just as dance imitates gesture (Article XII, Section VI). Indeed, Hutcheson seems to think that all art is imitative, insofar as the artwork imitates or copies the intention of the artist (i.e., an idea in the artist's mind; Article V, Section IV).

In the eighteenth century, the modern system of the arts was being consolidated—painting, poetry, literature in general, music, and sculpture came to be regarded as belonging to the same family of practices, the system of the fine arts or *beaux arts*.[3] Whereas for the Greeks, it sometimes seemed more natural to group music with mathematics, in the eighteenth century, music was the sister of painting and poetry.

Furthermore, the principle that unified all the disparate members of the family of fine arts was that of imitation. Thus, the category of Relative Beauty is especially important for Hutcheson; it is his way of grouping the beauties of art into a single, unified class of beautiful things.

Hutcheson does not deny that individual artworks can also have Absolute Beauty—that a painting can have a variety of figures, unified by pictorial balance and color patterns. But the beauty of the picture as an artwork is Relative Beauty—the beauty that is a function of the resemblance relation between two things: a representation and its referent. Likewise, a poem can have Absolute Beauty in virtue of containing many incidents and characters at the same time that it is unified by its possession of a narrative. But the beauty of the poem as an artwork, say Shakespeare's *Henry V*, is that it resembles the Battle of Agincourt.

As a result of his rambling though not exhaustive review of the major sorts of Absolute and Relative Beauty, Hutcheson confirms to his own satisfaction the hypothesis that the causal trigger that elicits the disinterested delight we call beauty is a compound ratio of uniformity amidst variety. It is this feature of objects that raises the idea of beauty in us—that activates our sense of beauty—and that often leads us to project our subjective feeling of beauty onto objects, of which we mistake beauty to be a property.

---

3. These arts were thought to belong to the same category insofar as they were all said to involve the imitation of the beautiful in nature.

However, here it is important not to misconstrue what Hutcheson is saying. He is not claiming that we see that some stimulus possesses a compound ratio of uniformity amidst variety and that we then go on to infer that it possesses beauty. Rather, the object has the property of uniformity amidst variety and that causes us to feel disinterested pleasure immediately. We do not, or at least we need not, realize what is causing the sensation of pleasure in us. That is, we are not nor need not be aware of what is eliciting the sensation of beauty; we feel it, oblivious to its causal origin. The affirmation—that "this is beautiful"—is arrived at non-inferentially.

Or, to put it differently, the compound ratio of uniformity amidst variety is the cause of our mental state, but not its object. Just as we sense the sweetness of the sugar without knowing the molecular structure that gives rise to it, so we feel disinterested pleasure without needing to know the precise factors of uniformity and variety that are bringing it about. Earlier Hutcheson argued that the feeling of pleasure we call beauty is cognitively impenetrable. Thus, knowing that an object possesses uniformity amidst variety does not make it feel more beautiful to us than knowing that the chemical composition of sugar makes it taste any sweeter.

Like Aristotle's theory of tragedy, Hutcheson's theory of beauty has a definitional part and an explanatory part where the explanatory part, also as in Aristotle, isolates that which functions to engender the effect in question—that is, it is the compound ratio of uniformity and diversity that causes the sensation of disinterested pleasure (a.k.a. beauty) in subjects.

In addition to isolating the causal trigger that explains the way in which ideas of beauty are raised in us, Hutcheson also suggests some laws with respect to the operation of the compound ratios of uniformity amidst variety. These laws include (1) that an increase in the variety factor in an object, while the uniformity factor is held constant, adds to our feeling of beauty; and (2) that an increase in the uniformity component in an object, while the variety component is held constant, adds to the sentiment of beauty. Thus, Hutcheson thinks not only that he has isolated the "original" of the sentiment or idea of beauty, but also that he has begun to chart its behavior.

Moreover, Hutcheson maintains that his discovery of the uniformity amidst variety principle suggests something about the nature of the opposite of beauty, namely ugliness or deformity. If beauty is a function of the presence of uniformity amidst variety, ugliness is its absence. Of course, it is hard to imagine many objects that have absolutely no uniformity or variety whatsoever. They would not be identifiable as objects if they altogether lacked unity, and if they have unity, they must have some variety that has been somehow unified. Hence, for Hutcheson, ugliness or deformity is not a matter of the total absence of uniformity or variety, but only the relative absence of such properties.

That is, on Hutcheson's account, deformity is a lack of appreciable degrees of uniformity or variety; it is a matter of beauty deprivation or privation, somewhat analogous to Augustine's conception of evil; ugliness is a function of possessing uniformity and variety in only the most meager degrees. Or, at least, this is the primary sense of ugliness or deformity for Hutcheson. When we say an object is ugly, we typically mean that it is not beautiful enough, a feeling we can explain by reference to its minimal or diminished possession of the properties of uniformity and variety for the kind of object it is. However, as we shall see, Hutcheson also allows that there is a second reason why we might find an object ugly or deformed, namely, if we have unpleasant associations with the object. But more on that in a moment.

As is perhaps already evident from the type of causal reasoning that Hutcheson employs in his explanation of the origin of the feeling of beauty, he is proceeding as if the same stimulus—replete with the same compound ratio of uniformity and variety—will elicit the same sentiment of delight from everyone. The faculty of beauty is a sense, strictly analogous to the sense of sight. Any normally sighted person will see red when exposed to the array of photons that give rise to the idea of redness.

Comparably, anyone equipped with the faculty of taste—the sense of beauty—will feel pleasure when exposed to objects sufficiently diverse, yet uniform. That is, if one is not altogether beauty blind, enough uniformity and variety will cause at least some feeling of pleasure in each of us, even though some may feel it more keenly than others. This much seems to follow from Hutcheson's conviction that the faculty for receiving sensations of beauty is a sense. That sense will be activated to some extent in everyone who has it—that is, when they encounter the right sort of objects, objects with the compound ratio of uniformity and variety. Hutcheson agrees that we may strengthen our active sense of beauty perception through practice and experience. But, on his view, we are building upon something native when we do this.

The sense of beauty is universal—or nearly universal, save for the beauty blind—and, for that reason, cross-cultural. This not only is implied by regarding beauty as a sense detector—functioning in the way that the tongue detects sweetness. Hutcheson also tries to bolster this conclusion with some anthropological evidence. He notes that the architecture and artifacts of all cultures possess beauty, once one scrutinizes them in terms of the uniformity amidst variety formula—that is, as long as one realizes that there are different ways in which artifacts from different cultures may instantiate that formula.

Chinese architecture employs different ratios of uniformity and variety than does Roman architecture; but once one becomes attuned to the Chinese proportions, one can see that they, too, are beautiful in accordance with the requirement of uniformity and variety, though they trade off uniformities and diversities differently than do Western examples. And similarly for the creations of other cultures worldwide. Thus, insofar as the artifacts—or at least some of the artifacts—of all cultures can be seen to abide by the uniformity amidst variety ratio, the idea of beauty is arguably a cross-cultural universal.

Moreover, Hutcheson might have reinforced this conclusion by means of another sort of observation. Although Hutcheson does not make this point himself, in defense of his position it might be observed that people throughout history have shown the ability to appreciate and to take pleasure in the artifacts of other cultures. One may be struck by the beauty of Chinese calligraphy or Mayan hieroglyphics without being able to read them. One might simply be delighted by the way they look.

Likewise, one may be struck by the elegance of what is actually an Eskimo fishing hook without knowing what it is used for. In such cases, it cannot be that our delight is explained by our having been culturally conditioned to savor these things, since we are outsiders—indeed, uninitiated illiterates—with respect to these examples. Nevertheless, they give us putatively disinterested pleasure. But if they give us pleasure, and this is not the effect of acculturation, what can be its basis? A likely conjecture is that they touch something nearly universal in us, something that transcends cultural specificity.

There can be no question that historically peoples of different cultures have been attracted to the artistic creations of "the Other." Nor can this be explained away simply by alleging that the colonized have always been forced to accept the standards of imperialist invaders, not only because sometimes it has been the imperialists who have been beguiled by indigenous beauties, but also because sometimes the exchange of beauties has been between alien civilizations of equal prowess.

Thus, to the extent that cross-cultural appreciation seems not only possible but flourishes frequently, the probability that there is *some* convergent or shared sensitivity with respect to beauty seems unavoidable. That is, it appears that the hypothesis that some feelings of beauty are universal or nearly universal has some substance, lest the phenomenon of taste convergence across alien societies would appear quite inexplicable. The proposal of near universality here appears to be the hypothesis that gives us our best explanation.

Hutcheson can explain this taste convergence in terms of a universal receptivity to compound ratios of uniformity and variety. Yet the apparent success of this conjecture itself raises questions since, although there is much convergence over the beautiful, there is also much disagreement. If the sense of beauty is universal, one would not predict much divergence of taste. But, of course, there is a stunning diversity of taste, not only between peoples of different cultures, but also among citizens of the same culture (something we will address in the next chapter on Hume). So, if one is impressed by how much convergence there is, one must also be impressed by how much divergence there is. And if one is like Hutcheson, convinced of the universality of taste, one must come up with some explanation for all this disagreement, which is inconsistent with the sense of beauty being a nearly universally distributed faculty.

Hutcheson's explanation of such disagreements rests on the possibility that, as mentioned earlier, the sense of beauty can be distorted by unpleasant associations. The Goths, for example, did not appreciate the classical unities of Roman architecture because they hated the Romans, whom they regarded as oppressors. They thought Roman monuments were ugly or deformed because they loathed the Romans. Their natural sense of beauty was distorted with respect to Roman artifacts because they associated negative, unpleasant memories with anything Roman. The Goths could not feel pleasure toward Roman buildings just because their troubled memories of their history of interactions with the Romans blocked the natural functioning of their sense of beauty. That is, their negative associations interfered with their ability to view Roman architecture disinterestedly. Their judgment of Roman architecture was distorted by their *interestedness*, in Hutcheson's sense.

Likewise, one might not be able to derive a sense of pleasure from an environment one finds inhospitable or threatening—an arctic icescape or a mountain of towering granite—not because the environment lacks uniformity and variety, but because one associates the unpleasant idea of danger with it. In such cases, the association of unpleasant ideas overwhelms the naturally functioning sense of beauty, suppressing feelings of disinterested pleasure with associations rooted in memories or predictions of personal disadvantage or harm that raise fears with regard to one's own interests.

Thus, Hutcheson freely concedes that there is a diversity of taste, that there is disagreement over beauty as well as consensus. Yet this does not compromise his proposal that the sense of beauty is nearly universal, since the dissent putatively occurs within the context of convergence. Convergence in sentiment is the norm; divergence can be satisfactorily explained away in terms of the aberrant interference of associations of unpleasant ideas rooted in vested interests. Or, so Hutcheson believes, thereby ostensibly neutralizing the most damaging counterevidence to his hypothesis.

By introducing the notion of the association of ideas, Hutcheson might appear to open the door to an explanation of our appreciative responses to beauty that runs in a direction opposite to his own theory. If the association of ideas can account for divergent opinions about beauty between the Goths and the Romans, might it not also account for why members of the same culture agree about what they find beautiful? Perhaps people are simply taught what is beautiful, just as the Goths taught their children what is ugly. Maybe what we call beautiful is merely a function of acculturation. If one can be indoctrinated into finding some things ugly, why can't it be the case that, likewise, what we find beautiful is also just a matter of education? That is, we learn what is beautiful, and that is what accounts for whatever consensus there is about beauty.

Hutcheson, however, denies this. He points out that for any process of cultural education to take hold, it must appeal to capacities that its inductees already possess. In order to be taught that certain objects are dangerous, the child must already have some intimation of fear. If a child has no quotient of fear, it will never be able to comprehend why her culture regards a certain group of objects as dangerous. Learning about what is dangerous depends on our being natively equipped with a capacity for fear. Culture then builds on that, teaching us more about what is fearsome. But we could not develop an intelligible category of fearsome things unless we already had a native sense of fear.

Similarly, neither culture nor custom can teach us what is beautiful, unless we already have a native capacity for detecting beauty—for taking pleasure, according to Hutcheson, from the compound ratios of uniformity and diversity.

Think of it this way. If it is the positive reinforcement through pleasure that culture and custom exploit in order to initiate us into their artistic practices, then we must antecedently possess the capacity to feel that pleasure—to have our sense of beauty caressed—by said objects. If we had no innate sense of beauty, then we would remain impervious to cultural conditioning, since cultural conditioning needs something on which to work—some regular source of stimulation upon which to build.

Culture and custom may expand our sense of beauty—that is, they may alert us to the wide range of beautiful objects available in a given society. But in order to do so, there must already be a sense of beauty for education to expand on. Likewise, Hutcheson might also have noted that in cases where alien cultures, sans education, admire each other's beautiful creations, that phenomenon might very well be the result of the triggering of some source of pleasure that preexists custom. For, we can be arrested and attracted by the beautiful artifacts of other cultures before we become *accustomed* to them.

Hutcheson also offers an account of why we have a sense of beauty to begin with. The explanation is both theological and teleological. Hutcheson argues that God endowed us with an internal sense of beauty because it enables creatures like us to navigate our environments successfully.

The sense of beauty takes pleasure in regularity and uniformity. We enjoy discovering it; we have a positive predilection for it; we search it out. This certainly puts us in an advantageous position in learning about the environment. Think of how much better off we are cognitively for taking pleasure in tracking regularities in nature. Such a disposition gives us a positive inclination to discover order in the universe.

God, on this account, has more than suited us for finding our way about the world in which he has placed us. He has, in his infinite benevolence, given us pleasure as a guide to the kinds of uniformities in nature whose identification serves us so well. The sense of beauty serves our ability to comprehend the very conditions of our natural existence. Our aesthetic sensibility, in other words, serves science.[4]

---

4. Perhaps this idea is related indirectly to Aristotle's notion of the pleasure in learning, while also suggesting a way of understanding the notion of scientific beauty.

Hutcheson's account is religious, but it can perhaps suggest a more naturalistic approach. Aristotle pointed out that imitation—the way humans learn—gives pleasure. A post-Darwinian might regard this as an adaptation that in organisms like us, who depend so much on education for existence, provides us with an evolutionary advantage, a hardwired incentive to do what we must in an energetically self-motivated fashion. In a similar vein, we might reread Hutcheson as suggesting that the pleasure we take from discovering uniformity is an evolutionary carrot, honed by the processes of natural selection, which facilitates our apprehension of important features of the natural world, like regularities, and thereby enhances our prospects for survival.[5]

Hutcheson, of course, outlines this phenomenon in terms of theology and teleology. However, he may be viewed in retrospect as a precursor of the view that a liking for beauty—understood especially in terms of uniformity—is a result of a natural (rather than a theological) process of selection, which though systematic, is not preordained in the strong teleological sense.

In this way, Hutcheson is able to elucidate why the sense of beauty is important to human life—to indicate its deep and abiding value. For not only does it, as he points out, encourage industry and progress, as we labor continuously to increase the beauty of our surroundings; it also, in a fundamental way, makes possible our understanding of the world around us, abetting the discovery of uniformities that themselves are all the more easily identified and stored in memory for being occasions for pleasure.

Assessing Hutcheson's Project

Hutcheson produced a formidable theory of beauty. He defined beauty, explained what caused it, and even speculated on why it is important by suggesting its value or significance for human life. Although in many ways his formulations are inadequate, he nevertheless began an important conversation, and many of his ideas, albeit in modified form, have exerted continuing influence on this tradition of philosophical research. And even if some of his answers were misbegotten, he certainly seems to have asked many of the right questions and to have suspected that these questions need to be systematically related to each other, including: What is beauty? What causes it? And what, if anything, is its value?

If we begin with the definitional part of his theory, perhaps the first thing we might wish to question is whether the sense of beauty is really a faculty, like the

---

5. In this regard, science, on Hutcheson's view, may owe a debt to the sense of beauty. Indeed, this is often acknowledged in the correlation that many scientists make between scientific discoveries and beauty. For example, Albert Einstein told Hans Reichenbach that he knew that his 1915 general theory of relativity was true before it was empirically verified by Arthur Eddington in 1919 because it was too beautiful not to be true.

faculty of sight or hearing or gustatory taste. Why imagine that there is a seventh sense? One reason to suspect that there is not is that, unlike the other senses, there is no specifiable organ, like the eye or the ear, or sense receptor, like taste buds, associated with it.

It might appear that Hutcheson deals with this problem by saying that it is an inner sense, but might not this consideration just as easily dispose us to say that this is a reason why we should refrain from calling beauty a sense at all? On Hutcheson's account, so many different kinds of things give rise to the sentiment of beauty; why suppose that there is a single faculty in operation here? The stimuli are so heterogeneous in contradistinction to the qualitative homogeneity of the stimuli received by clear-cut faculties like seeing and hearing. The objects of sight are all of a piece; they are all visible; save malfunction, we never mistake a sight for a sound.

But the objects of the alleged faculty of beauty are wildly various. Some are heard, some seen, some merely thought. Why claim that there is a single faculty here processing all this stupendously diverse input?

Thus, one worry is that Hutcheson is too quick to proliferate faculties. We do not postulate the existence of a sense of humor comparable to the sense of sight. Is the sense of beauty a real faculty or only metaphorically described as one, as is the case with what we call a sense of humor? The sense of humor has no specifiable receptor; there is no funny bone. It is only a "sense" in a figurative way of speaking. Is the sense of beauty anything more than a *façon de parler*?

Hutcheson is tempted to claim that it is so because it is immediate. Yet the same is often true with the so-called sense of humor. I accidentally put sugar on my pasta instead of parmesan cheese; I see what I've absentmindedly done, and I laugh. I don't infer that what I've done is funny because it is incongruous. I just have an immediate sensation of levity—a kind of pleasure. Humor often seems just like beauty with respect to an immediate, involuntary response. But if I am ill-disposed to hypothesize a faculty of humor or an organ of humor, why should I regard beauty differently?

Hutcheson, of course, maintains that the sentiment of beauty is also cognitively impenetrable. But one wonders whether he is really right about this. He says that knowledge cannot make something strike us as any more beautiful. However, it seems to me that if I learn about complex musical structures, I can indeed come to perceive beauty where before I only heard noise. Being taught about serial construction—learning about what constitutes uniformity in that type of composition—can yield delight, whereas previously there was disturbing boredom.

That is, knowledge can apparently superadd pleasure to the sensation of beauty. This presents at least one kind of problem to Hutcheson's claim that the sense of beauty is cognitively impenetrable. But as well there may be a further problem here, to wit: there may be cognitive pleasures to be had with regard to beauty—pleasures connected with *self-consciously* tracking features like uniformity amidst variety—that are themselves integrally connected to the pleasure Hutcheson calls beauty. Or, in other words, for Hutcheson the sensation of beauty is utterly noncognitive, whereas it may have, as Aristotle believed—at least some of the time—ineliminable cognitive dimensions.[6]

Hutcheson characterizes the idea of beauty as a disinterested pleasure. Inasmuch as all this means is that it is not the same as a pleasure connected to ownership, pride, or the prospect of personal advantage, this claim is not as controversial as it will be in the more complicated theories of subsequent philosophers like Kant. However, since this characterization is primarily negative—a statement of what the idea of beauty is not—it is rather uninformative.

Nor does it say something unique about beauty, since even Hutcheson himself thinks that virtue also engenders disinterested pleasure. Thus, disinterested pleasure is not a sufficient condition for identifying a genuine sentiment of beauty. Moreover, even if pleasure is required in order to call something beautiful, then beauty is not the only or even the most important attribute to consider when commending art, since not all art is predicated on eliciting pleasure.[7] Much modern art aspires to disturb and even to displease, while much of the religious painting that was known to Hutcheson emphasized pain and suffering.

To be fair to Hutcheson, he does not believe that beauty is such an omnibus concept, admitting that artworks may be commended for their grandeur or novelty in addition to their beauty. However, if one is tempted to think that beauty is the litmus test of all art or all good art, then whatever beauty means, it cannot be correlated simply to sensations of pleasure, disinterested or otherwise.

The explanatory part of Hutcheson's theory confronts even more difficulties than the definitional part. Hutcheson alleges that the cause of the idea of beauty in us is the compound ratio of uniformity amidst variety. However, strangely enough, he never addresses the issue that there may be factors other than these that *also* contribute to the sense of beauty.

Surely Hutcheson is right that uniformity and variety—separately and in tandem—are features that generally count in favor of calling something beautiful. Perhaps his myriad examples indicate that much. However, he never goes on to show that these are the *only* beauty-making characteristics. For example, often intensity is also considered to be a beauty-making characteristic. And perhaps sometimes it is the singer's energy or vivacity that leads us to find her performance

---

6. One such dimension might be the satisfaction of curiosity—the desire to know, for example, how the story will turn out or how this element contributes to the unity of the whole (perhaps functionally). The challenge for Hutcheson here will be to cut the difference between the disinterested pleasure to be had from the satisfaction of curiosity versus that of beauty.

7. To be fair to Hutcheson, he does allow that artworks may be dedicated to engendering responses other than beauty, such as a sense of grandeur.

beautiful. Is vivacity a matter of either uniformity or diversity, or is it some third thing? Hutcheson does not give us enough information to tell. Yet, more importantly, he has spent no effort demonstrating that uniformity and variety are the only levers relevant to engendering feelings of beauty. Therefore, at the very least, his argument is incomplete.

But there is also something arbitrary about his enumerative induction since the scope of what counts as uniformity and variety changes wildly as he proceeds. Sometimes uniformity pertains to a structural feature internal to an individual thing—like a harmony. But at other times it pertains to relationships between different things, like the resemblance between a portrait and the person who sat for it.

Likewise, variety sometimes pertains to an individual thing's having a number of component parts, but at other times it applies to many different individual things standing in some kind of relation. For example, having a number of different notes counts as a variety-making feature in a piece of music, whereas there being millions of members in a species is the relevant variety factor when it comes to animals. The variety pertinent to a geometrical theorem is its infinity of possible instantiations in an infinite number of figures, whereas variety in a peacock's plumage amounts to it having several different colors on the tail of a specific entity. With such loose notions of uniformity and variety in play, it is hard to imagine Hutcheson failing to find it wherever he wants, not because beauty is there, but because he uses these concepts like wild cards. At the very least, the liberality of his central concepts calls into question his induction. Because they lack any rigorously defined specificity, there is scarce guarantee that other researchers would be likely to replicate Hutcheson's findings.

The fact that Hutcheson's use of uniformity and variety is so promiscuous allows his formula to be confirmed by virtually everything. Everything, or nearly everything, has some uniformity and some variety, especially if we allow these concepts to range as freely as Hutcheson does. But we do not think that everything or nearly everything is beautiful. Thus, Hutcheson's formula does not truly isolate a sufficient condition for the source of beauty. The formula is too expansive; it includes way too much.

Indeed, the looseness of the formula will make it easy to come up with ugly things that will have uniformity and variety. What will Hutcheson say in response to cases like this? Perhaps he will agree with our examples but say that they do not possess enough uniformity and/or variety. But "how much" is "enough"?

At the same time, the formula is too exclusive. Because Hutcheson requires that sentiments of beauty be triggered by uniformity *and* diversity, he will not count single colors as beautiful. But this certainly runs counter to our ordinary way of speaking of beauty. Single colors and even single sounds might be called beautiful. But Hutcheson cannot do so, because they lack variety.[8] Following Hutcheson, we

---

8. But maybe Hutcheson was just mistaken about the science here because we know now that colors have complicated structures.

could not call a single-colored, monotone, minimalist painting beautiful, since it would lack variety (as well as a referent). But this seems wrong. Thus, Hutcheson's formulation does not identify a necessary condition for the elicitation of beauty, at least in terms of our standard use of that concept. It is too narrow.

Similarly, Hutcheson's conception of ugliness or deformity diverges from ordinary thinking. For Hutcheson, ugliness is merely the lack of beauty—the lack of uniformity amidst variety. This seems not only false since there are beautiful pure colors which lack variety. It also seems wrong because ugliness and deformity can be positive properties in their own right, and not merely the absence of beauty. For example, pit bulls are downright ugly and not just substandardly beautiful. Indeed, a big, hairy, golden-colored tarantula might have a great deal of uniformity and variety, and yet we still find it ugly, and not necessarily because we have unpleasant associations with it. The aversive response may be hardwired.

Hutcheson's account of Relative Beauty is also peculiarly at odds with our ordinary conception of beauty in art. He situates the locus of the beauty response in the resemblance relation between a representation—an imitation—and its referent. But we find pictures beautiful as pictures—as works of art—where we have no idea of what the referent looks like—no idea of whether the picture even vaguely resembles its model or even if it had a model. Surely representational pictures without models can be beautiful. So, the kind of uniformity Hutcheson requires for the beauty of imitations, then, seems to have nothing at all to do with what we normally think of as the beauty of pictures *qua* pictures.[9] We may admire the verisimilitude of a portrait, but admiring verisimilitude is categorically different from finding a picture beautiful since there can be accurate pictorial likenesses that are ugly.

Moreover, Hutcheson's notion of the importance of variety to the beauty of imitations has especially bizarre results. For example, a painting of a model will always be less beautiful than a photograph of the same model since there will only be two elements of variety in the case of the painting—the painting and the model—whereas, since the photograph can be reproduced a thousandfold, it will be necessarily more beautiful inasmuch as it accommodates far more variety—far more pictures—for the same amount of uniformity. Surely, this is an unacceptable result, one not only at odds with our ordinary concept of beauty, but absurd as well. Nor is this objection open to the charge of anachronism since prints and engravings were surely known to Hutcheson.

Though many would criticize Hutcheson's confidence that there is a nearly universal dimension to the human response to beauty, I am not sure that he is not onto something valuable, although it is in need of a more careful qualification than

---

9. It might be suggested that Hutcheson can invoke resemblance to the artist's intention here. But how could that be relevant to the response of spectators since they have no access to the image in the artist's mind that the picture supposedly resembles?

he provides. Perhaps there are certain sights and sounds and combinations thereof that garner universal, or nearly universal, responses of pleasure once our negative associations are factored out.

Biologists have discovered that certain kinds of symmetry patterns underlie judgments of beauty with respect to human appearance cross-culturally. And there is the phenomena of the untutored, cross-cultural appreciation of beauty—such as music and carving—from alien societies, which phenomena seems explicable most economically through the hypothesis that such examples touch a common chord. This does not explain all of our beauty responses, but it may be serviceable in the explanation of at least some of them.

Also, some landscape formations seem to be universally pleasing, like wide-open vistas, because, due to our primate heritage, they represent spaces where the onset of predators is readily detected and avoided. Some, but not all, beauty responses may be bred in the bone. To the extent that Hutcheson can be modified by claiming only that much, his approach may have some advantages over the more relativistically inclined approaches of many contemporary researchers.

Finally, Hutcheson's insight that culture and custom require some native ingredient of pleasure in order to tutor people in the beauties relevant to their practices seems right, since otherwise it appears difficult to understand how infants could learn consistently and creatively what to count as beautiful. Admittedly, Hutcheson goes too far in denying that culture and education can penetrate cognitively and augment whatever native powers of beauty detection we are born with. But perhaps in exaggerating the extent to which the sense of beauty—very narrowly construed as pleasure in the sensual dimension of things—has some basis in what is common to humans, Hutcheson has nevertheless perhaps performed a useful service by reminding us of an aspect of beauty too often ignored or repressed by current thinking, which overestimates nurture and culture over nature. *Of course*, Hutcheson goes too far in the direction of nature. But he knew that there was something about the beauty response that needed to be explained naturalistically and that may be something that we have forgotten or discounted to our own detriment.

Bibliography

Two sources were consulted for the quotations from Hutcheson in this chapter: (1) *Francis Hutcheson: An Inquiry Concerning Beauty, Order, Harmony, Design*, edited by Peter Kivy (Martinus Nijhoff, 1973); and (2) *An Inquiry into the Original of Our Ideas of Beauty and Virtue*, edited by Wolfgang Leidhold (Liberty Fund, 2004). All quotations are from the Liberty Fund edition.

Costelloe, Timothy. *The British Aesthetic Tradition*. Cambridge: Cambridge University Press, 2013.

Dickie, George. *The Century of Taste*. Oxford: Oxford University Press, 1996.
Guyer, Paul. *A History of Modern Aesthetics*. Vol. 1, *The Eighteenth Century*. Cambridge: Cambridge University Press, 2014.
Kivy, Peter. *De Gustibus*. Oxford: Oxford University Press, 2015.
———. "Hutcheson's Idea of Beauty: Simple or Complex." *Journal of Aesthetics and Art Criticism* 50 (1993): 243–45.
———. "The 'Sense' of Beauty and the Sense of 'Art': Hutcheson's Place in the History and Practice in Aesthetics." *Journal of Aesthetics and Art Criticism* 53 (1993): 349–57.
———. *The Seventh Sense: Francis Hutcheson and Eighteenth-Century British Aesthetics*. New York: Benjamin Franklin, 1976.
Korsmeyer, Carolyn. "The Two Beauties: A Perspective on Hutcheson's Aesthetics." *Journal of Aesthetics and Art Criticism* 38 (1979): 145–51.
Shelley, James. "Empiricism: Hutcheson and Hume." In *The Routledge Companion to Aesthetics*, edited by Berys Gaut and Dominic McIver Lopes, 41–54. London: Routledge, 2013.
Townsend, Dabney. "Hutcheson and Complex Ideas." *Journal of Aesthetics and Art Criticism* 51 (1993): 72–74.
———. "Lockean Aesthetics." *Journal of Aesthetics and Art Criticism* 49 (1991): 349–61.

Chapter 4

David Hume's "Of the Standard of Taste"

The topic of David Hume's essay "Of the Standard of Taste" is an important one, and it concerns something that probably most of us have encountered—namely, disagreements in taste between our friends and acquaintances. Hume's preoccupation in this essay is with the question of whether and how disagreements in taste can be adjudicated. This is not some remote, abstract debate, such as whether Forms exist in some supersensible world, but it is one that is as alive today as it was in 1756 when Hume entered the discussion.

For example, you may find yourself arguing with your partner, who thinks that *Sex in the City* is a better TV series than *Girls*, or you may plump for the superiority of Steve Reich as a composer, despite your best friend's conviction that Philip Glass is the best. These kinds of disputes happen all the time. Thus, the issue that Hume takes up in "Of the Standard of Taste" is hardly a dry, academic one. Moreover, whether or not you agree with Hume's position on the matter, you should be able to appreciate the utmost sophistication with which he handles the problem. Indeed, his treatment has seldom been surpassed.

David Hume is one of the giants of Western philosophy. He wrote in the eighteenth century and, along with Francis Hutcheson, was one of the leading, if not the most important, British empiricists (although he was Scottish). Hume is perhaps most noteworthy for his skepticism about causation. He never held an academic position, however, because he was widely suspected of being an atheist and, in those days, most universities were connected to religious institutions. Hume was considered for the chair of moral philosophy at the University of Edinburgh, but he was not awarded the position, given the widespread questioning of his religious beliefs (Hutcheson got the position).

According to one story, perhaps apocryphal, once Hume fell in the street in the mud; an elderly lady while helping him up, asked his name. When she heard it was "Hume," she dropped him back in the mud hissing, "atheist."

Instead of teaching, Hume plied his trade as a writer, and he was one of the first authors in the English-speaking world to support himself entirely by means of his pen. He was able to keep heart and mind together with his publications—albeit not his philosophical ones. He wrote a best seller—a six-volume history of England which every up-and-coming middle-class family of the day had to be sure to have on its bookshelf. Hume's book was a status symbol, among other things. And it was this historical writing with which he supported himself rather than his philosophical work.

As we saw in the last chapter, Hutcheson maintained that our sense of beauty, although subjective—that is, a feeling of pleasure *inside* the subject—was also objective (or intersubjective) in terms of being universal. Furthermore, if this claim to universality seems to be undermined by the divergent tastes of different cultures, Hutcheson claims that this is merely an *apparent* disagreement which can be readily dispelled by the notion of the association of ideas.

However, although Hutcheson does his best by means of this maneuver to explain away the apparent anomalies that his theory invites, it is nevertheless fair to take note of certain tensions in his view, namely, that what is given as subjective is in some sense objective and that, though there is the claim that taste converges on universal agreement about what is beautiful, there is also a great deal of evidence that there is a striking amount of disagreement about what is beautiful—more perhaps than the simple theory of the association of ideas can dispel. It is these sorts of tensions in Hutcheson's theory that Hume addresses in his essay "Of the Standard of Taste."

The Paradox of Taste

Hume begins his essay by setting out what he takes to be a paradox—indeed a paradox that some readers may have already felt haunts Hutcheson's theory, to wit: though we apparently agree that judgments of taste are subjective, we also appear to believe that some judgments of taste are right and others are wrong—that is, right and wrong for everyone. But isn't this a contradiction? How can it be that all such judgments are subjective and therefore ostensibly independent of any objective standard, at the same time that some judgments are right and the others wrong (where, of course, the very notion of rightness and wrongness appears to presuppose an objective standard)?

After a movie or a concert, one person will say the work was good, one person will say it was terrible, and the two will start to argue. This kind of behavior, the argument, is a sign that we think there is some fact of the matter available here. That is, rational argument presupposes an objective way of resolving it—that the argument can be reasonably resolved by, well, reasoning. We try to reason with each other and convert each other to our own point of view. Our behavior indicates that we actually think that there is some kind of objective standard here to which we can appeal. And yet we may do this at the same time that we repeat that these judgments are purely subjective.

But if they are truly subjective, then why don't we stop arguing? You don't argue if you like mustard and someone else prefers ketchup since this really does seem to be purely a matter of subjective preference. However, we do argue about, for example, whether George Clooney is a better actor than Philip Seymour Hoffman or Daniel Day-Lewis.

The structure of the "paradox of taste," as set out by Hume, takes the following form:

(1) If judgments of taste are subjective, then there can be no objective standards of taste.
(2) Judgments of taste are subjective.
(3) There are objective standards of taste.

There is a paradox here because though each of the propositions in this triad may appear to be true when viewed in isolation, nevertheless, when all three of them are put together, they yield a contradiction—namely: "There are objective standards of taste" and "There are no objective standards of taste," which follows from (1) and (2) above.

Hume's task in the essay on the standard of taste is to get rid of this contradiction. In order to banish this contradiction, of course, Hume will have to show that at least one of the propositions in this triad is false. By way of preview, let me say now that the proposition that Hume wishes to reject is (1). But before we start talking about how Hume intends to reject (1), it is instructive to review the way in which Hume sets forth this paradox.

The first seven paragraphs of the essay put in place the first two propositions of our self-contradicting triad. The conclusion of these first seven paragraphs is that though common sense and philosophy often disagree with each other, when it comes to matters of taste, they agree that there is no disputing such matters—or as the old Latin saying has it, *de gustibus non disputandum est*.[1] (Or, for those who prefer the French, *chacun à son goût*.)[2]

Hume begins by noting that common sense reveals to us that there is a wide variety of taste. That's what the first paragraph says. We notice that even among our narrow circle of friends, we often disagree about what is beautiful. And, of course, when we leave our narrow circle of acquaintances and go further afield—taking note of the judgments of beauty made, for instance, from persons of remote cultures—the apparent divergence of taste becomes ever more pronounced.

Having introduced the notion that there is a wide variety of taste, Hume immediately takes up an objection to this hypothesis concerning the apparently stunning diversity of taste. He suggests that perhaps there is more agreement about taste than his opening paragraph admits. After all, everyone agrees in applauding

---

1. Although sometimes attributed to Cicero via Quintilian, the origin of this platitude is disputed and is sometimes said to be of medieval rather than Roman provenance.

2. One might interpret this to mean that there's no disputing taste either because it's rude or it's pointless, given how very stubborn people are. However, Hume appears to interpret this platitude to mean that there is no disputing taste *because* assertions of taste do not involve matters of truth or falsity.

elegance—that is, everyone agrees that elegance is good. So how can divergence be as radical as the opening paragraph insinuates? For we all agree, as Hume observes, that elegance, simplicity, and spirited writing are good.

However, Hume believes that the kind of agreement that is invoked by these examples is an illusion. That is, people agree that what is elegant is good or laudable just because *elegant* is a term of commendation. To say that something is elegant is, in part, to say that it is praiseworthy. We agree that what is elegant is laudable because that is, in part, what the word *elegant* means. In other words, what we are agreeing about is the *definition* of elegant as a term of praise.

If you say to your friend, "what an elegant dress," as long as you are not being ironic, you are not saying, "what an ugly rag that is." But that we agree on what the word *elegant* means does not entail that we agree on the items to which this term of commendation applies. You think that certain things are elegant, and I may think some other things are elegant even though we both think that the term *elegant* means "laudable."

You think Fred Astaire's dancing is elegant, whereas I deny this and claim that Chubby Checker's dancing the Twist is elegant—something that you deny. Now in cases like this, we both agree that *elegant* means "laudable" or "good," but we disagree about what is in fact laudable. Thus, any appearance of agreement that seems to attach to our shared use of certain terms of commendation really masks a great diversity of taste—a wide range of disagreement over what things are in fact deemed praiseworthy.

This is the argument that Hume develops in the second, third, fourth, and fifth paragraphs of the essay using analogies to moral language. For example, Hume notes that both we and the ancient Greeks think that a virtue is a good character trait but recall that when it comes to picking out the virtues, the Greeks think pride is one whereas we think modesty is one—they think it is virtuous to blow your own horn, whereas we think it shows a flaw in one's character.

So, a simple exercise of common sense reveals to us that although we often use the same words to commend things, the fact that we share the same vocabulary of praise does not refute the claim of the first paragraph that there is a wide variety of taste—that we commend widely diverging things and that my commendations often conflict with your commendations.

In the sixth paragraph, Hume notes that all this disagreement in matters of taste makes us wish that we had a standard of taste we could use to adjudicate all our disagreements. But no sooner does Hume cite this wish than he asserts that philosophy shows that it can't be fulfilled. Thus, he begins the seventh paragraph by saying that "There is a species of philosophy which cuts off all hopes of success in such an attempt and represents the impossibility of ever attaining any standard of taste." What species of philosophy is this? Empiricism—the very school of philosophy to which Hume and Hutcheson subscribe.

Why is it that empiricism might be thought to preclude the fixing of a standard of taste of the sort that would adjudicate the disagreements and divergences of taste cited in the first seven paragraphs of the essay? Because, for the empiricist, as we saw in the discussion of Hutcheson, a judgment of taste, the judgment that something is beautiful, is really a feeling of pleasure—an inner sensation or *sentiment*, notably a sentiment of pleasure.

But a feeling of pleasure does not, as we noted in the last chapter, refer to the primary properties of objects external to the organism. A sentiment of pleasure is an event internal to the organism. It does not, as Hume puts it, represent what is really in the object that gives rise to it. A sentiment does not have reference to anything outside itself; it is purely subjective—that is, it is wholly within the subject. It is not something in the object; it is not something objective. Just as the pleasure is not in the Godiva chocolate bar, but in me, so beauty, understood as an inner impression of pleasure, is in the subject and not in the object that gives rise to it.

Moreover, my sentiment of beauty is in *me*; your sentiment of beauty is in *you*. If we disagree over what we judge beautiful, there is no external court of appeals before which we can argue our case. It's just your feeling against my feeling. It is analogous to the case where you like Pizza Hut and I like Domino's Pizza, or you prefer Burger King and I prefer McDonald's. We are both right in the sense that we have the feelings of preference that we have. But there is no objective fact of the matter here, no external standard, as there is in mathematics, which enables us to say that you are right, and I am wrong. This conclusion follows putatively from the view that a judgment of beauty is just an inner feeling—without reference to external facts.

Furthermore, if empirical philosophy tells us that judgments of taste are simply matters of feeling, then common sense concurs, showing us that among the members of the human race, there is an astounding diversity of such feelings. Nor can certain of these feelings be said to be better or more accurate than the feelings of others because *there is nothing for them to be more accurate about*. Feelings are just internal states. There isn't anything objective or external that can be used to assess them. They are by definition "inner." If different people have different feelings, all you can say is that they have the different feelings they have. It doesn't really make sense to argue about them—you have your feelings about what is beautiful, I have my feelings and *de gustibus non disputandum est*.

So, common sense and philosophy, notably empirical philosophy, for once agree that

(1) Judgments of taste are subjective.

and

(2) If judgments of taste are subjective, then there can be no objective standards of taste.

From which, of course, it follows that there can be no objective standards of taste, as was stated earlier as the first wing of the paradox.

Moreover, if there are no objective standards of taste, it really doesn't make any sense for us to argue about our differences of opinion regarding what is beautiful. Why? Because there is no way of settling such differences. Better to agree to disagree and to leave it at that: you have your taste, and I have my taste. This is the best we can do for the obvious reason that when we say something is beautiful, all we are talking about is our personal feelings.

Yet though this is the conclusion toward which everything in the first seven paragraphs leads, in the eighth paragraph, Hume abruptly changes gears. He writes:

> But though this axiom, by passing into a proverb ["*de gustibus* . . .], seems to have attained the sanction of common sense; there is certainly a species of common sense, which opposes it, at least serves to modify and restrain it. Whoever would assert an equality of genius and elegance between OGILBY and MILTON, or BUNYAN and ADDISON, would be thought to defend no less an extravagance, than if he had maintained a mole-hill to be as high as TENERIFFE, or a pond as extensive as the ocean. Though there may be found persons, who give the preference to the former authors; no one pays attention to such a taste; and we pronounce, without scruple, the sentiment of these pretended critics to be absurd and ridiculous. The principle of the natural equality of tastes is then totally forgot, and while we admit it on some occasions, where the objects seem near an equality, it appears an extravagant paradox, or rather a palpable absurdity, where objects so disproportioned are compared together.

Common sense appears to endorse the axiom that *de gustibus non disputandum est*, and yet common sense *also* behaves as if it really does not uphold this axiom. We think that it is just as obvious that John Milton is a better poet than John Ogilby, as that a mountain is higher than a molehill, and that the Pacific Ocean is larger than the mud puddle in my backyard. That is, certain judgments of taste—that Dostoevsky is a better novelist than Sidney Sheldon or Danielle Steel—seem to have the status of matters of fact. That *Hamlet* is a better play than *Phantom of the Opera* strikes us as having the same probative force as the true factual statement that the sun is larger than the moon. We're not disposed to chalk up these differences to "it's just your taste."

In the paragraph before the one on Ogilby and Milton, common sense seemed willing to go along with the philosophical view that everyone's judgment was on a par. For if a judgment of taste is simply a feeling of pleasure—a preference, a liking of this or that—then everyone's judgment is on the same footing—each person likes what they like and that's it. You like Yasujirō Ozu's film *Tokyo Story*, and I like the *Pokémon* cartoons. Neither one of us is right nor wrong. Apart from the fact that we take the pleasures we do where we find them, there are no other facts, notably external facts, to be had. And since there are no external facts to be had, there is no external standard against which we might address our differential responses. We are both in a sense right, where being right comes down to knowing what we like.

However, even though common sense is drawn in this direction, it is also drawn in the opposite direction. If I insist that *Pokémon* cartoons are better than Ozu's film *Tokyo Story*, then people are generally apt to say that I'm wrong and that I don't know what I'm talking about. I may know that I *like Pokémon* cartoons, but my judgment doesn't count for much. It can be dismissed. As Hume says in the eighth paragraph, "The principle of the natural equality of tastes is then totally forgot."

But, of course, if my judgment of the worth of the *Pokémon* cartoon show can be dismissed in this way, this presupposes that there is a standard of taste, an objective standard of taste in virtue of which some judgments are determined to be better than others and, indeed, in virtue of which some judgments may be dismissed as defective. And this, of course, advances the third proposition of the paradox of taste.

Thus, we seem to have argued ourselves into a paradoxical situation where, on the one hand, there appears that there can be no standards of taste, whereas, on the other hand, there must be a standard of taste. There are different ways to state the issue: taste can't be disputed/it can be disputed, or there are no standards/there are standards. Note the connection between the formulations. Also, note that the left side is the skeptical side. Now, in terms of Hume's overall line of attack, he wants to reject the idea—the *skeptical* idea—that there can be no standards of taste and to defend the position that there must be a standard of taste.

Solving the Paradox of Taste

We are led to the skeptical view that there can be no standard of taste on the basis of the assumption that if judgments of taste are subjective, then it makes no sense to presume that there are objective standards of taste. Hume's job in the rest of the essay is to show that it is not absurd to presume that there is an objective standard of taste even if judgments of taste are subjective, that is, even if they do not pertain directly to the features of objects in the world outside us.

Here it is useful to keep in mind that there are at least two different ways of drawing a subjective/objective distinction. There's what we might call the eighteenth-century way, which we don't use as much or as exclusively as they used it, and according to which x's being subjective means x is inside the subject. X is *objective*, on the other hand, means that x is outside the subject. So, the first way of marking the distinction hinges on the opposition: "in the subject" versus "in the object."

But there is another, more contemporary way of using these terms, where *subjective* means varying greatly from person to person, or idiosyncratic, and *objective* means intersubjectively verifiable. For example, we don't have any problem nowadays saying that the feeling of redness is in me and that it's not in some swarm of photons out in the world. The experience of the quality of redness is in me. On the other hand, saying that certain things are red—such as fire trucks in New York City—is typically intersubjectively verifiable. All of us, who are normally sighted, will look at the same objects and concur in calling them red. Thus, we will regard the redness of the pertinent items as an objective fact under the contemporary usage of "objectivity."

So, the two oppositions—the two ways of drawing the contrasts between *objective* and *subjective*—are not necessarily the same. One does not collapse into the other. It could be that we agree that all judgments of beauty are subjective in the sense that all these judgments are rooted in the subject; but this doesn't preclude the possibility of their being intersubjectively verifiable—that is, of their being objective in our second, more contemporary sense. So, the reason we may appear to have a contradiction here might be because the terms *objective* and *subjective* are not being used univocally. That is, they are not being used with the same meaning throughout the discussion. And recognizing this may give us an indication of the way in which Hume will attempt to deny the first proposition of the paradox of taste while retaining the second and third.

As noted, Hume is going to deny the first proposition of the paradox of taste. Thus, his position is as follows:

> It is not the case that if judgments of taste are subjective, then there can be no objective standards of taste. (For, taste is subjective in the sense that it is in the subject, but it may also be objective in the sense that there are intersubjective standards which can be used to evaluate personal preferences.)

How does Hume hope to overturn the first premise? He starts by introducing the idea of the rules of art. That is, Hume thinks that the existence of rules of art—recurring artistic structures that predictably cause certain sensations (like pleasure) in us—will somehow get us the standards of taste that we crave, albeit indirectly by attending to the responses of those whom Hume calls the "Ideal Critics" (a group of people on whom the rules of art will have maximal, unimpeded effect).

Nevertheless, this way of arguing for an objective standard of taste leaves us with two related problems. First, since these laws for the most part are not really known (they are certainly not written down), how, supposing they exist, are we to get access to them in order to help adjudicate disputes over taste? Second, if these laws operate as laws of human nature, how can there be so many disagreements in taste?

Unfortunately, Hume doesn't give any examples of rules of art in the essay "The Standard of Taste." And this has encouraged some commentators to suspect that there aren't any. But in other essays on art, Hume does give some examples of what he means by a "rule of art."

For example, in his essay "On Tragedy," he writes:

> Had you any intention to move a person extremely by the narrative of any event, the best method of increasing its effect would be artfully to delay informing him of it, and first to excite his curiosity and impatience before you let him into the secret.

That is, if you wish to draw a reader into a narrative, tell your story in such a way that the reader wants to know something in advance of your divulging it *and* then delay telling it. For example, there's a murder at the beginning of a mystery story; this raises the question of whodunit. The successful mystery story doesn't tell you right away. It draws you through the complications that Aristotle would have called the middle. And then the reader is drawn, excitedly, through the middle in anticipation that she will be told the secret by the end. Such is called a "page-turner." Thus, we have a rule here, namely,

> To draw a reader into a plot, alert her to something she wishes to know, and prolong the interval before she knows it.

Likewise, Hutcheson's notion that a compound ratio of uniformity and diversity will trigger a sensation of pleasure and Aristotle's hypothesis that a reversal of fortune will cause fear in the audience are probably the kinds of things that Hume would regard as rules of art.

Moreover, as Hume stresses in "Of the Standard of Taste," rules of art like this are only discovered through experience and practice. They are not known *a priori*; they are *a posteriori*; that is, they are known through experience. But Hume does think that there are rules of art.

Nevertheless, if they are for the most part unknown and so damnably difficult to excavate, how will they help to get us to a standard of taste? That is, how will the idea of a rule of art help Hume to undermine the view that there can be no standards of taste?

Here it pays to note the nature of the rules of art that Hume is advancing. Notice that these rules are not mere conventions, as are the rules about the number of lines in an English sonnet. They are more like laws, specifically laws of human nature. Notably, they are rules about how the structure of the stimulus causes, in general or lawlike ways, certain internal states in percipients. These states are *subjective* states, perhaps states of pleasure—states like the anticipation with respect to the mystery story that I've just discussed. The rules of art, in other words, are contingent generalizations that connect the structure of external objects to the affects of audiences, constituted as we are, in lawlike ways.[3]

---

3. In his essay "The Sceptic," Hume analogizes the ontology of beauty to that of color. Thus, it would appear that he takes beauty to be a response-dependent property like redness that provokes a predictable reaction from creatures like us.

Thus, these rules or laws of art bridge the subjective and the objective. They are laws concerning regularities between subjective states (of the percipients) and objective states (the structures of the artworks). According to these laws, such and such a variation in A (the stimulus, a.k.a. the artwork) will uniformly cause a variation in B (the audience). The state in B, when all the appropriate conditions are met, is what is standard or normal for human nature and, in that regard, B's state can supply us with a norm or standard of taste by telling us what is normal.

That is, given the reliable operation of the rules of art on suitably conditioned specimens of human nature, we can determine what the normal human response to a given stimulus should be and then use that as our norm or standard.[4] This norm or standard is a function of the responses of certain suitably conditioned persons who are Hume's Ideal Critics. And it is the converging responses of the Ideal Critics, which is due to the operation of the laws of art, that permits their responses to count as the norm—the normal, or correct, human response.[5]

The claim that if judgments of taste are subjective, then there are no objective standards rides upon a presumption that there are no regularities when it comes to subjective states. That, in other words, when it comes to subjective states—that is, what transpires in the subject—there is no connection at all between the subjective states and the objective stimulus. Yet this surely overstates the matter in the typical case. In the typical case, the state the subject is in depends on and is guided by the structure of the stimulus.

Moreover, the way in which the structure of the stimulus affects subjects may be *generalizable*. For example, letting readers know that there's a secret to be revealed in the story in a fairly reliable way prompts readers to continue reading in order to discover the secret. So, there may be a lawlike relation between the structure of the artistic stimulus and the internal state of the reader. But if there is a lawlike relation between our reactions and the structure of the stimulus, then there is something rather like a norm or standard of taste—a norm that predicts what *should* be the subject's reaction to the structure of the artwork. That is, a norm that tells us what is *normal*.[6] Thus, there is an *objectively discoverable standard against which the subjective responses of the participants can be assessed*—that is, a norm with respect to what pleasure or pain the suitably conditioned spectator should experience.

For example, in general, it is normal that readers will become involved if a narrative presents them with a question that they want answered *and* then prolongs

---

4. Since the term *rules* may suggest that they are conventional, it is better to think of these as *laws*, psychological laws of human nature.

5. "Normal" as in "all things being equal, all things being as they should be."

6. Normal as long as there are no features of the situation that interfere with the operation of the laws of art—such as the audience member bringing interests into the transaction, as Hutcheson claimed that the Goths did with respect to Roman architecture. See further comment on this below.

the delivery of the answer. This is the standard case. So, if I come along and, confronted by this sort of stimulus, I say that I am not engaged, then my claims that the mystery story is flawed need not be accepted at face value because they fly in the face of the typical operation of a rule (a law) of art. Subjective claims must be weighed against the authority of the workings of the rules of art. That is, in the case at hand, my judgments may be dismissed as abnormal if they are at variance with the proper functioning of the laws of art on suitably conditioned exemplars of human nature (the Ideal Critics).

The admission that feelings of beauty are subjective does not imply that there are no standards because the relation between certain stimulus objects—art objects—and our reactions are themselves susceptible to generalizations in light of the rules of art (which are laws of human nature). Moreover, in virtue of these regularities, some responses—such as the assertion that *Pokémon* cartoons are superior to *Tokyo Story*—are dismissible because they are at variance with the reactions that the operation of the rules of art predicts. My *Pokémon* responses are not normal responses in the sense that they are not the responses that the suitably conditioned audience member would evince as a result of the operation of the rules of art on the standard-issue human frame. To praise *Pokémon* over *Tokyo Story* is abnormal and, therefore, discountable.

Once we have granted that rules of art exist, how exactly do we use them to adjudicate disputes of taste? In the case of physical laws of nature, certain standing conditions have to be met for the law to operate. So, taking "matches light when struck" as an example of a physical law, notice that that law will only obtain when certain other things obtain, such as there being enough oxygen in the room, the matches being dry, and so on. These standing conditions must be met before a law will operate.

Similarly, Hume is going to claim the same requirement holds when we talk about the laws of art. There are laws of art and there are normal reactions that people should have (*should* is being used here in a causal sense) when exposed to certain stimuli. But just as is the case with natural law, we only get the normal results if the standing conditions are met. Thus, the reason that we find so many disagreements over taste between people with respect to what's good and bad and beautiful and ugly is that in most cases, the pertinent standing conditions are not met. That is, in the greatest number of cases, readers, listeners, and viewers are not suitably conditioned.

In a way, Hutcheson already suggested something like this with his idea of the association of ideas. The reason the Goths couldn't make what he considered to be the normal judgment about whether Roman architecture was beautiful was because they were like a room in which a match wouldn't strike due to a lack of oxygen. The Goths couldn't react normally, the way ordinary non-Goth people would react to the stimulus, because the Goths had a strong bias against all things Roman due to the Romans being regarded as their enemies and, therefore, threats to Goth interests. Hutcheson agrees that there is an arresting diversity of taste, but he believes that we can account for this divergence of taste in terms of the fact that people are often issuing their judgments when they have failed to meet the relevant standing conditions, specifically the standing condition of *disinterestedness*, discussed in the last chapter.

Of course, this way of explaining the diversity of taste calls for an identification of the appropriate standing conditions for issuing judgments of taste. In the tenth paragraph of the essay, Hume clearly has this in mind when he writes: "we require a perfect serenity . . . if any of these circumstances be wanting . . . we shall be unable to judge of the catholic and universal beauty." The "circumstances" he refers to are what I have termed "standing conditions." Furthermore, he is using the term *catholic* here not in the religious sense, but with its original meaning as "universal."

So far then we have been given an account of how there can be objective standards of taste in terms of the operation of rules (or laws) of art on suitably conditioned exemplars of humanity. Moreover, we have had explained to us how even though there are these regularities, there is, as a matter of fact, a great diversity of taste, for in order for these rules of art to do their work, certain standing conditions must obtain. But insofar as these standing conditions do not obtain, often with great frequency, there is a great diversity in people's judgments of taste. Thus, we have an explanation of the diversity of taste from within Hume's framework of rules of art acting on human nature.

However, doesn't this raise a problem for Hume on another front? If there is such an admittedly vast diversity of taste—that is, if people are so often responding deviantly to aesthetic stimuli—then how in the world can we ever hope to isolate these so-called rules of art functioning optimally in individual cases? In other words, if the operation of the laws of art are misfiring so often—perhaps even most of the time—how can we hope to track them down? How can we get access to them in such a way that we can use them to adjudicate disagreements with respect to judgments of taste?

What kind of state does a human being have to be in so that the laws of art will operate the way that they should operate across the human race? In other words, what are the criteria that have to be met in order to know that we have a case where the laws will operate properly? This is the point at which Hume resorts to the notion of the Ideal Critics.

The Ideal Critic is a person who satisfies the standing conditions required of the percipient if the percipient is to respond in a nondeviant way to the operation of the rules/laws of art with respect to a given artwork. That is, these Ideal Critics are, so to speak, flesh-and-blood detectors of the untrammeled operation of the rules of art.

So, even if we cannot state most of the rules of art—the laws that bring about certain regular effects in normal viewers under the right conditions—we can be sure that they are operating in full force on our Ideal Critics. Why? Because the Ideal Critics meet the standing conditions required for these laws to operate normally. They are, so to speak, perfect human samples.

Thus, we can adjudicate our disagreements by comparing our responses to the responses of the Ideal Critics. The joint verdict of these critics will constitute a norm against which we can measure our own responses. If you and I differ with respect to a particular artwork, the evaluation that best approximates the joint verdict of the Ideal Critics is the better one.

To isolate the proper functioning of the rules of art, observe how the pertinent artistic structures move Ideal Critics. Does such and such a work please the Ideal Critics—the critics cleared of all pertinent deficiencies? If so, then the work is pleasing and should please any normal human being who satisfies the relevant conditions.

However, this, in turn, raises another problem: suppose it is the case that the Ideal Critics' responses enable us to detect the proper functioning of the rules of art. *Nevertheless*, the question remains about how we are to detect or identify these Ideal Critics. The Ideal Critic must be suitably conditioned. But what precisely are these conditions?

The Ideal Critics

Many of the conditions which the Ideal Critics must meet are fairly straightforward and commonsensical. The critic must inspect the artwork in its proper circumstances of presentation. Painting should be viewed under ample lighting, music should be heard in acoustically hospitable situations, and so forth. Likewise, the critic herself should be physically shipshape. Her senses should be in working order; she should not have a distracting migraine or bellyache, and, if she is a critic of fine art, she should not be color blind or otherwise visually afflicted. Both the physical setting of the presentation of the artwork and the physical composure of the critic should be copacetic. However, in addition to meeting the aforesaid physical desiderata, Hume provides five more criteria for the identification of the Ideal Critics.

The Ideal Critics have the following five characteristics:

(1) They possess what Hume calls delicacy of taste.
(2) They are practiced.
(3) They should be involved in comparing and contrasting works of art.
(4) They should lack prejudice.
(5) They should have good sense.

The Ideal Critics are said to possess delicacy of taste, which for Hume amounts to the ability to make fine discriminations. For example, the Ideal Critic of painting ought to be able to discern which lines are strong and which are weak, which are elegant and which are clumsy and forced, and what colors belong together versus those that clash.

Delicacy of taste in the artistic realm is not altogether different from delicacy of taste in the gustatory realm. In order to make this point, Hume recounts the story from *Don Quixote* of Sancho Panza's kinsmen. They were vintners with reputations for remarkably discerning palates. On one occasion, they fell into a dispute over a certain cask of wine. One said that he detected a taste of leather in his drink; the other claimed it smacked of iron. Everyone had a good laugh at the expense of these supposed "experts." The townspeople supposed that the conflicting verdicts issued by Sancho's kinsmen proved that neither of them knew what they were talking about.

However, when the cask was broken open, an old key with a leather thong tied to it fell to the ground. The laughter stopped. Each of Sancho's relatives had in fact detected a quality that actually inhered in the wine.

Hume's point in telling this story has less to do with the difference between the two wine tasters and more to do with the contrast between the wine tasters and the rest of the townsfolk. He means the anecdote to confirm his conviction that there are people who have superior powers for sensing fine differences between things like flavors and shades of colors. Hume maintains that when it comes to artworks, there are those whose greater powers of discrimination set them above the rest of us. These people are the Ideal Critics.

The Ideal Critics are so perceptive that nothing escapes their scrutiny. The Ideal Critics grasp every ingredient in the composition. Hume believes that every quality in the art object has a natural tendency to produce determinate feelings in the humans who are prepared to receive them. To assess an artwork thoroughly, one must be receptive to every quality and structure in the artwork, while being open to all the feelings the artwork has to offer. This requires an exceeding level of delicacy of taste. The Ideal Critic can rise to this demand; she is able to suss out every relevant feature of the object and to respond to it in the way that human nature dictates, thereby informing the remainder of us how we would respond to what is available in the work, were we possessed of a comparable endowment of delicacy of taste.

In addition to possessing delicacy of taste, Hume contends that the Ideal Critics must be practiced, by which Hume means several different things. In the first instance, by "practiced," Hume has in mind that the Ideal Critics be practiced in the medium of which they are issuing judgments of taste. For example, the ideal judge of music is someone who plays an instrument, who can read music, and who understands music as a practitioner or insider. These are the people who will be most attuned to what is going on in the music.

But by "practiced," Hume also has the idea that the Ideal Critic will peruse the object of criticism more than once. Hume lays down this requirement in order to block several predictable ways in which a judgment of taste can go wrong. The Ideal Critic should see the play more than once, in order to ensure that she has not been overwhelmed on her first encounter with it. The work may initially appear confused, when it is only the critic who is befuddled. Or the work may be so flashy that although it seems monumental, it is really superficial. Thus, in order to get a sober and levelheaded fix on the object of criticism, Hume recommends that the Ideal Critic be one who revisits her judgment to assure herself that her first response was not a confused one.

Connected to the idea that the Ideal Critic be steeped in the art form she is criticizing is the notion that she is a person who is constantly comparing and contrasting the excellence available in the medium or art form that she has elected to judge. So, if she is evaluating dance, she should be someone with a wide experience of choreography of all sorts. She will not only be someone who has compared the virtues of the New York City Ballet, American Ballet Theater, the San Francisco Ballet, the Mariinsky Ballet, the Royal Ballet of London, and the Royal Danish Ballet, but she will also have seen modern dance, Bharatanatyam, postmodern dance, flamenco, tap, step dancing, and maybe even various styles of hip-hop and break dancing.

The activity of constantly comparing and contrasting the qualities available in a wide range of the artworks in the critic's field of vision, among other things, contributes to keeping the critic levelheaded. She won't think that just any performance of *The Sleeping Beauty* is wonderful simply because the greatness of the work shines through even in mediocre performances. Because she is always comparing and contrasting dance works, including different versions of *The Sleeping Beauty*, she will not be taken in. She will be able to assess each version of *The Sleeping Beauty* for what it is, as a result of having compared not only many *Sleeping Beauty* productions, but also other ballets and many other works of dance in different genres.

The dedicated pursuit of comparing and contrasting artworks with respect to their strengths and weaknesses also enhances the critic's ability to make fine discriminations. Delicacy of taste is partly a function of one's faculty of discrimination. By constantly comparing and contrasting the virtues of dances and dancers—by, for example, comparing a prima ballerina from American Ballet Theater with a featured soloist from the Alvin Ailey American Dance Theater—the seasoned critic can appreciate when one dancer does something effortlessly and without a discernible expenditure of effort while another dancer may be almost, but not quite, discernibly pushing it. In order to do this, the critic needs a fine eye, which, in part, is a cultivated or practiced eye, an eye practiced in comparing and contrasting the strengths and weaknesses within one's chosen field of expertise.

The Ideal Critic must also lack prejudice. Unlike Hutcheson's Goths, the Ideal Critics should not be encumbered by negative associations toward the works they are assessing. The Ideal Critic is free of any cultural grudges with regard to the works she assays. Nor should one's personal interests influence one's judgments. That the choreographer is your daughter should not influence your judgment.

Indeed, Hume has built into this notion of lack of prejudice (which is somewhat akin to Hutcheson's disinterestedness, albeit not exactly) the idea that the critic be somehow practiced at putting herself in the position of the intended audience for the work. To a certain extent, she has to have a historical or historicist sensibility. She has to be able, within limits (to be discussed), to position herself in a place where she can respond to the work as the intended audience would have responded, so as to let the structure of the artwork operate on her in the way in which it was intended.

Finally, the Ideal Critic must have good sense, by which Hume means that the Ideal Critic needs to be able to understand the relationship between the structure of the work and the purpose of the work—between the how and the what of the work, the relations between the parts and the whole. As Hume says, "It is well-known that . . . we must be able to judge how far the means employed are adapted to their respective purposes."

The good sense of which Hume speaks here is actually a matter of intellect, or of certain intellectual powers. Yet notice that these intellectual powers are not precisely what it is to have taste but are rather a prerequisite for the proper operation of taste. Reason is not part of taste. Reason is what is needed in order to get the right framework for engaging with the object, but correct reasoning is not what delivers pleasure to the subject. Reasoning is not a constituent of the pleasure we derive from artworks, although reason or good sense is a necessary condition for having that experience.

One needs good sense to be able to discern what the purpose of the work is and then to notice how the various choices the artist has made suit that purpose. For example, if the artist wanted to create a religious painting in order to evoke reverence, he wouldn't paint Saint Joseph in a way that resembles the countenance of Alfred E. Neuman on a cover of *MAD* magazine; if the artist did so, the Ideal Critic, exercising good sense, would be pained by the work and would pronounce the effort defective.

Good sense is not equivalent to good taste, since Hume is not speaking of the intellectual pleasure that one gets from figuring out what an artist is up to and how he has attained it. Hume is not talking about cognitive pleasure here. What good sense actually does is enable you to gain access to another kind of pleasure, which may be a feeling, such as one of completeness or unity or appropriateness, which you get when you apprehend how well the work is put together. In this respect, Hume echoes Hutcheson's distinction between the kind of pleasure we derive from beauty versus intellectual pleasure.

Hume is saying that the Ideal Critic (and/or the ideal audience member) requires good sense in order to be able to experience the pleasure that is available in an artwork, but the beauty response and the pleasure thereof are not identical to the intellectual satisfaction that may come of figuring out what the artist is after and how he got it. It is not that which gives you pleasure but is simply the level of understanding requisite in order to experience the pleasure the artwork is designed to produce.

The critic who has these properties, along with the properly functioning senses, freedom from pain and distraction, and access to the proper conditions of exhibition for experiencing the artwork, will be the ideal subject in the sense that the laws of art will operate on her in the right way—that is, in the way that human nature dictates. Subjects—notably the Ideal Critics—with these properties will respond to artworks as perfect specimens of humanity, inasmuch as they possess the kind of human frame the laws of art are suited to engage. When we seek to learn what it is that is normal in accordance with the rules of art, the Ideal Critics will be our, so to speak, laboratory test cases. Consequently, the convergence of their responses with respect to certain structures will provide the basis for our determination of how the rules of art should operate on the suitably prepared, standard-issue human beings.

The responses of the Ideal Critics show us the way in which the rules of art are supposed to mesh with the human frame in a particular case where all the relevant standing conditions are in place. In this way, the joint verdicts of the Ideal Critics will serve as our standards of taste. Indeed, the joint sentiments of these critics can function as objective standards of taste since, unlike our own judgments of taste, their conjoint sentiments are not rooted in our subjective experience, but in something outside of us, namely the Ideal Critics. Moreover, their joint verdict is a public affair—something we can investigate objectively, perhaps by polling them.

That is, though the sentiments of the Ideal Critics are *in* them, they are not *in* us and, thus, can function as objective—or external—standards for us. This is certainly an ingenious solution to the problem, given the logical constraints within which Hume is operating.

Because the Ideal Critics are immune to the problems that result in distorted sentiment—because they meet the standing conditions for the optimal interaction between the artwork and the audience—the Ideal Critics can function as a guide to what is correct and incorrect—to what is the norm or standard—with respect to particular artworks.

But there may be some ambiguity here. What is it precisely that the Ideal Critics discover? What is the standard of taste—a rule or a critical consensus? Is it that the Ideal Critics discover the rules of art which then function as the standard of achievement? Or is it that what they discover is whether the rules of art are functioning smoothly in a particular artwork? Commentators have argued for both interpretations. However, the notion that the standard of taste is a critical consensus strikes me as a better bet.

One reason for believing that Hume supposes this is that although he gives us some examples of what he has in mind as rules of art, we don't seem to have enough of them at our disposal to issue very many critical judgments nor to resolve most disagreements concerning taste. Second, a particular artwork is likely to involve many rules of art, all of them interacting in complex and subtle ways. In order to tell whether they are working together effectively, it is not enough to just know what rules of art are in play. One must know whether they are interacting successfully.

On the rule view, then, we would need higher-order rules of art, informing us about the interactions between different rules of art. Thus, there may be as many meta-rules of art as there are artworks, while at the same time, it is doubtful that we know many, if any, of these meta-rules.

On the other hand, the Ideal Critics can tell whether or not the rules of art are functioning successfully, even if they cannot articulate the pertinent rule or rules outright. They can tell us that the work is structured by the rules of art in such a way as to cause pleasure in anyone suitably prepared, as they are, to receive it properly. That is, they can tell us whether the work is good or bad—which just means that it will raise a feeling of pleasure in appropriately prepared spectators, on the one hand, or a sense of deformity, on the other hand, in sensitive observers.

And they can tell us this on the basis of the pleasure or pain they experience in response to the artwork since the Ideal Critics are precisely exemplars of the relevant sort of suitably conditioned subjects. Thus, any appropriate response should converge on their responses, and any disagreements in taste among the rest of us should be resolved in favor of those judgments of taste that correspond to or correspond most closely to those of the Ideal Critics.

That is, because of the way in which "Of the Standard of Taste" is written, Hume seems to suggest two alternative views: (1) that the standard of taste is a *rule*, specifically a rule of art, versus (2) the idea that the standard is simply a verdict issued by the "jury" of Ideal Critics. Do the Ideal Critics discover rules which can then be used to measure whether the work is good or bad? Or is it that they *respond* to the operation of the rules, which they may be unable to formulate, in certain works by feeling pleasure or displeasure such that against which we may then compare our own reactions.

If the latter, then it is their pleasure or displeasure that is the standard against which we measure our own pleasure and displeasure, attempting to bring our own response in line with theirs when we fall short, and using their responses to resolve our disputes with each other.

Of these two alternatives, as I've indicated, I favor the response, or verdict, view over the rule view simply because Hume doesn't really spell out how the rule view would go—in the essay on the standard of taste, he doesn't give us any concrete examples of how to apply a rule of the sort he may have in mind, especially in complex cases where a multiplicity of such rules may be operating simultaneously.

Instead, what the Ideal Critics seem to do is track the operation of the laws of art. Hence, when we disagree about a single case, we can compare our preferences with the joint verdict of the Ideal Critics. This verdict is objective. For, in the eighteenth-century sense of *objective*, it is outside the subject (outside me; outside you) where the parties to the disagreement are the pertinent subjects. The findings of the Ideal Critics are objective in such cases since they are based on their possession of the five qualities, something putatively as observable externally as the speed of a locomotive. So, the solution to the paradox of taste is that although taste is subjective, it is still the case that there can be an objective standard of taste, namely, the joint verdict of certain ideal human subjects or perfect samples of human nature (a.k.a. Ideal Critics) for the purposes of art evaluation. Therefore, the first premise of the paradox is false. Judgments of taste can be both subjective and objective (intersubjectively verifiable) at once.

Problematic Questions Concerning the Consistency and Possible Circularity of Hume's "Of the Standard of Taste"

After arguing that the convergence in the judgments of taste of the Ideal Critics provides us with an objective standard of taste, Hume goes on to acknowledge that there may be residual differences in the preferences of the Ideal Critics. But this raises the question of whether Hume is undermining the theory of objective, critical judgment that he has just labored so ingeniously to put in place. The potential trouble starts when Hume states:

> But notwithstanding all our endeavors to fix a standard of taste, and reconcile the discordant apprehensions of men, there still remain two sources of variation, which are not sufficient indeed to confound all the boundaries of beauty and deformity but will often serve to produce a difference in the degrees of our approbation or blame. The one is the different humours of particular men; the other, the particular manners and opinions of our age and country. The general principles of taste are uniform in human nature: Where men vary in their judgments, some defect or perversion in the faculties may commonly be remarked; proceeding either from prejudice, from want of practice, or want of delicacy; and there is just reason for approving one taste and condemning another. But where there is such a diversity in the internal frame or external situation as is entirely blameless on both sides and leaves no room to give one the preference above the other; in that case a certain degree of diversity in judgment is unavoidable, and we seek in vain for a standard, by which we can reconcile the contrary sentiments.
>
>   A young man, whose passions are warm, will be more sensibly touched with amorous and tender images, than a man more advanced in years, who takes pleasure in wise, philosophical reflections, concerning the conduct of life, and moderation of the passions. At twenty, Ovid may be the favorite author, Horace at forty, and perhaps Tacitus at fifty. Vainly would we, in such cases, endeavour to enter the sentiments of others, and divest ourselves of those propensities which are natural to us. We choose a favourite author as we do our friend, from a conformity of humour

and disposition. Mirth or passion, sentiment, or reflection; whichever of these most predominates in our temper, it gives us a peculiar sympathy with the writer who resembles us.

One person is more pleased with the sublime, another with the tender, a third with raillery. One has a strong sensibility to blemishes and is extremely studious of correctness; another has a more lively feeling of beauties, and pardons twenty absurdities and defects for one elevated, pathetic stroke. The ear of this man is entirely turned towards conciseness and energy; that man is delighted with a copious, rich, and harmonious expression. Simplicity is affected by one; ornament by another. Comedy, tragedy, satires, odes, each have its partisans, who prefer that particular species of writing to all others. It is plainly an error in a critic to confine his approbations to one species or style of writing and condemn all the rest. But it is almost impossible not to feel a predilection for that which suits our particular turn and disposition. Such performances are innocent and unavoidable, and can never reasonably be the object of dispute, because there is no standard by which they can be decided.

In this passage, Hume seems to agree that there may be persisting disagreements in taste even among those, the Ideal Critics, who are suitably conditioned to respond optimally to the operation of the rules of art. That is, even where the percipients have delicacy of taste, lack prejudice, and so forth, there may be different evaluations of particular works of art. This means that there may be differences in the assessments offered by Ideal Critics. Hume explains that this can occur because Ideal Critics may differ constitutionally. They may have different humours: one may be choleric and the other melancholic, as they said back in the day.

Or, to put it in contemporary parlance, the Ideal Critics may have different psychological dispositions—one being a hail-fellow-well-met and another being a pessimist. Moreover, Ideal Critics will often differ in age and, in consequence, differ in virtue of the temperaments typical of the different stages of life. Thus, a young man may prefer Ovid's *The Art of Love*, whereas the older critic may go in for sober histories, such as those of Tacitus.

Hume says that these disagreements are innocent, by which he appears to mean they are predictable and not problematic.[7] He also says there is no dispute between these judgments since there is no standard according to which we could adjudicate these divergencies of taste, presumably because there is no *joint* verdict in these cases.

But can Hume really be so casual about these ruptures in the consensus of the Ideal Critics? After all, if we subtract all the cases where critics possessed of the five identifying marks differ due to constitutional differences—including those of

---

7. It may be that Hume thinks these differences are harmless because the differences involve generally admitted great works. That one critic prefers one great work over another doesn't entail that either work is not great. In other words, the joint verdict of greatness obtains even if the Ideal Critics differ in their rankings of greatness. It's the joint verdict that the work is fine that counts.

diverging humours and those of different age-indexed temperaments—how many cases of agreement are going to be left over? Hume suggests that a lack of a common standard of taste here covering everyone is no problem, supposing, apparently, that a common standard will be available most of the time. However, given the constitutional differences between age groups that Hume allows for, plus the constitutional differences in the range of psychological types, why does Hume believe that there is enough consensus available that we may still speak confidently of the existence of a standard of taste?

In essence, I think that Hume is pointing out that critics, even Ideal Critics, may differ in their rankings. That is, they do not disagree, for example, that Ovid's *Art of Love* is good, but only over whether it is as good as some of its competitors. That is, the absolute judgments of taste—thumbs up or down—are convergent, although even Ideal Critics may differ about which artworks are the best and the better among the good works, on which all Ideal Critics are agreed.

Moreover, in order to keep this problem from undermining his theory altogether, Hume *might* offer the following possible solutions: First, as already indicated, he could note that it may only be a problem of ranking in these cases. The Ideal Critics may rank differently. But it is not the case that one Ideal Critic is saying a work—say, Ovid's *Art of Love*—is good, while saying another, for example, a history by Tacitus, is bad. There is no disagreement about the goodness of the pertinent works in such a case, but only a disagreement about the relative degree of goodness of the Ovid versus the Tacitus. Consequently, these kinds of differences between Ideal Critics, due to their differences in age and humour, do not compromise their ability to give us a reliable, convergent judgment on the good-versus-bad scale. Because of this, their differences are, as Hume says, innocent. That is, even allowing for divergences of taste of the aforesaid sort between the Ideal Critics, a fairly substantial standard of taste would remain intact.

And, in addition, Hume might defend the notion of objective standards of taste by relativizing such standards to different constitutional types. There is no objective standard of taste that pertains to the preference rankings of persons of all ages and all humours (a.k.a. psychological dispositions). But there may be objective standards of taste relative to the various, systematic, constitutional differences that, as a function of human nature, exist between people. Thus, if two people of the same constitutional type disagree in their judgments of taste, they may use the joint verdict of the Ideal Critics *of that constitutional type* as their standard of taste.

That is, if you are young and ebullient and you disagree with someone else who is young and ebullient, then it will be the joint verdict of the Ideal Critics who are constitutionally young in age and ebullient in disposition (humour) against whom you should measure your dispute.

For example, one young, fun-loving guy says *Dennis the Menace* cartoons are better than Shaw's *Pygmalion*, and another twentysomething counters vice versa. They can bring themselves before the court of young and ebullient Ideal Critics to adjudicate their dispute, and the judgment that most closely approximates those of the constitutionally apposite Ideal Critics is, in this instance, the superior evaluation.

Indeed, aspiring appreciators in this age- and humour-group, Hume *might* suggest, should strive to align their assessments with those of the Ideal Critics of comparable age- and humour-groups, if they wish—as one supposes they would—to get the most out of their engagement with artworks.

Hence, it may not be the case that all Hume can say about the differential verdicts of Ideal Critics is that they can only tell people that certain works are good or bad *period*, and nothing more. Perhaps Ideal Critics can also inform people about the degree of goodness of the work in question relative to the pertinent age-groups, personality types, and dispositions of disputants, where these differences are grounded in human nature and its regularities.

The idea—that some artworks are predictably more suited and more rewarding for some constitutionally defined groups of people rather than others—should be unproblematic. For example, consider what we call "children's programs." These are programs keyed to humans at a certain stage of biological development. *Teletubbies* is designed to appeal to very young, virtually infant, children. It is geared to the babies' level of biological development, including their cognitive powers. *Teletubbies*, let us say, is good relative to that group of people. It will appeal to them. It will not appeal to a Supreme Court judge, given her cognitive powers, level of emotional development, and maturity. *King Lear* is more likely to appeal to people like that. Conversely, *King Lear* is not suited for, nor will it appeal to, infants. We are entitled to assert this, moreover, on the basis of certain biological regularities that are rooted in human nature.

Likewise, Hume might claim that just as there are children's programs, there are also melancholic artworks that will appeal in a systematic way due to the operation of human nature to persons of a melancholic disposition, while young men, again due to their constitutional makeup, will prefer racier fare, such as Ovid's *Art of Love*. If members of such constitutionally based groups find themselves disagreeing about which works are better relative to their type of people, they should consult the joint verdict of the Ideal Critics—the critics who meet the five criteria—who are constitutionally like themselves in order to settle their differences. And if one wishes to hone one's taste, one might try to attune oneself to the judgments of the constitutionally indexed Ideal Critics so that gradually one's taste may improve by becoming more in synch with theirs.

People have different constitutional capacities. In Hume, these are called *humours* and *dispositions*. Artworks will affect people with different humours to different degrees. Horror stories appeal to people with morbid dispositions more than they appeal to people with optimistic dispositions. Presumably, horror stories will do so on a regular basis. So, if you wish to ascertain what are going to be the good, better, and best artworks for someone with a disposition (in this case, a taste for horror) like yours, what you do is look to the Ideal Critics with the same (morbid) psychological constitution that you have. They are reliable indicators or detectors of what people like you would most appreciate if the standing conditions were properly in place and the laws of art were operating without a hitch.

The Ideal Critic dominated by morbid humours will presumably prefer horror fictions over light operas and musicals (except for *Sweeney Todd*). So, if you wish guidance in ordering your artistic preferences, look to the Ideal Critics who are like you and try to take on board what their joint verdict recommends.

For Hume, it would appear that the variation in the humours and dispositions of these Ideal Critics can be taken to be lawlike—lawlike relative to certain regularly recurring psychological constitutions. Their verdicts are grounded in lawlike regularities, even where they diverge in their judgments of Ovid versus Horace versus Tacitus.

These verdicts are reliable and lawlike—they provide us with a solid standard of taste once you realize that it is a more complex standard than you might have at first expected. It is a standard that makes provision for lawlike variations relative to different populations of audience types in terms of their psychological makeup. This more complex standard can still give us objective results. For example, the joint verdict of the relevant group of Ideal Critics implies that for any x, if x is a suitably conditioned twentysomething with a buoyant disposition, Ovid will be best. That is, for such an audience member, Ovid will be better than Tacitus.

You can predict the optimal operation of the rules of art on the basis of the Ideal Critics so long as you look to the right subgroups of Ideal Critics and match them up with the kind of audience—in terms of its psychological constitution—that your predictions concern.

I present the preceding account of the different verdicts due to age and humour as a possible way, consistent with his views, that Hume might extend the discussion of the relevant differences between Ideal Critics. Whether we would ever have available psychological theories to carry it off is another, rather doubtful, matter.

Alternatively, remember that Hume doesn't think that *all* of the judgments of Ideal Critics provide us with a standard of taste, only the *joint* verdicts. Any judgments that do not elicit a joint verdict do not have the force of a standard. They are not aberrant, though; they are what Hume calls blameless. But they are not part of the standard of taste. These judgments fall outside the reach of the standard. So, the standard doesn't apply to everything—that is, not to every judgment or to every disagreement. But where it does obtain, it is objective.

Another place where the question of the consistency of Hume's "Of the Standard of Taste" arises concerns his parting remarks about moral defects in an artwork which he allows should count as a blemish in the work. Should the moral shortcomings of a work influence the Ideal Critics' evaluation of the work? Hume grants that an educated viewer can overlook details of style and manner peculiar to a work of a different time period and can even give a pass to its outmoded metaphysics, but he also states that

> where the ideas of morality and decency alter from one age to another and where vicious manners are described, without being marked with the proper characters of blame and disapprobation; this must be allowed to disfigure the poem, and to be a real deformity. I cannot, nor is it proper I should, enter into such sentiments; and however I may excuse the poet, on account of the manners of his age, I never can relish the composition. The want of humanity and of decency, so conspicuous in the characters drawn by several of the ancient poets, even sometimes by Homer and the Greek tragedians, diminishes considerably the merit of their noble performances, and gives modern authors an advantage over them. We are not interested in the fortunes and sentiments of such rough heroes; we are displeased to find the limits of vice and virtue so much confounded: And whatever indulgence we may give to the writer on account of his prejudices, we cannot prevail on ourselves to enter into his sentiments, or bear an affection to characters, which we plainly discover to be blameable.

This passage raises at least two issues. The first is whether Hume has violated the principle that Ideal Critics must lack prejudice by his willingness to count the moral defects of artworks as detracting from the overall goodness of the work. That is, is Hume's apparent moralism in this quotation consistent with his notion of the need for the Ideal Critics to be free from prejudice? And second, supposing that Hume can be exonerated from self-contradiction here, we would also like to know whether his view is correct—that is, should moral considerations play a role in judgments of taste?

Hume, like Aristotle, Plato, and virtually every other philosopher of art before the eighteenth century, thought that it was obvious that moral evaluation was relevant to assessing artworks. But, as we shall see in subsequent chapters, from the eighteenth century onward, a powerful tradition emerged in the philosophy of art which regards art as an autonomous realm, categorically discrete from other social realms and concerns, such as morality. This tendency, which gained increasing adherence in the nineteenth and twentieth centuries and has been variously called aestheticism, autonomism, and/or formalism, upholds the conviction that art is solely for the sake of art and not for the sake of morality, society, or anything else. Moreover, the influence of this art for art's sake tradition unavoidably forces those of us who have grown up in its shadow to interrogate the position Hume takes to be obvious and to ask whether his view of the relation of morality to the judgment of taste can be defended.

In terms of the first worry—that Hume's moralism with regard to art is inconsistent with his view that Ideal Critics should be unprejudiced—Hume may respond that our sense of moral indignation is not a prejudice; since on his view, moral sentiments are universal. To take moral umbrage at Achilles's treatment of the body of Hector in the *Iliad* is not on a par with being put off by the manners and fashions of another age. Moral issues strike at deep springs in human nature; moral responses are not mere prejudices based on local conventions. They are a function of human nature, they command universal assent, and, therefore, invoking moral convictions and emotional responses is not a matter of violating the strictures against sectarian bias.

One, of course, may dispute Hume's claims about the universality of moral sentiment, arguing that it is much more like fashion, manners, and metaphysics, as Hume conceives of them. However, that would remove the argument from the arena of the philosophy of art to that of ethics. Undoubtedly, this may be a worthwhile debate. Nevertheless, from the perspective of the philosophy of art, we can say that there is no inconsistency between Hume's demands that the Ideal Critics be free of prejudice while also encouraging them to take account of the moral defects of artworks when issuing their judgments of taste. For, Hume does not regard our moral assessments of the works to be a matter of prejudice but of a universal response, bred in the bone. So, at the very least, Hume is not inconsistent.

As already indicated, Hume's willingness to admit the moral assessment of an artwork into the critic's overall evaluation of it is apt to rub the wrong way the sensibilities of many modern aestheticians. For many of them, it is a category mistake to count the moral defects of an artwork as an aesthetic defect in that work since aesthetics and ethics are necessarily twain. Does Hume have anything that he can say to the modern aesthetician?

For Hume, the judgment of taste is based on subjective feelings of pleasure and pain. If the artwork provokes pleasure, it is good; if it engenders pain, it is bad. The point of the artwork, putatively, is to elicit pleasure. If it fails to evoke pleasure or causes pain, the work is defective as an artwork.[8] Presenting immoral actions unqualified, or worse, endorsing them will cause pain in the reader, viewer, and/or listener. And that, of course, will amount to a defect or a blemish in an artifact whose function it is to induce a pleasurable response. The immoral features of the work, in other words, will block the intended uptake of the work, causing pain rather than pleasure. That is, the moral defects in the work cripple the capacity of the piece to serve up pleasure, thereby thwarting the aesthetic purpose of the artwork.

When a work of fiction presents us with an action, it mandates that we imagine it in a certain way. But our imaginations resist entertaining evil as good. For example, for normal, morally sensitive audiences, it is impossible to enter into the world of a fiction where torturing innocent children is good. It is like the impossibility of

---

8. Of course, the language of pleasure and pain is too reductive to canvas all of our reactions to artworks. However, for purposes of discussing Hume's position, I will not dispute it here. Nevertheless, for the record, let me state that I find it to be extremely questionable because it is overly simplistic.

imagining that something is funny when it is not. Thus, part of Hume's reason for counting moral blemishes as aesthetic defects may be that representing evil actions as good awakens imaginative resistance in the spectator, which resistance in turn impedes the spectator's full enjoyment and engagement with the work, perhaps to the point of causing psychological pain. That is, as Hume might put it, the pain evoked by the moral blemish blocks the possibility of taking pleasure in the work.

Unlike what we will encounter in the work of Kant and his would-be followers, who only regard disinterested pleasure as pertinent to the judgment of taste, Hume finds morally interested pleasure and pain to be relevant to such judgments. Thus, where Kant might dismiss moral concerns as germane to assessments of the beautiful, Hume will accept them in the critic's assessment because, without Kant's commitment to a very draconian concept of disinterested pleasure, the interested pleasures and pains of morality are legitimate ingredients in judgments of taste and, thus, figure naturally in the capacity of the beautiful object to either instill or undercut the sensations the artwork was designed to promote.

Note that this is a major difference between Hume and many of the aestheticians, like Kant, who will succeed Hume. As we will see at length in the next chapter, Kant would regard pleasure or displeasure, taken on the grounds of morality, to be interested. A judgment of taste made on such grounds would not be a true judgment of taste. In contrast, Hume allows for certain "interested" pleasures, such as those connected to morality, to count in the judgment of taste, whereas this is precisely what Kant and his followers disallow. Throughout the nineteenth and twentieth centuries, many Kantian theorists of art regarded their position as an advance over Hume's, although by now in the early twenty-first century, the notion of disinterested pleasure à la Kant is again hotly debated, and Hume's moralism is gaining a second hearing.

Another potential problem for Hume's account is circularity. In order to pick out the Ideal Critics, it is alleged, we must already know which artworks are beautiful. For how can we know if a critic exhibits delicacy of taste unless we see that she is responding to beautiful artworks with the appropriate delicacy? Yet how can we know that the pertinent artwork is beautiful prior to the joint verdict of the Ideal Critics?

That is, Hume maintains that the mark of an Ideal Critic is that she exhibits delicacy of taste. That means that the critic is attending to the correct features of the aesthetic stimuli. But how can we know that unless we already know that the work in question is beautiful (successful or good)? However, we can't know an artwork is successful or good without the collective judgment of the Ideal Critics, and, of course, we cannot know that until we know who the Ideal Critics are. According to this argument, in order to know whether someone evinces delicacy of taste we would have to already know which artworks are good, bad, or ugly. But that is supposedly what observing the critic is supposed to tell us. So, the proposal looks like it is inadmissibly circular.

Nevertheless, it might be said: surely, we can tell whether or not someone exercises delicacy of taste without having to know anything about artworks per se. For whether or not someone has refined powers of discrimination can be determined without reference to artworks. Being able to tell whether someone can discriminate between Prussian blue, cerulean blue, and navy blue does not require that we know which artworks are the good ones. Delicacy of taste, understood as discriminatory prowess, can be adjudged without reference to artworks or to judgments thereof.

Furthermore, whether one has good sense—the ability to understand means-ends relationships—also presupposes nothing about art and our judgments concerning artworks. And the same applies to the quality of a lack of prejudice.

Finally, there is no problem of circularity in determining whether a critic is practiced and has wide knowledge of her field of expertise. One can tell whether a critic has a grasp of the relevant comparisons and contrasts germane to her field by examining the way in which she conducts her criticism and the references she makes therein. And one can determine whether a critic is a passable practitioner in the art form she criticizes by listening to her play musical instruments, examining the pictures she's painted, the poems she has written, and so on. Remember, we only need to establish that she is practiced, not that her artworks are good.

Thus far then, Hume seems immune to some of the criticisms of which he is commonly accused. But he is not off scot-free. Let us review some further objections.

Lingering Problems for Hume

We have just attempted to exonerate Hume from the charge of circularity by arguing that one can determine whether a candidate for the title of "Ideal Critic" can be certified to possess the five qualifying properties for that status without reference to beautiful artworks.

But our argument might be countered by saying that someone could have each of those properties and, nevertheless, not be a reliable critic. In terms of the ways in which we interpreted those properties above, a handyman might have good sense when it comes to fixing things, delicacy of taste when painting things, like barns and outhouses, and not have a prejudiced bone in his body (he respects everyone). He may also be a passable singer as well as someone who listens to music on the radio on a regular basis.

Yet does this guarantee that he will be an Ideal Critic of songs? Surely, we could imagine that this might not be the case. So, even if the five qualities that Hume singles out can be seen to be noncircular, necessary conditions of the station of Ideal Critic, it is not evident that we have a list of jointly sufficient, noncircular qualifications for that role.

At times, Hume seems to regard critical judgment as equivalent to feelings. But certainly, there is more to a critical judgment than a feeling, pro or con. Surely, the feeling needs to undergo some cognitive monitoring. Nor can it be, as Hume sometimes suggests, that a feeling of pleasure (or pain) is always a necessary condition for issuing a genuine judgment of taste. For isn't it possible to judge an artwork accurately sans any tremors of pleasure? Aren't purely cognitive judgments of artworks possible?

For example, we can make critical judgments with reference to the category to which the artwork belongs, declaring it to be good of its kind, without any associated feelings of pleasure. One could know that a certain mystery story or romantic story is good of its kind just by knowing the aims of that kind of art and then by recognizing that the work in question realizes them.

For instance, one might not like the genres of horror fictions or tearjerkers, yet still be able to accurately identify a good instance of the kind in question. That is, one can render correct critical evaluations not only where one feels no pleasure but also where one has an outright disliking for the kind of works under scrutiny.

By choosing the gustatory model for critical judgment, Hume, like Hutcheson, fails to allow for the degree to which such judgments may be partly or even wholly cognitive. Of course, it is true that Hume gives good sense a role in critical judgment, but that role is purely ancillary. Good sense is a precondition for genuine critical judgments, but it is not part of the critical exercise itself.

Indeed, with his emphasis on feelings, Hume makes it sound at times as though the object of the critical judgment is the experience of pleasure or pain we and the Ideal Critics alike undergo. But surely the object of the critical judgment must be the artwork and not the feelings the artworks evoke. The object of critical judgment is *The Tempest* and not my response to *The Tempest*, no matter how ideal a critic I am.

Changing the direction of our criticisms so far, let us suppose that Hume is right—that there are Ideal Critics, identifiable in the way he stipulates. Moreover, imagine that we can find these critics by using Hume's five characteristics as a guide, and we can discover the cases where they agree. Should we then treat them as the standard of taste?

Perhaps that is good advice if we ourselves lack the five qualities that define the Ideal Critics. But what if we realize that we ourselves instantiate these characteristics as well as anybody else does? What need then would we have for the *joint* verdict of these critics. Wouldn't consulting them be redundant? For, if I had the qualities that define an Ideal Critic, I would be an Ideal Critic myself and could, therefore, rely on my own verdicts as decisive. Instead of waving in the direction of the assembly of joint critics, I could point to myself as an exemplary critic as the grounds for the authority of my judgment of taste. Or that, at least, is what the next philosopher on our docket, Immanuel Kant, suggests.

Bibliography

The text that I used in the preparation of this chapter was *David Hume: Selected Essays*, edited by Stephen Copley and Andrew Edgar (Oxford University of Press, 1993).

Carroll, Noël. "Hume's Standard of Taste." *Journal of Aesthetics and Art Criticism* 43 (1984): 181–94.
Cohen, Ted. "Partial Enchantments of the *Quixote* Story in Hume's Essay on Taste." In *Institutions of Art*, edited by Robert J. Yanal, 145–56. University Park: Pennsylvania State University Press, 1993.
Costelloe, Timothy M. *The British Aesthetic Tradition: From Shaftesbury to Wittgenstein*. Cambridge: Cambridge University Press, 2013.
Dickie, George. *The Century of Taste*. Oxford: Oxford University Press, 1996.
Guyer, Paul. *A History of Modern Aesthetics*. Vol. 1, *The Eighteenth Century*. Cambridge: Cambridge University Press, 2014.
———. "Humean Critics, Imaginative Fluency, and Emotional Responsiveness." *British Journal of Aesthetics* 48 (2008): 445–56.
Kivy, Peter. *De Gustibus*. Oxford: Oxford University Press, 2015.
———. "Hume's Neighbor's Wife: An Essay on the Evolution of Hume's Aesthetics." *British Journal of Aesthetics* 23 (1983): 195–208.
———. "Hume's Standard of Taste: Breaking the Circle." *British Journal of Aesthetics* 7 (1967): 57–66.
———. "Recent Scholarship and the British Tradition: A Logic of Taste—The First Fifty Years." In *Aesthetics: A Critical Anthology*, edited by George Dickie and Richard Sclafani. New York: St. Martin's, 1977.
———. "Remarks on the Varieties of Prejudice in Hume's Essay on Taste." *Scottish Journal of Philosophy* 9 (2011): 111–14.
Korsmeyer, Carolyn W. "Hume and the Foundations of Taste." *Journal of Aesthetics and Art Criticism* 35 (1976): 201–15.
Mothersill, Mary. "Hume and the Paradox of Taste." In *Aesthetics: A Critical Anthology*, edited by George Dickie, Richard Sclafani, Ronald Roblin. New York: St. Martin's, 1989.
Shelley, James. "Empiricism." In *The Routledge Companion to Aesthetics*, 2nd ed., edited by Berys Gaut and Dominic McIver Lopes, 41–53. London: Routledge, 2002.
———. "Hume's Double Standard of Taste." *Journal of Aesthetics and Art Criticism* 52 (1992): 437–45.
———. "Hume and the Nature of Taste." *Journal of Aesthetics and Art Criticism* 56 (1998): 29–38.
Shiner, Roger A. "Hume and the Causal Theory of Taste." *Journal of Aesthetics and Art Criticism* 54 (1996): 237–49.
Townsend, Dabney. *Hume's Aesthetic Theory: Taste and Sentiment*. London: Routledge, 2001.
Wieand, Jeffrey. "Hume's True Judges." *Journal of Aesthetics and Art Criticism* 53 (1995): 318–19.
———. "Hume's Two Standards of Taste." *Philosophical Quarterly* 34 (1983): 129–42.

CHAPTER 5

Immanuel Kant's *Critique of Aesthetic Judgment*

Generally considered one of the giants of modern philosophy in the West—if not *the* giant—Immanuel Kant lived from 1724 to 1804 and wrote the *Critique of Judgment*, the third of his three *Critiques*, in 1790. He lived as a philosophy professor in Konigsberg, Prussia, where he spent his entire life. During Kant's lifetime, Prussia was a part of Germany, but it is now a Russian enclave called Kaliningrad, near Poland. The topic of this chapter, the *Critique of Aesthetic Judgment*, is part I of the third *Critique*, and it has had an immense influence on the course of aesthetics throughout the subsequent two centuries and beyond. However, it is his *Critique of Pure Reason* on which his reputation primarily rests.

In the preface to his *Prolegomena to Any Future Metaphysics*, Kant wrote that he had been "awakened from his dogmatic slumbers" by David Hume. Hume claimed that we have no way of knowing that natural regularities—patterns of cause-and-effect—that obtain today will obtain tomorrow. Hume maintained that such knowledge would have to be demonstrable by *a priori* argument or by empirical argument.

Hume could not find an *a priori* argument to this end and he argued, furthermore, that an empirical argument to this conclusion would perforce be inadequate. For, in order to reliably predict future events—the cause-and-effect patterns of tomorrow—induction would have to be justified since we base causal judgments on induction. But as Hume argued, the only thing that could justify induction empirically is induction itself. That is, the reason we believe that the future will be like the past is that in the past, the future has been like the past, which empirical argument is inadmissible as it is circular. Moreover, Hume also maintained that we cannot tell by observation alone that one event is the cause of another event, as opposed to the two events merely being correlated—merely appearing sequentially in space and time. That is, does the wayward baseball cause the window to break, or is it that the window just happens to shatter on its own as the baseball enters its spatiotemporal coordinates?

Hume's skepticism about causation, Kant says, roused him to respond. Kant believed that he could show knowledge of causation to be necessary. In his *Critique of Pure Reason*, Kant argues that causality is an *a priori* concept, one we must bring to any experience, if the experience is to be intelligible to us. That is, we can know that everything we experience will have to abide by causal laws because the category of causation itself is a component of the mind. The mind comes equipped with certain forms and categories, such as space, time, and causality. Experience will only be intelligible or comprehensible if it fits into these molds. The mind is a filtration system; the only thing that gets through to us is what fits this filtration system. So anything we experience as intelligible must abide by the forms of space and time, and the categories, such as causality. They are the conditions that make any experience possible for us.

So, Kant's answer to Hume's skepticism regarding causation is that we can be sure that causal regularities will continue into the future—we can be sure that they hold necessarily—because this is the necessary requirement for any experience, including any future experience. If we experience anything in the future, then it must abide by causal laws.

The form of this argument is a transcendental argument: an argument that asks what must be the case if such and such is the case? It is a type of argument to the best explanation, which is to say, a form of induction. Given that such and such holds, what has to be the case? For example, if experiences are intelligible, what makes that possible? In part because experience is organized by the principle that everything has a cause.

This argument is at the center of Kant's greatest book, *The Critique of Pure Reason*. By *critique*, Kant does not mean just "criticism" in our contemporary sense. Rather, he also means an investigation into the conditions that make something possible. When Marx offered a critique of political economy, he was asking what makes capitalism possible. His answer was surplus value.

Kant asks in the *Critique of Pure Reason* what makes theoretical reason possible? What must be the case if theoretical thinking, like "matches burn when struck," is possible? Part of the answer is that our mind is structured in the terms of the category of causation. This strategy of relocation of the solution of problems like that of causation in the mind—this subjective turn—was christened by Kant as his "Copernican revolution."

The *Critique of Pure Reason* is referred to as the *First Critique*. Kant's work concerning aesthetics is the *Critique of Judgment*, known as the *Third Critique*. The *First Critique* asks what makes judgments like "matches ignite when struck" possible. The *Third Critique* also asks questions about the possibility of certain kinds of judgments, namely aesthetic judgments such as "this rose is beautiful." This is the leading question in the part of the *Third Critique* on which we will be focusing. Teleological judgments are the subject of the second part of the *Third Critique*, although this is beyond our purview.

In between the *First* and *Third Critiques*, there is a *Second Critique*—the *Critique of Practical Reason*. Its question is What makes moral judgments possible? So we see that there are *Critiques* for the putatively three major kinds of judgments that we make: theoretical (or scientific) judgments, or judgments of pure reason based on concepts; moral judgments, or practical judgments related to purposes; and aesthetic judgments—judgments about whether or not certain things are, for example, beautiful or sublime.

The purpose of the *Critiques* is to explain what is distinctive about each of these kinds of judgments and to show how they are possible—to show or to reveal the grounds we have for making legitimate (a.k.a. correct) theoretical, moral, and aesthetic judgments. This is an especially pressing issue with respect to aesthetic judgments because there is something especially peculiar about them. For as Hutcheson and Hume maintained, such judgments are based on our experiences of pleasure, which are subjective. Yet, as Hume tried to argue, we think that they should elicit agreement from other people, which, as we've seen, implies that we think that they are objective. But how is that possible if we've only got a single case—our own reactions—to go on? That is the question that dominates the first part of the *Critique of Judgment—The Critique of Aesthetic Judgment*.

One way to situate this text is to read it as if it is an answer to Hume's paradox. How can a judgment of taste—what Kantians count as one species of aesthetic judgment—be objective (i.e., command the assent of others), if it is based solely on subjective experience? The word *aesthetic* in Kant's time pertained to perception and sensation; so, an aesthetic judgment is not at all different from the judgment of taste that Hume analyzes.[1] Moreover, Kant wants to discover how these judgments are not only objective but also necessary. That is, in Kant's way of putting it, aesthetic judgments are said to command universal assent. Yet since the ground for this necessity is not immediately apparent, Kant aims to establish it.

Though the question being posed is Hume's, Kant comes up with a different answer. As we've seen, Hume refers us to the joint verdict of the Ideal Critics—critics in the plural—as the ground for judgments of taste. Kant tries to argue that the objectivity of the aesthetic judgment can be founded on the authority of my own case, my own feeling of pleasure, my own experience. There is not, for Kant, any need to consult a body of critics. Implicitly, Kant's criticism of Hume is that if a person could ascertain that she has the pertinent subjective feelings (notably disinterested pleasure), then the Ideal Critics are redundant.[2]

There are other ways that Kant differs from Hume. They agree that the judgments are based on feelings of pleasure, but like Hutcheson, Kant implicitly parts company with Hume insofar as Hume does not qualify the kind of pleasure that is relevant to such judgments—judgments of the form "X is beautiful." Like Hutcheson, Kant maintains that the relevant sort of pleasure is disinterested

---

1. The word *aesthetic* was introduced by Alexander Baumgarten in order to encompass roughly the domain of sensitive cognition, i.e., cognition through the senses. It gradually came to be associated with the kind of experience afforded by artworks, perhaps due to Baumgarten's examples, which chiefly were works of art, notably poetry. The word *aesthetic*, from the Greek *aisthetikos*, meaning roughly "relating to sense perception." For Kant, it applies to judgments made on the basis of subjective feelings.

2. Note: Kant also differs from Hume in that from Kant's point of view, Hume's willingness to allow morality to enter into the judgment of taste disqualifies it as a judgment of free beauty.

pleasure. And disinterestedness, in turn, is important for accounting for the objectivity of such judgments.

Kant's account of aesthetic judgments is not, however, just a repetition of Hutcheson's. Some differences include the following: (1) Kant makes no commitment to a faculty of taste. (This was perhaps a rather strained idea anyway. Would we postulate a sense of humor just because comic amusement can be triggered involuntarily?) (2) Hutcheson tries to offer a formula for what in the object causes disinterested pleasure in the percipient. Hutcheson proposes what Hume would call a rule of art—that a ratio of variety amidst uniformity putatively causes delight in observers. But, as we'll see, Kant denies that we can formulate such rules, a point he makes by saying that we can't make judgments of taste with respect to free beauty by subsuming the relevant object under a concept; although Kant does agree with Hutcheson that the relevant pleasure is not a cognitive pleasure, that is, pleasure that results from subsuming a particular under a concept.[3]

The central project of Kant's analysis, then, is Hume's project, the question of the objective grounds for issuing judgments of the form "this rose is beautiful." There are two kinds of judgments that Kant thinks one can make about the object that we commend as being beautiful: there are judgments of free beauty—of which natural beauty is the paradigm—and there are judgments of dependent or accessory beauty.

As the text opens, Kant is initially speaking primarily of free beauty with respect to nature and not the beauty we would ascribe to an artwork. There are cases in which judgments of free beauty can be made about works of art, but what the theory of free beauty will work best for is judgments like "this sunset is beautiful" or "look at that peacock's tail, isn't it beautiful?"

Aesthetic Judgments of Free Beauty

Kant's theory is the most complicated one that we will study. Its parts are intricately related in often multiple ways that often require our doubling back to earlier points in order to trace the ways in which Kant refines them, making new connections and developing them in new directions. Thus, our exposition, like Kant's own presentation, is sometimes repetitious. This makes reading sometimes difficult. Given this, perhaps the most useful way in which to begin to expound Kant's theory of judgments of free beauty is to state the theory outright and then to present Kant's arguments for each of its parts.

---

3. Kant's noncognitivism in his analysis of beauty also stands in stark contrast to the dominant approach of the aestheticians who preceded him in Germany (who advocated what might be called Rationalist Aesthetics). Following Leibniz, these philosophers—including Baumgarten, Mendelsohn, and Wolff—regarded the experience of beauty as a clear but indistinct cognition of perfection which they thought could be characterized in terms of formulas like unity in diversity.

The following is Kant's theory of judgments of free beauty, which may also be called pure aesthetic judgments or judgments of taste. The theory that Kant puts forward in the "Analytic of the Beautiful"—Book I of the *Critique of Aesthetic Judgment* is as follows:

> X is beautiful (where X stands for a singular term, e.g., "this rose") is an authentic judgment of taste (a genuine aesthetic judgment) if and only if it is a (1) subjective, (2) disinterested, (3) universal, (4) necessary, and (5) singular judgment concerning (6) the contemplative pleasure that everyone ought to derive (7) from the free play (and the quickening) of the faculties of the imagination and the understanding in relation to (and in response to) (8) forms of finality (forms of purposiveness, or purposiveness without a purpose).

This is undoubtedly a formidable and obscure sounding formula. So, let us go over each part of the formula one at a time. Moreover, as we go over it, we will also note why Kant thinks such judgments are objective (in the sense of intersubjectively and normatively valid).

First, judgments of beauty are subjective. The judgment is rooted in one's own subjective experience—an idea that we are familiar with from Hume and Hutcheson. The judgment is based on an inner feeling of pleasure. It is also part of the subjectivity of aesthetic judgment that it is necessary to experience the object face-to-face in order to judge it. In Kantian terminology, this is usually glossed as "not by inference, but presentation." The judgment is rooted in an experience and that experience is in the subject. Kant makes this clear on numerous occasions. For example, in the First Moment, in "A Judgment of Taste Is Aesthetic," he states that

> if we wish to decide whether something is beautiful or not, we do not use understanding to refer the presentation to the object so as to give rise to cognition; rather, we use imagination (perhaps in connection with understanding) to refer the presentation to the subject and his feeling of pleasure or displeasure. Hence a judgment of taste is not a cognitive judgment and so is not a logical judgment but an aesthetic one, by which we mean a judgment whose determining basis cannot be other than subjective. But any reference of presentations, even of sensations, can be objective (in which case it signifies what is real [rather than formal] in an empirical presentation); excepted is a reference to the feeling of pleasure and displeasure—this reference designates nothing whatsoever in the object, but here the subject feels himself, [namely] how he is affected by the presentation.

To say that the judgment in question is not cognitive is to say that it is not an inference from a general premise. To say that it is aesthetic is to say that it is based on subjective feeling; it is a judgment of sense or intuition. It cannot be based on a chain of reasoning or on the testimony of someone else. It has to rest on a subjective, firsthand experience. It couldn't be derived from a chain of reasoning of the following sort: all roses are beautiful; the thing in the black box in front of you is a rose; therefore, the rose in the black box is beautiful. That would be a judgment of pure reason, a product of the intellect or understanding.

To make an aesthetic judgment, you have to have a feeling of pleasure from the stimulus itself, and this requires that you have a close encounter of the third kind. You cannot declare this or that to be beautiful based on the testimony of someone else, including a critic of the highest authority. Such judgments must be rooted in your own direct experience of the object.

Second, the judgment is disinterested. To say that a judgment is disinterested is to say that it has no connection with purpose. This concept is already familiar from Hutcheson. But Kant's notion of disinterestedness is much broader than Hutcheson's. It does not only extend to matters of personal advantage but requires that disinterested judgments be divorced from all considerations of purpose.[4] For Kant, the pleasure felt must not be connected to any advantage or utility, including the utility of moral goodness (which, of course, is different from Hume's position on evil in artworks).

Kant titles the second section in First Moment "The Liking That Determines a Judgment of Taste Is Devoid of All Interest." Kant makes this claim in stronger terms than Hutcheson: "In order to play the judge in matters of taste, we must not be in the least biased in favor of the thing's existence but must be wholly indifferent about it."

Here, Kant offers a test to determine whether a judgment is truly disinterested. If you are indifferent to an object's existence, then you do not *care* whether it exists; if you do not care if it exists, then you do not like it because of some use you could put it to. For, if you wanted to put it to some use, you would care if the thing in question exists.

If you say, "That palace is beautiful," then you may not be indifferent to its existence. You might be making that judgment because you would like to live in the palace or to be invited there, or you might have some other ulterior motive. According to Kant, you can be certain that you do not have an interest in it, only if you do not care at all whether it exists. Even if the palace were a mirage, you would still say it is beautiful, supposing your pleasure in it is disinterested. On the other hand, if you do care about whether or not a thing exists, you no longer have a purely aesthetic attitude toward it. You are not genuinely disinterested.

---

4. Perhaps one reason that Kant disconnects judgments of taste from purposes is that any link with purposes would allow for inferential judgments of the sort disallowed by Kant's first condition on aesthetic judgments of free beauty, namely, that they be grounded in an immediate experience of pleasure rather than any form of reasoning. Perhaps part of Kant's reason for excluding the resort to concepts in judgments of taste is that concepts typically come with subtending purposes.

Kant opposes pure aesthetic judgments not only to judgments of the good (which depend on the purposes/concepts), but also to judgments of the agreeable. For, we are concerned with the existence of the agreeable—we want the object of our liking to exist because we desire more of the same, as is the case when we like or find agreeable a certain kind of food. That is, we care whether or not the ice cream sundae before us exists.[5] Judgments of the agreeable are aesthetic judgments since they originate in the senses, but they are not pure aesthetic judgments. They depend on our own personal preferences and cannot command the assent of others. My liking for sour pickles, for example, cannot be universalized.

The third feature of a pure aesthetic judgment of the beautiful is that it is universal, in the sense that anyone should be capable of making the same judgment. That is, if we experience the stimulus, cleared of all of the interests that differentiate us, then it seems likely that our judgments will converge. So, if our judgments of taste are truly disinterested, they should reflect what *anyone* would *feel* being subjected to the relevant stimulus because we have factored out what is unique to each of us.[6] In Section 6 of the Second Moment, Kant writes, "For if someone likes something and is conscious that he himself does so without any interest, then he cannot help judging that it must contain a basis for being liked that holds for everyone."

The reason for the introduction of the idea of disinterestedness is now evident. Kant intends to claim that if I can factor out all of the interests that make people different from one another and can ensure that all that is in play in my judgment is, more or less, what we have in common (notably, our human powers of the imagination and understanding), then we all have the capacity to render the same judgment. For we can be sure that what differentiates and particularizes us, our individual interests and preferences, have been factored out in such a way that we ought to be able to say that if I feel pleasure, you, too, can feel a comparable pleasure as well. The idea underlying this is that what are being activated are the cognitive, perceptual, and psychological processes that we all have in common in virtue of our shared human nature.

Thus, if you could be sure that those faculties are operating, so to speak, in their pure state—that is, in the way they would be operating in everybody were they disinterested (because you have subtracted out what makes everybody different, namely their interests and personal preoccupations)—then you would get a picture of how everybody with the same psychological makeup would respond to the stimulus in question, descriptively speaking.

---

5. Note also that the indifference-to-existence test also precludes the derivation of the judgment from a concept since it may be assumed that no concept will be instantiated by something we suppose does not exist. The indifference-to-existence test also putatively distinguishes aesthetic judgments from judgments of the good since no one should be indifferent to the existence of the good.
6. Because the structure of human *feeling* is putatively common to all, the feeling is subjectively universal.

The fourth condition for an authentic aesthetic judgment is necessity. Kant does not merely say that everyone's cognitive and psychological states can be operating in the same way under certain conditions; he also says that they *ought* to be, normatively speaking. The genuine aesthetic judgment commands the assent of all. If I have uttered an authentic aesthetic judgment—one that is disinterested—then everyone else ought necessarily to agree with it. Everyone should have the same experience. Why? Because the grounds for personal divergences have been factored out insofar as the judgment is disinterested.

Kant introduces this idea in the Second Moment and argues for it in the Fourth Moment. He points out that "we think of the beautiful as having a necessary reference to liking."

He argues for the particular kind of necessity here as follows:

> If judgments of taste had a determinate objective principle, then anyone making them in accordance with that principle would claim that his judgment is unconditionally necessary. If they had no principle at all, like judgments of the mere taste of sense, then the thought that they have a necessity would not occur to us at all. So they must have a subjective principle, which determines only by feeling rather than by concepts, though nonetheless with universal validity, what is liked or disliked.

This necessity is not the logical necessity of, for example, a geometrical proof, but it is exemplary necessity. We can think of this by analogy to pure chemical samples. If you know that you have a pure sample of a chemical, then you should be able to say that the properties possessed by your sample will be had by everything else that it is a sample of and that everything with those properties will behave in the same way when subjected to various processes.

Similarly, what Kant is claiming is that when you make a pure aesthetic judgment, if it is genuinely disinterested, then you are a pure sample. You are a pure sample of how this stimulus will affect the human cognitive systems of the understanding and the imagination. In virtue of being a pure sample, you are able to say how any disinterestedly functioning system like yours will be (or ought to) respond. Thus, the necessity of an aesthetic judgment is exemplary necessity, which presupposes the idea of a perfect example.

The universality claim in condition three is descriptive or predictive. If my judgment is disinterested, then everyone else like me will (or should in the sense of would or will) have the same response. But in condition four we are being told that others should have the same response in the normative sense. They ought to have the same liking. When we reflect on the universal grounds of our response, our likings, then we also realize that we have grounds to command the assent of all. What grounds the exemplary necessity, in addition to the universality? As we shall see, Kant will base this on the supposition that there must be a *sensus communis*, a common sense rooted in our common human nature. Kant argues that our faculties, imagination, and understanding must be the same given that we are able to communicate our inner states to each other (such as the cognition that the stone just broke the window).

Fifth, the judgment must be a singular judgment—"this (particular) rose is beautiful." This stems from several parts of the theory. Kant may have built this into his picture of the aesthetic encounter as a direct experience in which one confronts a specific object and reacts to it. This notion also dovetails with the notion that the judgment is not mediated by concepts but is based on the feeling or experience of a singularity, that is, based on experience—the feeling of pleasure induced by a single object. The judgment is not based on cognitive concepts, but on the token couplet of a feeling in response to a single object or presentation, and not on knowledge about a class of objects.

In Section 9 of the Second Moment, Kant specifies that "a presentation that, though singular and not compared with others, yet harmonizes with the conditions of the universality that is the business of the understanding in general, brings the cognitive powers into that proportioned attunement which we require for all cognition and which, therefore, we also consider valid for everyone who is so constituted as to judge by means of understanding and the senses in combination (in other words, for all human beings)." Thus, though singular, the judgment can be universal inasmuch as it mobilizes common human psychological powers.

The sixth condition holds that the pleasure involved in the aesthetic transaction is contemplative pleasure. In Section 5 of the First Moment, Kant states that "a judgment of taste . . . is merely contemplative, i.e., it is a judgment that is indifferent to the existence of the object: it [considers] the character of the object only by holding it up to our feeling of pleasure and displeasure. Nor is this contemplation, as such, directed to concepts, for a judgment of taste is not a cognitive judgment (whether theoretical or practical) and hence is neither based on concepts, nor directed to them as purposes."[7]

Kant's seventh condition contends that this contemplative pleasure must come from the free play of the faculties of imagination and understanding, where these faculties are not tethered to concepts or purposes. The pleasure does not come from subsuming an object under a concept. When the cognitive faculties are in free play, they are searching for a concept, but not settling on one. In Kant's words, "When this happens, the cognitive powers brought into play by this presentation are in free play, because no determinate concept restricts them to a particular rule of cognition. Hence the mental state in this presentation must be a feeling, accompanying the given presentation, of a free play of the presentational powers directed to cognition in general" (Section 9, Second Moment).

Also, Kant adds, "If the given presentation that prompts the judgment of taste were a concept which, in our judgment of the object, united understanding and

---

7. In terms of our earlier schematization of Kant's theory of judgments of free beauty, what we have added by means of the sixth condition is the requirement of pleasure.

imagination so as to give rise to cognition of the object, then the consciousness of this relation would be intellectual (as it is in the objective schematism of judgment, with which the *Critique* [*of Pure Reason*] deals). But in that case the judgment would not have been made in reference to pleasure and displeasure and hence would not be a judgment of taste. But in fact, a judgment of taste determines the object, independently of concepts, with regard to liking and the predicate of beauty. Hence that unity in the relation [between the cognitive powers] in the subject can reveal itself only through sensation. This sensation, whose universal communicability a judgment of taste postulates, is the quickening of the two powers (imagination and understanding) to an activity that is indeterminate but, as a result of the prompting of the given presentation, nonetheless accordant: the activity required for cognition in general" (Section 9, Second Moment).

Thus, the contemplative pleasure arises from these faculties humming together. Note that there are actually two levels of pleasure: one, the play of the faculties and two, pleasure in their harmonization with each other and the forms of finality—our pleasure in the realization that our faculties are suited for each other and the world and vice versa—which is pleasurable because it provides experiential confirmation that practical activity is possible.

The first order of pleasure is similar to the pleasure you get when you take a good run or you swim, and you feel like all your muscles are working together perfectly. In the case of aesthetic judgment, it is the combined faculties of imagination and understanding that are working together perfectly and afford something like a mental burn that is akin to the pleasurable physical burn we experience after robust exercise.

The second level of pleasure is a kind of meta-pleasure.[8] It is the pleasure we take in the fact that our faculties fit the stimulus so well. The first-order pleasure

---

8. This meta-pleasure has special meta-philosophical significance for Kant. Kant thought that there was a certain tension between his first two *Critiques*. The first *Critique* involves a fully determinate nature with no apparent room for the sort of freedom presupposed by the second *Critique*. In his introduction to the third *Critique*, Kant suggests that it may provide some reconciliation to that tension. In addition to the section of the third *Critique* that deals with teleological judgment, it is in the preceding discussion of the free play of the faculties where he sees some promise of reconciling the tension. First of all, the faculties are in *free* play (i.e., free from concepts), intimating the possibility that nature is open to alternative views and, thence, possibly to alternative actions. Also, aesthetic experience suggests that nature is conducive to operations of our faculties, which further supports our faith that it is open to our formulation of alternative lines of thinking and action. That is, the experience of beauty encourages our conviction that nature is purposive with respect to our conception of it, which conviction underwrites our commitment to the idea of moral freedom. The experience of free beauty, of course, does not prove this. Rather it reinforces this conviction experientially.

Since the role of beauty in the project of the three *Critiques* is not primarily germane to the history of the philosophy of art, I will not be dwelling on it in this chapter. It is really beyond the purview of this book.

we take in contemplating the stimulus tells us that our faculties are suited for the world, and we take a second-order pleasure in this fact.

It may be useful at this point to provide some background on Kant's conception of these cognitive faculties. The understanding is the faculty by which we categorize things. "That's a horse," for example, is a judgment issued by the understanding. The imagination is the faculty we use to fill out and construct the objects we encounter in the world. For instance, we all suppose that the back portions of objects continue to exist even when we are not currently looking at them. The faculty of mind that fills things out, that can construct and make the world complete, is the imagination, according to Kant.

In judgments of free beauty, the faculties of imagination and understanding are in free play when they are stimulated by an object that gives rise to a feeling of beauty. That is, they are involved in discovering patterns, but they are not required, as they ordinarily would be in our practical lives, to fit these things under concepts. When you look at the beautiful plumage on a peacock, your mind is not necessarily working to determine what kind of bird you are looking at. Your imagination is tracking the patterns observable in the bird's tail and filling them out without having to identify what the thing is.[9]

Likewise, when standing before a landscape in foliage season, you detect all kinds of recurring motifs of color running through the arbors dotting the landscape. You notice all sorts of patterns: first you organize the manifold by focusing on the red leaves; then you reorganize the field by making the brown ones the center of your attention; then you note the way in which the red leaves give way to the orange ones, then to the yellow ones, and finally to the brown; and so on. But you are not under pressure to subsume these patterns under concepts, let alone under one determinate concept—that is, you do not make a judgment of the understanding about them.

Nor is it the case that in determining that a landscape is beautiful that you have resorted to some kind of formula like that of perfection as parsed by rationalist aestheticians like Christian Wolff in terms of uniformity amidst diversity, which formula you can identify as at work in the landscape. Rather, you let your mind and eyes together rove over the stimulus and if the stimulus is rich enough, they work together like a purring automobile engine. That is what Kant means by the term *quickening*. You are exercising the cognitive powers that you have—your powers of observation and your powers for constructing patterns of organization in objects—but you are doing so in a playful way. You can just let your faculties run free, and the stimulus will exercise them in a way that will give rise to pleasure.

---

9. This does not entail that you may not know the kind of bird you are observing, but only that that knowledge plays no role in the delight you feel as you explore the rich patterns in its plumage. In this, Kant represents a strong contrast with Aristotle, who locates the relevant source of pleasure in the acquisition of knowledge through learning.

Consider cloud gazing. You look up at the sky. First you see a cloud as a mountain of mashed potatoes, then as a giant puff of cotton, then you see a face in it. Your imagination and understanding play with various alternatives, never settling on one, as would the determinative judgment that the cloud is a member of the class cumulonimbus. Moreover, the play of the imagination and understanding in this manner generates pleasure.

This pleasure is noncognitive. Unlike Aristotle, Kant does not regard the primary form of aesthetic pleasure to be cognitive in the sense of discovering what is true or false. However, although aesthetic pleasure is noncognitive for Kant, it derives from the interplay of cognitive faculties, albeit cognitive faculties operating as if on a holiday from their usual occupations, that is, those of issuing theoretical, practical, and moral judgments. In short, what Kant has done here is to reorient the usual conception of the relation of cognition to aesthetic experience away from an emphasis on the direct product of cognition in terms of the discovery of some truth to emphasis indirectly on the process of cognition, that is, on the interplay of the cognitive faculties. So, although a noncognitivist with respect to aesthetic experience, Kant nevertheless finds an indispensable role for cognition, as a process, in his account of aesthetic judgment.

The eighth and last criterion required by a judgment of taste is that your attention in cases of genuine aesthetic judgments be directed toward forms of finality, or forms of purposiveness without a purpose. If something has a form of finality, it looks to us as though it possesses a final cause in the Aristotelian sense, although we do not actually determine what that final cause is. This phenomenon may also be described in terms of an object's possession of a form of purposiveness that can be understood in terms of the object appearing as though it was created with an intention (purpose), although we suspend curiosity about the exact nature of that intention (purpose).

Kant explains that the judgment is directed toward mere forms of purposiveness:

> A Judgment of Taste is Based on Nothing but the *Form of Purposiveness* of an Object (or of the Way of Presenting It). Whenever a purpose is regarded as the basis of a liking, it always carries with it an interest, as the basis that determines the judgment about the object of the pleasure. Hence a judgment of taste cannot be based on a subjective purpose. But a judgment of taste also cannot be determined by a presentation of an objective purpose....
>
> ... Therefore the liking that, without a concept, we judge to be universally communicable and hence to be the basis that determines a judgment of taste, can be nothing but the subjective purposiveness in the presentation of an object, without any purpose (whether objective or subjective), and hence the mere form of purposiveness, insofar as we are conscious of it, in the presentation by which an object is *given* us. (Section 11, Third Moment)

This is a very formal conception of our response to the object. For example, you might be looking at a piece of farmland that is being cultivated for industrial agricultural purposes, and in order to satisfy those purposes, it might have a very specific, very striking contour and design. Yet, you might not know what that the purpose is; you may just find the look of it engaging to your cognitive and imaginative powers. You take delight in looking at it in terms of discerning different patterns in it, but you are not looking at it in terms of its actual purpose. In this, you are attending to the apparent purposiveness in the array, with no thought of its actual purpose. You are tracking the patterns before you without an interest in the exact purpose that said patterns were designed to serve. That is, you are attending to the *form* of purposiveness without regard to the actual purpose of the object. In this sense, the object of aesthetic attention is formal.

To say that something strikes us as possessing the form of finality or the form of purposiveness is to indicate that the stimulus strikes us as the product of intention or design without our knowing—or, at least, without our thinking about—what it has been designed for. Thus, we may be arrested by the pattern or apparent purposiveness or pattern of the markings on the back of a snake without having any inkling of the function that design subserves. That is, we contemplate it apart from its purpose, which, of course, entails that we view it with no concern for whatever interests attach to those purposes.

Of course, in many cases, we may know the purpose of the object of our attention. However, the experience of the object may still be aesthetic in Kant's view just in case the pleasure we take in it is not that of delight in the suitedness of its design to its actual purpose, but its appearance of "designedness" or purposiveness.

This view of the object of aesthetic attention also contributes to Kant's reasons for thinking that the aesthetic judgments we make in this state will be exemplary judgments. For, in effect, by discounting the relevance of actual purposes, the content of whatever we are experiencing has been factored out, thereby ensuring that we are not attending interestedly to things in terms of their purposes, but only in terms of the impression they yield of purposiveness. So anything in the object, the content, which would make our reaction differential, has been subtracted out because the target of our attention is solely the form of purposiveness.

Therefore, there is nothing in the subject (who is disinterested) and nothing in the object (which is examined only in terms of its form of purposiveness) that could give rise to a differential response. In that sense, this judgment must be exemplary, and if it is exemplary, then I ought to be able to command others to converge on and agree with my judgment. Just as I say that others ought to refrain from immoral action, even if people are behaving immorally, so I can say of others that they should like—take pleasure in—the expanse of foliage I claim to be beautiful, even if they disagree with me. The necessity in the judgment derives from its, so to speak, normative "oughtness" or "bindingness."

This is the basic idea of Kant's theory of aesthetic judgments of free beauty. With this background in hand, let us look a bit more closely at some of its details.

Further Observations about Kant's Theory of Aesthetic Judgments of Free Beauty

We have just compared the aesthetic judgment of free beauty to the moral judgment. But, of course, the moral judgment differs from the aesthetic one. Suppose you are in a classroom and you and all of your friends are misbehaving, say you are talking loudly to each other. I say you ought to be quiet. I'm not reporting what you are doing, but what you ought to be doing, what morality requires, what morality says is necessary. On what basis do I do this?: in virtue of the purpose of the rules of classroom order—rules whose purpose is to facilitate class instruction. So, the oughtness or the necessity of my claim is based on a rule that is connected to a purpose. Rules and purposes ground my claim that others ought to assent to my command. Yet, since there are no rules with respect to aesthetic judgments, the question arises: From whence does its oughtness come?

As already noted, Kant calls the necessity here "exemplary necessity." However, what does this mean? That I see myself as a fair specimen of what is common to all humans. That is, my judgment is disinterested and based on the normal functioning of our common faculties, our common (or shared) sense or *sensus communis*. Consequently, in this regard, I am a fair specimen of a certain common human core. Thus, my response should be standard for everyone constituted as I am (given the principle of the same causes, same effects). Once I realize this much, then I have the basis to demand that others respond as I do—that they should delight in the foliage as I do.

Why? Again, because I am a fair sample of the basic human response, which is the disinterested response. I am the standard of taste, as Hume might put it. However, for Kant, I don't need a collection of Ideal Critics. I can issue the judgment on my own. The authority for my judgment and its claim on others derives from my presumption that I am a fair sample of the standard, disinterested human response.

I am, in other words, a perfect example— an untainted sample. That's why the necessity is exemplary. It is in virtue of being an undistorted, uncontaminated, disinterested example that I claim that others should respond normatively in the same way that I do.

I base this claim not only on the fact that my liking is disinterested—it passes the indifference-to-existence test—but also on the fact that, as a result, the relevant pleasure arises from the play of the standard-issue human faculties, namely the imagination and the understanding. These are faculties that all humans putatively possess.

In the ordinary course of affairs, these faculties are what enable us to subsume particulars under concepts. The imagination enables us to construct particulars in such a way that the understanding can apply concepts (or purposes) to them. For example, when we judge that "This is a spruce tree," this is a matter of filling-out patterns, which we then see fit certain concepts. The imagination and the understanding work together to identify certain patterns and then slot that which instantiates said patterns under certain categories (concepts and purposes).

What happens in aesthetic experience is different, however, than what happens in ordinary cognitive experience. In ordinary cognitive experience, the imagination and the understanding are committed to subsuming particulars under definite, determinate concepts, for example, the concept of bachelor. The name of the game in the typical situation is to find the category to which the particular belongs. In this way, concepts determine the activity of the imagination and the understanding.

But aesthetic judgment is reflective judgment. This is different from the ordinary sort of operation of reason, which involves subsumption under a concept. We apply the general concept to the particular where the general concept is already in our repertory. In reflective judgment, you have to search for or discover the concept. The paradigm of reflective judgment is scientific discovery. Isaac Newton had to discover the concept that would unify earthly and celestial motion—he had to construct the concept; he had to find it. It was a matter of searching and striving. Of course, he finally did discover it. The aim of reflective reason is discovery; when that aim or goal is achieved or satisfied, we feel pleasure.

Similarly, in aesthetic judgment there is a search, but a determinate concept is not found which could unify the presentation. Nevertheless, in the course of the search we come to be aware that our faculties are suited for each other— they work in concert—and that they are suited for negotiating the world, for tracking purposiveness or pattern, just as the world is suited for the faculties in that it affords the patterns to be tracked. That is, the mind and the world are suitable for each other.

We think this because of the pleasure that arises from the interplay of the faculties in relation to forms of finality. Our powers match the world (the stimulus), and the world matches our powers—affords us detectable patterns. The world is amenable to our faculties. The world is, so to speak, made for our faculties and this reassures us, at the level of felt experience, that it is possible for us to realize the aim of reflective judgment—discovery.[10]

In addition, when we realize that our faculties are suited for the world and vice versa, this experientially confirms for us that the conditions for practical reason are in place. That is, we couldn't reason practically unless the world was suited for our faculties and our faculties for the world. So, we take added pleasure from

---

10. Perhaps here we may detect shades of Hutcheson, who also correlated the sense of beauty with the capacity to discover pattern.

the harmonious functioning of our faculties exemplified in aesthetic experience because it indicates to us that the aims of reflection and practical reason are within our reach. The harmonious play of the faculties confirms this in experience, and this provides an additional layer of pleasure that derives from the exercise of the faculties.

To understand the origin of this pleasure, recall that the faculties are attending to forms of finality. We are focusing on a form of finality when we receive the impression that the objects of our attention are designed or intended. We have the impression that they serve a purpose even though we do not know what that purpose is. As previously noted, we can call this feature "purposiveness"—or purposiveness without a purpose. Even though we do not subsume the object under a purpose, we nevertheless detect what appears to be a purposive patterning of phenomena. This detection gives us pleasure when we experience such objects because it conveys the impression that the objects have been designed for the cooperative interplay of our cognitive powers—that the aim of reflection can be realized by the world inasmuch as one condition for this possibility is in place, namely, that our cognitive powers are suited to the world. This yields pleasure since the aim of reflective cognition is disclosed to be realizable. Indeed, the suitability of our faculties to the world ratifies experientially our conviction that the conditions for practical activity can be met.

In aesthetic experience, the understanding and the imagination are in free play. They are not governed by the aim of finally placing the particular under a determinate category, concept, rule, or purpose. They search for categories—trying out different ways of organizing our perception of it—but without having to come to closure and without having to lock in on a determinate concept. It is a reflective, contemplative activity. Our pattern-detecting capacities, in other words, are operating, but they don't have to come to a determinate conclusion about how to classify the particular whose presence is activating them. It is a bit like running the engine of a fine automobile—in this case, our pattern-detecting engine—and listening to and enjoying the engine hum without throwing it into gear.

In the aesthetic experience the faculties function together harmoniously—they hum along like a well-functioning motor finding alternative patterns but not having to settle on one. This gives us a sense of well-being, a sense of life (of the life force), a sense that all is well since our faculties are in fine fiddle. As the faculties move together in concert, meshing together, locating patterns and then finding new ones, we feel pleasure, pleasure derived from the smooth operation of standard human faculties. Moreover, since these are faculties that I share with all other humans, I can expect other humans, insofar as they are cognitively constituted just like me, to be able to partake of the same pleasure when encountering the same stimuli that I do.

Of course, Kant not only claims that judgments of taste are universal. He also claims that they are necessary. But this raises the question of how I can demand the necessary assent of all solely on the basis of my own experience—the subjective experience of a lone individual. How is that possible? Thus, Kant must demonstrate the possibility of pure judgments of taste. How does he do that?

With the discussion of the universality of aesthetic judgments of free beauty, Kant has given a description, or perhaps a definition, of aesthetic judgments. He will then show how the elements of this definition can be assembled into an argument for the objectivity of taste.

He makes this argument in Section 38:

> If it is granted that in a pure judgment of taste our liking for the object is connected with our mere judging of the form of the object, then this liking is nothing but [our consciousness of] the form's subjective purposiveness for the power of judgment, which we feel as connected in the mind with the presentation of the object. Now, as far as the formal rules of judging [as such] are concerned, apart from any matter (whether sensation or concept), the power of judgment can be directed only to the subjective conditions for our employment of the power of judgment as such (where it is confined neither to the particular kind of sense involved nor to a[ny] particular concept of the understanding), and hence can be directed only to that subjective [condition] which we may presuppose in all people (as required for possible cognition as such). It follows that we must be entitled to assume *a priori* that a presentation's harmony with these conditions of the power of judgment is valid for everyone. (Section 38)

The phrase "required for possible cognition as such" is important. It means that the mental powers that we have to use for any cognition, the understanding and the imagination, are what the judgment of taste is based on, and it is these powers that we may presuppose to be in operation in all people since they are required for the possibility of cognition as such. Thus, the aesthetic judgment of free beauty is being based on what we presuppose everyone has as part of his or her cognitive psychological makeup. It follows that we must be entitled to assume *a priori* that a presentation's harmony with the conditions of the power of judgment is valid for everyone. In other words, it seems that when in judging an object of sense, if we feel this pleasure (through the discernment of subjective purposiveness of the presentation in relation to our standard-issue, human cognitive powers), we must be entitled to require this response of pleasure from everyone who is constituted similarly.

Why does Kant believe that everyone must have the same cognitive makeup? He relegates his reasoning to a footnote to the preceding argument. He says:

> To be justified in laying claim to universal assent to a judgment of the aesthetic power of judgment, which rests merely on subjective bases, one need grant only the

> following: (1) that in all people the subjective conditions of this power are the same as concerns the relation required for cognition as such between the cognitive powers that are activated in the power of judgment; and this must be true, for otherwise people could not communicate their presentations to one another, indeed they could not even communicate cognition.

Here, Kant is claiming that we are entitled to think that we must have the same psychological makeup, since if we did not, we would not be able to communicate mental or cognitive states of knowledge to one another. That is why we have to presuppose that we all have the same basic cognitive machinery. Kant believes that he had proven this in his first *Critique*, although it seems to be a plausible enough claim in its own right. That is, it appears reasonable to suppose that we can communicate our cognitions to each other as when we concur that the window over there just shattered because it was hit by a baseball.

Kant's next argument is that if there is a certain pleasure that arises from the pertinent psychological machinery working disinterestedly in perfect harmony, and we all have the same machinery, then if I feel pleasure, others ought to be feeling disinterested pleasure as well, assuming that their cognitive machinery is also working perfectly. This form of necessity is exemplary necessity, and it is in virtue of this sort of necessity that Kant thinks that genuine aesthetic judgments of free beauty—judgments that lay claim on the assent of all—are possible.

A formalization of his argument (from Section 38) goes like this:

(1) If I can know others are psychologically constituted exactly like me, then if I feel disinterested pleasure in the free play of my faculties, in response to the relevant forms of purposiveness, then I know others should necessarily feel comparable pleasure.

(2) If others can communicate cognition, both to me and to each other, then I know they are psychologically constituted exactly like me.

(3) Others do communicate cognition both to me and to each other.

(4) Therefore, others are psychologically constituted exactly like me.

(5) Therefore, if I feel disinterested pleasure in the free play of my faculties in response to the relevant forms of purposiveness, then I know that others should necessarily feel comparable pleasure.

(6) I do feel disinterested pleasure in the free play of my faculties. (ex hypothesi)

(7) Therefore, I know that others should feel necessarily comparable pleasure.

(8) If I know others should necessarily feel comparable pleasure, then that justifies my commanding them to do so.

(9) Therefore, I am justified in demanding them to do so.

(10) If I am justified in so demanding their assent, then genuine aesthetic judgments of free beauty are possible.

(11) Therefore, genuine aesthetic judgments of free beauty are possible.

Moreover, an answer to Hume's paradox about the objectivity of judgments of taste despite their origin in subjective pleasure follows from Kant's demonstration of the possibility of aesthetic judgments. If aesthetic judgments are universal and necessary, then they are objective in the sense of being intersubjectively valid in principle. Thus, because our subjective constitution is the same, where the differentiating factors like human interests and the content of the stimulus have been subtracted from the presentation, our responses should be converging. Moreover, we can rely on our own disinterested experiences when issuing aesthetic judgments without consulting the tribe of Ideal Critics. For Kant, such critics are redundant since I can justify my particular aesthetic judgments solely with reference to myself and my disinterested pleasure.

How exactly do I justify particular judgments of taste—my occurrent judgment now that "X is beautiful"? How can I confirm that? Supposedly, I realize that others are constituted as I am— that they have the same faculties of imagination and understanding that I do. They must because we are able to communicate inner states to each other. That is, a common psychological constitution must be the case because otherwise, such communication would be impossible. But since the communication of inner states happens, it is possible. Thus, all of us must be constituted in the same way. Moreover, if I realize this, then I am in a position to expect others to experience pleasure when I do insofar as my pleasure is based on common faculties functioning disinterestedly. So, I solicit the assent of all. And where others coincide with my example, I get confirmation of my feeling. The confirmation of my feeling is that it is matched by the feeling of the others. In this way I can confirm that my particular judgment of taste is objective in the sense of being intersubjective.

Disinterestedness is the key to making the argument for the objectivity of taste. This includes factoring out moral differences, contra Hume. Morality is taken out of the judgment of taste—or, at least, it doesn't figure in the judgment. However, this does not mean that Kant thinks that morality and aesthetics have nothing to do with each other. It is just that, for Kant, the relation is not based merely on the moral content of beautiful things. Rather there are other types of relations between beauty and morality. One, as we shall see, is the claim that "the person who experiences beauty in nature shows a good character."

Judgments of Dependent Beauty

In Kant's third *Critique*, there are two major categories of aesthetic judgment: judgments of beauty and judgments of the sublime. Before we leave the subject of judgments of beauty and move on to the discussion of the sublime, there is one additional point to make about judgments of beauty. For Kant, there are two kinds of judgments concerning beauty. We have been discussing free beauty. There is also another sort of beauty that Kant examines called dependent beauty (or sometimes adherent or accessory beauty; Section 16, Third Moment). Free beauty does not presuppose an idea of what the object is meant to be; accessory beauty does presuppose such a concept, as well as the object's perfection in terms of that concept. Accessory beauty is dependent beauty; it depends on a concept. Free beauty is free of or independent of concepts.

Dependent beauty is beauty of a kind. We judge something to dependently beautiful when it is good of its kind, as in the case of judging that this horse is a beautiful Tennessee Walker. A Tennessee Walker belongs to the category *racehorse*. It is a good-making feature of racehorses that they be long-legged. If a racehorse has short legs, it is not likely to be a good racehorse. Given that this Tennessee Walker has long legs, it follows, all things being equal, that this is a good Tennessee Walker, that is, a (dependently) beautiful racehorse.

Similarly, when experts make judgments at flower shows about American Beauty roses, they have a concept of an American Beauty rose; they have criteria of what counts as a good American Beauty rose. In virtue of such criteria, someone might declare that this is a perfect American Beauty rose. But this sort of beauty depends on there being a concept of an American Beauty rose that this particular flower approximates perfectly. So, there is beauty in terms of perfection, but that kind of judgment of beauty must be related to a concept. If judgments of free beauty are pure, then judgments of dependent beauty are impure.

With judgments of dependent beauty, you have an object or a presentation. It belongs to a certain kind, and it is beautiful, if it is a perfect instance of that kind. This is dependent beauty, so-called because it depends on the concept of the kind of thing it is. It is conditioned beauty. It has as its condition of application that it meets the criteria of whatever kind it belongs to. In Kant's terms, it is accessory to the concept, meaning that it is dependent on the concept. Free beauty, on the other hand, does not involve concepts, only feelings, notably feelings of disinterested pleasure which ground judgments of independent beauty.

Kant's examples (Section 16) of free beauty are the foliage on the border of wallpaper, a fantasia (a freely structured composition of instrumental music), crustaceans, flowers, and so forth. Notice that artworks, properly so called, are not the primary or most prominent examples of sources of free beauty. To an appreciable extent, beauty in artworks will be dependent or accessory beauty. This is because the artwork will typically belong to a certain genre. It may be a representation or a comedy, that is, something that meets certain criteria. For example, a mystery story will have certain criteria in order for a work to count as a member of the genre. In the case of tragedy, Aristotle gave us a definition, or rules for making a good tragedy, so if you refer to *Oedipus Rex* as a beautiful tragedy, you are probably saying of *Oedipus Rex* that it is a perfect example of its kind.

Works of art can possess free beauty as well as adherent beauty. Suppose we are looking at an artwork and it is a representation. Imitations or representations have certain purposes. There are certain criteria for what counts as a good representation, for example, verisimilitude. So, something could be a beautiful representation in terms of satisfying the concept of representation. It could be a perfect representation.

But it could also possess free beauty. There may be features of the painting—perhaps the way the color is splashed on the canvas—that might give you a feeling of pleasure apart from the content. So, you might make a dual judgment with regard to a painting and say it is beautiful with respect to dependent beauty, and it is also beautiful with respect to free beauty. Kant points out that many of the disagreements people have about works of art have to do with the fact that one party to the disagreement may be evaluating it in terms of dependent beauty, and the other party to the disagreement may actually be evaluating it in terms of independent or free beauty.

Since artworks belong to genres and kinds, judgments of beauty regarding artworks almost always call into play at least some considerations of concepts. However, as we have seen, we may also judge a particular work of art to be beautiful just because of some feature of it that is not essential to the kind of work that it is. It may be the powerful brush strokes in a painting by Van Gogh that give you a great deal of pleasure, where this feature is not essential to the kind of representational painting it is, but which nevertheless delights you.

But, given this possibility, an unavoidable question is how you would make an all-things-considered judgment of such a painting. That is, suppose there is a painting that you can judge in terms of free beauty and in terms of dependent beauty. How are you supposed to combine these judgments?

Kant is not always so helpful about situations like these, and this is a considerable source of technical disagreement. But one idea that can be justified by the text is that to make an all-things-considered judgment in cases like these, the judgment of free beauty has to be constrained by the judgment of dependent beauty. That is, you cannot call the object beautiful overall if it is an artwork, belonging to a certain kind, unless it meets the concept or discharges the purpose of that kind of artwork. It is not beautiful overall unless its articulation has been constrained in terms of the relevant conditions for its possession of dependent beauty. For example, if a pictorial artwork is meant to be a portrait, then the pleasing color patterns in it should not obscure the features of the person it is intended to represent.

Another, perhaps less cumbersome way of putting the point is that an artwork is beautiful all things considered only if it is at least adherently or dependently beautiful, or, alternatively, adherent or dependent beauty is a necessary condition for an artwork to be beautiful overall. So, if an artwork is independently beautiful in certain respects that must also be consistent with its being dependently beautiful with respect to the concept of the kind to which the artwork belongs. Its free beauty should not conflict or impede the work's satisfaction of the conditions of dependent beauty required by the kind of artwork it is. If the shading in a painting affords an experience of free beauty, for example, it should not occlude recognition of the outline of the figure the painting is designed to represent.

The Sublime

For Kant, as already indicated, there are two major classes of aesthetic judgments: judgments of beauty and judgments of sublimity. The sublime became an important notion in the eighteenth century. It involved the recognition of a dimension of taste that had been previously neglected or ignored, at least in terms of theory. The eighteenth century is when people really begin to talk about the sublime a great deal. Beauty, people became convinced, was not a capacious enough of a category to encompass all of our aesthetic judgments.

Kant gives some examples of the things that counted as sublime: thunderstorms, towering mountain ranges like the Alps, the rough and violent side of nature as opposed to the placid and calm side of nature. People also began to appreciate artists such as Antonio Rossi, who tried to capture that aspect of nature.

In the eighteenth century, it was fashionable for middle-class and upper-class Englishmen to take a year out of their life and to make a grand tour of Europe during which they would seek out the great artworks, including architecture, gardens, and landscapes on the Continent. And by mid-century, the grand tour began to include visits to violent waterfalls and dark, brooding forests in Germany and the Alps. At that time, Western culture began to realize that it needed an additional aesthetic category beyond beauty since the pleasure associated with things like storms at sea did not fit into the category of beauty. Another concept was needed, and the concept that critics and theoreticians alike began to cobble together was that of the sublime.

The sublime could not be part of the concept of beauty since it involved an element of displeasure as well as pleasure. A clap of thunder, for example, brings with it a twinge of anxiety. That is, there are some kinds of things in which we take pleasure—in that we feel positively toward them—but that also elicit a touch of displeasure or distress. Gothic tales and horror stories are two examples.

Insofar as these items did not appear to be conceptualized appropriately in terms of beauty (since they involved *displeasure* mixed with pleasure), it seemed as though an entire aesthetic category was missing from the discussion.[11] In the

---

11. Another factor in the emerging theoretical interests in the sublime was undoubtedly the rediscovery of Longinus's classical text *On the Sublime*. With respect to Kant, this is interesting since Longinus located the sublime in the subjectivity of the artist, i.e., her mind.

eighteenth century, theorists such as Edmund Burke realized that in terms of the kinds of delight that we take from the arts and nature—or in terms of the positive reactions we have thereto—there are some items that have a tincture of displeasure as a recurring feature; moreover, this displeasure is not a negligible feature with respect to our response. Rather, it is ineliminable from the experience.

In the case of tragedy, for example, undergoing this displeasure is part of our overall positive judgment. Thus, it was felt that the category of the sublime was needed to cover this range of aesthetic experience and, thereby, to supplement the concept of the beautiful. Kant addresses this new category in the "Analytic of the Sublime."

What is the sublime? Kant emphasizes that, like beauty, it is an experience, specifically a subjective experience. As with beauty, people often attribute sublimity to objects, but Kant argues, it is really a certain sort of experience. The sublime is in us and not in objects. Kant divides the sublime into two types—the mathematically sublime and the dynamically sublime.

First, let us look at the Mathematical Sublime. The mathematical sublime can be found in response to things verging toward the infinite, such as the starry night sky. This experience occurs when we are presented with something of enormous scope. It is an experience of something large beyond comparison, something indeterminately large, so large that we cannot get a sense of its unity. We cannot construct an image of it in our minds because it is too big; it frustrates the imagination. Close your eyes and try to imagine an infinite expanse; such an expanse always exceeds the mind's eye; we cannot visualize it; it is too large to be contained on the stage in the theater of the mind. We cannot imagine its totality, though we think it is a totality. This causes displeasure and, in that sense, frustration. This is the first (unpleasant) moment of the sublime.

However, though the imagination cannot grasp the stimulus, it can be grasped by reason, by an idea of reason—namely, totality. Through reason, we can grasp the idea of infinity and manipulate it, as we do, for example, in calculus.

And even where we cannot grasp immensity so determinately, we still are struck by reason's drive to grasp totalities. Thus, we find ourselves in awe of reason and its vocation—the vocation of humanity (which is to comprehend totalities). When we experience these indeterminately large stimuli, we realize from our encounter that our own reason has infinite scope. We come to be awestruck by the power of reason in us.[12]

Kant describes the experience of the mathematical sublime as follows: the "sublime is what, even to be able to think through, that the mind has a power

---

12. When postmodernists like Jean-François Lyotard talk about the postmodern sublime, they invoke the idea of something so immense that it is unrepresentable by means of the imagination. However, they omit Kant's characterization of the way in which the experience of the sublime also provokes our sense of awe with regard to reason.

surpassing any power of sense" (Section 25). That is, the sublime arises from the effort of the imagination to comprehend infinity or what appears infinite. But the attempt to image the infinite by means of sense or imagination falters. However, while in the very grip of that frustration, we become aware of another faculty in us—that of reason, which faculty is a supersensible one (i.e., not merely a faculty of sense) and which faculty does have the capacity and the vocation to comprehend totalities, even totalities of infinite scope. Our readiness to negotiate, or at least to attempt to negotiate infinity, in turn, causes wonder in us—awe at a supersensible aspect of ourselves, a capacity or capability or, at least, a readiness to attempt to comprehend phenomena of infinite scope.

Not only does the mind have the power to comprehend totalities, it is its vocation to do so—its aspiration. It is reason's aspiration to understand the world. Once we see that we have this power and this vocation, we feel pleasure, and we feel awestruck at what it is to be human. This is the source of sublimity on Kant's account—the recognition of the power and vocation of reason that underpins our capacity for reflective judgments.

Such, then, is the mathematical sublime. Confronted by the suggestion of infinity or vast scope in nature, like the expanding universe, we come to be aware of a part of us that is more than adequate to the task of comprehending it—that is our supersensible faculty of reason, something in ourselves that is literally awesome.

Likewise, exposed to an infinite series of numbers, we are not able to imagine it—to image it—to hold it in our mind's eye. In contrast to beauty, which is bounded, the sublime is unbounded. Yet despite this displeasurable frustration of our imaginative powers, we realize that we can compute it, we can compare it to other large series of numbers, and we can manipulate it mathematically. Thus, though our imagination can't handle the notion of infinity (as well as indeterminately vast physical processes), our reason can. Once we appreciate this power in us, we feel awestruck. The judgment of the mathematical sublime is based on this feeling of awe we have when we come to realize that we possess this supersensible faculty and that we have the breathtaking human ambition to comprehend totalities.

Now let us turn to the Dynamical Sublime. Where the mathematical sublime is a response to the scope or scale of things, the dynamical sublime occurs when we encounter aspects of nature where nature's power is most demonstrable. Examples include storms at sea, volcanoes, lightning, and any other situations through which nature exhibits awesome power. The experience of dynamical sublimity occurs when we encounter nature in all its might, but at the same time, are not finally terrified by it. We look out over the tempest-tossed sea, hear the thunder crash, see the lightning streak, and, though perhaps initially frightened (displeasure), we are not ultimately afraid for our own lives.

Reason scrutinizes the vast power of nature but does not cower before it. We can stand back and think about the laws that bring such natural upheavals about. We do not feel terrorized by nature, despite its power. This makes us aware that there is a part of us that nature cannot touch or that is impervious to the power of nature, a part of us where, as Kant says, nature's "might has no dominion over us."

Kant describes the dynamical sublime in Section 28, where he emphasizes nature as a might. This is probably one of the most impressive literary flights in Kant. He writes:

> Consider bold, overhanging and, as it were, threatening rocks, thunderclouds piling up in the sky and moving about accompanied by lightning and thunderclaps, volcanoes with all their destructive power, hurricanes with all the devastation they leave behind, the boundless ocean heaved up, the high waterfall of a mighty river, and so on. Compared to the might of any of these, our ability to resist becomes an insignificant trifle. Yet the sight of them becomes the more attractive the more fearful it is, provided we are in a safe place. And we like to call these objects sublime because they raise the soul's fortitude above its usual middle range and allow us to discover in ourselves an ability to resist which is of a quite a different kind, and which gives us the courage [to believe] that we could be a match for nature's seeming omnipotence.
>
> For although we found our own limitation when we considered the immensity of nature and our inability to adopt a standard proportionate to estimating aesthetically the magnitude of nature's *domain*, yet we also found in our power of reason, a different and nonsensible standard that has this infinity itself under it as a unit; and since in contrast to this standard everything in nature is small, we found in our mind a superiority over nature itself in its immensity. In the same way, though the irresistibility of nature's might makes us, considered as natural beings, recognize our physical impotence, it reveals in us an ability to judge nature and reveals in us a superiority over nature that is the basis of a self-preservation quite different in kind from the one that can be assailed and endangered by nature outside us. This keeps the humanity in our person from being degraded, even though a human being would have to succumb to the dominance [of nature]. Hence if in judging nature aesthetically we call it sublime, we do not do so because nature arouses fear, but because it calls forth our strength (which does not belong to nature), to regard as small the [objects] of our natural concerns: property, health, and life and because of this we regard nature's might (to which we are indeed subjected to in these [natural] concerns) as yet not having such dominance over us, as persons, that we should have to bow to it if our highest principles were at stake and we had to choose between upholding or abandoning them. Hence nature is here called sublime merely because it elevates our imagination, [making] it exhibit those cases where the mind can feel its own sublimity, which lies in its vocation and elevates it even above nature.

Here, Kant is characterizing the sort of experience we might have witnessing a lightning storm from a safe place. When we are not in danger, the storm can be very exciting. At first, you may shudder under the force of the thunderclaps, but then you begin to relish the experience. This is a signal that you are not intimidated, that to some degree you feel apart from nature, and that you do not feel threatened by it. You are not just an animal being; you do not run and hide, as a cat might; you overcome your initial fear and enjoy spectacular nature.

The significance of this is that it reveals to us that there is a part of us that stands outside nature—a part of us that is free—a part of us that is autonomous. This is a supersensible part, a part of the mind, that cannot be subdued by danger, and which inhabits a realm of freedom outside of causal categories. It is an inhabitant of what Kantians call the noumenal realm, as opposed to the phenomenal realm, that, among other things, is subject to the laws of causality.

The dynamical sublime arises because the initial fear followed by calm when confronted with the might of nature reveals something about us—that we possess a supersensible dimension—that there is a part of us that is free or autonomous. And this calls forth a feeling of respect, respect for our own freedom, or autonomy, which is awe inspiring, which is sublime.

Consider this comparison of the experience of the sublime versus the experience of free beauty.

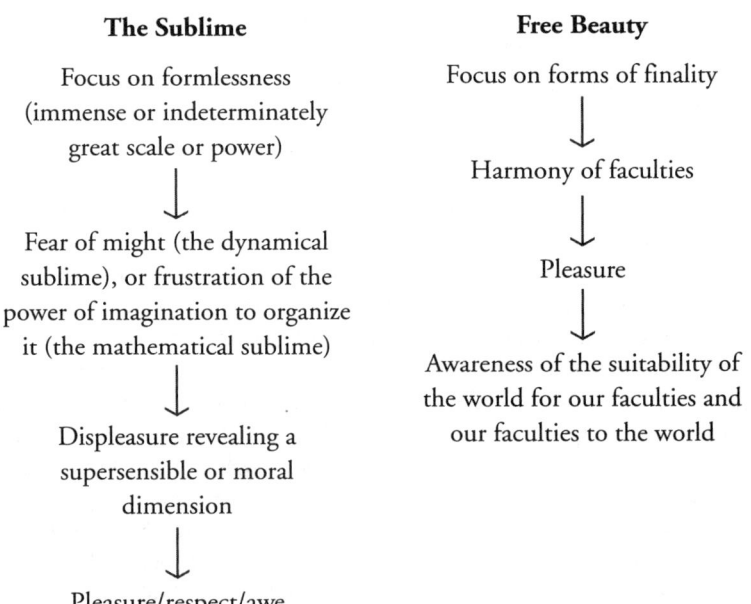

In the dynamical sublime, the initial spectator response is fear, whereas in the mathematical sublime, it is the frustration of the imagination. But, you can then also derive a kind of meta-pleasure from this experience as it discloses our possession of a supersensible dimension—one of autonomous reason and freedom.

With respect to the experience of free beauty, there is also a level of meta-pleasure since when you attend to the pleasure that you get as the faculties harmonize, you access a further pleasure due to your own awareness of this harmony because it reflects the fact that our faculties are suited for each other and the world. In the case of beauty, the species of pleasure is more of a kind of serene, calm pleasure, whereas with respect to the sublime, the pleasure is more like a thrill as we stand in awe of ourselves.

Notice that built into these analyses is an attempt to offer an account of the significance of aesthetic experience—to say why it is important to have it. For example, according to Kant, in the experience of the dynamical sublime, we come, experientially, to the realization that we are free (from nature). The experience is significant because it provides a palpable confirmation that the presupposition of morality—human freedom—is justified. It does not prove it, of course, but it does give a feeling of freedom, which is what is presupposed by morality.

The dynamical sublime, then, is a kind of experiential confirmation of the possibility of morality. The experience of beauty, on the other hand, brings an awareness that we are built in such a way that the world is suited for us, and we are suited for it in terms of our mental powers. And this is an experiential confirmation of the possibility of practical reason.

Just as judgments of free beauty are necessary, so are judgments of the sublime. But before turning to Kant's grounds for believing this, recall what he contends with respect to the experience of beauty. The experience of beauty is a function of a certain limitation, the limitation of the understanding to find a concept under which to subsume the object. From this, a search ensues, and that is when the faculties begin to work together, giving us a feeling of pleasure. This is pleasure in the fact that the world and our faculties are suited for each other. This is important because it assures us that a condition for the exercise of practical reason is in place. If our faculties and the world were not so synchronized, the exercise of practical reason would be impossible. However, it all (our faculties and the stimuli) works together perfectly. Furthermore, we think this is part of the grounds to make demands on other people because everyone should be interested in confirmation of the possibility of practical reason. Other people should be interested in the objects that we point to as beautiful because we all should have an interest in the experiential confirmation of the possibility of practical reason.

The experience of the sublime is a little different. A limitation also prompts it, but this time it is a limitation in the case of the mathematical sublime of the imagination. This does not initially cause pleasure, but rather displeasure. It is an inhibition, but this inhibition in turn makes us aware of another feature in us—the urge within us to encompass totalities (in the case of the mathematical sublime). This is what Kant calls the vocation of reason—the vocation of man or humanity—to go beyond the limitations of the imagination. This is the urge to go beyond the limitations of empirical experience (the senses). Thus, our experience of the limitations of the imagination gives rise to the recognition of a power in us.

Similarly, in the case of the dynamical sublime, the sense of threat and the accompanying displeasure gives way to the discovery that there is something in us that is apart from nature. Consequently, there is some part of us that is beyond or not part of the sensible world—the world of nature. That is, there is a supersensible dimension to us. This realization causes pleasure, which takes the form of a kind of awe or respect for our powers of mind, which are greater than nature, or at least not subservient to nature. The experience also yields pleasure through the satisfaction of an intellectual interest. The experience signals that there is a supersensible dimension—a free dimension—a part of us that is autonomous with regard to natural determination. This part is reason. This reassures us that the conditions for practical reason—freedom—are in place and that the vocation of humanity is possible.

And these recognitions putatively give the judgment of sublimity the force of necessity. On the one hand, we are able to command the assent of all to our judgments because it is reasonable of us to ask of all other persons that they have an interest, albeit an intellectual interest, in the vocation of humanity. On the other hand, others should have an interest in confirmation of the freedom of the human being and the glory of the human vocation to use reason, both to act morally and to understand the universe.

Finally, at this point, there are three parting comments on the Kantian sublime that may be useful to consider. First, Kant's notion of the sublime supplements the idea of beauty, adding a new aesthetic category; there are now two kinds of aesthetic judgments. Second, though the sublime is usually thought to involve the feeling of humility, specifically of humanity as small in contrast to nature as large, Kant is reversing that, finding nature to be dwarfed in a way by humanity's awe-inspiring reason. Third, Kant is offering a nontheological account of these experiences of awe that we often undergo when in the presence of spectacular natural scenes. Whereas many Christians heretofore would have attributed that awe to an intimation of the handiwork of God in nature, Kant reinterprets it as awe in response to our own powers of reason.

Traditional theologians of Kant's day would have seen a moral message written on the face of nature. They would see the work of God there, or at least, his presence. Because nature is the cipher of God, they would argue, we feel a thrill in its presence. Kant, on the other hand, argues that the thrill we feel is at the awakening of our own powers—our power of reason which stands apart freely from nature.

This, too, has moral significance inasmuch as the experience of the sublime experientially confirms for us that a precondition for moral experience—autonomous reason (reason free from nature [instinct])—is in place. This experience gives us faith in the possibility of moral judgments, just as does the experience of beauty, which persuades us experientially that disinterestedness is possible. Both the experiences of the sublime and beauty then have moral significance, though not directly by sending messages with specific moral content to people, but rather by what they imply about the possibility of morality. Both intimate experientially that the preconditions of morality are possible.[13]

Aesthetics and Ethics

We've just seen that with respect to the experiences of beauty and sublimity, Kant sees a connection between aesthetics, including art, and morality. So we are back to an issue we encountered with Plato—the relation of art (and the pleasures it affords) to morality.

Roughly speaking, Kant is opposed to the view that we might call direct, didactic moralism—the sort of view we might associate with Plato. This would be the opinion that works of art and aesthetic feelings have some sort of direct impact on percipients by teaching some moral lesson to either the mind (in the form of a principle) or to the heart (in the form of an emotion). The direct moral didact supposes that art or other aesthetic objects have some moral content—an ethical proposition or some belief-inducing moral message or some specific ethico-emotional impact—and, furthermore, the aforesaid didact maintains that the moral significance of art and other aesthetic objects are to be gauged by determining the degree to which the emotions or belief-inducing messages directly delivered by art and other aesthetic objects are morally correct. So, for the didact, art is morally significant to the degree that it conveys admirable or upstanding moral messages and/or emotions which, in turn, are usually thought to have behavioral consequences.

Kant, of course, does not want to deny that works of art are sometimes designed to implement these ends. However, Kant does contend that the deepest significance of the aesthetic realm for ethics is not that it delivers morally correct beliefs and moral emotions directly. Rather, he sees the significance of aesthetics to morality

---

13. Notice that in Kant's accounts of aesthetic experience (i.e., of beauty and sublimity), cognition (reason), and morality have roles, albeit the roles are not as direct as in traditional beliefs about the triplicate of Truth/Goodness/Beauty. Kant, in other words, does not entirely give up the triplicate, but complexifies it. In terms of the relation of aesthetics to ethics, it would be a mistake to think that Kant holds there is no relation. Rather, he eschews typical views of a direct relation between the two: the notion that art or the beautiful promote morality or result in good or evil behavior. Yet Kant finds numerous indirect ways in which beauty is connected to ethics. Kant challenges that simple, direct view of beauty and morality just as he also challenges the view that truth and beauty go together in that the beautiful is constantly correlated with the production of truth.

in a series of what might be called indirect relations (of which the text suggests at least five or six). Here are some:

(1) That the experience of free beauty confirms the harmony of our faculties and the suitability of our faculties to the world and vice versa.
(2) That the experience of beauty in nature shows a good character and, perhaps, helps build a good character—a good moral character.
(3) That the experience of the sublime reveals to us that there is a part of us which is separate from physical nature, impervious to its might, and in some sense superior to it. This aspect of us is reason, or the supersensible, and it is free.
(4) That taste makes moral ideas, as one sort of aesthetic idea, sensible.
(5) That beauty is the symbol of morality.

Let's analyze each of these claims in somewhat more detail.

(1) That the experience of beauty confirms the harmony of our faculties and the suitability of our faculties to the world and vice versa. That is, as we have already noted, the experience of beauty—the pleasure caused by the quickening of the interplay of the imagination and the understanding—provides an occasion where we have a palpable feeling not only of the harmony of our faculties and their suitability for each other, but also a feeling of their "fittingness" to the object of their attention, namely, purposiveness without a purpose. In other words, our faculties are suited to detect and track purposiveness and pattern as such. The corresponding palpable feeling of aesthetic pleasure is morally significant because such synchronization between the faculties and their objects in the world is a condition for practical reason in general. For, we could not act were not these very conditions met. In this way, then, the experience of beauty provides us with a palpable feeling which reinforces our confidence that the basic presupposition of practical reasoning and, therefore, of morality obtain.

(2) That the person who experiences beauty shows good character. Why? In Section 42, Kant says, "I do maintain that to take a *direct* interest in the beauty of nature (not merely to have the taste needed to judge it) is always a mark of a good soul; and that, if this interest is habitual, if it readily associates itself with the *contemplation of nature*, this [fact] at least indicates a mental attunement favorable to moral feeling." The connection Kant sees between interest in the beauty of nature and moral feeling is that both involve taking pleasure in something independent of the satisfaction of any preexisting desire. Moreover, Kant trusts an interest in the beauty of nature over an interest in the beauty of art because the latter is more susceptible to social influence. Indeed, the experience of the beautiful may even tutor us and thereby prepare us for disinterested love in general (see "General Comment on the Exposition of Aesthetic Reflective Judgment).

Perhaps, here we have a suggestion of the closest or most direct relationship between morality and aesthetic experience that we find in Kant. It amounts to this: the experience of the beautiful prepares us—builds up in us—a propensity for disinterestedness, which, of course, is crucial for moral judgment. So, one way in which the experience of beauty is related to morality is that the experience of beauty accustoms us to the sort of disinterestedness that is a prerequisite for moral judgment, and thereby prepares us for the difficult task of superseding personal interests in the way that genuine moral judging presupposes.

This notion of cultivating the person in terms of some form of disinterestedness is as direct as Kant gets in the relation of beauty to morality, but it is still not as direct as views like Plato's that claim that works of art inculcate specific moral emotions, like cowardice, in percipients. So, ironically, for Kant, the notion of disinterestedness factors out morality, only to bring it back in somewhat indirectly.

(3) The moral significance of the experience of the sublime. In the experience of the sublime, as observed previously, we find experiential affirmations of certain of the preconditions of morality—we feel or come to find in our experiences a phenomenological affirmation of the existence of a supersensible element, autonomous reason that, of course, is a presupposition of moral activity. So, once again, an aesthetic experience, in this case the experience of the sublime, reinforces morality by supplying a palpable feeling that bolsters our conviction that certain preconditions of moral judgment hold.

(4) That taste makes moral ideas, as one class of aesthetic ideas, sensible. In order to explicate this relation between aesthetics and ethics, we need to make a substantial detour and discuss Kant's notion of art.

What is art, or specifically fine art, for Kant? It is *beautiful* art (in German, the word is *schön*), or the *beaux arts*. In order to approach Kant's view of such art, let us recall what we know about Kant's view of beauty, especially free beauty.

Remember that on Kant's account of free beauty, it engages the mind, but not in terms of concepts. There is no definition of beauty on the basis of which we can say that such and such is beautiful because it meets such and such a formula. There are no formulas when it comes to beautiful art in regard to free beauty. Whereas Hutcheson and certain Rationalist or Leibnitzian aestheticians suggest that there might be a formula for beauty—a certain compound ratio between unity and diversity—Kant is opposed to the notion that there could be any kind of definition or formula, at least with respect to what we are calling free beauty. So, there are no formulas for what we are calling fine art understood as the art of free beauty.

But if art—beautiful art—is not produced by means of formulas, how is it produced? According to Kant, it is produced by means of genius. Kant titles Section 46 "Fine Art Is the Art of Genius." There Kant offers what he takes to be a proof that the fine arts must be considered arts of genius:

> For every art presupposes rules, which serve as the foundation on which a product, if it is to be called artistic, is thought of as possible in the first place. On the other hand, the concept of fine art does not permit a judgment about the beauty of its product to be derived from any rule whatsoever that has a concept as its determining basis, i.e., the judgment must not be based on a concept of the way in which the product is possible. Hence fine art cannot itself devise the rule by which it is to bring about its product. Since, however, a product can never be called art unless it is preceded by a rule, it must be nature in the subject (and through the attunement of his powers [of imagination and understanding]) that gives the rule to art; in other words, fine art is possible only as the product of genius.

So, the beautiful is the stimulation of pleasure, but this cannot be captured by means of a formula applied mechanically. It arises from the play of the imagination and understanding. But how does art achieve this, if not by way of the application of a determinate concept?

Art does this via the artist's stimulation of her own imagination and understanding in the process of creation which she is then able to pass on to us. The artist possesses a special innate or natural talent for sustaining the play of the common human faculties imagination and understanding. Thus, the artist is able to tap into these common human resources subconsciously in the process of creating art in a way that can stimulate a comparable engagement of the faculties of the rest of us. Not only does the artist invite us to participate in her play of imagination and understanding, the artist also encourages us to embark on our own free play.[14]

The artist does not use a rule or a determinate concept to engender beauty. She uses her own nature—her own human nature—to produce beautiful art. Thus, when Kant discusses the "innate mental aptitude through which nature gives the rule to art," we can understand this as claiming that (human) nature as subconsciously enlisted by the artist is what gives the rule to art—that is, discovers what gives disinterested pleasure to us in virtue of our common humanity. Fine or beautiful art is the art of genius because there is no algorithmic formula for the beautiful. What produces the experience of beauty can only be apprehended by genius in the very process of creation, ungoverned by explicit rules or concepts. There is no science of beauty. Beauty can only be found in the practice of geniuses who are, in effect, natural beauty detectors (by dint of their human nature) for the rest of us.

The common core of humanity may be lawlike, but most of us do not have access to it. The artistic genius, so to speak, executes those laws—but intuitively, not self-consciously—through her exercise of her imagination and understanding.

Kant's view is similar to but not the same as Socrates's view in *Ion*. There art was not the product of knowledge (or craft), but of inspiration, specifically divine inspiration. Kant has dropped off the idea that the inspiration is divine—instead it is a natural talent that he calls genius. Just as Ion does not, according to Socrates,

---

14. In this way, the art of genius can be said to cultivate taste in the audience.

know where his beautiful recitation comes from, so too Kant's genius produces beautiful things but does not know exactly how or, at least, could not summarize it in a tidy algorithm. Obviously, this is a romantic view of art.[15]

Kant defines genius in Section 46. He explains that "genius is the talent that gives the rule to art. Since talent is an innate productive ability of the artist and as such belongs itself to nature, we could also put it this way: Genius is the innate mental predisposition through which nature gives the rule to art." The genius uses herself to detect beauty—she doesn't use formulas. One consequence of this view is that artistry cannot ultimately be taught—at least not in the same way that scientific knowledge can be taught—that is, allegedly, by rote imitation.

One cannot learn artistry through mere imitation since there are no routines or algorithms for churning out beautiful things. Genius is a necessary condition for the production of beautiful art. Artistry must come primarily from inborn talent. But artists do serve apprenticeships, and some of these apprenticeships result in producing great artists. If beautiful artmaking can't be learned by simple imitation, what is going on in these cases?

The genius of those students who possess genius is awakened by the exposure to the master. He doesn't imitate the master, but, as in the case of Manet and then Picasso copying Velasquez, has his own ideas sparked by exposure to the master's work. Genius, so to speak, awakens genius.

What is the nature of these ideas—the ideas that the master has embodied in her work and the ideas the apprentice formulates in response to the master's ideas? These are what Kant calls aesthetic ideas. Whether we are speaking of the master or the apprentice, what genius produces are aesthetic ideas. Indeed, in Comment I of his "Dialectic of Aesthetic Judgment," Kant says that it is the aim of the genius to produce aesthetic ideas. But what are aesthetic ideas?

In Section 42, Kant writes, "By an *aesthetic idea*, I mean a presentation of the imagination that prompts much thought but to which no determinative thought whatsoever, i.e., no (determinate) *concept*, can be adequate." What is going on here? Recall what is involved in the experiences of beauty. Understanding and imagination are in free play. The play is free because the mind is under no pressure to find a concept under which to subsume the stimulus.

Likewise, the product of genius will engender the quickening harmonization of the faculties in response to a presentation that exhibits purposiveness without a purpose—without recourse to any determinate purpose that the object might actually possess.

If this is too obscure, perhaps the example of metaphor may be helpful here. Romeo says, "Juliet is the sun." This is an aesthetic idea. Why? Because it invites the mind to play with it, to test it for different meanings. To explore it. There is

---

15. It is interesting to draw a correlation here between Kant and Longinus since in Longinus, the genius is the source of the sublime.

no fixed meaning to this metaphor. There are as many meanings as you can find in it. For instance, you may read it as saying Juliet is the center of my universe; or Juliet is the light of my life; or, she is my source of warmth; or she's hot; and so on. There is no point of closure, so to speak; no point where you can say you have fully exhausted all the available associations between Juliet (the target of the metaphor) and the sun (the source of the relevant associations).

This is not to say that you can draw just any association between Juliet and the sun. "Juliet is a gaseous orb" is clearly inadmissible. But we can never be sure that all the legitimate associations between what we may call the target domain and the source domain of a living metaphor have been excavated. There is no algorithm for decoding a metaphor—no final, determinate concept in terms of which the target domain of the metaphor can be decisively subsumed. Living metaphors, as opposed to dead ones, are permanently open to exploration. They are aesthetic ideas.

Similarly, genuine artworks, for Kantians, are aesthetic ideas. Such artworks are structured in such a way that they invite extended thought but are open-ended or open-textured. They allow the mind to try out different viewpoints on the work. Consider *Citizen Kane* by Orson Welles. The film involves the search for the meaning of the dying word of Charles Foster Kane. He said "rosebud." As the investigation proceeds, the reporter/narrator frequently returns to the theme that no one word could sum up a human life.

Yet, in the concluding shots of the film, we are shown the source of "rosebud"— it is the name decaled on one of Kane's childhood snow sleds. Moreover, this tempts us to interpret the enigma of Charles Foster Kane in terms of the childhood that was lost when he was parted from that sled and became a ward of the bank.

So, the film then invites us to explore the idea of a human life—is a human life as complex and unfathomable as the reporter/narrator alleges or can it be interpreted by means of a key like "rosebud" or a formula like "lost childhood"? The film does not come to a conclusion. It entices us to explore both possibilities in light of the details of the story that it unfolds.

Citizen Kane does not force a determinate concept upon the viewer. It does not subsume the narrative under the formula "Human life = x, y, z." It bids us to reflect on possible interpretations without closure—without summoning us to fix on one final interpretation. In this way, it is an aesthetic idea.[16]

---

16. As this example indicates, aesthetic ideas mandate an active response on the part of readers, listeners, and viewers. They ask for a playful response in the sense of the free play of the faculties. In the preceding instance, it is a matter of interpretive play. Undoubtedly, the notion that artworks *qua* aesthetic ideas call forth the interplay of imagination and understanding finds its origin in Kant's notion of contemplative play. Moreover, the idea that artworks are permanently open to further interpretations probably also stems from Kant's notion that artworks are aesthetic ideas—perpetually open to further exploration without algorithmic closure.

But what does this have to do with morality? Simply this: that many of the aesthetic ideas that artistic geniuses explore are ones of moral significance. In Section 42, Kant writes that the genius "takes [things] that are indeed exemplified in nature, such as death, envy, and all the other vices, as well as love, fame, and so on; but then, by means of an imagination that emulates reason in reaching [for] a maximum, he gives these a sensible expression in a way that goes beyond the limits of experience, namely with a completeness that cannot be found in nature . . . thereby the presentation aesthetically expands the concept in an unlimited way."[17] And, of course, where the concept in question is moral, engaging it aesthetically has moral significance.

For instance, consider *King Lear*. One thing that Shakespeare explores in this play is what it means to be a good daughter. Perhaps, this is obvious in the contrast between Cordelia, Goneril, and Regan. But arguably, the play does not have a simple answer. For is it really self-evident that Cordelia is a good daughter? After all, had she indulged her father's requests in the opening of the play, all of the ensuing death and destruction could probably have been averted. Is Cordelia truly admirable or is she the sort of prig whose moral vanity is condemnable? Shakespeare leaves us to think about it and, in doing so, enlarges our thinking about what it is to be a virtuous daughter without reducing that idea to a determinate concept.

Beautiful artworks are aesthetic ideas. These ideas are aesthetic because of the way in which they bring about pleasure by engaging the faculties in the harmonious free play of thought with regard to a sensible presentation (i.e., one apprehensible by the senses) without closing down thinking in terms of a determinate conclusion. Geniuses have the capacity to create these ideas, although not by recourse to explicit rules. Moreover, they enable the rest of us to exercise our minds comparably in terms of taste, which is the spectator's correlative to the artist's genius. Thus, taste gives us access to aesthetic ideas and where those aesthetic ideas are generally moral in nature, concerning, for instance, mortality, virtue, and vice, etc. Consequently, art facilitates our exploration of them in terms of sensible manifestations that enlarge our comprehension.

That which artists—artistic geniuses—create engages our exploration of these ideas in a way that results in pleasure because it puts our faculties of imagination and understanding through their paces. In other words, art activates taste. This is precisely what disposes us to call these artworks beautiful or fine. It also enables us to see as the artistic genius sees and to expand our power to see how the artist sees. Here, beauty is the result of the expression of aesthetic ideas.

Each of the arts has a different medium for embodying aesthetic ideas. Poetry is based on word and speech; the visual arts are based in the optical and gesture; and music rests on tone and the play of sensation. Each art, via the genius of the artist, can make morality sensible to the taste of readers, viewers, and listeners through

---

17. Note: all of the themes Kant mentions can have moral significance.

the alchemy of aesthetic ideas. Thus, one of the primary offices of art with respect to ethics is that by engaging taste it makes moral ideas *qua* aesthetic ideas sensible in a way in which they may become objects of reflection.

(5) Beauty as the symbol of morality. This is perhaps the most obscure, but also the most important, relation that Kant sees between aesthetics and morality. What does it mean to say that beauty is the symbol of morality and what, in any event, leads Kant to make the claim? Why is this idea important?

Kant maintains that concepts require intuitive or experiential basis. In Section 59, entitled "On Beauty as a Symbol of Morality," Kant claims that "establishing that our concepts have reality always requires intuitions." Morality is an abstract concept; therefore, the concept of morality needs some intuitive basis. According to Kant, this can take the form of either a schema or a symbol. Kant maintains that beauty is a symbol of morality. But what is meant by *symbol* in this context?

Kant says, "Symbolic exhibition uses an analogy . . . in which judgment performs a double function: it applies the concept to the object of sensible intuition; and then it applies the mere rule by which it reflects on that intuition to an entirely different object, of which the former object is only the symbol." What Kant is suggesting here, I think, is that a *symbol*, in the sense he is using it, is a metaphor. This interpretation is warranted, in part, by his invocation of the notion of analogy in his account of what he intends by the notion of a symbol and also by his suggestion that the source domain of the metaphor plays a double role by characterizing a different object (the target domain).

That is, as we saw earlier, metaphors are structured in terms of two parts: a target domain and a source domain. In the metaphor Richard the Lionheart, King Richard is the target—what the metaphor is about—and lions are the source domain, the source of the attributions that are intended to characterize Richard. In this case, Richard is said to be lionlike because of his strength, his bravery, his kingship, and so forth. Richard is being analogized to lions with respect to certain properties lions are said to possess. Lionheartedness, then, would be a symbol of Richard, in Kant's terminology.

An example that Kant uses to illustrate his idea of the symbol is that an absolute monarchy is a hand mill. The target domain here is absolute monarchy, and the source domain includes various properties of hand mills such as that hand mills crush things (viz., grains), they are mechanical rather than organic, they serve to manipulate things for purposes other than their own (it is not the purpose of grains to be ground), and so forth.

Following this pattern of understanding Kant's notion of a symbol then when Kant asserts that beauty—or, maybe more accurately, judgments of beauty—are the symbol of morality, he means that judgments of beauty are metaphors for morality. That is, beauty is the source domain of certain associations that illuminate pertinent features of morality. Which ones?

The four that Kant enumerates are (1) that judgments of beauty are independent of preexisting desires; (2) that said judgments involve a direct liking for their object; (3) that such judgments are free; and (4) that they are universal. That is, the judgment of beauty experientially grounds the abstract concept of morality by tying certain of its features—such as desire-independent pleasure, felt freedom, and universality—to analogous intuitions or sensations that we undergo during aesthetic experiences. Beauty—the judgment of free beauty—is a symbol of morality in the sense that it is a metaphor for the abstract concept of morality. It supplies that abstract concept with an intuitive or experiential analog that helps us grasp—by means of feeling—the nature of morality.

In this way, Kant is able to construct a relation between aesthetic experience and morality, but, in contrast to the Platonic view, it is an indirect relation. It is not that art and aesthetic pleasure are to be understood as instruments that communicate moral beliefs and emotions for good or ill effect. The relationship is not consequentialist, but is instead symbolic. There is a relationship between aesthetics and ethics, but it is not directly didactic. Rather aesthetic experience serves as a metaphor, rooted in experience, for the concept of moral goodness, which is not otherwise something available to us via intuition. Aesthetic experience is an experiential analogy—something with a phenomenological basis—that we can use in order to reflect on the concept of morality, in order to get a handle on it, in order to reassure us experientially of its possibility.

That is, via the experience of beauty, we can represent moral goodness metaphorically. The judgment of taste phenomenologically affords us an experience, a palpable feeling, which we may employ to represent vividly moral goodness to ourselves insofar as we have a feeling that gives us a grasp of the concept of moral goodness. This doesn't prove that there is moral goodness; but rather encourages our grasp of the concept by matching it with a feeling we have that illuminates the concept experientially. The experience of beauty concretely illuminates aspects of our concept of moral goodness, grounding its possibility by means of phenomenological analogs. The experience of beauty corresponds to our concept of moral goodness by associating it to something that we palpably feel and thereby reinforcing our confidence in its possibility. And in this way, aesthetics serves ethics, but not in the straightforwardly didactic manner presupposed by most moralists, beginning with Plato.

The Antimony of Taste

In the opening section of this chapter, it was suggested that one way to think about Kant's *Critique of Aesthetic Judgment* is to regard it as a response to Hume's paradox of taste. This is somewhat speculative, since Kant does not refer to Hume explicitly. However, toward the end of the *Critique of Aesthetic Judgment*, Kant does broach something very close to Hume's paradox of taste, although Kant frames it under the title of the "Antinomy of Taste" (Sections 56, 57).

Like Hume, Kant notes that it is commonplace to observe that everyone has his own taste and that there is no disputing taste. From this, Kant surmises the thesis that the judgment of taste is not based on concepts (since, were it based on concepts, then such judgments could be disputed). Yet, again like Hume, Kant notes that we often do argue about judgments of taste. However, argumentation presupposes that one side of the debate may be able to compel the necessary assent of the other side and, of course, this would appear to require concepts. So, tracing a path of reasoning not unlike Hume's, Kant reaches an antinomy—two propositions each of which appears plausible in isolation, but which yield a contradiction when placed next to each other.

Kant expresses this antimony in the following way:

> Thesis: A judgment of taste is not based on concepts; for otherwise, one could dispute about it (decide by means of proofs).
> Antithesis: A judgment of taste is based on concepts; for otherwise, regardless of the variation among [such judgments], one could not even so much as quarrel about them (lay claim to other people's necessary assent to one's judgment).

That is, a judgment of taste must refer to some concept; if it did not, it could not solicit the necessary consent of all. But, as Kant has argued throughout the "Analytic of the Beautiful," the judgment of taste—"this rose is beautiful"—cannot be derived from a concept but must be based on a subjective experience of disinterested pleasure. We do not, in other words, possess a definition of beauty which when applied to a particular rose proves that this rose is beautiful. Instead, genuine aesthetic judgments are based on feelings, not concepts.

Nevertheless, on the other hand, concepts must be involved in such judgments, since the arguments we have with regard to them presuppose that one of the disputants may be in a position to require agreement from the other disputants inasmuch as he is right.

So, concepts are involved in judgments of taste; and concepts are not involved. Which is it? Kant perhaps surprisingly answers both. How can that be? Kant suggests that there are two different notions of *concepts* at play in the antinomy and that the failure to qualify the difference between them is what gives birth to the appearance of contradiction here. That is, the antinomy rests upon an equivocation between two distinct ideas of concepts that have been heedlessly run together.

What are these two sorts of concepts? They are, as Kant labels them, determinate and indeterminate concepts. The determinate concepts are undoubtedly the more familiar of the two. It is useful to think of them in terms of definitions like "A bachelor is an unmarried man." This sort of concept figures in reasoning such as:

(1) All bachelors are unmarried men.
(2) Pope Francis is a bachelor.
(3) Therefore, Pope Francis is an unmarried man.

Concepts of this sort, determinate concepts, are concepts of the understanding. They figure in precisely the kind of reasoning that Kant disallows as a model for judgments of taste. It is the deployment of this type of concept that Kant invokes in his "Thesis of the Antinomy of Taste."

Nevertheless, this is not the only sort of concept, according to Kant. There are also indeterminate concepts (or ideas). These are ideas or concepts that must be presupposed by reason. One such concept is that of a supersensible substrate underlying all intuition. Reason must presuppose such a transcendental concept, but we cannot say anything very determinate about it. For, as we have seen, it belongs to the noumenal rather than the phenomenal realm. That is, in order for reason to proceed, reason must presume that there is a supersensible substrate of humanity—as we might say, a common cognitive architecture or common core—a universally distributed panoply of faculties or powers of judgment suited to detecting and tracking nature's purposiveness for creatures like us.

Concepts or ideas of this sort Kant calls concepts or ideas of reason. The idea of morality, as we've seen, is such an idea; no sensible intuition can be given for it. The supersensible substrate of humanity is also like this. It is not cognizable by the understanding. Thus, it is unexpoundable, indemonstrable, and indeterminate. Moreover, it is this indeterminate idea, the *sensus communis*, as we have seen, that grounds our command of the assent of all in judgments of taste.[18] Consequently, the antithesis of Kant's antinomy is, by Kant's lights, true, but it does not contradict the claims of the thesis because there is no contradiction involved in asserting that judgments of taste do not involve determinate concepts, although they do involve indeterminate concepts.

Furthermore, although not stated outright, we can see that Kant also has available the means for a solution to Hume's challenge to account for the possibility of the objectivity of judgments of taste. Kant can argue that

(1) If the judgment of taste is universal, it can be objective (in the sense of intersubjectively valid).
(2) If there is nothing about the percipient's response and nothing about the stimulus objects that would trigger a differential reaction, then the judgment of taste can be universal.

---

18. That we are willing to argue about matters of beauty indicates that we are presuming that there is something like the *sensus communis* that we can appeal to.

(3) Since the percipient's response is disinterested and based solely on common human faculties, there is nothing about the percipient that would trigger a differential response.

(4) Since the relevant stimulus objects of judgments of taste are merely forms of finality, there is nothing about the object that would trigger a differential response.

(5) Therefore, the judgment of taste will be universal.

(6) Therefore, the judgment of taste can be objective.

Moreover, this consequence follows neatly from Kant's characterization of the judgment of taste in his "Analytic of the Beautiful."

Potential Problems for Kant

As we have seen, Kant's aesthetic theory is extremely complex. It also offers a highly ingenious account of how, despite their peculiarity, judgments of taste are possible. Nevertheless, this very impressive intellectual edifice is not without some potential weaknesses. Here are a few to ponder.

Ascertaining that one's aesthetic judgment is disinterested is crucial to the possibility of commanding the assent of others with respect to one's own judgment of taste. Yet how is this to be done? Kant proposes the indifference-to-existence test. But is this test reliable? Might we not have some unconscious interests? That is, we think we are disinterested and indifferent to the existence of the object in question, but we really have an interest of which we are unaware. Isn't this possible? Doesn't it compromise the efficacy of the indifference-to-existence test? At the very least, it would seem as though this test is not sufficient to determine disinterestedness.

Moreover, contemporary psychologists have discovered that we are possessed of all sorts of unconscious biases. Perhaps when I think that I am experiencing disinterested pleasure in response to George Balanchine's ballet *Stars and Stripes*, I am unconsciously feeling patriotic pleasure. Moreover, not only do we not know all of our unconscious (and interested in Kant's sense) biases now, we have no idea of what unconscious biases we and our descendants will form in the future. Furthermore, we not only cannot know our own unconscious biases, we also cannot know whether or not the judgments of taste of others—past, present, and future—are interested.

So, even if authentic judgments of taste are in some sense metaphysically products of disinterested pleasure, we can never know this. Epistemically then, we are never, contra Kant, entitled to demand the assent of others to our judgments of free beauty. Nor is anyone else. Indeed, all the consequences that Kant thinks flow from the claim that aesthetic judgments of free beauty are unavailable to him.[19]

There is also the question of whether the notion of indifference to existence is necessary for disinterestedness. Suppose a Chinese vase that I do not own but deem to be beautiful is about to tip over, and I rush to save it from shattering on the stone floor of the museum.[20] Does that imply that my judgment of its beauty is not disinterested? Would not even a Kantian concede that I am still issuing a genuine, disinterested aesthetic judgment even as I hurry to intercept its downward trajectory?

Kant maintains that the pleasure requisite for genuine judgments of taste emerges from the free play of the faculties of understanding and imagination as they explore the stimulus object, but these faculties are finally unsuccessful in discovering a determinate concept adequate to the object. However, ordinarily would not such a failed search end in frustration rather than pleasure? Doesn't Kant owe us a clear account of why we are not frustrated when dealing with the beautiful? Perhaps, he will say that our being disinterested makes a difference here.

But the disinterested mathematician who is consistently thwarted in her search for the proof of a theorem is unlikely to be delighted. She will not exclaim "how beautiful," as is her wont when her cogitation results in success. So, why aren't we similarly frustrated when we cannot secure closure with respect to the sorts of beautiful stimuli that interest Kant?

The notion that forms of purposiveness are the objects of authentic judgments of taste is simultaneously too broad and too narrow. It is too broad because everything, or very nearly everything, may exhibit a form of purposiveness. The dripping snout of a dirty, ancient pig suggests a form of purposiveness, but it is not beautiful.

Kant connects the experience of beauty to the operation of the cognitive faculties of the understanding and the imagination. Why doesn't he explore the perhaps more likely possibility that the response to beautiful stimuli activates some non-cognitive faculty? In contemporary jargon, isn't it more probable that the beauty response is less a function of the prefrontal cortex and more an affair of lower recesses of the brain?

Kant claims that genuine aesthetic judgments are not based on concepts. Our claim on the assent of everyone else is based on what he calls exemplary necessity.

---

19. Perhaps Nietzsche was getting at something like this regarding all inward judgments in his book *Daybreak*, 116. Similarly, aesthetic experience—characterized as experiences valued for their own sake—are similarly unavailable given the unavoidable human tendency to perennially suffer unconscious biases.

20. Suppose as well that we for some reason know that we will never be able to view the vase after we save it.

But isn't this itself based on the concept of causation—the notion that like causes will have like effects on like subjects? Nor does this law seem indeterminate.

Kant maintains that in the case of valid aesthetic judgments, we must directly experience the stimulus we declare to be beautiful. This is connected to his idea that such judgments are singular. But suppose that on the basis of a completely reliable source, I can know that the Persian rug in the next room is exactly like the one in this room—the one that I declare disinterestedly to be beautiful. Surely, I should be able to infer validly that the one in the next room is beautiful, although I have not encountered it directly. Remember that we are assuming that the report about the identity between the two rugs is completely reliable. But when that is assumed, shouldn't we be able to issue valid aesthetic judgments on the basis of inference? It may be that in reality we are never entitled to that assumption. But if we could, why not make the inference? Moreover, if Kant allows that we could, but asserts that this would not be a valid aesthetic judgment, he may be open to the charge that he is begging the question. At the very least, cases like this indicate that Kant allows some room for inference with respect to aesthetic judgment.

Connected to the requirement that judgments of taste be based on face-to-face encounters with the relevant aesthetic stimulus is the question of whether we can find musical compositions—as opposed to performances of musical compositions—to be beautiful. Unless we are like Mozart and can look at a score and hear it in our heads, in what way can we say that we experience, for example, Brahms's Fourth Symphony directly? But wouldn't that be the unavoidable, if deeply counterintuitive, consequence of Kant's theory.[21]

Kant associates various meta-pleasures with the experiences of beauty and the sublime. The experience of beauty is said to provoke pleasure at the experiential confirmation that the conditions for practical reasoning have been met, while the experience of the sublime reinforces phenomenologically our faith in the vocation of autonomous reason. But how plausible is it to attribute such conclusions to most people who nevertheless undeniably experience the beautiful and the sublime? That is, the experience of the beautiful and the sublime are putatively within the reach of all human beings. They are not recondite. Nevertheless, who but a philosopher could derive the meta-pleasures that Kant attributes to these experiences?

Kant contends that beauty is a symbol of morality. Moreover, he also appears to treat the notion of a symbol as a form of metaphor where such metaphors, for him, seem to simply involve analogs or similarities between two objects, like absolute monarchies and hand mills. Yet, in ordinary language, similarities alone do not establish that we are dealing with a metaphor. We look for evidence that a speaker intends us to take his locution as a metaphor, and then we look for pertinent similarities. But with the experience of the beautiful in nature, there is no intention to be had since nature has no intentions. So, the experience of beauty in response to

---

21. I owe this suggestion to Marilynn Johnson.

nature—what Kant appears to regard as the highest form of aesthetic experience—cannot be a symbol of morality, since it cannot be a metaphor for morality.

Moreover, since it is a truth of logic that everything is like everything else in some respect, many things other than beauty may also be symbols of morality. Beauty may be a symbol of morality, but other candidates could probably be made to serve in this way. However, wouldn't this undercut the ambitiousness of the claim Kant intends to be making?

Kant thinks that aesthetic judgments are reflective—that is, they involve searching for a concept. He refers to this process as *contemplation*. But is contemplation the right concept here? Isn't contemplation more a matter of a non-searching disposition—a matter of being at ease and perusing something in a leisurely and unexcited way. Isn't it more a matter of sampling than searching? Thus, might not Kant's characterization of being touched by beauty be far too strenuous to be captured by the notion of *contemplation*?

Concluding Remarks

Although we have acknowledged a series of potential problems with Kant's aesthetic theory, one cannot deny its immense influence on the course of the philosophy of art in the West over the last two centuries. His concept of aesthetic judgment in terms of disinterestedness, very broadly construed, has served as the historical basis of one of the most enduring conceptions of aesthetic experience in Western philosophy—namely, the notion that aesthetic experience is valued for its own sake. Kant's suggestion that the appropriate objects of aesthetic attention are forms of purposiveness, moreover, has served as an impetus to what is often called formalism. And, as we shall see, due to the way in which figures like Arthur Schopenhauer and Clive Bell, among others, have developed the Kantian perspective, Kant's thinking has provided ingredients for various conceptions of the autonomy of art, including the notion of art for art's sake, aestheticism, the aforesaid formalism, and, in our own day, the aesthetic theory of art. Admittedly, these developments may well represent misinterpretations of Kant's intentions. Nevertheless, it is difficult to imagine their taking root without Kant providing at least some of the spadework.

Bibliography

The translation used in this chapter for Kant's *Third Critique* is *Critique of Judgment*, translated by Werner Pluhar (Hackett, 1987). Another excellent translation is *The Critique of the Power of Judgment*, edited by Paul Guyer and translated by Paul Guyer and Eric Matthews (Cambridge University Press, 2000).

Allison, Henry. *Kant's Theory of Taste*. Cambridge: Cambridge University Press, 2001.
Beiser, Frederick. *Diotima's Children*. Oxford: Oxford University Press, 2009.
Clewis, Robert. *The Kantian Sublime and the Revelation of Freedom*. Cambridge: Cambridge University Press, 2008.
Cohen, Ted, and Paul Guyer, eds. *Essays in Kant's Aesthetics*. Chicago: University of Chicago Press, 1982.
Crawford, Donald. *Kant's Aesthetic Theory*. Madison: University of Wisconsin Press, 1974.
Guyer, Paul. *A History of Modern Aesthetics*. Cambridge: Cambridge University Press, 2014.
———. *Kant and the Claims of Taste*. Cambridge, MA: Harvard University Press, 1979, 1997.
———, ed. *Kant's Critique of the Power of Judgment: Critical Essays*. Lanham, MD: Rowman and Littlefield, 2003.
———. *Kant and the Experience of Freedom*. Cambridge: Cambridge University Press, 1993.
———. *Values of Beauty*. Cambridge: Cambridge University Press, 2005.
Hughes, Fiona. *Kant's Critique of Aesthetic Judgement*. London: Continuum, 2010.
Kemal, Salim. *Kant and Fine Art*. Oxford: Oxford University Press, 1986.
Nietzsche, Friedrich. *Daybreak: Thoughts on the Prejudices of Modernity*. Edited by Maudemarie Clark and Brian Leiter. Translated by R. G. Hollingdale. Cambridge: Cambridge University Press, 1997.
Wicks, Robert. *Routledge Philosophy GuideBook to Kant on Judgment*. Abingdon, UK: Routledge, 2007).

CHAPTER 6

G. W. F. Hegel's *Introductory Lectures on Aesthetics*

Georg Wilhelm Friedrich Hegel was born in Stuttgart, Germany, in 1770. He died in 1831. He was Kant's most illustrious successor. Some might even argue that G. W. F. Hegel surpassed Kant.

One often hears of a distinction between what is called "Analytic" or "Anglo-American" philosophy versus something called "Continental" philosophy. In many ways these terms do not make a great deal of sense, since so many different kinds of philosophers are gathered together under each of these labels—often including philosophers who are diametrically opposed to each other. However, as a rule of thumb, one way to get a sense of who gets grouped where is that the Continental philosophers are typically thinkers who take Hegel seriously, whereas the Analytic philosophers generally (although there are significant exceptions) do not; some even dismiss him outright.

This is not to say that Continental philosophers always agree with Hegel. Many of them, like Karl Marx and Michel Foucault, are highly critical of Hegel. But that criticism testifies to the fact that they take him seriously, whereas Hegel does not belong to the canon of most Analytic philosophers. Students in so-called Analytic Philosophy Departments are not required to take courses in Hegel or qualifying exams about him. Kant is the last philosopher to appear on the required reading lists of both Analytic and Continental philosophers. Thus, Hegel represents a kind of turning point in the evolution of Western philosophy.

Kant and Hegel

One useful way in which to initially orient the discussion of Hegel is to contrast him with Kant. A leading difference between Hegel and Kant is that whereas Kant thinks that some things are unknowable, Hegel is more sanguine. You will recall from the last chapter that one of Kant's greatest achievements was his subjective turn, his vaunted Copernican revolution, whereby he claimed that the mind filters its inputs so that everything we experience is shaped in terms of certain forms and categories, such as space, time, and causality. But that implied for Kant that there was something unfiltered that was being filtered. This something in its unfiltered state, Kant argued, is unknowable since knowledge requires being processed (filtered) by the mind. So there is a noumenal realm, the realm of the notorious thing-in-itself, and the phenomenal realm—the realm of phenomena, the realm that we experience via the forms and the categories.

In the *Critique of Judgment*, we encountered this noumenal realm under the rubric of the *supersensible*. Kant thought that we could know that there is a noumenal realm, but that we cannot know anything specific about it, since knowledge would involve the application of the mind's categories, whereas the noumenal, by definition, is that which is unprocessed by the mind. Perhaps you know the old song by the Doors that proclaimed, "Break on through to the other side." Kant argues that there is an "other side" and that we can know that it exists, but that we can't break on through to it.

Although attracted to parts of Kant's philosophy, many German philosophers, like Johann Gottlieb Fichte, were unhappy with the conclusion that there was something unknowable; so, they created metaphysical systems designed to show that our knowledge is not limited in the way Kant maintained. Nothing riles philosophers more than the claim they can't know something (except maybe the claim that you can know something which, of course, vexes the skeptics). Thus, many of Kant's successors, like Arthur Schopenhauer, developed elaborate philosophies intended to demonstrate that we could have knowledge of Kant's unknowable. Hegel's project is perhaps the most formidable attempt in this vein.

Hegel is an Idealist. He maintains that ultimately reality is mental, and that we can have access to it through consciousness. That is, since ultimate reality is consciousness, we can come to know and understand reality because that is a matter of understanding our own nature. Thus, a leading difference between Kant and Hegel is that Hegel thinks we *can* have knowledge of reality in itself.

A second important difference between the two philosophers has to do with their analysis of the mind. Kant thinks that the categories—the things the mind uses to organize its input—are transhistorical. Our categories—like causation—are fixed; they do not change over time. The mind of a Neolithic hunter-gatherer and my mind employ the same basic structures.

Although many thinkers have been drawn to Kant's idea that the mind organizes our experience in terms of categories, there is less agreement regarding the claim that these categories are historically and culturally invariant. We encountered Kant's view of the invariant structure of the categories when we discussed his notion of the *sensus communis* in his *Third Critique*. Other thinkers, however, have argued that the categories that the mind uses to organize experience are subject to change. They argue that these categories vary as you move from one culture and/or historical period to another.

Undoubtedly you have heard the assertion, often advanced by cultural anthropologists, that different cultures see the world or organize the world in terms of different fundamental categories. The idea is Kantian, at least in the sense that it holds that the human experience of the world is structured in light of the categories that the mind brings to the world. But the view is ultimately not Kantian, since cultural anthropologists typically think that the structures the mind deploys are diverse across the various human tribes.

Hegel is one of the most important figures to have made people sympathetic to the view that, in a certain sense (to be discussed), the mind changes historically. Hegel contends that the mind evolves over time—that people understand the world differently in different historical epochs. Hegel argues that the mind—human consciousness—undergoes transformation in the course of history and that part of his task as a philosopher is to chart those transformations.

Moreover, Hegel believes that this process of transformation takes a specific direction—that it is evolutionary, that it is progressive. Specifically, Hegel contends that the human mind becomes more and more conscious of its own nature as time goes on. Like Socrates, Hegel took the most important precept of life to be "Know thyself." However, Hegel applies this precept to human conscious itself, rather than to particular individuals. Hegel thinks that the quest for self-knowledge—for consciousness to become conscious of its own nature—is *the* primary task of human history. The vocation of Mind with a capital *M* is to understand itself, to understand its own nature. And this is why art is so important in his system since art has a crucial role to play in the evolution of humankind's self-understanding or self-consciousness. What role? Art has the capacity to reflect the human mind and can show us, as a mirror reflects our face, the nature of the human mind, including the ways in which the mind changes from one period to the next.

So the contrast between Kant's view of the invariant structure of the mind versus Hegel's conception of its evolutionary nature gives way to Hegel's notion of the significance of art. Since the mind or consciousness (or, in Hegel's idiom, *Spirit*) changes from one period to the next, what art does is—at each point in the evolution of human consciousness—to give us the measure of the mind's understanding of itself.

Since art is so bound up with the evolution of consciousness over time, it is useful to say something about Hegel's conception of the historical process in which art plays such an integral role.

Hegel and History

So far, I've been using the term *mind* a lot. Clearly, since I've been talking about it changing over substantial expanses of time—evolving from epoch to epoch—I am not, as Hegel is not, referring to individual minds—to my mind or your mind. Our minds do not persist from epoch to epoch. We die. Consequently, when Hegel speaks of the human mind—of the human mind evolving—he is speaking in a corporate or collective sense, not in an individualistic one. He is referring to the mind of the human race as it evolves—the history of human mentality, if you will—a process in which we are all participating in the broadest sense. Hegel has several different ways of alluding to this phenomenon, including *Mind* (with a capital M), *Consciousness, Spirit, Absolute Spirit,* the *Divine Nature,* and even *God* (though in a somewhat Spinozistic sense).[1]

Hegel's fundamental premise regarding Mind or Consciousness or Spirit is that it undergoes change throughout the historical process. Hegel's greatest book, *The Phenomenology of Spirit* (1807), is an account of the way in which the human mind has evolved through history (from immediate awareness and sensation through perception and eventually to concept) on its way to realizing its destiny—Consciousness's self-understanding of its own nature.

As already indicated, Hegel's picture of history is essential to what he has to say about art since he believes that art is a reflection of Mind or Spirit. Therefore, the history of art is a reflection of the human mind as it strives to realize its vocation. Moreover, since the mission of the human mind is to know itself *and* since art is a primary way in which we can come to know ourselves, art has a virtually indispensable role to play in the process of our coming to understand the nature of human consciousness—a process that we may also describe as a matter of consciousness becoming conscious of its own nature, a process that, by definition, is one of self-consciousness or self-awareness.

This process spans the history of the human race from ancient times to Hegel's own day. As time goes on, Hegel argues, the human mind or Spirit comes to understand itself with ever more lucidity and refinement. At each stage of development, art reflects through its various media—such as stone, for example, if it is sculpture—the corresponding level of understanding of itself that the mind has reached at that point in its evolution.

Art reflects mind. Therefore, art history reflects the evolution of the mind, its history. That history takes a certain direction; it has, so to speak, a certain destiny. It gravitates toward greater and greater self-consciousness. It is driven by a tendency to aspire always toward a better understanding of its own nature. Thus, the history of art evinces greater and greater self-consciousness. The history of art recapitulates the history of consciousness.

But art does not do this simply in a passive manner. Art makes a contribution to the evolution of human consciousness.

How?

Think again of a mirror analogy: you hold the mirror up to your face in order to comb your hair. But once you see how you look, that knowledge enables you to rearrange how you look. Looking into the mirror enables you to change your appearance. Similarly, when consciousness, in a manner of speaking, looks into the mirror of art, it not only sees how it is but that self-understanding makes possible further

---

1. Throughout, I will be treating Mind or *Geist* as human consciousness. This is a humanistic interpretation. An alternative type of interpretation is to treat Mind as something superhuman such, as mentioned above, as God.

refinement. In this way, art does not merely record what we are, it also serves as an instrument or agency for further evolution.

Because art is so intimately related to the history of consciousness, it pays to speak in some detail about Hegel's specific view of the evolution of human consciousness before turning directly to his *Introductory Lectures on Aesthetics*.

Roughly history follows this path. In the beginning, there is Matter and there is Spirit or thought. This is *the* basic distinction between things. Matter is heavy; Spirit is light. Matter is subject to physical laws; matter is fully determined by causal principles. Spirit is distinct from matter. In what way? Because in principle, Spirit or Mind is free—not fully determined by laws. That is the ultimate nature of Spirit—that it is free.

As already established, Hegel thinks that the history of consciousness is the story of Mind or Spirit or Consciousness *coming* to know itself. But what is the nature that comes to be known over the course of history? It is the realization that Spirit or Mind is free. But Mind does not grasp everything this implies all at once. It takes time and reflection in order to gradually comprehend what this involves. So the historical process is a series of successive approximations regarding our freedom—a series of increasing refinements about that to which human freedom amounts.

What does it mean to say that humans are free? That we create ourselves. But what does that mean?

Consider the contrast with animals. Animals have fixed natures. Putatively, they are completely programmed by nature—by instinct. Humans are in a constant process of re-creating themselves. How do we do this? Through our cultures, including importantly our material cultures, and our practices.

A beaver is preprogrammed to make a dam—throughout history, beavers have been instinctually preprogrammed to build the same damn dams. Humans are different. Confronted by different environments, we figure out how to adjust in different ways, and the practices we evolve to accommodate to our varying situations change the kinds of people we are—hunter-gathers, say, in contrast to agricultural or industrial workers.

Through our practices, we free ourselves from nature. The freedom that Hegel emphasizes is first of all, freedom from nature—freedom from instinct and freedom from its burdens. By freeing ourselves from nature through our practices, through culture (including material culture), we, in turn, create ourselves as certain kinds of peoples—peoples who have realized their potential to be free in certain respects and to a certain extent. This is not something that happens with transparent self-awareness. It is an unplanned consequence of our specific practices in which all or nearly all participate. There was no grand blueprint to create Homo Consumer. That is just what we have become—in contrast to Homo Faber—as a result of a social organization that we assembled almost blindly, at least with respect to its ultimate outcome.

In large measure, each culture attains the level of freedom that it enjoys through the coordination of the energies and efforts of its members—that is to say, through its social organization. Freedom from nature is bound up with politics—with social organization—that is, through the coordination of activities (in terms of chains of commands, obligations, the distribution of power, rights, wealth, and the like) of the members of society. Human freedom from nature is connected to the political organization of a culture, the distribution of power and responsibility, and material goods. Thus, in an important sense, political culture reflects the level of human freedom at any given point in human history. Moreover, political culture creates people specific to its mode of organization—knights and serfs, for example. Statecraft is soul craft.

The level of human freedom—as well as the awareness of that freedom—changes over time with changes in political organization. Hegel is famous for offering a tripartite history of the evolution of human freedom from ancient times to his own day. Reduced to a slogan, Hegel claims that history moves from a state of affairs where one is free to a state where some are free and finally to the point where all are free.

Concretely, what Hegel has in mind is that in Asiatic civilizations, one is free—the emperor, the pharaoh, or the rajah. In classical civilization, some are free, the citizens of the polis in Athens, for example. That is, the people who do the talking in Plato's *Republic*. However, only some are free in ancient Athens; only some have political agency. Many within the walls of the city are disenfranchised, including women, foreigners, and slaves. The same is true of ancient Rome, although Rome, with its codification of law, adds to the prospects for freedom of more people than just the citizenry because a system of settled laws affords increasingly extensive protections.

So in the first epoch of the history of freedom, one is free (one who is usually identified as a god). In the next phase, some are free. Thus, perhaps predictably, in the last stage, all are free, specifically in the sense that all are equal.

This last stage starts with the Christian idea that everyone is equal in the eyes of the Lord. Everyone has a soul. For example, Saint Paul argues that everyone can be a Christian—Gentiles as well as Jews. With Christianity, the principle of equality emerges in terms of religious doctrine. But this idea then begins to be expanded beyond religion into the political realm until the idea of liberal democracy in our own time *seems* to have become an almost universal ideal.

Of course, it is not true that all are free—neither in our own day nor in Hegel's. But Hegel means only that the notion that all have a right to be free has come into its own as an expectation—perhaps as a dominant expectation—in the modern world. It is an idea that underwrites the various civil rights movements in our own times, for example. So even though it is not yet the case that all are actually free, the ideal of universal freedom is abroad and healthy in the world today. Admittedly this ideal still faces resistance; nevertheless, things are arguably trending in that direction, which is basically what Hegel is suggesting.

Earlier I noted that according to Hegel, human history involves an increasing awareness or self-consciousness of its own nature, which needless to say, Hegel believes to be a matter of freedom. However, so far, we've only discussed the expansion of freedom and not our self-consciousness of freedom—the self-consciousness of our own true nature as free beings. Where does the notion of self-consciousness fit into Hegel's history of freedom?

Each society achieves a certain level of freedom through its practices. Each culture empowers its members to a certain extent and in certain ways. This is perhaps most evident in its forms of political, social, and economic arrangements. But the level of freedom is also reflected by and reflected on by other aspects of the culture, such as philosophy, art, and religion.

For example, religion reflects the level of freedom in a culture for Hegel inasmuch as he takes divinity to be a symbol of Spirit. In Asiatic society, one is free, the emperor or pharaoh. This is reflected by the religion of the times in which the pharaoh is also a god. Divinity in such cultures stands for a conception of humanity—a projection of humanity onto a theological plane. In Asiatic societies, only the emperor is truly human, truly free, and this is represented by portraying the emperor as a god. Ancient religion, then, gives us a limited conception of human spirit; it reveals that Spirit is free, but its conception of that freedom is blinkered insofar as it sees that freedom only extends to the one.

In ancient Greek religion, all the gods take on a human form as opposed to the allegedly animal-fusion gods of Asian societies, such as Ganesh, the elephant-headed Hindu deity. Nor are the Greek gods literally natural forces, although they may be associated with them, as Apollo is associated with the sun. Indeed, Greek gods even behave like humans, given as they are to petty rivalries.

As a reflection on *human nature*, Greek religion putatively represents the divine—the symbol of humanity—as divorced from, as separate from, nature. Greek religion, that is, is a reflection on the nature of human spirit, and it employs the language of myth to register a new insight into the nature of human spirit, namely, that human spirit is something apart from brute nature, as signaled by the fact that the gods are ageless and immortal.

In this way, Greek culture not only involves an increase in human freedom, but its religion implicitly reflects on this advance in human freedom, as does its art and its philosophy. Art, philosophy, and religion are expressions of the advance in human freedom and thereby provide objective correlatives for the evolution of freedom, opportunities for us to meditate on and become self-aware of our growing empowerment, where such self-awareness itself becomes a condition for further empowerment, which leads to further self-awareness, and so forth.

However, Hegel does not think that this is a never-ending process. He thinks that we will reach a point where we can fully comprehend our nature as free beings—a point at which self-consciousness will fulfill its mission, an end of history (i.e., an end of the developmental history of consciousness's quest to understand itself).

Indeed, Hegel felt, albeit immodestly, that that historical moment was reached with the publication of his *Phenomenology of Spirit* in 1807.

Of course, one may dispute Hegel's declaration that history ended circa 1807. Nevertheless, one can do this without abandoning Hegelianism altogether. One might think that the process has not been completed but is still going on. Nowadays, many would reject even this view on the grounds that it conceives of history as a progressive project—a progress toward greater freedom and an awareness thereof. Yet it does seem difficult to flatly deny that in certain respects, there has been—over the course of history—an increase in humanity's freedom from nature and an increase in political freedom. That is, there does appear to be more of both.

Be that as it may, it is within the context of this overall philosophical theory that we need to approach Hegel's conception of art since art has a role to discharge in the evolution of consciousness's self-understanding. Art abets this realization. But this raises the question of the way in which consciousness becomes aware of itself.

Consciousness becomes aware of itself by externalizing itself—by manifesting what is inside outside—by *expressing* itself. Humankind learns about its own nature by acting and then by reflecting on what it has done. In order to grasp what we really are, we must observe what we have done. This is not only how others come to understand us, it is how we come to understand ourselves. We understand ourselves through our works and by reflecting on our works. That is the way in which we come to understand ourselves and our conceptions of ourselves.

Consider how, as an individual, we try to figure out who we are. We might start by closing our eyes and peering inward. But all we are likely to "see" is a void dotted by phosphenes.[2] If we really want to learn about ourselves, we should look to our behavior—to our actions—which will reveal our interests and what we value. So, too, is it, Hegel suggests, with society at large.

Look at what humanity creates and what it destroys, what it worships and abominates, what it builds and how it transforms nature. Humankind objectifies itself, sculpting the world in its own image. We project ourselves into objects, into the world. Nowadays it is difficult to find anyplace on earth that has not been modified by human endeavor. If you want to know what modern society values look at our roads and bridges—they express who we are; they signal our desire to get from here to there. The built environment is, for Hegel, a mirror of the human spirit at each stage of its development.

Hegel writes that

> man is realized for himself by *practical* activity, inasmuch as he has the impulse, in the medium which is directly given to him, and is externally presented before him, to produce himself, and, therein at the same time to recognize himself. This purpose

---

2. Recall how Hume reported that when introspecting, he was unable to catch any glimpse of a "self."

he achieves by the modification of external things upon which he impresses the seal of his inner being, and then finds repeated in them his own characteristics. Man does this in order as a free subject to strip the outer world of its stubborn foreignness and to enjoy in the shape and fashion of things a mere external reality of himself. (XLIX)[3]

Consciousness or Spirit objectifies or externalizes itself through its activities—through its practices such as, we have seen, religion. It presses its imprint upon nature as it shapes the world to serve Spirit's own needs, desires, and values. By examining what we have produced and our practices of production, we can learn about our nature where the very processes themselves involve an increase in or expansion of human freedom. That is, not only do our practices free us from the dominion of matter/nature, but by contemplating those practices in terms of what they express, we acquire further freedom through self-consciousness.

Art, of course, is one of our practices. Indeed, as we saw with respect to Kant's notion of aesthetic ideas, it is a medium for the expression of our deepest human themes, such as ideas of morality. Thus, on this view, art is an undeniable source for learning about human nature. For Hegel, artistic practices were one of the primary sources of consciousness's expression of its evolving nature over centuries. Through its art, each society expressed the level of its consciousness of the nature of consciousness-as-freedom.

Hegel writes:

> Fine art . . . has become simply a mode of revealing to consciousness and bringing to utterance the Divine Nature, the deepest interests of humanity, and the most comprehensive truths of the mind. It is in works of art that nations have deposited the profoundest intuitions and ideas of their hearts; and fine art is frequently the key—with many nations there are no other—to the understanding of their wisdom and their religion.
>
> This attribute which art shares with religion and philosophy, only in this peculiar mode, that it represents even the highest ideas *in sensuous forms*, thereby bringing them nearer to the character of natural phenomena, to the senses, and to feeling. (XII–XIII)

Art, for Hegel, enables consciousness to reflect on itself by embodying Spirit (Consciousness, the Divine Nature, the Absolute, etc.) in sensuous forms.[4] It is because these forms are sensuous that they are the subject of aesthetics. By externalizing consciousness in its various stages, art, so to speak, puts consciousness

---

3. All quotes are from Hegel's *Introductory Lectures on Aesthetics*.
4. For Hegel, art, religion, and philosophy are primary ways in which Consciousness becomes aware of itself; art deals in the sensuous, religion in sensory inner imagery and feeling, and philosophy in concepts.

in a position where it can be observed or self-observed. Art takes the abstract ideas of a culture—ideas perhaps that the culture itself could not articulate philosophically—and makes them concrete objects, like statues, where they are available to intuition, that is, to the senses.

Sometimes this process can be referred to as alienation. Consciousness or Spirit alienates or estranges itself by assuming an alien, externalized, or objectified form, a sensuous form that can be scrutinized because it has been articulated in shapes that can be grasped by intuition—that is, by the senses—and where it's essential nature can be sized up. Where Kant thought beauty was the symbol of morality, Hegel thinks art is the sensuous symbol of freedom.

In its role as a reflection of the nature of consciousness, art stands alongside philosophy and religion. In fact, in the earliest stages of this evolution, prior to the advent and sophistication of philosophy, art, generally in concert with religion, has a dominant role to discharge in the expression of consciousness's self-understanding. And throughout *much* of history, art continues to hold a special position.

Each of our practices addresses certain human needs. Art is a human practice. So it too addresses a need. Hegel maintains that

> the universal need for expression in art lies, therefore, in man's rational impulse to exalt the inner and outer world into a spiritual consciousness for himself, as an object, in which he recognizes his own self. He satisfied the need for this spiritual freedom when he makes all that exists for himself *within*, and in a corresponding way realizes this his explicit self *without*, evoking thereby, in this reduplication of himself, what is in him into vision and into knowledge for his own mind and for that of others. This is the free rationality of man, in which, all action and knowledge, so also art has its ground and necessary origin. (L)

As this indicates, for Hegel, art has an absolutely central function to perform in human history. For that reason, he treats art with far more seriousness than most philosophers. But before expounding on that significance at length, Hegel needs to tell us what art is.

What Is Art?

Hegel's *Introductory Lectures on Aesthetics* is literally an introduction to a four-volume series of lectures that has been published with titles such as *The Philosophy of Fine Art* or *Aesthetics: Lectures on Fine Art*. This four-volume study is a philosophical account of the history of art and its various forms and genres. It contains some of the most brilliant philosophical art criticism ever produced. It was not, however, a book that Hegel himself completed; rather, it was culled from Hegel's notes for several different lecture series that Hegel delivered during his lifetime, and it was edited and published posthumously by his student Heinrich Gustav Hotho.

Although Hegel has a reputation for obscurity, he was reputedly a splendid lecturer. Wealthy folk sent their valets to his lectures to take notes so that they could join in sophisticated conversations about his philosophy in their salons and soirees. Maybe one of the reasons for Hegel's tarnished reputation as an author can be explained by the fact that much of the writings by him that have come down to us were derived from his lecture notes—and, as most professors will admit, their lectures notes, which are usually just personally encoded reminders of what they want to say, are very often intelligible only to themselves.

Hegel's *Introductory Lectures on Aesthetics*, then, introduces his massive exploration of the nature and purpose of the arts as revealed over the history of humankind. As such, it performs the usual tasks of such introductory enterprises—defining and defending its scope, fending off possible objections to the project, defining its subject and its significance, giving a summary overview of the vast history it is about to survey, and so forth.

In the first chapter Hegel, like most authors, tells us what his book is about. He is going to deal with aesthetics, the realm of the perceptible—of sensation and feeling—including especially the beautiful. Hegel is not particularly comfortable with the label *aesthetics* nor alternatives, like *Kallistics* (recalling *kalon*); but rather than coining a new nomenclature, he prefers to stipulate his area of interest. He only intends to deal with artistic beauty—with fine art (with the *beaux arts*). That is, unlike Hutcheson and Kant, natural beauty is not within his purview.

Hegel thinks that he is justified in this move for several reasons. First, he maintains that every science has the prerogative to stipulate its domain of inquiry. Here Hegel uses the term *science* in the European sense to describe his inquiry. In this usage, *science* refers to any knowledge-seeking project, not only, as in the Anglo-Saxon sense, to natural science.

The second reason Hegel screws his attention to fine art rather than nature is, in his words, because "artistic beauty stands *higher* than nature. For the beauty of art is the beauty that is born—born again, that is—of the mind" (II). Thus, because it is of Spirit born—produced by the mind—it has more to tell us about the nature of Consciousness than does nature.

Hegel also defends his focus on fine art versus nature by suggesting that natural beauty is too indeterminate a subject to sustain scientific investigation, for "in dealing with natural beauty we find ourselves too open to *vagueness*, and too destitute of a *criterion*" (IV). That is, since natural beauty is not the product of mind—is not the product of intentional activity—it lacks determinate criteria of appreciation. For this reason, natural beauty lacks objectivity in the sense of an objective standard of taste. What counts as natural beauty is too irretrievably subjective and, therefore, it is too epistemically unruly to be susceptible to scientific inquiry.

Having demarcated his domain of inquiry—and defended his choice of focus—Hegel pauses to ask whether fine art really deserves to be the subject of scientific inquiry. In particular, he foresees two objections to the worthiness of his project. The first objection is rather puritanical. It charges that art is not weighty enough to warrant scientific study. Art is not part of the serious business of living. Art is about relaxation and amusement. It is too unimportant—too frivolous—to spend precious philosophical brain cells contemplating it.

The second challenge echoes Plato. Art is accused of dealing in illusions. Its stock and trade are deceptive appearances.

Hegel deals with the puritanical dismissal of art by reminding readers of the role art plays in the self-disclosure of Spirit to itself. He argues that "just as little does art elude philosophical consideration by unbridled caprice. As has already been indicated, it is its true task to bring to consciousness the highest interests of the mind. Hence it follows at once with respect to the *content* that fine art cannot rove in the wildness of unfettered fancy" (XXII). That is, fine art is hardly a lightweight affair. Rather it is part and parcel of *the* central human drama. It is not a mere amusement; its true task is revealing our highest interests, a project of which no other is more serious, according to Hegel. This, of course, is not meant by Hegel to deny that some art is, in fact, amusing, but only to stress that art in its highest vocation—the sort of art that Hegel is most intent on analyzing—is part of the serious history of humanity.

Hegel parries the charge that fine art is suspect because it traffics in illusions in a way that is reminiscent of one of Aristotle's rebuttals of Plato. Hegel argues that

> art liberates the real import of appearances from the semblance and deception of this bad and fleeting world, and imparts to phenomenal semblances a higher reality, born of mind. The appearances of art, therefore, far from being mere semblances, have the higher reality and the more genuine existence in comparison with the realities of common life.
>
> Just as little can the representations of art be called a deceptive semblance in comparison with the representations of historical narrative, as if that had the more genuine truth. For history has not even immediate existence, but only the intellectual presentation of it, for the element of its portrayals, and its content remains burdened with the whole mass of contingent matter formed by common reality with its occurrences, complications, and individualities. But the work of art brings before us the eternal powers that hold dominion in history, without any such superfluity in the way of immediate presentation and its unstable semblances. (XIV)

That is, in the same way in which Aristotle claims that poetry was closer to philosophy than history, so Hegel asserts that art is more suited to getting at the essence of the historical process than historical inquiry is, since art cuts through the details to the heart of the matter. Art does not commerce in deceptive illusions but delivers higher truths, truths born of the mind, truths about Consciousness's journey to self-realization. Although working through appearances, art is capable of bringing us into contact with general (Hegel says eternal) features of events, whereas ordinary history confronts us with the clutter of messy, transient particularities.

Having defined his project and defended it, Hegel is prepared to get down to business, starting with the matter of defining art. Although he makes certain suggestions about the nature of art in the first chapter—implicitly classifying artworks as intentionally made, sensuous (or perceptible) things—the definition of art is directly engaged in the second chapter of the book.

Hegel begins, as most philosophers do, by complaining about previous theories, arguing that they have been either too general or too narrow. His own definition starts to take off in Section XXXI. Hegel reminds us that his subject is artistic beauty—fine art (recall that *kalon* can refer to either the beautiful or the fine). He has established that *art* is an intentionally made thing. So the next order of business is to parse the operative notion of beauty in the formula artistic *beauty*. That is, what essentially is beauty?

Hegel answers this question by citing the philosopher Aloys Hirt, and defines *beauty* as *perfection*. But what is perfection? Again alluding to Hirt, Hegel says the perfect is "that which is adequate to its aim" (XXXI). A steak knife that is sharp enough to cut through a piece of beef is adequate to its aim and is a perfect steak knife. So a beautiful artwork will be such that it is adequate to its aim.

But what is the aim of art? For Hegel, the aim of art is to present a certain content to the senses. So a beautiful artwork will be about something—will have content—that is given form in a manner adequate to its aim. Hegel says of art that it "involves in the first place a *content*, as, for instance, a particular feeling, situation, incident, action, individual, and secondly, the *mode* or *fashion* in which this content is embodied in a representation" (XXXI). So, for Hegel, the beautiful artwork is comprised of form and content, where the content is presented in a form adequate or suitable to it.

Here, the notion of form is akin to that which we find in expressions like the "human *form*." Thus, another way of getting at what Hegel is claiming is to say that the beautiful artwork is an intentionally made thing that possesses content—that is about something—that is *embodied sensuously* in a form adequate, or suitable, or appropriate to whatever it is about.[5] That the beautiful artwork is an intentionally made artifact distinguishes it from natural beauty. But what sort of artifact is it? One that is about something—that has content—where content is presented in a manner adequate, appropriate, or suitable to that content.

In medieval Catholicism, the house of the Lord was meant to draw our thoughts to heaven; thus, its vaulting ceilings beckon our eyes upward. The form of Gothic cathedrals—their architectural embodiment—is adequate to expressing this transcendent meaning, whereas a low ceiling would be an inappropriate choice. It

---

5. The idea of the beautiful as the appropriate, of course, returns us to one of the definitions canvassed in the *Hippias Major* by Socrates, which was eventually rejected.

would not advance the meaning the church aspires to project (indeed, it might even impede it), whereas the verticality of the Gothic nave reinforces the message of Christian doctrine that the building was intended to subserve.

For Hegel, the form of the work of art is suitable only when "so much ought to enter the work of art as belongs to the display, and, essentially, to the expression of that content and no other; for nothing must announce itself as otiose and superfluous" (XXXI). That is, the artwork should be an organic whole. Every element in the artwork should contribute to the expression of whatever the artwork is about. There should be nothing in the artwork that does not enhance the content of the work. If the work contains rhymes, they should not be merely ornamental; they should support the meaning of the poem, perhaps by accenting its key ideas.

In order to discharge the aim of displaying some content, the work must deploy the means at its disposal—its means of presentation (such as lines and colors, if it is a painting, or words and gestures, if it is a drama)—in a way that gets the content of the work across to the audience. That is, the form of the work of art must function in such a way that it presents its content effectively. Ideally, in order to achieve this, the artwork should contain only what is required to express or advance the content of the work.

This content can also be called the *significance* of the work or the principle of the *characteristic* of the work. These phrases are names for what the work is about. And, for Hegel, artworks necessarily have content. They are necessarily about something.

But, of course, if we are talking about artworks, which are intentionally made, *sensuous* objects, that content must be manifested somehow. It must have form (in the sense of the human form, i.e., perceptible form). And for the artwork to be beautiful, in terms of perfection, that form must be adequate to the content of the work. And that, too, is necessary for artistic beauty, that is, for something to be a work of fine art.

So, Hegel's definition of a work of fine art is

> X is a work of fine art if and only if (1) X is an intentionally made, (2) perceptible (sensuous) object, which (3) is about something (X has content), that (4) has a form (a form of embodiment) that is adequate or suitable or appropriate to its content.

Each of these conditions is individually necessary for something to count as a work of fine art, and together, they are jointly sufficient to grant a candidate for artistic status said status. That is, when all four conditions are met, that is enough to call the work a work of fine art (or beautiful art).

Consider Jacques-Louis David's *Oath of the Horatii*. Two male figures in Roman garb dominate the picture, which is meant to celebrate patriotic resolution. The two men and their swords form a virtual X on the picture plane which directs the viewer's eyes to precisely the point in the painting that marks the swearing of their patriotic oath—the most important element in the visual array—thereby reinforcing the content or theme of the work by means of its perceptually compelling design. This is one way in which the form of the painting is adequate to what it is about. But at the same time, the clear, solid structure of the design projects the qualities of clarity and firmness, echoing the resoluteness of the commitment of the Horatii—the feeling of their commitment resonating throughout the work. This, too, contributes to embodying the work in a form perfectly suited to its content.

Hegel says that "we find distinguished as the elements of the beautiful something inward, a content, and something outer which has that content as its significance; the inner shows itself in the outer and gives itself to be known by its means, inasmuch as the outer points away from itself to the inner" (XXXIII). That is, the work of art has a content—something inward, its significance, its meaning—which is embodied in something outer—its mode of presentation—which points to, or is about, or comments on, or is otherwise suitable to its content. The form of the work—its embodiment—makes the content (some idea) sensuously available to audiences. Music, architecture, sculpture, and painting make ideas immediately accessible to the senses through images that are adequate or not to the content. Poetry and literature do this through figurative language and the description of perceptible things, characters, and actions that call forth mental images which we scrutinize like inner pictures and which we also call images.

So far, the definition of fine art gives us a very abstract notion of what a work of fine art is. This definition could be satisfied by very trivial artworks, like the movie *The Hangover*. Certainly it has a form adequate to its (comic) content. But the definition doesn't tell us why art itself is important, nor does it instruct us in how to tell which works of fine art are the noteworthy ones. In order to learn that, we must attend to the works that answer humankind's need to produce art. And, of that need, Hegel writes:

> Art appears to arise from the higher impulse and to satisfy the higher needs, at times, even the highest, absolute need of man, being wedded to the religious interests of whole epochs and peoples and to their most universal intuitions respecting the world. . . .
>
> The universal and absolute need out of which art, on its formal side arises has its source in the fact that man is a *thinking* consciousness, i.e., that he draws out of himself and makes explicit *for himself,* that which he is. (XLVII–XLIX)

That is, the need for art is derived from our need to understand our own human nature, our need to be become conscious of our nature as Spirit. What makes certain works of art important, then, is that they are about Absolute Spirit or Consciousness. That is the content of noteworthy works of fine art. Art makes this content sensuously manifest. Indeed, noteworthy art is art in which the form of embodiment of the content is appropriate to what it is about, namely, Spirit.

> In art these sensuous shapes and sounds present themselves not simply for their own sake and for their immediate structure, but with affording in that shape satisfaction to higher spiritual interests, seeing that they are powerful to call forth a response and echo in the mind from the depths of consciousness. It is thus that, in art, the sensuous is *spiritualized*, i.e., the spiritual appears in sensuous shape. (LVIII)

Thus, important fine art, on Hegel's view, makes Spirit manifest to the senses by means of sensuous forms that are adequate to, supportive of, or which enhance its content, which, in the case of noteworthy art, is the nature of Consciousness itself as free.

For example, Shakespeare's *Romeo and Juliet* marks the emergence of the freedom of the individual from the domination of clan and tribe, since Romeo and Juliet choose to marry each other, rather than to bow to a choice dictated by their respective families. Romantic love, and its advocacy, in plays like Shakespeare's, celebrate individual free choice and thus the evolution of Spirit's emerging, concrete understanding of the scope of human freedom.

It is worth noting that Hegel's views contrast sharply with Kant's in several respects, including the following: (1) For Hegel, significant artistic beauty is not simply about feeling; it is not simply subjective. It has an objective content, namely, Absolute Spirit. (2) Artistic beauty is related to a determinate concept, the nature of consciousness; in this respect, engagement with art is more directly cognitive than what we find in Kant since, as in Aristotle's account, it is truth tracking. (3) Art is more important in Hegel than it is in Kant inasmuch as it is plays an indispensable role in the fulfillment of human destiny, its quest for self-knowledge. This places art alongside philosophy and religion in the category of humanity's highest endeavors.

The Philosophy of Art History

As we have seen, something is a noteworthy work of fine art only if (1) it is about spirit (or, its content is the nature of self-consciousness), which it (2) makes manifest or embodies in a form that is appropriate to it (spirit, self-consciousness). However, as discussed earlier, Hegel does not think that Consciousness comes to know its own nature all at once. It is a matter of unfolding—occurring in stages—over the course of human history.

Self-consciousness is a process. It takes time. Consciousness has many layers or aspects, and these must be unpacked gradually.[6] A perhaps useful analogy might

---

6. Narrative is the ideal form for doing this, as Hegel shows. Narrative is the best way to come to a self-understanding of ourselves as individuals; similarly, narrative is the best method for discovering the nature of the self-consciousness of the human race.

be to think of psychoanalysis, a narrative investigation into the self that can extend over years. Similarly, consciousness's-as-such interrogation of its depths takes millennia. It comprises the whole of human history up to Hegel's time before Spirit is in a position to understand itself fully and with total clarity. Hence, fine art, too, must mirror Consciousness's emerging self-understanding as it evolves.

That is, since spirit's self-understanding of itself changes over time—by becoming more and more refined—the specific content of art at each stage of the development of art changes. Thus, with each shift in Spirit's level of self-consciousness, the corresponding artistic forms of embodiment must alter in order to discover a form of presentation appropriate to the pertinent stage of self-consciousness. In this way, Hegel is able to explain the change of artistic styles from epoch to epoch. With each epoch, there is new content which, in turn, calls for the creation of new forms that will be adequate to the articulation of the new content.

Roughly speaking, humanity moves from sensation to conceptualization or intellect, beginning in the confusion and contingency of immediate awareness and sensation and arriving finally in the lucidity of pure thought. Art, in Hegel's narrative, will both mirror and enable this development, at least up until its last stage of evolution.

The evolution of art proceeds in step with the evolution of consciousness, mirroring it, while also drawing it onward. Moreover, as we have seen, on Hegel's account, Consciousness's conceptions of itself do not change helter-skelter. They have a destination—a path to self-consciousness, involving a more and more refined understanding of the nature of Spirit as freedom. This is a developmental process, akin to the growth of the infant into a child and then into an adult. Its stages of self-understanding correspond to the growth of human freedom. As consciousness achieves greater levels of freedom, this is reflected in the content and, consequently, the correlative forms of works of fine arts. Different historical epochs achieve different levels of freedom, and this is reflected in the fine art of the relevant epoch.

In his *Introductory Lectures on Aesthetics*, Hegel singles out three major stages in what we may call the philosophical history of *noteworthy*, fine art. These stages correlate with the three stages in the development of freedom that we discussed earlier (from one is free to some are free to all are free). These three stages of art history are, respectively, (1) the symbolic stage, (2) the classical stage, and (3) the romantic stage. With each of these stages, the content of consciousness mutates and, with these changes in content, the forms of artistic embodiment are transformed in a suitable fashion.

The earliest stage in Hegel's philosophical history of art is the symbolic stage which Hegel associates with the art of ancient China, India, Mesopotamia, and Egypt (CV α). At this point in human history, Spirit's understanding of itself is obscure. This obscurity is mirrored, for instance, in the form of its architecture. The pyramids supposedly express Spirit's understanding that it is majestic, even sublime; they communicate this through their monumental form. Yet this is not ultimately a completely satisfactory portrayal of spirit in sensuous form, since the pyramids give no sense of having an inside and, therefore, afford no intimation of the inwardness or interiority of spirit. Nevertheless, these structures are sublime, according to Hegel, since they strive to represent something that is unrepresentable (Spirit) by material means (like blocks of solid stone) that are not up to the task.

As noted previously, Spirit putatively attempts to work out its understanding of itself through its images of divinity. The medium of religion comprises the inward or mental images of the godlike as embraced by each successive civilization, and art, whose medium is sensation, brings this inward imagery outward, where it is available to perception. Symbolic art becomes the primary vehicle of religion in this initial period of history because, at this point in time, there is no theology to speak of.

At the symbolic stage of development, Spirit is uncertain of its relationship to the animal kingdom—uncertain of the significance of its own animal nature. For this reason, it represents itself in animal forms—as gods that are part human and part animal, like the Hindu monkey-god Hanuman or the falcon-headed Egyptian god Horus or the Great Sphinx at Giza (which is a human-headed lion). Hegel also interprets gods represented as distortions of the human form—such as the multiple arms (e.g., Shiva as Nataraja) and grotesqueries of Indian gods and goddesses (e.g., Kali/Durga)—as evidence of Spirit's extremely imperfect comprehension of its own nature, as is also the representation of divinity symbolically by means of eggs or lotus blossoms.

Classical art, the art of Greece and Rome, is the next major stage in the coevolution of art and spirit's self-consciousness (CVI β). As we have already seen, Spirit's understanding of the freedom that is its essence advances at this historical juncture.[7] This is reflected in classical art. As Hegel observes, Greek gods are represented in human form, thereby anthropomorphizing Spirit. This way of representing divinity evinces that Spirit has come to a better comprehension of itself. No longer is it symbolized by forms that are part animal and part human. Now the gods—like Zeus, Hera, Athena, Apollo, and others—are represented as fully human, thereby identifying the proper locus of Spirit in humankind.[8]

The art of the classical stage indicates that the human form is the proper object of reflection on which Spirit should now concentrate in its pursuit of

---

7. For Hegel, as one stage of history reaches its limit, the possibility of a new stage that will address that limitation opens up.

8. Hegel's treatment of the gods of classical art versus those of symbolic art indicates the often highly and suspiciously selective cast of Hegel's account. With respect to animalistic representations of the divine, Hegel appears to neglect Zeus's shape-shifting proclivities (into such things as bulls and swans), not to mention that classical mythology is populated by creatures such as centaurs and satyrs who were either gods, demigods, or descended from gods.

self-consciousness. By representing itself as human, Spirit acknowledges its biological nature at the same time that it ceases to conceive of itself in terms of animality, but instead becomes self-conscious of itself in terms of mind.

Moreover, the statues of the classical period are remarkable for their harmonious (idealizing) proportions, which Hegel takes to symbolize spirit's recognition of the unity of the human and the divine (the ideal) and, for that reason, as the physical form that corresponds to mind.

If architecture is the signature art of the symbolic stage of artistic development, sculpture performs that function in the classical stage. Furthermore, Hegel regards this transition as a gain in freedom inasmuch as sculpture is more free than architecture since it is, putatively, less subject to sheer natural forces, like gravity and solidity. That is, sculpture is less an affair of mechanics. In this way, sculpture, notably the eminently more malleable, harmonious sculpture of the classical stage, represents serene human nature (a.k.a. the divine) as extracted from the very nature that Mind/Spirit is in the process of conquering.

Nevertheless, although classical art overcomes some of the limitations of symbolic art, it has its own liabilities. Though it achieves the best—most perfect, most harmonious—manifestation of spirit possible in perceptible form, this is only the best of a critically limited thing. For, ultimately, spirit cannot be restricted to sensuous form. Not all the characteristics of spirit can be limned in terms of bodily characteristics. So, if spirit is going to discover an artistic form that better articulates it, it must go beyond the achievements of classical statuary, no matter how perfect its harmonious proportions appear.

So, just as some of the central problems of symbolic art were solved by classical art; likewise, the problems of classical art are addressed by the next period of artistic development, namely romantic art (CVII γ), The central problem of classical art, according to Hegel, is that it remains indissolubly wedded to the physical inasmuch as the gods are still conceived of in terms of the external form of the human body. But Spirit or Mind ultimately transcends the physical. And that thought only begins to be artistically articulated clearly with the onset of romantic art.

Specifically, romantic art begins with Christianity. Hegel maintains that

> now Christianity brings God before our intelligence *as spirit*, or *mind*—not as particularized individual spirit, but as absolute, in *spirit* and in truth. And for this reason Christianity retires from the *sensuousness* of imagination into intellectual inwardness, and makes this, not bodily shape, the medium and actual existence of its significance. (CVII)

That is, with Christianity comes the notion of God as a disembodied Consciousness, thereby disclosing the genuine nature of Spirit.

Christianity inaugurates the epoch of romantic art.[9] Its content, first and foremost, is the passion of Christ, his crucifixion and resurrection, where the resurrection especially symbolizes the transcendence of spirit over matter. Christ, God-incarnate, represents humanity as such, and the fact that he could transcend death promises that Spirit is not chained to the body—not only in the case of Christ, but for humans in general. That early romantic art took the incarnation and the passion of Jesus as its content is amply testified to by all those pictures of the birth of Jesus, his infancy in relation to his mother, the Madonna Mary, the stations of the cross, his execution, and his subsequent apotheosis. Christ's life and death function as an allegory of the triumph of spirit over physical existence. The task of romantic art would be to find a form of embodiment adequate to this conception of Spirit.

Thus, the history of art charts an itinerary from mirroring an originating stage of indeterminacy—of animism sunken in nature—to determinacy: to the transcendence of nature as encapsulated at first in the birth and death of Jesus.

Alongside the preceding story of the evolution of art, which has primarily emphasized the changing content of art through the ages, Hegel has a parallel story to tell about the evolution of art in terms of its various media (art *forms*).[10] Architecture is the exemplary medium of the symbolic stage of art. But it is not ultimately adequate as a perceptible vehicle for reflecting the true nature of Spirit, for it is involved too deeply with matter. Its principles are too mechanical and are subject inextricably to natural laws, such as gravity.

Classical art represents a correction and an improvement as a means for projecting Spirit. Of course, it also deals with matter, but it uses matter via sculpture to present the harmoniously proportioned human form in order to express something spiritual. Classical art, in this way, combines humanity with nature in a way that forges a reconciliation of the spiritual with the material. This is achieved by fusing the idealized human form with stone, thereby imprinting matter with Spirit.

The romantic arts, in turn, surpass architecture and sculpture by successively "dissolving" the material dimensions of artistic media. Whereas architecture and sculpture are three-dimensional, painting, a paradigmatic romantic art, is two-dimensional. Representational painting represents the three-dimensional world of matter in two dimensions, making the third dimension dependent on the viewer's imagination. The so-called illusionistic space of the picture plane is allegedly a literal departure from the material world, addressing the mind and,

---

9. In its relation to religion in the case of Christian art, the subject of art exceeds the externality of classical art and thus incorporates inwardness and feeling.

10. By explicating the nature of the various art forms, Hegel supplies his followers with the means to evaluate artworks. Artworks succeed if they realize the function of their art forms and fail otherwise.

thereby, engendering deeper contact with subjectivity. In this way, painting can putatively connect with inner feelings, such as serenity, as embodied, for example, in portraits of the baby Jesus embraced in the lap of his loving mother, Mary.

Music, as a primarily temporal art, is putatively even further "distanced" from the three-dimensional realm of matter. Although physically produced, Hegel does not believe this is relevant to comprehending it. Thus conceived as dematerialized, music allows the exploration of the realm of feelings—the pulse of our inner life—in terms of its rhythms of expansion and contraction, of ebb and flow, of tension and release, of gathering and dispersing, and so forth. However, insofar as music, especially pure orchestral music, is supposedly limited to the realm of feeling, it is inadequate to revealing the depths of Spirit fully insofar as Spirit is mind.

Like music, poetry is also allegedly dematerialized, but in virtue of language, it can plumb human subjectivity even more deeply than music. In the epoch of romantic art, tragedy is the paradigmatic form of poetry, modeled on the passion of Christ, but evolving in modern times with a focus on the suffering and passions of individuals, like Hamlet, whose exploration of feelings poetry is able to pursue with more penetration and perspicacity than music alone.

Of course, Hegel recognizes that tragedy was also a feature of Greek culture, but he distinguishes between the tragedies of the ancients and those of the modern romantic epoch. For whereas, on Hegel's view, the subject of ancient tragedy was the conflict of social forces—such as the clash between the claims of the tribe versus the claims of the state as exemplified by *Antigone*—the focus of modern tragedy is the feelings of individuals, specifically in terms of suffering.

Poetry is finally the emblematic art of the romantic epoch. Unlike sculpture and painting, it points to something not perceptual, not visualizable. Therefore, it points to the ultimate nature of spirit. Nevertheless, poetry is still tied to figurative expression. It still appeals to the sensuous, even if it is the sensuous (or imagistic) imagination. Thus, in this respect, poetry is finally limited in its capacity to adequately disclose the true nature of Consciousness.

Indeed, inasmuch as fine art, by definition, is an affair of embodying ideas in sensuous form, the possibility of its fully revealing the nature of Consciousness to itself was foreclosed, so to speak, in principle, from the get-go, insofar as spirit is irreducibly immaterial. However, that limitation only becomes evident in the course of the historical process with the plight of romantic art. Thus, Hegel concludes that in his own day, art has come to an end. It has taken its project as far as it can and must now turn over the task of clarifying the nature of Spirit to theology and philosophy.

The End of Art

In the very first chapter of his *Introductory Lectures on Aesthetics*, Hegel declares:

> In all these respects art is, and remains, for us, on the side of its highest destiny, a thing of the past. Herein it has further lost for us its genuine truth and life and rather is transferred into our ideas than asserts its former necessity or assumes its former place in reality. (XVIII)

That is, art in terms of its highest vocation—the revelation of the nature of consciousness to itself—is over, is a thing of the past. The reason for this is made clear as the book proceeds, arguing that the project of illuminating immaterial spirit by sensuous means is self-defeating in the long run, although it is only by charting the long run that this becomes clear, finally in the epoch of romantic art.

Hegel's point in introducing the end-of-art thesis in the first chapter of the book is methodological. Hegel believes that phenomena only become susceptible to philosophical analysis when they have come to an end. As he says in his *Philosophy of Right*, "Minerva spreads its wings at dusk," by which he means that we can only see the subject clearly when it is over, in the twilight of its heyday. It is for that reason that aesthetics is possible in Hegel's own day, since it is only in his own day that art has reached the end of its tenure as a mirror to mind. That is why, Hegel believes, that a "scientific" study of its nature—of course, as conducted by him—has only become possible in the first part of the nineteenth century.

Needless to say, Hegel is not saying that art ceased altogether to be made in the 1820s. In fact, probably more artworks have been created since Hegel declared the end of art than ever before. Rather, Hegel is saying that art in pursuit of its highest vocation is no longer feasible. Art has gone as far as it can, given the means at its disposal, to reveal the nature of Consciousness. As Hegel notes, "The form of art is enough to limit it to a restricted content" (XVI).

Why? Because spirit or mind has evolved an extremely abstract understanding of itself in modern times. Consider Kant's *Critique of Pure Reason*. Art is not up to delivering reflection on the nature of the mind of that level of generality, since among other things, it is locked into particularity. Isadora Duncan was famous for bragging that she intended to choreograph Kant's *Critique of Pure Reason*. She never did so and, according to Hegel, she never could have. For artworks are particular and concrete, and for that reason, not suitable for reflecting the abstract self-understanding that Spirit/Mind has evolved by the time of Kant and Hegel.

> The spirit of our modern world, or to come closer, of our religion and our intellectual culture, reveals itself beyond the stage at which art is the highest mode assumed by man's consciousness of the absolute. The peculiar mode to which artistic production and works of art belong no longer satisfies our supreme need. We are above the level at which works of art can be venerated as divine and actually worshipped; the

impression they make is of a more considerate kind, and the feelings which they stir within us require a higher test and a higher confirmation. Thought and reflection have taken flight above fine art. (XVI)

That is, consciousness has reached the stage of pure spirituality and abstractness. Yet art by its nature is connected to sensuous media. Consequently, it cannot fully reflect Spirit while at the same time remaining art. Spirit, in a manner of speaking, has gone to a "place" where art cannot follow. At an earlier stage of development, art could serve, along with religion and philosophy, to mirror Mind. Indeed, in the beginning, art had an edge in this regard since theology and philosophy were still in their nascent stages. But as Mind increasingly realizes itself as irreducibly immaterial spirit, art can no longer perform the service of articulating it, although religion and philosophy still can.[11] Thus, art drops out of the triad, leaving to religion (theology?) and the philosophy the highest vocation of humanity—coming to know its own nature.

Whither Art?

Although by Hegel's day, the project of art in terms of its highest vocation has ended, art continues to be created. This raises the question of the end of art—its role or purpose—after the *end of art*—that is after its world-historical role has been carried forward as far as possible. That is: What is the end (in terms of its purpose) of fine art in modern culture after fine art has reached the end (in terms of the culmination) of its historic project?

Throughout history, as we have seen, Hegel maintains that there is an opposition between sensuousness and Spirit, between the particular and the universal. However, in modern times, Hegel contends, this tension has become especially acute and disturbing. Hegel writes:

> These antitheses . . . have from all time and in manifold forms preoccupied and disquieted human consciousness, although it was modern culture that elaborated them most distinctly, and forced them up to the point of most unbending contradiction. Intellectual culture and the modern play of understanding create in man this contrast, which makes him an amphibious animal, inasmuch as it sets him to live in two contradictory worlds at once; so that even consciousness wanders back and forward in this contradiction, and, shuttlecocked from side to side, is unable to satisfy itself

---

11. However, religion, as it is practiced by the faithful, arguably also should defer to philosophy as the highest expression of self-consciousness's understanding of itself because that practice involves entertaining sensuous mental imagery. The theological element of religion, insofar as it is philosophical, may be another matter. But shouldn't Hegel concede the "end" of exoteric religious worship making a contribution to the refinement of the nature of self-consciousness?

as itself on the one side as on the other. For, on the one side, we see man a prisoner in common reality and earthly temporality, oppressed by want and poverty, hard driven by nature, entangled in matter, in sensuous aims and their enjoyments; on the other side, he exalts himself to external ideas, to a realm of thought and freedom, imposes himself as a *will* universal laws and attributions, strips the world of its living and flourishing reality and dissolves it into abstractions. . . . Such a discrepancy in life and modern culture and its understanding demand that the contradiction be resolved. (LXXIII)

It is the task of modern philosophy to reconcile this opposition—to reconcile the abstraction of contemporary intellectual life with the particularity of existence. Art, in turn, whose vocation remains the revelation of truth in sensuous form, must represent the preceding, philosophically reconciled antithesis. Moreover, since the revelation of truth in sensuous form has always been the essential role of art, the representation and exhibition of this philosophical reconciliation is an intrinsic purpose of art.

In Part II—"The End of Art," of chapter 3, Hegel takes up the issue of the end (the purpose) of art and rejects the usual suspects, including imitation, the purification of the emotions, instruction, improvement, profit, and fame. These are all aims that are extrinsic to the work of art as such, which aims as a matter of its essence at the revelation of truth by means of sensuous form. Thus, in the modern period, where philosophy reconciles the abstract with the particular, the role of art is to project that truth and, thereby, to participate in the reconciliation of the antithesis that disturbs modern culture.

The problem that art at the end of art addresses is how to live with the abstractions of spirit/reason in the world of the mundane existence. Specifically, how can the abstract idea of autonomy be reconciled with everyday life where autonomy is embodied in the ethos of particular cultures? Art can contribute to this reconciliation since, inasmuch as its medium is sensuous forms, it can embody abstract ideas of autonomy by representing the ethos of nations and peoples.

For example, Dutch art celebrates *their* ethos, *their* form of autonomy. Through the genre of the still life, Dutch painters seek to endow apparently trivial content—foodstuffs and kitchenware—with radiant human feeling. Their paintings from ordinary life are, in an important sense, celebrations of their way of life, their ethos, that is, their version of autonomy. It involves an affirmation of their comfortable, bourgeois *modus vivendi*. With its emphasis on the pleasures of the table, it expresses self-respect without vanity by exhibiting with pride the products of their own industry. The simplicity of their art exemplifies their thrift and their self-reliance, as does the genre of Dutch landscape painting whose ratio of earth to water recalls to mind their heroic seizure of much of their country quite literally from the sea. In these ways, Dutch painting functions as an externalized hallmark of bourgeois freedom of the Netherlandish variety—their variation on the autonomy of Spirit.

Fine art does not explore as deeply and as abstractly as philosophy does the nature of spirit, but it is not dispensable either, especially in modern culture, because it represents the reconciliation of the antithesis between the abstract and particular in a way not available to, for instance, philosophy. For, since it is perceptible, its sensuous materiality is able to address that part of our amphibian nature in a way philosophy doesn't.

Critical Questions for Hegel

Hegel's philosophy of art is a monumental endeavor. Needless to say, questions concerning his exegesis of the historical significance of art forms, genres, and particular works of art arise at every turn. His virtually allegorical glosses of the "meaning" of artistic media, like painting and music, seem particularly forced, tailored all too conveniently to suit Hegel's pageant of world history. But perhaps it is more philosophically productive to attend critically to some of the most abstract features of his theory rather than to dote on the specifics of Hegel's more fanciful interpretations.

Hegel's definition of art is at the heart of his philosophy. But is it convincing?

Fundamentally, Hegel maintains that something is a work of fine art if and only if (1) it has content and (2) it has a form of embodiment that is appropriate to its content. Its form of embodiment, in other words, is suitable to its content where its content is to be understood in terms of its meaning. The content condition and the form condition of this formula are each necessary requirements for art status, and together, they are jointly sufficient to count something as art. However, the theory is arguably too narrow insofar as it excludes many works that would normally be considered artworks.

Consider the content requirement. If content is a matter of meaning, surely there are artworks that are, in a manner of speaking, "beneath meaning." Think of artworks that are dedicated exclusively to the pleasurable stimulation of the senses—mere decorative art. Such art could be either visual or aural—pure orchestral music that just thrills one with its intricate sonic structure and ornamentation, but which advances no ideas; or, abstract visual designs that your eye enjoys viewing but which carry no message. Can Hegel deny that these are artworks properly so called? But that would appear to violate our normal usage of the concept of art, including our common understanding of the notion of the fine arts. Of course, Hegel acknowledges that there is decorative art. The question is whether his definition of art is consistent with his acknowledgment of decorative art.

There may also be reason to challenge Hegel's form-of-embodiment condition. In the twentieth century, a type of art appeared that has been referred to as the found object or the readymade. A famous example is *Fountain* by Marcel Duchamp. This is an ordinary urinal, turned upside down, perhaps to indicate that it is not in use, and signed R. Mutt. The presentation of this urinal as an artwork was intended to affront prevailing conceptions of art which Duchamp rejected. In other words, it possessed a meaning. But did it possess a form of embodiment appropriate to that meaning? Wasn't its form precisely the form of an ordinary urinal—a form, moreover, adequate to the usual function of such devices—rather than a form with anything remotely connected to Duchamp's intended meaning? Duchamp used it for his own polemical purposes, but did his repurposing of the urinal literally change its form? If anything, wasn't it the contextual features surrounding Duchamp's actions that gave *Fountain* its significance rather than the physical form of the object?

Another readymade proffered by Duchamp was an ordinary metal canine grooming comb. This rather dull-looking object had exactly the form required to clean the hair on the back of a dog. But like *Fountain*, it was also meant to throw down the gauntlet to its contemporary art world. Yet in what way could its specific form of embodiment be said to articulate that meaning? Indeed, isn't the point of the readymade that the relation between the meaning of a readymade and its form is arbitrary?

The Hegelian, here, might be tempted to say that found objects are a category of art that appeared only after Hegel's theorizing and that were beyond his ken. True enough. However, insofar as Hegel's definition is apparently intended to capture the eternal essence of art, that response is not available to him. Hegel may deny that the works in question are artworks, but that would seem to fly in the face of more than a century of art history. Isn't the record settled on the matter of Duchamp's place in the canon?

Consequently, the burden of proof belongs to those descendants of Hegel who wish to defend each of his requirements for art's status. One problem with those conditions is that they are not inclusive enough. The formula excludes putative artworks without meaning, on the one hand, and artworks with meaning but without a unique form of embodiment, on the other hand. These apparent shortcomings need to be repaired by aspiring Hegelians.

Not only are these conditions too exclusive. Conjoined, they are too inclusive. For example, many commercial advertisements will satisfy Hegel's formula, such as the breathlessly paced, sonorously narrated, and seductively photographed videos of high-performance, luxury vehicles that nowadays are screened in many cinemas before the featured presentations. Hegel, of course, can deny that these count as important art. But how can he deny that they are fine art? Their form of embodiment—like the form of the automobiles they hawk—suits their message.

The content condition and the form condition together do not appear to be jointly sufficient to exile such candidates from the order of art. If one is tempted to be Hegelian in this matter, one needs to address this problem.

A second fundamental tenet of Hegel's approach is the end-of-art thesis. For Hegel, art reflects the spirit of its age. As human consciousness or spirit progresses—becomes more and more aware of its own nature—fine art reflects this new content (this emerging level of greater self-awareness) by developing new artistic forms of embodiment. Art forms, like opera, emerge that celebrate the feelings of the individual. However, this process of development supposedly reaches a limit with the romantic art of Hegel's own day, because consciousness allegedly becomes too abstract to be projected by embodiments in sensuous forms. How would one translate Kant's theory of mind into pictures—even word pictures? Thus, Hegel contends that art must relinquish its highest vocation and turn over the task of articulating spirit's self-consciousness to theology and philosophy.

But might not certain types of art that arose after Hegel's death complicate this diagnosis? With respect to painting, the twentieth century saw the birth of abstract art—paintings by artists like Hilma af Klint, Wassily Kandinsky, Kazimir Malevich, and Piet Mondrian, who, in different ways, aspired to discover forms capable of embodying the absolute. Perhaps, each failed in his/her effort. But their failures do not show that abstract art must be limited in the way that the representational art that Hegel knew about was putatively limited.

Another art form scarcely on Hegel's radar screen was the novel. In the twentieth century, a prominent number of novelists, like Robert Musil and Thomas Mann (and dramatists like Samuel Beckett), took a philosophical turn. Might not novels and plays of this sort have the resources to continue the pursuit of the highest vocation of art?

A work like Jean-Paul Sartre's *Nausea* presents a conception of human freedom. It articulates a view of freedom that is parallel to the views that Sartre propounds in his more philosophical writings, such as *The Transcendence of the Ego* and *Being and Nothingness*. Indeed, Sartre was familiar with some of Hegel's writing. Moreover, Sartre's emphasis on freedom is very Hegelian, as is Sartre's conviction that it is the nature of consciousness to be free. Why isn't the philosophical novel a counterexample to Hegel's end-of-art thesis?

Again, Hegelians cannot respond that the philosophical novel was beyond his purview, since he barely contemplated the novel in his account of the march of art history. For, the end-of-art history was not for Hegel a mere historical observation; it was intended to obtain necessarily. Moreover, shouldn't it have been obvious that this was possible even in Hegel's own day since literature trades in words, and, therefore, it always had the capacity to express abstract ideas? That is, works like Sartre's were not utterly unimaginable even in Hegel's time.

Concluding Observations

Few philosophies of art are as totalizing as Hegel's. Nor do many grant art as integral and as important a role in the unfolding of human history. Of course, a great deal of what Hegel says about art depends on accepting his conception of human history which—maybe, it goes without saying—is highly controversial, especially in light of its progressive, inevitable, unidirectional, altogether-too-neat picture of human development toward greater and greater levels of freedom, not to mention his commitment to philosophical Idealism. But despite Hegel's metaphysical excesses, much of the approach to art history that Hegel put into practice has had an abiding influence on the way in which the history of fine art is still studied.

That is, much art history today is conducted in an effort to discover what art reveals about the society that produces it. Of course, we do not align those societies in a sweeping historical trajectory devoted to elaborating a grand unifying theme like freedom. But we do frequently take art to be evidence of the ethos of nations. Indeed, we often regard our own art as a mirror to our reigning values and interests. That is, we continue to decipher art in an effort to discern who we are. In that respect, we remain Hegelian.

Bibliography

The translation used in this chapter is G. W. F. Hegel's *Introductory Lectures on Aesthetics*, edited by Michael Inwood and translated by Bernard Bosanquet (Penguin, 1993).

Bungay, Stephen. *Beauty and Truth.* Oxford: Clarendon Press, 1987.
Guyer, Paul. *A History of Modern Aesthetics.* Cambridge: Cambridge University Press, 2014.
Hegel, G. W. F. *Aesthetics: Lectures on Fine Art.* Translated by T. M. Knox. 2 vols. Oxford: Clarendon Press, 1975.
Houlgate, Stephen, ed. *Hegel and the Arts.* Evanston, IL: Northwestern University Press, 2007.
Inwood, Michael. "Hegel." In *The Routledge Companion to Aesthetics*, edited by Berys Gaut and Dominic McIver Lopes, 71–82. London: Routledge, 2005.
Kaminiski, Jack. *Hegel on Art.* Albany: State University of New York Press, 1962.
Pippin, Robert. *After the Beautiful.* Chicago: University of Chicago Press, 2013.
Rutter, Benjamin. *Hegel and the Modern Arts.* Cambridge: Cambridge University Press, 2010.
Wicks, Robert. "Hegel's Aesthetics: An Overview." In *Cambridge Companion to Hegel*, edited by Fred Beiser, 348–77. Cambridge: Cambridge University Press, 1993.

CHAPTER 7

Arthur Schopenhauer's *The World As Will and Representation*

Arthur Schopenhauer (1788–1860) was born in Danzig (now Gdansk) to a prosperous German family. Educated initially for a life in business like his father's—a career not to Arthur's taste—Schopenhauer was freed to pursue other interests after his father's suicide in 1805. Studying at Gottingen and then Berlin, Schopenhauer completed his doctoral dissertation—"On the Fourfold Root of Sufficient Reason"—in 1812. Although he tried his hand at teaching, he was not successful in it. He regarded Hegel as his great rival and scheduled his classes at the same time Hegel did. But his lecture hall remained empty, while Hegel's was full. Nevertheless, Schopenhauer's inheritance was large enough so that he could retire from teaching and no longer work for a living.

In 1818, he published the first volume of his pessimistic masterwork, *The World As Will and Representation*. It was not an immediate success; however, after 1850, the book began to be widely read, not only because many regarded it as a user-friendly introduction to Kant, which was not exactly correct, but also because of its high literary quality. Schopenhauer is undeniably an excellent writer, one whose resounding rhetoric often tends to persuade more with sound than sense, which is probably a major reason for the continuing popularity of his philosophy. He was also an important influence on the composer Richard Wagner and on the young Friedrich Nietzsche.[1]

Compared to most, Schopenhauer led an eminently comfortable life. He rose in the morning to a large breakfast, read his favorite English newspapers at his club, where he enjoyed lunch and conversation with friends, took a long walk in the afternoon, had a sizable dinner, and then read Hindu and Buddhist texts before going to sleep. His was an extremely agreeable life replete with full meals, good

---

1. Although Nietzsche initially was impressed by Schopenhauer's philosophy, he eventually rejected it, including Schopenhauer's aesthetics. For whereas Schopenhauer ultimately saw art as a means of escaping life, Nietzsche came to endorse the view that art should help us engage it. Nietzsche's overall perspective was life-affirming. He eschewed the notion that art should be detached or disinterested, a refuge from living, and he, Nietzsche, even approved of what he regarded as the illusionistic dimension of art insofar as it contributed to enhancing our ability to persist. In terms of this book, Nietzsche is a heteronomist as opposed to someone like Schopenhauer who is an arch-autonomist. For Nietzsche, art is the great stimulant of life; it is not an escape from it (*Twilight of the Idols*, 24).

conversation, and constant access to art. Though unlucky in love and embittered over being eclipsed in reputation by Hegel, Schopenhauer's own experience of suffering hardly seems commensurate with the dour and pessimistic view of human life that he is notorious for propounding, notably in *The World As Will and Representation*. Personally, confronting little that any of us would count as extraordinary hardship, Schopenhauer argued that ours is the worst possible existence, stretched on a rack of unrelenting pain, unfulfilled desire, and boredom. Since these convictions seem scarcely motivated by Schopenhauer's personal experiences, it is to his metaphysics that we must turn for an account of his deep pessimism—his view of existence as perpetual suffering, relieved only on occasion for many of us by aesthetic experience and, for the very few, by the life of ascetic renunciation.

Schopenhauer's Metaphysics

For Schopenhauer, the philosophies of Kant and Plato, along with various Hindu and Buddhist writings, provide major sources of inspiration. Though critical of many of the details of Kant's philosophy, Schopenhauer accepts Kant's distinction between the phenomenal and the noumenal and uses it as the foundation of his own philosophical system. That is, for Schopenhauer, the world can be comprehended under two aspects: the way it appears to us (the phenomenal aspect) and the way the world is in itself (the noumenal aspect). The world as it appears to us is the world as idea or representation; the world as it is in itself is the world as will. Just as we may perceive the well-known, reversible duck-rabbit figure as either a duck or a rabbit, so we may comprehend the world either as representation or as will. Let us take up these aspects one at a time.

What is it to comprehend the world as representation? It is to encounter the world, due to the structure of the human mind, in terms of certain categories, namely: the categories of space, time, and causality (which Schopenhauer derives from Kant) and the category of the subject-object relation (which Schopenhauer introduces to supplement Kant's inventory).[2] Schopenhauer calls these categories—these mental filters—the principle of sufficient reason. Because the mind is structured in terms of these categories, all ordinary experience, and ordinary knowing falls under them and is organized by them.

The mind, so to speak, structures experience in terms of these categories insofar as it only accepts as intelligible input that which is amenable to these categories. Thus, in any experience, we organize the objects that we encounter in terms of space and time—we place them in space and time—and we see them as standing

---

2. This feature of experience had already been introduced by Karl Leonhard Reinhold in his 1789 treatise *New Theory of the Human Faculty of Representation* which Schopenhauer may have read.

in causal relations to each other and also to us (where we fall under the category of the subject, and they fall into the category of object). All ordinary experience is structured in terms of these categories. They are the categories in accordance with which we ordinarily cognize or come to know the world. Anything that eludes these filters—that fails to fall into these categories—would not be cognizable—not be knowable or capable of being experienced—in the ordinary sense (which includes scientific knowledge).

Why are these categories called the principle of sufficient reason? Because these categories supply the basic reasons or answers that we have to the questions that we ask about the objects of ordinary experience, such as "Where are they?" (space), "When are they?" (time), and "Why or wherefore are they?" (causality). It is because our minds organize or construct the world as representation in terms of these categories; moreover, that ordinary experience is of a plurality of individual things, separated in space and time, and as causes as distinct from effects and subjects as distinct from objects. Thus, the world as representation is governed by the principle of individuation (the *principium individuationis*); that is, in ordinary experience, phenomena appear to us as individual things—the horse over there, the tree next to me, the stone that crashes through the window.

The phenomenal world (the world of phenomena) is the world as representation, a world experienced as composed of individual things due to the fact that our minds are structured in terms of the principle of sufficient reason. It is the world as it is familiar to all of us. But, like Kant, Schopenhauer is not convinced that this is the whole story. The world as representation is the world as it appears to us. But how is the world in itself—apart from cognition in terms of the principle of sufficient reason? We say that the mind constructs the world in virtue of the aforesaid categories. But from what or out of what is the mind constructing this world? On what are these categories operating? What is the input that they are organizing? If these categories are being applied, it must be the case that they are being applied to something. Therefore, there must be a way the world is in itself, a way apart from the manner in which our experience of it structures it categorically.

Schopenhauer, along with Kant, thinks of this as the noumenal aspect of the world, in contrast to the phenomenal aspect—that is, in contrast to the world as it appears to us due to the nature of our minds. For Kant, however, although we can know that there is this noumenal aspect to the world—that there is a way the world is in itself—we can know nothing specific about it. Why not? Because to know, in the ordinary sense, about the content of the noumenal realm would be to apply our categories of understanding—the principle of sufficient reason—to noumena in the way we treat phenomena. But if we proceed in that fashion, we will no longer be talking about the noumenal realm but about the phenomenal realm—the world as it appears to us given the structure of our minds.

If to know is to apply the principle of sufficient reason, then we cannot cognize the noumenal realm, since, by definition, the noumenal realm is that which is inaccessible to the relevant categories. If anything is susceptible to cognition, understood in terms of the categories, then it is phenomena, not noumena. Consequently, for Kant, apart from knowing that there is something in itself, nothing else can be said of it.

Subsequent philosophers, including Schopenhauer, found this conclusion frustrating. As we saw with Hegel, there is nothing more effective for provoking the philosophical imagination than telling a philosopher that something is impossible. Thus, Schopenhauer set out to discover a means for knowing about the way the world is in itself that could circumvent the epistemological obstacles that Kant had identified.

In a nutshell, Schopenhauer's challenge was this: all ordinary knowledge is connected to the categories. These categories individuate things in space and time and organize them in causal relations. Presumably, the way the world is in itself might not be like this—it might not be comprised of things that are individuated in space and time and connected causally. Perhaps the world in itself exists in some non-plural state, a state in which objects are not distinct from each other or from subjects, nor are causes and effects independent existents. But since space, time, and causality are our categories of knowledge—because anything we can be said to know must be cognized on their terms—how can we know anything about a realm where these categories are necessarily inapplicable?

Clearly, an important presupposition here is that the limits of our knowledge are coextensive with what is cognizable in terms of the categories. But if there is some sort of knowledge that is independent of the categories, then that might open up the possibility that that sort of knowledge can be had of the way the world is in itself. This is the key to Schopenhauer's solution of the Kantian problematic. Schopenhauer agrees that we organize and know of external experience—our experience of phenomena, of the world outside us—in terms of the categories. But there is another dimension of experience, an inner dimension, and our knowledge of this inner dimension does not seem organized in terms of the principle of sufficient reason.

When we experience ourselves, so to say, from the inside, our experience is not shaped by the categories. I do not experience my inner self as located in space, nor does the subject-object relation appropriately describe self-consciousness. As we experience ourselves inwardly, subject and object are one; we are not objects to ourselves as subjects. Nor are our motives experienced as alien causes. So, to an appreciable extent, our experience of ourselves falls outside the principle of sufficient reason. When we know ourselves from the inside, the principle of sufficient reason is far from fully operational.

But this then implies that we do have a degree of access to something outside the phenomenal—to something apart from the world as representation. We have access to ourselves from the inside, and this experience and knowledge appear in important ways to lie outside the categories (of space, causality, and the subject-object relation, though arguably not time). That is, we have access to the things in themselves—albeit limited access—just because we are, in virtue of our inner lives, inhabitants of the world in itself, the world outside the categories. We can know about the world in itself because, in part, we live there—or, more technically, because we are noumenal ourselves.[3]

That is, ordinary knowledge of what we experience as outside ourselves—representational knowledge—is governed by the principle of sufficient reason. But there is another kind of knowledge, the knowledge to be had from the inside of ourselves. This knowledge is not altogether mediated by the principle of sufficient reason. We know ourselves inwardly through direct acquaintance. And to the extent that this self-knowledge by direct acquaintance is not exclusively governed by the categories, we can have some knowledge of the way the world is in itself. Furthermore, Schopenhauer suggests, we can use this epistemic foothold in the noumenal realm to extrapolate generalizations about the world in itself. That is, we can extrapolate from what we discover about ourselves through introspection in order to say something about the nature of the world in itself, since, again, we are directly acquainted with it through self-consciousness.

Schopenhauer concedes that we cannot be absolutely certain that what we extrapolate about the nature of the world in itself from our inner experience of ourselves is a fully reliable guide to the world in itself, but he maintains that it is the best (perhaps it is the only) way that we can hope to learn anything about the world in itself. Schopenhauer's intellectual honesty here is certainly admirable, but given the confident tone in which he goes on to characterize the world in itself, one wonders whether he has not vastly overestimated what one could be entitled to say of the entire noumenal world on the basis of such a small sample of it, notably, our own self-consciousness.

Nevertheless, Schopenhauer plunges ahead with his program. Encouraging us to introspect along with him, he bids us to ask ourselves: What is the nature of our inner life? What is distinctive about it? What are our essential inner features? For if we can answer these questions, we can, he believes (probably with insufficient warrant), hypothesize fruitfully that those are also essential features, across the board, of the world in itself.

So, looking inward, what do we find? Among other things, that we control our bodies. What does this tell us about what are we? In a word, Schopenhauer says "will"—not just the will to move, but in moving the will to live, to expand ourselves, to preserve ourselves, to appropriate things, to forestall our own deterioration and

---

3. Of course, in the third section of his *Groundwork of the Metaphysics of Morals*, Kant also points out that we have internal insight into the true nature of ourselves, but he identifies that true nature as reason—quite a different finding than Schopenhauer's, as we'll soon see.

dissolution, to keep ourselves intact, and to multiply.[4] Our inner life shows itself to be involved in incessant striving to acquire what we need to continue to go on, and then to acquire ever more in order to augment our dominion.

Reflecting on the only specimen of the world in itself to which we have access—namely ourselves—Schopenhauer invites us to conjecture that the world in itself is *will*: the will to be, the will to life, the will to self-preservation and expansion, a sort of cosmic life force, which, moreover, is indivisible since it is not susceptible to the principle of sufficient reason (which accounts for the division of things into separate entities).

The world in itself is will. Furthermore, since the world in itself is not plural, not divided—since it is all will—and since it is the world in itself that provides the necessary ground for everything that appears in the world as representation, we can hypothesize that everything—every individual thing—has an aspect of will. Here Schopenhauer is not only thinking of living things, such as plants, animals, and people, but of inanimate things as well, such as rocks.[5]

For example, look at the suspension bridge resisting, as we are wont to say, the buffets of the hurricane; it resists breaking apart; it holds together, "struggling" to maintain itself, attempting to preserve its integrity. In this regard, it manifests the will to self-preservation. Notice how easily we apply volitional language to inanimate objects, like bridges, walls, and even riverbanks. For Schopenhauer (though perhaps not for all of the rest of us), these terms—*resisting, holding, struggling, attempting*—are not merely metaphors. Thus, on the basis of such thinking, including the tendency of things to remain intact, he concludes that everything in the world as representation—every individual thing—is a manifestation of will.

What is the relation of the world as representation—the world of individual things—and the world as will—the world of relentless, indivisible striving? For Schopenhauer, each thing that appears to us phenomenally is an objectification of will. That is, every individual object that appears to us is, at ground, a configuration or objectification of will, a coalescence of will predicated on preserving itself. Here a simile may be useful: each individual thing that appears to us is like a temporary wave on the surface of the ocean of will, gathering itself momentarily together into a temporary form, and striving to sustain its integrity, before eventually dissolving and reuniting with the ocean of indivisible will, of which it is only a transitory manifestation.

These objectifications of will, moreover, come in different grades. The quotient of will in a stone is less than the quotient of will in an animal, which, in turn, is less than the will objectified in a human being. Higher grades of will involve greater

---

4. The association of the will with preservation and expansion perhaps suggests the influence of Spinoza.

5. Although Schopenhauer starts with the conjecture that will is a distinctive feature of consciousness, it turns out that it is a feature of everything.

amounts of will, more complexly organized. However, by taking the appearance of individual things, these objectifications of will must ultimately be thought of as illusions. The world as representation is a veil—Schopenhauer refers to it in the Hindu idiom of Maya—since it is not the way the world is in itself. In itself, the world must be conceived of as unitary willing, the pure force of striving. The principle of individuation that governs the world as representation is finally an illusion arising from the objectification or expression of different grades of the indissoluble world-will that constitutes the very nature of the world in itself.

Schopenhauer's Pessimism

So far, Schopenhauer's analysis has yielded a view of reality as possessing two aspects: the world as representation and the world as will. But, as yet, we have not encountered Schopenhauer's vaunted pessimism. How does that enter the picture? In short, Schopenhauer believes that pessimism follows from an analysis of what is involved in willing as such. He writes:

> All willing springs from lack, from deficiency, and thus from suffering. Fulfillment brings this to an end; yet for one wish that is fulfilled there remain at least ten that are denied. Further, desiring lasts a long time, demands and requests go on to infinity; fulfillment is short and meted out sparingly. But even the final satisfaction itself is only apparent; the wish fulfilled at once makes way for a new one; the former is a known delusion, the latter a delusion not as yet known. No attained object of willing can give a satisfaction that lasts and no longer declines; but it is always like the alms thrown to a beggar, which reprieves him today so that his misery may be prolonged till tomorrow. Therefore, so long as our consciousness is filled by our will, so long as we are given up to the throng of desires with its constant hopes and fears, so long as we are the subject of willing, we never obtain lasting happiness or peace. Essentially, it is all the same whether we pursue or flee, fear harm or aspire to enjoyment; care for the constantly demanding will, no matter in what form, continually fills and moves consciousness, but without peace of calm, true well-being is utterly impossible. Thus, the subject of willing is constantly lying on the revolving wheel of Ixion is always drawing water in the sieve of the Danaids, and is the eternally thirsting Tantalus. (Section 38)[6]

Through introspection, Schopenhauer believes (perhaps overconfidently) that we can discover the nature of the world in itself. It is will. Now, by further introspection and analysis, Schopenhauer encourages us to ask, "What is it to will?" (at least, for individual beings). To will, he argues, is to desire. To desire, in turn, is to be conscious of a lack or a privation, the object of desire. But consciousness of

---

6. All quotations are from the edition of *The World As Will and Representation* cited in the Bibliography.

a lack is painful; it involves suffering. Therefore, all desire is a form of suffering. It is our essential nature to desire inasmuch as we are essentially creatures of will. Therefore, desire saturates every moment of our life. Therefore, our life, through and through, is bound up with suffering.

Moreover, through reflection on our inner nature, we can gain insight into the nature of reality in itself. Therefore, the world in itself is ultimately an ordeal of suffering. That much follows from the presupposition that the world as will is one of ceaseless striving (of ceaseless desire). Furthermore, since we are contemplating it from outside the protocols of the principle of sufficient reason, this relentless, indivisible striving and suffering is not explicable; since it cannot be rationalized in terms of the principle of causality, the world as will has no cause. Suffering is the nature of the world in itself insofar as it is an incessant process of inexplicable (and, therefore, senseless, meaningless) striving.

Suffering is a virtually inexpungible curse on human life. Why? Human life is a life of desiring. Desires are either fulfilled or they go unfulfilled. If they are not fulfilled, we continue to endure pain. If they are fulfilled, satisfaction is fleeting; it lasts for but a moment and is soon followed by more rampaging desires and, therefore, more pain. Desires have a tendency to give birth to more desires, more desires than can ever be quenched, and even when desires are momentarily met, the pleasure of fulfillment (if it is not immediately disappointing) is small in comparison to the amount of pain suffered in the antecedent interval of time in which we anticipate the realization of our desires. Think of the child who awaits her Christmas presents for months (an interval of pain, by definition, according to Schopenhauer) and then plays with her new doll for a few minutes before lurching toward her next gift.

Moreover, the cessation of desire, if it ever occurs, is most likely to give rise to a state of boredom, itself an unhappy experience, which, in turn, prompts the production of new desires (including artificial ones, such as the craving after fashion) and, of course, these new desires bring with them more pain. Desire, pain, boredom, pain, more desire, more pain—human life is an inescapable circle of suffering. We are like rats on a treadmill, constantly striving, but always finding ourselves in the same place, the place of pain.

It is noteworthy that Schopenhauer attempts to convince us of our sorrowful plight primarily by deduction, rather than by an empirical review of all the horrible features of human existence (from war, famine, and earthquakes to competition, envy, and hatred). However, Schopenhauer's argument may not be as compelling as it appears at first glance.

There may be several gaps in the deduction. For example, Schopenhauer connects desire with privation; but surely we can desire things that we do not lack: I may desire my wife, but I may be already happily married. Likewise, Schopenhauer associates desire with pain. But, in ordinary language, desire need not be painful; it may be a source of pleasure.[7] Sometimes we prolong the consummation of desire just because it is pleasurable. Desire is only always painful under a technical definition, such as Schopenhauer's, which stipulates that any desire, any consciousness of a lack, is painful. Thus, Schopenhauer's conclusion that all is suffering because desire is ever present may ride on an equivocation: the pain and suffering that Schopenhauer invariably associates with desire may be merely stipulative and, consequently, should not be regarded as a necessary, unpleasant concomitant of all desire in the ordinary sense. For example, tonight I may have two desires—to see a movie or a play. If I choose the movie, one would not ordinarily say that I was in pain. To say that I am in pain, in normal circumstances, would be a very strained way of speaking.

Furthermore, although Schopenhauer correctly observes that desiring is a continuing feature of human life—since we rarely cease desiring—he forgets that there is a difference between the fact that the life of desire does not cease and the claim that desires (specific desires) are never satisfied. Although I will be thirsty again tomorrow, my thirst right now may be sated agreeably with a cool beer. For these and other reasons, Schopenhauer's argument may not be as conclusive as he presumes.

Nevertheless, even if human life is not as miserable as Schopenhauer contends, a reasonable case might still be made that things are pretty bad. And whether human life is consummately deplorable, as Schopenhauer alleges, or merely pretty bad, it raises the unavoidable question of whether there can be relief from all the suffering—solace from all the senseless and painful striving. To this end, Schopenhauer makes two suggestions: that life can be palliated, at least temporarily, through aesthetic experience; and that entire lives, albeit the lives of the very few, can be substantially ameliorated through the path of ascetic renunciation. Since the life of renunciation is available to almost no one, let us turn to the way in which aesthetic experience can afford a respite from our misery.

Schopenhauer's Aesthetics

Since ascetic renunciation is such a demanding discipline, aesthetic experience is, for most of us, our primary avenue of release from the wheel of striving. Moreover, since art makes aesthetic experience particularly accessible, art is of singular importance in Schopenhauer's philosophical system. Perhaps no other major philosopher accords art as high a status as Schopenhauer does. For him, art is nothing less than a source of salvation, albeit temporary.

How can art perform this function? According to Schopenhauer, although ordinary knowledge is in the service of the will, there is nevertheless another kind

---

7. Perhaps Schopenhauer might have realized that had he not been so unlucky in love.

of knowledge that can release us from our implacable striving. This is knowledge of Platonic Ideas. Since Platonic Ideas exist timelessly, if we sink ourselves into the contemplation of them to the point where they fully occupy our consciousness, then we will lose ourselves in these Platonic Ideas, forget our individuality, and—like the Platonic Ideas that occupy our minds—transcend the bonds of time. Such aesthetic experiences can occur in response to natural beauty, but works of art are particularly effective conveyors of Platonic Ideas and, for that reason, they afford the opportunity to escape the principle of sufficient reason and the principle of individuation. Illuminating this process with respect to natural beauty, Schopenhauer writes:

> Raised up by the power of the mind, we relinquish the ordinary way of considering things, and cease to follow merely their relations to one another, whose final goal is always the relation to our own will. Thus, we no longer consider the where, the when, the why, and the whither in things, but simply and solely the what. Further, we do not let abstract thought, the concepts of reason, take possession of our consciousness, but instead of all this, devote the whole power of our mind to perception, sink ourselves completely therein, and let our whole consciousness be filled by the calm contemplation of the natural object, a crag, a building, or anything else. We lose ourselves entirely in this object, to use a pregnant expression; in other words, we forget our individuality, our will, and continue to exist as pure subject, as clear mirror of the object, so that it is as though the object alone existed without anyone to perceive it, and thus we are no longer able to separate the perceiver from the perception, but the two have become one, since the entire consciousness is filled and occupied by a single image of perception. If, therefore, the object has to such an extent passed out of all relation to the will, what is thus known is no longer the individual thing as such but, the [Platonic] Idea, the eternal form, the immediate objectivity of the will at this grade. Thus, at the same time, the person who is involved in this perception is no longer an individual, for in such a perception the individual has lost himself; he is *pure* will-less, painless, timeless *subject of knowledge*. (Section 34)

The event described here has two sides: the side of the object, the Platonic Idea, and the side of the subject, the pure, will-less subject of knowledge. The Platonic Idea is not the idea of an individual thing, like a rose, but is rather an idea of "roseness." Platonic Ideas are said to have greater objectivity than ideas of individual things because they are clearer manifestations (objectifications or expressions) of will than are individual things. They are also alleged to stand outside the framework of the principle of sufficient reason since Platonic Ideas—unlike individual roses—do not inhabit a specific place or time. Rather, they are akin to the idea of a species and, like the species "rose," they exist in no one space or time. Nor can the idea of a species enter into causal relations; "roseness" is neither a cause nor an effect. So, the knowing subject, by turning his or her consciousness over to the Platonic Idea, becomes like it, a veritable mirror image, thereby exiting the principle of sufficient reason and its service to striving.

Our encounter with the Platonic object, for Schopenhauer, is a matter of perception, not conceptualization. Platonic Ideas, for him, are like images, not concepts.

The subject may arrive at this state through two routes: the object, whether a work of art or a particularly exemplary instance of some natural species, may arrest me perceptually in a strikingly compelling way that suddenly puts this series of events in motion; or, as a result of my putting myself in a certain contemplative attitude, an aesthetic attitude, the object comes to fill my consciousness entirely. Then I lose myself in the object; I sink myself into it perceptually; I open myself fully to the object and effectively merge with it.

But since my object of attention here is a Platonic Idea, and since a Platonic Idea stands outside of space, time, and causality, the subject takes on this aspect of the Platonic Idea; and as that happens, the division between the subject and the object dissolves. I leave my individual identity behind, along with the rest of the framework of the principle of sufficient reason and, in shedding my individual identity, I transcend my individual will, becoming what Schopenhauer calls a pure will-less, timeless subject of knowledge. Through contemplating the Platonic Idea and fusing with it, I enjoy a kind of knowledge independent of the principle of sufficient reason, which framework, of course, serves the designs of the individual will. Thus, knowledge of the Platonic Idea releases me from the realm of individual willing and striving.

For Schopenhauer, there are different modes of knowledge. Ordinary knowledge is born of the needs of the will; it is governed by the principle of sufficient reason. Science is the systematization of this kind of knowledge. But there is also knowledge of Platonic Ideas. This can be had from nature, but for most of us, it is more readily available from art. But how exactly does art put us in contact with Platonic Ideas?

Art is the product of genius. A genius is a person with the capacity of knowing the world independently of the principle of sufficient reason. This is why, Schopenhauer comments, artistic geniuses are impractical and so bad at math; they are closer to lunatics than they are to scientists, thus perhaps recalling the idea of divine madness. The genius is capable of deriving Platonic Ideas from nature by using his or her imagination to complete nature—to glean the essential features of a species from a particular, imperfect instance of it. All of us have this capacity to some extent, as is demonstrated by the fact that we can be responsive to the products of artistic genius. But only the very few are capable of doing this with consistency. These are the artistic geniuses who enable the rest of us to see the world through their eyes—eyes not governed by the principle of sufficient reason—thereby affording us the opportunity to undergo temporary release from the endless cycle of striving.

This process of immersion in Platonic Ideas, as relayed to us through works of genius, is pleasurable. But it is important to note that it is pleasurable in two distinct ways. Just as the process has two sides—the subjective and the objective—the process yields two kinds of pleasure: (1) a species of objective pleasure that is cognitive and that comes through contact with the Platonic Ideas, granting us special insight into the nature of the world as will; and (2) a species of subjective pleasure that is affective and involves the feeling of release from the striving and pain of human existence.

Inasmuch as this second sort of pleasure involves freedom from practical concerns, it bears some relation to Kant's notion of disinterested pleasure; however, Schopenhauer's account differs from Kant's insofar as Kant regards disinterestedness as a condition for aesthetic experience, properly so called, whereas, for Schopenhauer, detachment from the practical is a central point or aim of aesthetic experience.

That is, for Schopenhauer, being disinterested (free from practical concerns, free from willing) is itself a form of pleasure—it is a matter of relief from the importunings of the individual will, where relief itself is a type of pleasure, like the relief we might experience from a medicinal painkiller. For Kant, on the other hand, *disinterest* merely modifies the term *pleasure*; disinterestedness is not a particular kind of pleasure at being lifted above the stream of everyday life, as it would appear to be for Schopenhauer.

This transformation in the conception of disinterestedness or detachment from a condition for aesthetic experience to the aim of art is a momentous event in the development of the philosophy of artistic autonomism, since it identifies the function of art as the liberation from all the concerns of life, including practical concerns, morality, politics, and so on.

That Schopenhauer holds that aesthetic experience affords cognitive pleasure through the apprehension of Platonic Ideas may seem diametrically opposed to Kant's view that pleasure taken in free beauty has nothing to do with determinate concepts. However, the difference turns out to be not so stark when one realizes that Schopenhauer's Platonic Ideas are not concepts, let alone determinate concepts. Rather, they are objects of perception. The domain of art is the senses; art gives us sensitive or sensuous knowledge via perception.

Like Aristotle, Schopenhauer believes that a major portion of the pleasure to be had from art is cognitive—that is, pleasure derived from learning about the world as will. However, although this knowledge reaches us through perception, it is a form of general knowledge or knowledge of types rather than knowledge of particular things.

How is this possible? Perhaps here it is best to consider an analogy between the illustrations or diagrams in dictionaries and Schopenhauer's Platonic Ideas. A dictionary illustration of a sparrow is an idealized depiction of a sparrow, not a picture of a specific sparrow. The dictionary illustration provides knowledge of the essential features of the type or the species, and it does this by addressing perception. Similarly, the Platonic Ideas give us knowledge of different grades of the objectification of will at the level of the type or the species through idealizations that engage perception.

For Schopenhauer, the cognitive pleasure available through art can be thought of in terms of beauty. Since this pleasure is connected to knowledge, beauty is a function of the clarity with which the work of art presents the type or Platonic Idea to perception. This is a crucial determinant of the pleasure that the work of art yields, but it is not the only determinant. Since what works of art provide are idealizations of different grades of the objectification of the will, the pleasure that they offer will vary in direct proportion to the degree of will being manifested or expressed through the work of art in question. The higher degree of will manifested or presented by the work of art, the more pleasure it yields. So, since a stone has less will than a man, a picture of the Platonic Idea of a man will manifest a higher degree of objectified will than that of a stone and, therefore, the picture of the man, all things being equal, will elicit greater pleasure than the picture of the stone.

Schopenhauer provides us with several dimensions along which we may plot the pleasure afforded by a work of art. For example, of any work of art we can ask the following: (1) Is the pleasure it affords predominantly affective (the negative pleasure of release) or cognitive (the positive pleasure of knowledge)? (2) How high is the objectification of will embodied in the artwork (for the greater the level of objectification, the more pleasure it yields)? Moreover, with these distinctions in mind, Schopenhauer also proceeds to rank the various forms of art hierarchically.

Architecture makes manifest the lowest grade of the objectification of the will—the conflict between gravity and rigidity (where rigidity resists gravity). This is not a particularly high level of objectification; it is not deeply revelatory of the true nature of the world-will; so, the pleasure that architecture affords is primarily affective—a matter of feeling a release from striving. The same can be said of spectacles of moving water, such as fountains. Landscape painting and still lifes portray living things. In that respect, they present us with higher objectifications of will and, therefore, more cognitive pleasure than architecture, while animal painting and sculpture stand higher still because animals involve a greater objectification of will than fruits, vegetables, and foliage. Since human beings express the lineaments of will more clearly and forcefully than any other animal, paintings and sculptures of people provide more cognitive pleasure than any other form of visual art.

Poetry, however, ranks higher than visual art because it can present more aspects of the human objectification of will than painting and sculpture, thereby providing more profound insight into the nature of the world as will. And of the various forms of poetry, tragedy is the highest since it gives us, in perceptible form, the clearest image of the deepest truth about human existence—that it is, at root, suffering, a matter of unspeakable pain. In this way, tragedy cuts to the essence of will in a powerfully revelatory manner.

Thus far, Schopenhauer has regarded forms of art in terms of their capacity to imitate or represent different grades of the objectification of the will. But this raises a question about where to place music in the hierarchy of the arts since music—pure orchestral music—is not straightforwardly an imitative art. In Schopenhauer's language, it does not imitate this or that degree of objectification of the will. However, rather than banishing music from the order of the arts for this reason, Schopenhauer uses this feature of music to its advantage. He writes:

> Thus music is as immediate an objectification and copy of the whole will as the world itself is, indeed as the Ideas are, the multiplied phenomenon of which constitutes the world of individual things. Therefore music is by no means like the other arts, namely a copy of the Ideas, but a copy of the will itself, the objectivity of which are the Ideas. For this reason the effect of music is so very much more powerful and penetrating than is that of any of the other arts, for these others speak only of the shadows, but music of the essence. (Section 52)

Whereas the other arts give us cognitive access to the will at various levels of objectification, music, through its tempos and rhythms, permits insight into the whole nature of the will as such, tracing its very pulsations, in a manner of speaking, by means of its melodies, harmonies, dissonances, cadences, and the like. Music affords perceptual acquaintance with the pulse of the world as will, thereby not only lifting us out of the world as representation but also enabling us to know its inner dynamism directly. Schopenhauer admits that he cannot prove this, but thinks that if we reflect on this hypothesis, we will come to concur with him.

A Digression: Asceticism

Although the topic of asceticism is not properly a component of Schopenhauer's philosophy of art, it is useful to examine it because it provides a telling comparison to what is involved in an aesthetic experience. After all, aesthetic experience is, in part, a miniature version of the species of ecstasy afforded by asceticism.

For the vast majority of humans, art—and most especially music—provides us with our only prospect of respite from the wheel of striving. But there is also another, far less traveled route, namely ascetic renunciation. The natural inclination of human beings is egoism, the pursuit of one's own interests and desires. But this, according to Schopenhauer, is the source of human suffering. In order to avoid suffering, then, one must attempt to deny desire, to deny the will: "those who have once attained to denial of the will, strive with all their might to keep to this path by self-imposed renunciations of every kind, by a penitent and hard way of life, and by looking for what is disagreeable to them. . . . [Asceticism is] this deliberate breaking of the will by refusing the agreeable and looking for the disagreeable, the voluntarily chosen way of life of penance and self-chastisement, for the constant mortification of the will" (Section 68).

However, practices of fasting, chastity, and other forms of self-denial alone will not bring release. Knowledge is also required. Recall that the release that constitutes aesthetic experience is in large measure a function of the transcendence of the principle of individuation, which also correlates with insight into the nature of will. Similarly, if an entire life is to approach this sort of salvation, it, too, must involve transcending the principle of individuation in such a way that one perceives the true nature of will—that it is indissoluble and unitary, and that the distinction between our individuality and that of others is an illusion. Moreover, once such a person—call her a saint—realizes this, the clamoring of her individual will after her own interests subsides, and she sacrifices herself to others inasmuch as she regards their lives as her own (for we are all indissolubly of the same world-will).

Schopenhauer writes:

> Now, if seeing through the *principium individuationis*, if this direct knowledge of the identity of the will in all its phenomena, is present in a high degree of distinctness, it will at once show an influence on the will which goes still farther. If that veil of Maya, the *principium individuationis*, is lifted from the eyes of a man to such an extent that he no longer makes the egotistical distinction between himself and the person of others, but takes as much interest in the suffering of other individuals as in his own, and thus is not only benevolent and charitable to the highest degree, but even ready to sacrifice his own individuality when several others can be saved thereby, then it follows automatically that such a man, recognizing in all beings his own true and innermost self, must also regard the endless suffering of all that lives as his own, and thus take upon himself the pain of the whole world. No suffering is any longer strange or foreign to him. All the miseries of others, which he sees and is so seldom able to alleviate, all the miseries of which he has indirect knowledge, and even those he recognizes merely as possible, affect his mind just as do his own. It is no longer the changing weal and woe of his person that he has in view, as in the case with the man still involved in egoism, but, as he sees through the *principium individuatioinis*, everything lies equally near him. He knows the whole, comprehends its inner nature, and finds it involved in the constant suffering. Wherever he looks, he sees suffering humanity and the suffering animal world, and a world that passes away. Now all this lies just as near to him as only his own person lies to the egoist. Now how could he with such knowledge of the world, affirm this very life through constant acts of will, and precisely in this bind himself more and more closely? Thus, whoever is still involved in the *principium individuationis*, in egoism, knows only particular things and the relation to his own person, and these then become the ever-renewed *motives* of his own willing. On the other hand, that knowledge of the whole, of the inner nature of the thing-in-itself, which has been described, becomes the quieter of all and every willing. The will now turns away from life; it shudders at the pleasures in which it recognizes the affirmation of life. Man attains to the state of voluntary renunciation resignation, true composure, and complete will-lessness. (Section 38)

That is, once one sees through the principle of individuation, one accepts one's identity with all suffering, and this quiets the will and leads one to turn away from it, sacrificing for others insofar as one draws no distinction between oneself and others. Desires are renounced, once the saint has perceived the true face of suffering that inheres in her, and her energy is dissipated by acts of self-mortification and self-sacrifice. This provides a route to more enduring solace than occasional encounters with works of art. But it is clearly an option for the very, very few. The names of Jesus and Buddha spring to mind, perhaps along with other rare mystics and holy persons. But it is not a vocation that most can shoulder. For us, there is the life of desire and merciless pain, leavened only by soothing intervals of aesthetic experience.

Concluding Observations

Schopenhauer's metaphysics are complex and often hard to fathom. What exactly is the relationship of ordinary objects in the world of representation to Platonic Ideas? They are of different grades of objectification, but how exactly are we to understand that? How are Platonic Ideas objects of perception if they are not in space? Why is it that once the saint gives up desire, she is not stricken with boredom? And how exactly is one able to turn away from the world-will when one is disgusted by its ferocity? It is not clear that Schopenhauer's system can consistently support all of the various scenarios that he proposes.

Similarly, the mechanics of aesthetic experience that Schopenhauer advances are often hard to square with his metaphysics. Supposedly, an encounter with architecture will momentarily lift us out of the world of striving since when submerged in Platonic Ideas of rigidity and gravity, we are outside the principle of sufficient reason. But how can that be? Surely, these particular Platonic Ideas, supposing that there are such things, must have something to do with tensile strength. Thus, how can we contemplate the idea of rigidity versus gravity outside the framework of the principle of sufficient reason since tensile strength involves causality.

And comparable points can be made of other forms of art. Can there be narrative, let alone tragedy, without causality? And can there be music without thinking of time—without thinking of movement through time?

But it is not only the details of Schopenhauer's ontology that are perplexing. As already noted, the derivation of the ultimate nature of being as suffering from the phenomenon of desire is flawed at several points. Thus, it is perhaps not surprising that Schopenhauer has few followers among contemporary philosophers.

Nor do Schopenhauer's aesthetics mesh neatly with generally accepted views of our commerce with artworks. For Schopenhauer, the cognitive pleasure we derive from art has to do with the generalizing grasp it affords of Platonic Ideas. Undoubtedly, there is some art that engenders pleasure, including cognitive pleasure, by giving us purchase on generalizations (let's drop the notion of Platonic Ideas). Yet this is not the whole story because we also take pleasure, including cognitive pleasure, in artworks that feature what is unique and particular in its subjects. But Schopenhauer's theory has no accommodation for that dimension of our engagement with artworks.

Furthermore, Schopenhauer locates our pleasure in artworks solely in their capacity to enable us escape from ordinary experience, which for him, of course, is the experience of striving. Yet, with the arts as we know them, a frequent source of other value we place on certain artworks is that they encourage our participating with affairs on this side of the veil of Maya. This is often the point of realistic art that holds a mirror up to society for the purpose of motivating social change. But Schopenhauer has no legitimate room for this sort of art in his philosophy. Perhaps, he would dismiss its claim to art status. But what do we have greater reason to accept: realism of the previous sort or Schopenhauer's metaphysics?

Despite these problems, Schopenhauer's influence is still felt in the philosophy of art. In addition to his suggestive comments about various forms of art, his notion that aesthetic experience is a release from practical striving has exerted a continuing effect on the tradition and has been adapted by art theorists and philosophers such as Clive Bell, as we shall see in the last chapter of this volume, and autonomists, like Monroe Beardsley. Indeed, even where many philosophers of art would deny his influence, Schopenhauer's idea that aesthetic experience involves a separation from everyday affairs and their interests has penetrated their subconscious as is shown by their alleged "intuitions" that aesthetic experience is divorced from morality, politics, the arousal of emotion, and so forth.

Because of this influence, questions about the cogency of Schopenhauer's philosophy must continue to be raised since his view of artistic detachment, as it recurrently echoes in contemporary aesthetics, permits no allowance for the possibility that some art, properly so called, is about connecting us to the worldly existence and not separating us from it, ecstatically or otherwise. And surely, we have more grounds to believe that this, too, can be a legitimate function of art than we have to believe that the world is finally naught but a single orb of throbbing pain, worthy only of escape.

Appendix: A Brief Note about Friedrich Nietzsche

Friedrich Nietzsche's first book, originally entitled *The Birth of Tragedy Out of the Spirit of Music* (1872), was profoundly influenced by Schopenhauer's philosophy. Nietzsche presented Greek tragedy as the result originally of two forces operative in Greek culture: the Dionysian and the Apollonian. The Apollonian drive, named after the god of light, was the drive for form that imbued appearances with the illusion of order; the Dionysian drive, named after the god of wine, drunkenness, and frenzy, was the drive to dissolve into primordial ecstasy. Thus, Greek tragedy combined elements of Schopenhauer's world as idea—in the Apollonian illusion of form—and the world as will in Dionysian intoxication, excess, the transgression of boundaries, and the dissolution of self and the *principium individuationis*. The Apollonian dimension of tragedy was rooted in its poetry. The Dionysian dimension was sounded by the chorus and its music that fostered a feeling of unity between the actors and the audience as well as between the audience members themselves.

Greek tragedy, in this respect, was the very embodiment of Schopenhauer's philosophy of human existence. Moreover, insofar as the protagonist of the Greek tragedy was typically destroyed, Greek tragedy bore witness to the horror of human life as Schopenhauer portrayed it. Human striving leads inevitably to a terrible end. That is the lesson of tragedy. Thus, tragedy gave the ancient Greeks insight into the primordial futility of being.

But for Nietzsche, this does not result in pessimism. Rather, this insight into the nature of human existence gave the Greeks strength—the strength to persist. The insight into Dionysian reality was in part made tolerable by the Apollonian illusion of form. So rather than being an opportunity to escape, as Schopenhauer would have it, the travails of human existence, the experience of tragedy and its ultimately appalling revelations, for Nietzsche, gave the Greeks the strength to forge on, due to its wrapping of the apprehension of Dionysian reality in the Apollonian form.[8]

Although this difference of opinion between Schopenhauer and Nietzsche is significant in terms of cultural history, it is not a continuing debate among contemporary philosophers of art and, since it is not part of their narrative, it will not be pursued further herein.

---

8. Nietzsche maintained that Greek tragedy eventually declined as a result of Euripides, whom Nietzsche believed diminished the contribution of the Dionysian chorus. According to Nietzsche, this obscured insight into the awfulness of human life in favor of what he regarded as Socratic optimism, a trust in rationality rather than an acknowledgment of the fundamental, primordial irrationality of reality.

When Nietzsche originally published *The Birth of Tragedy*, he thought the original power of tragedy might be restored by the Wagnerian *gesamkunstwerk* with its promise of challenging the phenomenology of the *principium individuationis*, although subsequently, Nietzsche lost his faith in Wagner.

Indeed, in his book *Twilight of the Idols* (24), Nietzsche commends tragedy for its life-affirming tendency to encourage bravery in the face of catastrophe.

Bibliography

The translation used in this chapter was Arthur Schopenhauer's *The World As Will and Representation*, two volumes, translated by E. F. J. Payne (Dover, 1966).

Carroll, Noël. "Arthur Schopenhauer." In *The Blackwell Guide to Continental Philosophy*, edited by Robert C. Solomon and David Sherman, 30–42. Oxford: Blackwell, 2003.
Gardiner, Patrick L. *Schopenhauer*. Harmondsworth, UK: Penguin, 1983.
Guyer, Paul. "Back to Truth: Knowledge and Pleasure in the Aesthetics of Schopenhauer." *European Journal of Philosophy* 16 (2008): 164–78.
———. *A History of Modern Aesthetics*. Vol. 2, *The Nineteenth Century*. Cambridge: Cambridge University Press, 2014.
Hamlyn, D. W. *Schopenhauer*. London: Routledge, 1980.
Jacquette, Dale. "Idealism." In *The Routledge Companion to Aesthetics*, edited by Berys Gaut and Dominic McIver Lopes, 83–95. London: Routledge, 2001.
———, ed. *Schopenhauer, Philosophy, and the Arts*. Cambridge: Cambridge University Press, 1996.
Janaway, Christopher. *The Cambridge Companion to Schopenhauer*. Cambridge: Cambridge University Press, 1999.
———. *Schopenhauer*. Oxford: Oxford University Press, 2007.
Magee, Bryan. *The Philosophy of Schopenhauer*. Oxford: Clarendon Press, 1993.
Neill, Alex. "Aesthetic Experience in Schopenhauer's Metaphysics of Will." *European Journal of Philosophy* 16 (2008): 179–93.
Neill, Alex, and Christopher Janaway, eds. *Better Consciousness: Schopenhauer's Philosophy of Value*. Oxford: Wiley-Blackwell, 2009.
Nietzsche, Friedrich. *The Birth of Tragedy*. In *The Birth of Tragedy and The Genealogy of Morals*. Translated by Francis Golffing. Garden City, NY: Doubleday, 1956.
———. *Twilight of the Idols*. Translated by Richard Polt. Indianapolis: Hackett, 1997.
Safranski, Rüdiger. *Schopenhauer and the Wild Years of Philosophy*. Translated by Ewald Osers. Cambridge, MA: Harvard University Press, 1989.
Shapshay, Sandra. "Schopenhauer: Aesthetics." In *Stanford Encyclopedia of Philosophy*. Stanford University, 1997–. Published May 9, 2012; updated June 4, 2018. https://plato.stanford.edu/entries/schopenhauer-aesthetics/.
———. "Schopenhauer's Aesthetics and Philosophy of Art." *Philosophical Compass* 7 (2012): 11–22.
Tanner, Michael. *Schopenhauer, Metaphysics and Art*. London: Orion, 1998.
Wicks, Robert L. *European Aesthetics: A Critical Introduction from Kant to Derrida*. London: Oneworld, 2013.
———. *Schopenhauer*. Oxford: Wiley-Blackwell, 2009.
Young, Julian. *Schopenhauer*. London: Routledge, 2005.

Chapter 8

Leo Tolstoy's *What Is Art?*

Of the many illustrious figures whom we have discussed thus far, Leo Tolstoy, if not the best known, is probably the one who has been read by more people than any of the other authors we've canvassed. His works, such as *War and Peace* and *Anna Karenina*, are among the foremost novels of the nineteenth century, if not of all time. *What Is Art?* is a text that Tolstoy wrote late in his life, and, in many respects, it is a recantation of much of his earlier career, disavowing, for example, the great novels that are the primary reason for which he is remembered today. To say the least, *What Is Art?* was a scandalous book, censored in its own time.

The book stigmatizes not only *War and Peace* and *Anna Karenina* but also many other canonical works of art, including the plays of Aeschylus, Sophocles, Euripides, Aristophanes, Shakespeare, Ibsen, and Maeterlinck; the poetry of Dante, Tasso, Milton, Goethe, and Baudelaire; the painting of Raphael, Manet, Monet, Renoir, Pissarro, and Sisley; the music of late Beethoven, Liszt, Berlioz, Wagner, and Brahms, not to mention a large swath of Bach; the novels of Zola and Kipling, in addition to his own; and so on.

Tolstoy either disenfranchises so many of what most of us would regard as major artistic achievements, or he declares them downright bad, that many have regarded his judgments as the ravings of a crank. But behind many of these artistic evaluations, however apparently eccentric, lays a highly developed theory that was itself threatening to the czarist regime that ruled Russia when the book was published in 1898. For Tolstoy argues that art, properly so called, has a legitimate social role to play *and*, furthermore, he contends that if it does not play that role, it should be either discounted as inferior and socially suspect or not be apprized as genuine art at all, and rather demoted to the status of a noxious parasite. Moreover, by Tolstoy's estimate, much of the "art" that catered to the tastes of the nobility and upper classes of czarist Russia—such as the opera and the ballet—fell precisely into these categories.

Nowadays, we would call Tolstoy an antielitist. The art that his theory celebrates encompasses the kind of rudimentary forms of articulation associated with the simple folk—or, in his day, the peasantry. That is, lullabies and folk songs fare better than operas; country dances are superior to ballets; and folktales beat Symbolist poetics. For him, a paradigmatic work of art is a peasant boy honestly recounting a story that expresses his fear of a wolf.

Tolstoy's *What Is Art?* is implicitly a document of social criticism. Tolstoy excoriates the injustices of czarist Russia, which exacts great sacrifices from the masses in order to support the pleasures of the aristocracy—pleasures on which Tolstoy casts a satirical, defamiliarizing gaze, lampooning operatic conventions, like people conversing in recitative, and treating balletic costuming—or the lack thereof—as virtually pornographic. Thus, the czarist authorities were not wrong to see in Tolstoy's highly revisionist aesthetics a threat to their way of life. Tolstoy attacks the status quo in existing society by attacking the status quo in its art, notably its *high* art.

Unlike Schopenhauer, who recommends art as a means to escape life, Tolstoy represents a return to the idea that art has a social role, which, for Tolstoy, is the communication of the best human feelings. Like Plato, Tolstoy is a moralist. And like Plato, he identifies art in terms of its addressing feeling and emotion. But unlike Plato, he does not question art's connection to the emotions; rather he endorses artworks that engender the very un-Platonic feelings of compassion and sympathy.

For Tolstoy, art has an important social vocation—to promote fellow feeling. Like Hegel, Tolstoy believes that art has a historic mission, namely, to abet human progress by transmitting the very best human emotions, the emotions that bond humanity in contrast to the emotions, like xenophobia, that divide us. That is why the arts that perpetuate class divisions—as Tolstoy believes the ballet and opera do—are highly suspect.

How is art related to the emotions? For Tolstoy, art *expresses* emotion. Art brings what is inside, outside. *Expression* comes from the Latin word *exprimo*, which means "to squeeze or to press out," as one squeezes out the juice from the inside of a grape. In this respect, Tolstoy's emphasis on expression is another way in which he recalls Hegel. However, on Tolstoy's theory, what gets expressed by art is not the collective spirit of the age or mind, but the feelings of individuals, albeit in the best of cases, their feelings of universal brotherhood. That is, it is not the spirit of a particular civilization that art expresses, but the feelings of specific people—you, me, Rainer Maria Rilke, Philip Larkin, and Sylvia Plath.

In terms of the history of the philosophy of art, Tolstoy is classified as an expression theorist of art, in contrast to Plato and Aristotle, who are characterized as imitation theorists. That is, whereas Plato and Aristotle putatively regard *imitation* as key to identifying objects and performances as works of art, for theorists like Tolstoy, *expression*—specifically for him in virtue of the communication of feelings—is the most important factor. The difference between imitation theories and expression can be explicated in terms of their contrasting domains: the domain of imitation (what gets imitated) are objects, people, places, events, and actions; the domain of expression (what gets expressed) are feelings, affects, emotions, moods, emotional qualities, and points of view.

Expression theories, such as Tolstoy's, began to emerge as a distinctive viewpoint in the eighteenth century in the writings of Thomas Reid and Jean-Baptiste Dubos. The popularity of such views was possibly influenced by the rediscovery of Longinus's *On the Sublime*, an ancient text which located the source of sublimity in the outpourings of the genius-artist whose creative process was inextricably bound up with deep emotions. In the nineteenth century, the identification of art with the expression of feeling became an article of faith for the Romantics; William Wordsworth, for instance, claimed that "poetry is an overflow of powerful feeling."

Expression theories of art are generally thought to be a reaction formation to imitation theories of art. A likely impetus for the emergence of expression theories was the development of absolute or pure orchestral music. Although absolute music was beginning to lay claims to an exalted cultural status through the achievements of figures like Beethoven, one was hard put to say what, if anything, such art imitated. Surely it was art, but in virtue of what? One proposal was in virtue of its expression of emotion.

For the expression theorist, art is not about the representation of the outer world of things, but an expression of the inner, psychological realm. The imitation theory of art located the value of art in its ability to provide knowledge of things (e.g., Aristotle). However, by the end of the nineteenth century, connecting art to the production of knowledge of the world of things implied a lowered status for art, since by then art could no longer compete with natural science as a source of knowledge of the objective world. The value of art had to be located elsewhere. Expression theories of art, arguably in response, propose that the value of art is in the access it gives us to the subjective world of feeling, in contradistinction to the access science gives us to the objective world of knowledge.

This view—the expression theory of art—is probably the one most people hold pre-theoretically even today. Though it has lost favor among contemporary philosophers, it was the leading viewpoint for the first five or six decades of the twentieth century. Tolstoy, John Dewey, R. G. Collingwood, and, arguably, Susanne Langer are among its most forceful philosophical proponents. It is clearly the view of art that underwrites most popular fictions about artists who are constantly represented as in search of self-expression, often agonistically. Of course, it is possible to be an expression theorist while subtracting out the angst.

Although we can gather a sizable collection of theories under the rubric of *expression theories*, they can differ widely in their particulars. Tolstoy's theory, for example, possesses many features that are absent from other leading theories, as we shall see.

What Is Art?[1]

By way of preview, in *What Is Art?*, Tolstoy poses two major questions: (1) What is art? and (2) What is good art? Tolstoy's answers to both these questions, as we shall see, involve the idea of the expression or communication of feeling. Before proceeding, we might diagram his theory this way, as a kind of road map to where we are headed.

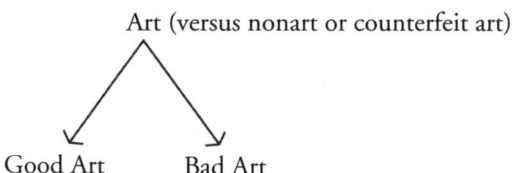

As this diagram indicates, Tolstoy's first order of business is to distinguish art from nonart. This makes sense, since before we try to establish which artworks are good, we need to know what kinds of things we are talking about. Presumably, we cannot say what makes for a good hammer until we know what a hammer is. Ditto art.

However, even at this early point in the discussion, it is worthwhile to pause a moment to try to understand exactly what Tolstoy is after with the question, What is art? By asking it, one could be looking for an account of all of the interconnected activities that make up the social practice of art—what kinds of institutions does it comprise, what are its rules and conventions, who plays what roles and when, and so forth.

But that is not the sort of answer that Tolstoy is looking for. Rather, Tolstoy wants to know what feature or features something must possess in order to count as an instance of art. That is, what distinguishes an artwork from other things, like ordinary bicycles, carpentry tools, washing machines, vegetables, constitutions, swimming pools, galoshes, and so forth? In this respect, his project recalls Aristotle's aim of defining tragedy. Tolstoy, that is, wants to define art—to say on what

---

1. The question—"What is art?"—began to become increasingly pressing in the nineteenth century with the advent of succeeding modern art movements. Whereas previously most educated people could tell art by looking, when art began to depart from various preexisting canons—as the paintings of Édouard Manet, the poetry of Charles Baudelaire, and the music of Hector Berlioz did—the need for a definition appeared to become urgent and has seemed even more so as time has gone by. Tolstoy, among other things, I think, sensed this, which, along with his reformist aims, provided a motivation for his theory, although given those reformist aims, he was not disposed to incorporate the products of the emerging avant-garde into his theory. But the theory, I contend, was nevertheless a response, albeit a negative one, to the developing crisis that seemed to call for some way of identifying art amidst revolutionary change.

grounds something can be categorized as an artwork rather than as something else. He is not attempting to describe the practice of art, but rather to identify the conditions that a discrete particular thing or performance must meet in order to be classified as a work of art.

We can tell that this is what Tolstoy is after, given the way that he rejects certain rival accounts of art status. For example, Tolstoy rejects the notion that art correlates with beauty on the grounds that there are many *things* that are beautiful that are not artworks. Sunsets, for example, are beautiful, but they are not art—not artworks. Similarly, Tolstoy eschews attempts to define art in terms of pleasure since that, too, fails to distinguish a lot of things that are pleasurable, like horseback riding, from artworks, properly so called. That is, neither beauty nor pleasure is sufficient to guarantee that a candidate is an artwork.

Tolstoy's aim is to isolate precisely those features which an object or a performance must possess in order to count as an artwork. For example, he will attempt to define, probably unsuccessfully, what distinguishes artworks from speech acts. To be exact, Tolstoy means to set out the criteria that anything must satisfy in order to be legitimately called an artwork; he wants to provide a formula for cleaving art from nonart—or, as he perhaps misleadingly calls it—"counterfeit art."[2]

Tolstoy begins his investigation by emphasizing the amount of time, energy, labor, and lives that art costs in order to ask, "What is the point of this?" This may seem like a strange way to begin to define art. But Tolstoy proceeds in this manner in order to attempt to establish that whatever we arrive at as a definition of art, it must make evident why art is important if it is to be a satisfactory definition. That is, for Tolstoy, an account of what art is must explain why the sacrifices that are made for its creation deserve all of the effort. Why do people think the cost of art in human terms warrants the blood and treasure spent on its production?[3] For Tolstoy, then, a constraint on saying what art is, is that such a definition makes it apparent why art is worth the trouble, or, as Tolstoy puts it, why art is important for human life. He says:

> For the production of every ballet, circus, opera, operetta, exhibition, picture, concert, or printed book, the intense and unwilling labor of thousands of people is needed at what is often harmful and humiliating work. It were well if artists made all they require for themselves, but, as it is, they all need the help of workmen, not only to produce art, but also for their own usually luxurious maintenance. And,

---

2. "Counterfeit" may be the wrong word here because it suggests that the candidate in question is presenting itself spuriously as art, whereas the things that actually fall into Tolstoy's category are not simply what might be called "phony art," but things that are neither art nor pretend to be art, like potatoes. Phony art, of course, falls into this category, but so does much else.

3. This, of course, supports Tolstoy's social criticism; he believes that the aristocratic art of czarist Russia does not warrant the sacrifices made in its behalf.

one way or other, they get it, either through payments from rich people or through subsidies given by government (in Russia, for instance, in grants of millions of rubles to theaters, conservatories, and academies). This money is collected from the people, some of whom have to sell their only cow to pay the tax and who never get those aesthetic pleasures which art gives. It was all very well for a Greek or Roman artist, or even for a Russian artist of the first half of our century (when there were still slaves and it was considered right that there should be), with a quiet mind to make people serve him and his art; but in our day, when in all men there is at least some dim perception of the equal rights of all, it is impossible to constrain people to labor unwillingly for art without first deciding the question whether it is true that art is so good and so important an affair as to redeem this evil.

If not, we have the terrible probability to consider that while fearful sacrifices of the labor and lives of men, and of morality itself, are being made to art, that same art may be not only useless but even harmful.

And therefore it is necessary for a society in which works of art arise and are supported, to find out whether all that professes to be art is really art, whether (as is presupposed in our society) all that which is art is good, and whether it is important and worth those sacrifices which it necessitates. It is still more necessary for every conscientious artist to know this, that he may be sure that all he does has a valid meaning; that among whom he lives which excites in him the false assurance that he is doing a good work; and that what he takes from others for the support of his often very luxurious life will be compensated for by those productions at which he works. And that is why answers to the above questions are especially important in our time.

What is this art which is considered so important and necessary for humanity that for its sake these sacrifices of labor, of human life, and even of goodness may be made? (pp. 15–16)[4]

So, for Tolstoy, an adequate account of art must make clear how art is worth the sacrifices that everyone winds up making for it. Tolstoy's approach is quite distinctive in this regard since this is not a customary desideratum of most theories of art. In this, Tolstoy returns us to the way of thinking that we encountered in Plato and Aristotle. Like them, Tolstoy thinks that art has social responsibilities.

Despite its deviation from modern practice, for Tolstoy, any theory of art must meet this social criterion of adequacy. Moreover, Tolstoy uses this presupposition dialectically, deploying it to defeat competing theories of art. For example, Tolstoy believes that the leading theory of art in his day was the beauty theory or pleasure theory, as derived, probably by way of misinterpretation, from the Kantian notion of free beauty. Moreover, Tolstoy maintains that this sort of theory does not stack up well against his criterion of adequacy. Mere pleasure, he argues, is too trivial to merit great labors made in the name of *art*.

---

4. All page numbers are from the edition of *What is Art?* cited in the Bibliography.

Also, there is wide subjective variation in who takes pleasure in what. Pleasure, that is, does not afford an objective criterion of art status; it is too subjective. Pleasure would not provide a stable way for all people to agree on what counts as art, and if that is the case, it cannot explain how there could be any consensus on why everything that winds up being called art is worth the costs that art incurs.

Tolstoy introduces his own preferred theory of art this way: "The inaccuracy of all these definitions arises from the fact that in them all (as also in the metaphysical definitions) the object considered is the pleasure art may give, and not the purpose it may serve in the life of man and of humanity" (p. 49).

Here is an outline of his argument:

(1) Either art is a means to pleasure, or it is a means to intercourse/communication (Tolstoy's preferred view).[5]

(2) However art is characterized, it must be considered essentially as a condition of human life. (That is, it must be thought to be vitally important.)[6]

(3) Since the mere production of pleasure is not a condition of human life—this is just too trivial a purpose—art is not a means to pleasure.

(4) Therefore, art is a means to intercourse/communication (which *is* something worthy of being considered important and a condition of human life; indeed, human life would be impossible without it).

However, this argument, if successful, gets us only so far as the proposition that art is at least a form of intercourse or communication. But this does not yet give us a full account of what art is, since there are many things that are forms of human intercourse and that involve communication, but that are not art. My lectures, I hope, are communications, but not even my loving mother thinks they are art. So, what has to be added to Tolstoy's basic theory of art (that *art* = communication) in order to introduce the distinction between artworks, properly so called, and things like my lectures?

In order to get at this, Tolstoy discusses the difference between what he takes to be the two major forms of communication—speech and art:

> Speech, transmitting the thoughts and experiences of men, serves as a means of union among them, and art acts in a similar manner. The peculiarity of this latter means of intercourse, distinguishing it from intercourse by means of words, consists in this, that whereas by words a man transmits his thoughts to another, by means of art he transmits his feelings. (p. 49)

---

5. This opening premise is arguably flawed insofar as it does not seem to cover all the alternatives.

6. This requirement implicitly draws a contrast with Kantian-derived theories of art that characterize art in terms of the affordance of aesthetic experience, a.k.a. disinterested pleasure.

Here Tolstoy presumes that speech and art belong to the same genus—communication. Indeed, they neatly partition that genus between them. What differentiates them is a matter of *what* they communicate. Speech acts communicate thoughts or ideas; artworks communicate feelings. Adding then the fruits of this analysis of the contrast between speech and art to the opening argument about the human purposes of art, we get an initially broad statement or outline of Tolstoy's answer to the question of what art is, namely, *art is the communication of feelings*.

This is a *broad* outline of Tolstoy's theory. I call this a broad outline of the theory because it is still somewhat vague—it is difficult to apply because we still don't really have a handle on what Tolstoy means by communication nor on what he means by feeling.

First, let's deal with his idea of communication. He requires that a communication involve a sender and a receiver. Roughly put, Tolstoy thinks of communication as a matter of a sender having something that she gives or transmits to the receiver. What is it that the sender has? A mental state—a thought or a feeling. And what the sender gives or transmits to the receiver is the *same* mental state.

So, for Tolstoy, for Jones to communicate something A to Smith is for Jones to undergo some mental state A—to have some thought or feeling—and then to somehow get Smith to undergo the same mental state—to have the same thought or feeling.[7]

Tolstoy pictures communication thusly:

Jones (mental state A) → Smith (mental state A)

You could call this the contagion or infection model of communication. Tolstoy thinks of communication along the lines of a communicable disease. One has a certain kind of germ and then transmits the same kind of germ to someone else, only here, it is a mental state that is transmitted. Indeed, Tolstoy even uses the concept of *infection*.

Or, to opt for a different analogy, Tolstoy thinks of communication as involving a kind of union between the sender and receiver. They become as one in feeling. Call this the communing or *communion*[8] view of communication. Moreover, that which is communicated with respect to art is an affective mental state. Sender and receiver share the allegedly selfsame feeling. Tolstoy states that "it is upon this

---

7. The influence of this way of conceiving of artistic communication continued into the twentieth century. To cite one example, consider Tolstoy's fellow Russian, the filmmaker Sergei Eisenstein, whose extremely well-known theory of montage explicitly claims to involve this transfer of the selfsame affect from the director/editor to the viewer.

8. Insofar as Tolstoy was a committed Christian, we may assume the religious overtones here are no accident.

capacity of man to receive another man's expression of feeling and experience those feelings himself, that the activity of art is based" (p. 50).

Furthermore, Tolstoy believes this concept of communication has straightforward implications about the nature of the kind of feelings that are communicated (where one thinks of communication in Tolstoy's terms). Tolstoy envisions communication as the transmission of a feeling from one person to another—where communication involves one person being in a mental state and then bringing about the *same* mental state in the receiver. Tolstoy maintains that this then entails that the feeling or experience that the sender transmits must be one that she *literally underwent* herself. That is, the feeling that she transmits is *sincere*—a feeling that she, the sender, herself, actually or *genuinely* underwent. The claim that artworks transmit *sincere* feelings then follows, Tolstoy believes, from his conception of communication.

Moreover, Tolstoy thinks that it is obvious that if a feeling is sincere, then it will be individual insofar as each person's actual emotional experience is personal and, therefore, unique.[9] So it is a natural consequence of transmitting sincere emotions that the emotions in question will be individualized emotions. They will be personal, not, so to speak, generic. They will carry the affective texture of the artist's personal experience—as does the tale of the boy's fear of the wolf, that Tolstoy references, as distinct from *Paranormal Activity 3*, where its very number suggests that it traffics in a very mass-produced sort of feeling, namely, the same feelings afforded by *Paranormal Activity 1* and *2*.

Thus, Tolstoy appears to think that it follows from the fact that the artist is involved in communicating her feelings that the feelings in question must be sincere—must be feelings the artist herself actually experienced. Moreover, he thinks that if the feeling in question is sincere, it must be individualized. Indeed, he even claims that insofar as the emotion conveyed is sincere, this will "impel" the artist toward a clear expression of it:

> I have mentioned three conditions of contagiousness in art, but they may be all summed up into one, the last, sincerity, i.e., that the artist should be impelled by an inner need to express his feeling. That condition includes the first; for if the artist is sincere he will express the feeling as he experienced it. And as each man is different from everyone else, his feeling will be individual for everyone else; and the more individual it is—the more the artist has drawn it from the depths of his nature—the more sympathetic and sincere will it be. And this same sincerity will impel the artist to find a clear expression of the feeling which he wishes to transmit. (p. 141)

This is the reasoning that also leads Tolstoy to the attribution of clarity as an ingredient in artistic expression. However, it probably involves Tolstoy's changing

---

9. Of course, it is worth asking whether it follows from an emotion's being personal to its being unique.

the sense in which we are to understand the concept of sincerity in the argument. For in saying that sincerity leads to clarity by some natural pathway, Tolstoy must have in mind that a *sincere* emotion is not just an emotion that someone actually underwent, but an emotion that involves *a desire to be as open and as frank as possible.*

Tolstoy believes that insofar as an artwork involves the expression of sincere emotions, it follows that artworks gravitate toward the clear expression of the pertinent emotions. For, he seems to presuppose that a sincere emotion is one that is naturally open and accessible and, thus, strives, so to speak, for clear expression. Here, "sincere emotion" means more than "one that is literally or genuinely undergone"; it also means one that is honest, forthright, and forthcoming.

So far then, by specifying Tolstoy's conception of communication and by reflecting on what he takes that conception to entail, we can begin to flesh out his view of the nature of art more precisely. An artwork is not just a communication of feeling; it is at least the clear transmission of an identical, sincere, individualized feeling from a sender (an artist) to a receiver (an audience). The boy articulates his particular fear of the wolf, and we are infected by the selfsame fear.

But how are we to construe the operative notion of feeling in this account? On that issue, Tolstoy's presentation is somewhat loose. For our purposes, the domain of feelings would appear to include visceral feelings, emotions, moods, attitudes, and even affectively charged points of view. These are what comprise the transmissions characterized in the preceding paragraph.

However, even a characterization of this degree of precision is not yet fine-grained enough to differentiate artworks from nonart. Why not? Consider a case like this: a young woman is awaiting the results of an audition; the cast list is to be posted in the green room momentarily. Our aspiring actress nervously awaits the results, standing near the bulletin board upon which the results will be displayed. Unconsciously she starts to pace back and forth. As you stand by, you begin to sense her feeling, her nervousness, her anxiety. It is contagious; you *catch* it. When the results are posted and she gets the part, she raises her arms above her head involuntarily in a triumphant gesture. And again, you share her feeling; you sense her elation. Note in both cases that the woman's gesticulations fit Tolstoy's theory of art as we have stated it so far, but surely nervous tics and involuntary explosions of joy shouldn't count as artworks. How can we exclude cases like this from the order of art?

By requiring that the communication in question be *intentional*. In the example that we have just imagined, the woman's gestures were involuntary. Thus, in order to block cases like this from counting as art, we can add to our formula that art is not merely the communication of feeling; it is the *intentional* communication of feeling.

Tolstoy perhaps thinks that he can also block cases like this by adding to his formula the stipulation that the communications of feelings in question must be "by means of movements, lines, colors, sounds, or forms expressed in words" (p. 51). Obviously, what Tolstoy is trying to do with this qualification is, in effect, to stipulate that the relevant communications must involve a known artistic genre or medium, such as music (sounds), lines/colors (paintings), forms expressed in words (poetry), and movements (dance and pantomime). Thus, our perambulating, aspiring actress's fretting and strutting would not count as an artwork (a performing artwork), because it does not belong to an established art form/genre.

But, of course, Tolstoy can't say outright that for something to be art, it must be the communication of feeling in a known artistic form/genre, since such a characterization of art would be circular. It would be a definition of art that depends on making reference to art—to *art*istic forms/genres—before the term *art* itself has been defined.

So to avoid the appearance of circularity at the same time that ordinary, everyday, intentional, conventional expressions of emotion are excluded from the order of art, Tolstoy talks more broadly of communications of feeling by means of lines, colors, sounds, movements, and forms expressed by words. However, when we turn to looking at Tolstoy's definition of art more critically, we will have to determine whether this talk of lines, colors, sounds, and so on will really do the work Tolstoy wants it to do.

Earlier, we stated that in broad outline, Tolstoy's answer to the question of what is art is "art is the communication of feeling." We are now in a position to flesh out that theory more amply and with greater exactitude. Summarizing the position so far, we can say that for Tolstoy:

> X is art => X is the (1) intentional, (2) clear (3) transmission from a sender to a receiver (4) of the identical, (5) sincere, (6) individualized (7) feeling (by which Tolstoy means an emotion, an attitude, or a point of view) (8) by means of lines, colors, sounds, movements, or forms of words.

This formula fills in what I earlier called the broad sketch of Tolstoy's conception of art. It draws out and makes explicit what Tolstoy believes is implied in saying art is the communication of feelings as well as adding a certain necessary qualification to that formulation. Expanded thusly, Tolstoy's theory is fairly intricate. It has a lot of parts. But what I'd like to stress is that every part is there for a reason. That is, Tolstoy has an argument or a reason for each one of the components in the formula.

There may be a difficulty, however, in Tolstoy's exposition of his theory that needs to be addressed. At one point, Tolstoy states that "art . . . is not the expression of man's emotions by external sign" (p. 51). This may appear to suggest a contradiction. For isn't the claim that art is not the expression of emotion by an external sign inconsistent with the claim that art is the communication of emotion?

Yet perhaps one way to erase the impression of inconsistency here is to ask whether or not the phrase "expression of emotion" comes to the same thing as the phrase "communication of emotion." For some expression theorists, like Collingwood, the expression of emotion need not require an audience; the poet, for instance, clarifies her emotion for herself. Moreover, she may do this by rehearsing her verse mentally, never putting pen to paper. She need not be aspiring to infect another with her feelings; she need not even make it available for others to read. That is, expression in this sense need not involve an external sign.

On the other hand, Tolstoy—whose theory always emphasizes the social—maintains that it is not art without an audience. Art is *communication*—which requires a sender *and* a receiver. Expression, under certain contrasting views, requires only an artist, such as a poet, who is exploring her emotion for herself, including only reciting it in her mind's ear, sans any external sign.

So, given this possible distinction, then, between expressing emotions or feelings and communicating emotions or feelings, we might give the preceding troublesome passage a noncontradictory reading. In saying that art is not the expression of feeling by external signs, Tolstoy is saying that it is not really art if it is simply a matter of an artist exploring her feelings for herself; in order to be art, it must be social; it must be a matter of an artist conveying a feeling to an audience. Art is communication and communication is social. No social dimension, no art.

This, needless to say, is a plausible assumption for Tolstoy to make since he wishes to develop a definition of art that will explain why society is willing to bear art's costs. And communication—including the communication of feeling—is a vital human need.

Nevertheless, the question of whether art requires receivers is a substantive issue that must be considered in any critical assessment of Tolstoy's theory. We must ask specifically: Can there be art just for the artist alone or must art, properly so called, be social, that is, be available to an audience?

This should clarify any initial questions about Tolstoy's definition of art. However, before examining Tolstoy's definition of art critically, let us look at the part of his theory concerned with the evaluation of art.

What Is Good Art?

So far, we have been looking at the way in which Tolstoy negotiates the top tier of the theory—how he tells art from nonart (or what he calls counterfeit art). Now let's look at how he deals with the question of how to determine whether art is good or bad. When we turn to the text, it is quickly apparent that the question of whether an artwork is good or bad is somewhat complicated because there are at least two independent standards of evaluation in Tolstoy's account. There is one standard for evaluating artworks independent of their content—or, as we might say, formally—and there is another standard for evaluating artworks in terms of their content.

Consider our outline of Tolstoy's theory, now expanded:

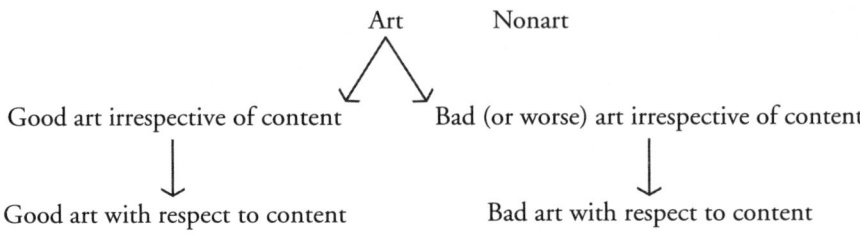

Let's first turn to the standard of evaluation irrespective of content.

In order to evaluate an artwork, you first have to be sure that what you're evaluating is an artwork. That can be determined by using the list of criteria established earlier. That list tells you that if you're dealing with a real, live artwork, then it has the properties of sincerity, individuality, and clarity. It has each of these attributes to some degree.

Moreover, we can, in principle, gauge the degree of sincerity, individuality, and clarity of an artwork's projection of a feeling without approving or disapproving the emotion in question. That is, whether a feeling is positive or good (say, brotherly love) or negative or bad (say, racial hatred), we can ascertain whether it is sincere, individualized (personally unique), and/or clear. In other words, we can gauge the sincerity, individuality, and clarity of the projected emotion without evaluating the emotion—that is, the very content of that which the artwork communicates, whether the feeling be, for example, one of fellowship or racism.

On Tolstoy's view, in terms of evaluating artworks irrespective of content, the *more* sincere, individualized, and clear an artwork is, the better it is. Note two things about this first standard of evaluation. First, it implies that anything that is an artwork is to some, if only minimal extent, good. Why? Because in order to be an artwork, a communication must cross some minimal threshold of sincerity, individuality, and clarity and, therefore, must have some quotient of each of these attributes and, hence, must be good to at least the extent it possesses some magnitude of each of these attributes. Second, looking back at Tolstoy's definition, note that it is only the degree terms—sincerity, individuality, and clarity—in that definition that come to play a role in the evaluation of the artwork, irrespective of its contents.

Nevertheless, even though artworks, properly so called, possess these characteristics, they may not possess them to a sufficient degree. For example, they may be obscure, as in the case of some of Beethoven's late works, Berlioz's *Symphonie Fantastique*, or Schonberg's atonal compositions. Or they may not be individualized; they may be more or less formulaic, like Horatio-Alger bromides or mass-produced pornography. Or, they may be manipulative and cynical rather than sincere, as in the case of a great many tearjerkers.

However, it is crucial to notice as well that although Tolstoy does concede that artworks can be evaluated irrespective of their content, this is not the most important standard of evaluation for Tolstoy. The most important standard of evaluation for Tolstoy concerns the way in which we assess artworks when we are attending to their content. But how do we evaluate artworks in terms of their *content*—that is, in terms of the emotions they express (since clearly the content of an artwork, for Tolstoy, is whatever emotions it transmits)? This, of course, comes down to the question: What emotions should artworks transmit? Tolstoy's brief answer is that the standard we use is and should be *religious*.

According to Tolstoy, when we are assessing art in light of its content, then we tell good art from bad art on the basis of the specific feelings they transmit. Art has a function—to communicate feelings. Just as language putatively functions ideally to communicate the *best* thoughts that humans of each age have had, art likewise ideally transmits the best feelings.

Both art and speech supposedly have a historic role to play in the evolution of human culture (shades of the Hegelian idea of progress here). That role is to transmit the best achievements in thought and feeling that humans have had. Art has an indispensable humanizing function—to transmit feelings, to educate people in the best feelings, and thereby to humanize people. This function is only fully realized when art transmits the very best feelings. Artistic content can be evaluated in terms of whether or not art is performing its historic function ideally—that is, transmitting the best emotions. But what are the best emotions? Those cultivated by religion, not institutional religion, but the faith of humble, true believers.

Whereas Hegel sees the progress in the history of art in terms of the enlargement of self-consciousness, Tolstoy measures the progress in terms of the way in which art contributes to the expansion of fellow feeling. Tolstoy's position is nevertheless Hegelian and not just because it advances a progressive view of history. For like Hegel, Tolstoy also connects progress with religion as a vehicle that transmits the deepest feelings of a culture at any given time. And, like Hegel, Tolstoy emphasizes that art can work in concert with religion to inculcate the deepest—Tolstoy would say "the best"—feelings of an age to its audience.

Tolstoy conceives of human history as an evolution toward perfection, although unlike Hegel, this is an evolution of feelings rather than of self-consciousness. Art has a role or function in that evolutionary process; it performs that function well when it engenders the best feelings, thereby hastening perfection. Each age or epoch has or develops more perfect feelings. It is the task or role of art to transmit these ever more perfect feelings, presumably until we arrive teleologically at the kingdom of God on earth. The key feelings of each epoch—the feelings that bring us ever closer to this perfection—are embodied in religion—not organized religion, but the religious faith of the common people (Tolstoy distrusts organized religion).

Now the religion of our own age, according to Tolstoy, is Christianity. The feeling that is central to it is what Tolstoy calls—employing a narrowly sexist idiom—the brotherhood of man under the fatherhood of God. The good art of our times, then, will be the art that transmits Christian feelings—that is, feelings of the *unity* of peoples under God.

This can be done in two ways:

(1) Directly—one can evoke explicitly Christian feelings—the unity of all human persons in the family of God's children. Tolstoy thinks that Charles Dickens's *A Christmas Carol*, Victor Hugo's *Les Misérables*, and Harriet Beecher Stowe's *Uncle Tom's Cabin* do this. That is, they evoke explicitly Christian feelings. Consider in Stowe's novel how often she emphasizes Tom's faith in the Christian God and the salvation story of Jesus. Gospel songs might be another example here, although not one that Tolstoy explicitly cites.

(2) Indirectly—artworks can be good by evoking Christian feeling indirectly—by instilling a sense of unity and sympathy among people without making direct or explicit reference to Christian theological tenets. This can be done by dealing with basic human experiences and thereby enlarging the emotional area in which humans feel togetherness or solidarity, but without directly alluding to Christianity. Tolstoy gives as examples of this: *David Copperfield*, *Don Quixote*, and the comedies of Molière. Had Tolstoy lived to see them, I think that he would have included the comedies of Charlie Chaplin in this category—that of things that abet fellow feeling and sympathetic union among peoples *without* explicitly evoking Christian doctrine. Tolstoy refers to this as *universal art*, which contrasts with Christian art as exemplified by works like *Uncle Tom's Cabin*.

Tolstoy states:

> The task for art to accomplish is to make that feeling of brotherhood and love of one's neighbor, now attained only by the best members of society, the customary feeling and the instinct of all men. By evoking under imaginary conditions the feeling of brotherhood and love, religious art will train men to experience those same feelings under similar circumstances in actual life; it will lay in the souls of men the rails along which the actions of those whom art thus educates will naturally pass. And universal art, by uniting the most different people in one common feeling, by destroying separation, will educate people to union, will show them, not by reason but by life itself, the joy of universal union reaching beyond the bounds set by life. (pp. 190–91)

So, in terms of content, artworks can be good either directly, that is, they transmit explicitly Christian feeling; or, they can be good if they instill a sense of unity among people (and are thus what he terms *universal art*), whereby they indirectly engender ideal Christian feeling among people without being explicitly Christian. Moreover, if artworks are good with respect to content for *encouraging* fellow feeling, a.k.a. love of thy neighbors, very broadly construed, then they are *bad* to the extent that artworks abet divisiveness and hatred among people, that is, to the extent that they discourage fellow feeling.

Bad art includes *propaganda* that trumpets that my country or my religion or my race is superior to the exclusion of all others. Such art is divisive and therefore bad, according to Tolstoy. This includes patriotic works such as Leni Riefenstahl's 1935 film *Triumph of the Will*. Likewise, art that reinforces social divisions either by celebrating the upper classes (e.g., portraits of the nobility) or by catering to their special interests and tastes (allegedly ballet) is bad to the extent that it exacerbates class stratification. Religious art that promulgates one religion over others or that declares that God is on our side ("*Deus vult!*") is bad precisely because it drives a wedge between peoples.

Similarly, elitist art designed for the consumption and consolidation of a single social class to the exclusion of others is also bad. Perhaps for Tolstoy, what we think of as avant-garde art, art made for the express purposes of affronting the sensibilities of the masses and for confirming the taste of specialized artistic coteries would be considered bad (if he would consider it art at all). In Tolstoy's experience, the poems of Baudelaire would probably fall into this category. Or, from our own time, consider the notorious example of Andres Serrano's *Piss Christ* as it was understood by the general public.

To summarize, then, Tolstoy offers us two standards for evaluating whether art is good or bad. The first standard assesses art irrespective of content. According to this standard, art is good or better insofar as the emotions it communicates are more sincere, individualized, and clear; art is less good or worse where the degrees of sincerity, individuality (mass art), and clarity (avant-garde art) it contains falls below some undefined threshold. Works that are obscure or formulaic, if they count as art at all, will be consigned to the rank of bad art.

This first standard of goodness is not as weighty for Tolstoy as the second standard of artistic evaluation—the evaluation of artworks in terms of their content, specifically in terms of their emotional content. Evaluated in terms of their emotional content, artworks are good if they either explicitly or implicitly promote Christian feeling—that is, artworks are good if they directly promote explicit Christian love of others under the godhead or insofar as they indirectly advance this end by engendering fellow feeling among peoples.

In terms of this second standard of artistic evaluation in terms of content, artworks are bad where they thwart fellow feeling by being divisive—either directly or indirectly. They may explicitly promote antipathy between peoples, as is the case of wartime propaganda, or they may do so implicitly by suggesting the superiority of the institutional religion they represent over all others.

So, a complete diagram of Tolstoy's theory looks like this:

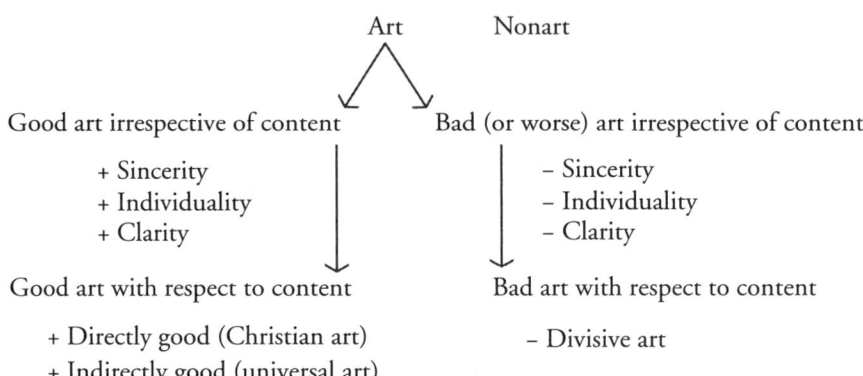

The first standard of evaluation—good irrespective of content—is obviously connected with Tolstoy's definition of art. But perhaps a case could also be made to the effect that there is a thematic relation between Tolstoy's definition of art and his second standard of evaluation—the content standard. For if one looks at Tolstoy's definition of art, one notes that it is underwritten by a view of emotional communication as a sort of communion. That is, artistic communication is a form of emotional sharing or communion. One might say that underlying the specific emotions shared through works of art, there is also a general emotion of sharing, communion, union, or sense of togetherness that all authentic works of art engender.

In other words, all genuine artworks engender an emotional sharing or feeling of union. In this respect, one might try to hypothesize that an emotion of communion or fusion with others or fellow feeling—the sharing of feeling or solidarity—is part and parcel of any authentic work of art or, at least, follows from what is thereby involved in being one.

Thus, if you buy this way of talking, Tolstoy's second standard of evaluation may also appear linked to his definition of art. For his definition of art might be read as implying that art, properly so called, has the function of promoting fellow feeling and, from this, the second standard of evaluation may seem to follow—that is, art is good insofar as it discharges the function of abetting fellow feeling.

Admittedly, there may be some problems with this attempt at grounding Tolstoy's way of evaluating content. For the inferential leap from communication/communion to fellow feeling may be too hasty. Moreover, the way in which this account suggests that we are to ground the notion of bad art seems murky. Recall that bad art is nevertheless art inasmuch as it has the properties of sincerity, individuality, and clarity to some, albeit insufficient, degree. Yet that entails that it communicates, at least to some degree. But doesn't it appear curious to associate bad art with respect to content with fellow feeling in any degree? For bad art in this sense is, by definition, divisive.

However, in any event, Tolstoy may not need to depend on the aforesaid inference since, as we have seen, he has at his disposal an explicit argument in terms of the progressive historical evolution of feeling to bolster his content standards of evaluation. Summarized from our previous exposition of Tolstoy's view of history, his argument may be presented as follows:

(1) If there is progress in human feeling, then it is the purpose of art to abet that progress by transmitting the best of the accumulated feelings of the past and the present. (Premise)

(2) There is progress in human feeling. (Premise)

(3) Therefore, it is the purpose of art to abet human progress by transmitting the best of the accumulated feelings of the past and the present. (From 1 and 2.)

(4) If a work of art performs its purpose, then it is good. (Premise)

(4a) If a work of art does not perform its purpose, then it is bad. (Premise)

(5) Therefore, if a work of art transmits the best accumulated feelings of the past and the present, then it is good. (From 3 and 4.)

(6) Religion defines the best accumulated feelings of the past and the present for each epoch. (Premise)

(7) Christianity is *the* religion of the present epoch. (Premise)

(8) Therefore, Christianity defines the best accumulated feelings (e.g., fellowship) of the past and present for the current epoch. (From 6 and 7.)

(9) Therefore, if a work of art in the present epoch transmits Christian feelings (e.g., fellowship), then it is good. (Roughly from 5 and 8.)

(9a) Therefore, if a work of art in the present epoch does not transmit Christian feelings, then it is bad. (The argument as it would have proceeded from 4a.)

A Critical Review of Tolstoy's Theory

Now that we have Tolstoy's entire theory before us, we can begin a critical examination of its details. We can start with his definition of art. Perhaps needless to say, since the theory is so aggressively revisionist, it should come as no surprise that it does not square with the prevailing contemporary consensus among art historians about that which belongs to the category of art. Nevertheless, it is informative to assess Tolstoy's theory in light of current views, if only to cast its radicality in bold relief.

In order to get a sense of Tolstoy's departure from reigning concepts of art nowadays, we can begin by going through his definition condition by condition, questioning their necessity, before turning to an assessment of the whole.

Tolstoy requires that artistic expression be intentional. One counterexample of this may be the Surrealist practice of the exquisite corpse. Surrealist poems were sometimes produced corporately. One poet would write the first line of a poem on a piece of paper, fold the paper over without telling anyone what she had written, and then pass it on to the next poet, who would do likewise. This process could last until every poet in the room had contributed at least one line to the poem. Or, they could start a second round.

Clearly, the resulting poem in terms of whatever emotion, if any, it expressed was not the intention of any one of the contributors to the poem. Nor was the express emotion—again, if any—the result of a group intention, since the poets were not in communication with each other. Moreover, not only were the Surrealists interested in composing poems in this way, they also produced drawings by means of a comparable procedure. Contemporary art historians regard the results of these processes as artworks, but obviously, Tolstoy cannot.

Similarly, Tristan Tzara, the Dadaist poet, is said to have composed poems by cutting words out of newspaper articles, putting them in a hat, and picking them out of the hat randomly. In such a case, it cannot be said that he intended to communicate a particular emotion—the poem and its mood would be the result of the luck of the draw; indeed, it cannot even be said that he intended to communicate any emotion whatsoever, since he could have had no idea whether the resulting concatenation of words would congeal into a coherent emotion.

Other avant-garde experiments in aleatoric techniques abound. The choreographer Merce Cunningham composed his dances by throwing the runes of the *I Ching*. Often these strategies are adopted in order to present the audience with an open-structured text, one where the audience is meant to supply its own interpretation of the work. But this sort of structure is not compatible with Tolstoy's view, since it renders the author's intention irrelevant in terms of the audience's reaction, affective or otherwise.

In these cases, one might say that since the authors still intend to make art, they do not violate Tolstoy's intention requirement. That is not clear, however, since he is more fine grained regarding what that intention aims to bring about. Nevertheless, some contemporary commentators may go so far as to deny the necessity of an intention to make art, or even to communicate, inasmuch as they accept that it is possible for very young children to make art, not to mention certain animals, such as chimpanzees and elephants. Yet it is not evident that children, chimps, and elephants possess the cognitive wherewithal to form the requisite intentions.

In any event, Tolstoy's requirement that the artistic communication be intentional in some sense may be the strongest claim for acceptance of all his conditions. His further claims are even less acceptable from the viewpoint of contemporary art history.

The demand that the artistic communication be clear has been intentionally violated by many movements in the modern period, including, for example, Symbolism which opted for diffuse and ambiguous affect. Subsequent movements such as Surrealism and Dadaism also strived willfully for obscurity. In their film *Un Chien Andalou*, Luis Buñuel and Salvador Dalí claim to have reedited their images whenever they felt the sequence started to make sense.

Moreover, as observed earlier, Tolstoy appears to suppose that the sincerity of the artist will involve an aspiration to clarity or even that sincerity entails a commitment to clarity. But this is a dubious inference. I doubt that Tolstoy questions Christ's sincerity, but Christ's parables were often not particularly clear. Christ wants his listeners to interpret them—to work at understanding them. Furthermore, this seems like a legitimate artistic aim—to employ indirection, ambiguity, and irony to encourage the reader, listener, or viewer to actively respond to an artwork by searching for its hidden meaning. Since Christ did it, would Tolstoy want to foreclose that avenue of address to authors less divine?

Tolstoy requires that the artistic communication involves a sender and a receiver. This clearly is inconsistent with the aesthetics of modernist art according to which artists may create for themselves—audiences be damned—in a gesture, among other things, of defiance with respect to the dominant forms of commercial mass art. But modernist aesthetics aside, arguably a poem is metaphysically still a work of art even if the poet writes it for her eyes only.

Surely, art status doesn't depend on the work having an actual audience. If a painting were destroyed on the way to the gallery before anyone besides the painter sees it, it would still be an artwork, wouldn't it? It sounds like magic to suppose that it only becomes art when at least one audience member looks at it.

Of course, Tolstoy might respond that all he requires is that it is intended to be presented to an audience, not that it is actually presented. But that seems questionable. If the poet writes a poem and burns it immediately, it seems unlikely that she intended to present it to an audience. Yet it is (was) still art. What else would it be?

Tolstoy contends that the feeling communicated by the artist must be identical to the feeling experienced by the reader, viewer, or listener. This appears to deny that there can be a divergence between the author's emotion and the audience's. Among other problems, this does not allow for irony on the part of the author. Jonathan Swift's *A Modest Proposal* is designed to provoke a feeling of approbation in its complacent readers, whereas Swift's attitude toward them is one of moral contempt.

Of course, irony may not be the only motivation for an asymmetry between what the artist feels and what his audience feels. The artist may be commissioned to work on a project for which he has no sympathies. He may be an atheist cast as a believer in a faith-based film. He may feign devotion in a religious doctrine to which he feels no attraction—and even possibly some loathing—and yet he may elicit a feeling of reverence in viewers. His performance may be manipulative, but that does not discount its status as art.

Some actors may claim that it is impossible to be convincing without feeling the emotion of the character. But that is just superstitious. As Sir Laurence Olivier said to Dustin Hoffman—when, during the filming of *Marathon Man*, Hoffman asked him what he needed to be feeling in a certain scene—"just try acting."

The preceding case, of course, also raises questions about Tolstoy's requirement that the feelings communicated in the artistic exchange be sincere. As a child, I once heard Boris Karloff tell a scary story to a group of us who attended a screening of *The Raven*. He sent chills up our spines, but I doubt that he was frightened. Indeed, he probably derived some pleasure—and perhaps chuckled inwardly—at his well-practiced capacity to make our hair stand on end. One can readily imagine unsentimental authors commissioned to write romance novels who nevertheless succeed in making their readers weep because they know the most effective strategies for eliciting the relevant responses.

Here, it may be claimed that even if the authors do not feel the sentiments they aim to engender while writing, they must have felt it at some time or another. But this seems to me controversial. Again, think of the atheist playing a redeemed sinner. Suppose that he was raised by atheists, such that he never experienced a religious moment in his entire life. Why imagine that such an actor, if talented enough, could not arouse devotion in an audience of believers?

Art forms have recurring strategies for eliciting certain emotions. Those strategies will perform their function whether or not the artist currently has or ever had the feelings in question. This often happens with respect to commissioned art. But there is no reason to suppose that if the artist is not sincerely communicating his feelings, the work is not art.

Tolstoy might respond to some of these examples by reminding us that he requires that the feeling communicated by the genuine artwork must be individualized. It cannot be generic. But this does not seem to correspond to art as we know it. Tragedy and comedy each appear to have certain emotions that they aim at eliciting. As we saw, according to Aristotle, Greek tragedies were intended to elicit pity and fear. But did Sophoclean pity and fear differ from the Euripidean variety?

You might claim that they did in virtue of possessing different objects. But on those grounds, virtually every numerically different emotional state would differ from every other state, which would be too easy a way to claim any one of them was individualized. That is, this would render vacuous the notion of an individualized feeling.

Tolstoy claims that what is communicated by a work of art is a feeling. Even though he appears to have a generous notion of that which constitutes a feeling, it is not generous enough. Some artworks are intended to communicate ideas. Much modern art, for example, is intended to communicate ideas about art. For example, Andy Warhol's *Brillo Box* metaphorically makes the point that art, especially in the contemporary art world, is a commodity. The work does not communicate a feeling about this. It does not express outrage. It just presents an idea in pictorial form.

Tolstoy defended the notion that art communicates feelings by drawing a contrast between art and speech. However, that distinction is not compelling since, on the one hand, some speech—poetry, hate speech, patriotic oratory, prayer, and so on—communicates feeling, while, on the other hand, some art communicates ideas, such as the chapters on history in Tolstoy's own *War and Peace*, and the chapter on whales in *Moby Dick*, not to mention the social criticism in novels such as *Brave New World, 1984, Fahrenheit 451*, and so on.

Tolstoy stipulates that artistic communication is expressed by means of lines, colors, sounds, or forms expressed by words. Obviously, by including "forms expressed by words" in this qualification, Tolstoy appears to undermine the distinction he draws between speech and art, unless by "forms expressed in words," he is drawing a distinction between speech and some distinguishable effect of speech. But it is hard to see what that might be since every trope available to poetry, for example, would also be available to rhetoric.

Moreover, as indicated earlier, the work Tolstoy appears to intend for this stipulation may be circular. That is, the formula looks like an attempt to identify established artistic forms without introducing their names: painting, music, and poetry. However, this will not do the work Tolstoy appears to want done, since nonart practices, such as advertising, will also employ these media. The clear-cut way for Tolstoy to close this lacuna would be for him to say that the communication of feeling he has in mind must be expressed by means of some genuinely *art*istic medium, but this would be circular since it is the very notion of *art* that he is attempting to define.

Each of the conditions that Tolstoy presents as necessary or required for something to count as a work of art is controversial. But the formula is also jointly insufficient to pick out all and only items that we would typically consider artworks. It is too exclusive—it will not pick out all the artworks for the reasons we have just seen; Tolstoy's criteria exclude works that we would consider bone fide works of art, such as Symbolist and Surrealist artworks. But it is also too inclusive. It will categorize things as artworks that we would not.

Consider a letter written to an ex-lover who has betrayed you. You wish to express your contempt for your ex. You intend your ex to feel precisely as small and slimy as you regard him/her to be. Your writing is emotionally charged, blisteringly clear, sincere, highly personal, withering. Your ex feels terrible. You infect your ex with your loathing. Your ex hates himself/herself as much as you do.

It would appear that such a letter would have to be a work of art according to Tolstoy's account but would not be so classified by art historians. Thus, in addition to not categorizing as art much that art historians would, Tolstoy's theory has the potential to find art in places where we would never look, including joyful home videos of birthday parties, love letters (and hate letters), Sunday sermons, and so on. That is, combining the conditions in Tolstoy's definition is not conjointly sufficient for picking out all and only art.

Thus, Tolstoy's definition fails to pick out the extension of much that we currently regard as art, while also countenancing as art some things that we would never regard as such. Of course, this is perhaps to be expected since Tolstoy's theory is avowedly revisionist. Consequently, although the preceding counterexamples may satisfy us as refutations of Tolstoy's view, they would not likely move him. Indeed, he would regard many of the avant-garde examples as counterfeit art due to their intentional obscurity, while those that survive that test are apt to rank badly due to their divisiveness—their commitment to outraging the bourgeoisie along with everyone else who does not belong to their visionary company.

So, is it possible to challenge Tolstoy's theory in a way that might convince him of its inadequacy? Perhaps we can demonstrate to the satisfaction of someone attracted to Tolstoy's definition of art that crucial aspects of it are self-defeating, given the aims of anyone sympathetic to Tolstoy's overall project.

Earlier, we noted that the requirement that the artist and her audience share the same feelings is open to question in terms of irony. Irony is often a useful strategy for the purpose of social criticism. We cited Swift's *A Modest Proposal*; but Swift means to entrap English readers into feeling positively about a program that Swift himself regards as outrageous in order to unmask his audience's evil. Does Tolstoy wish to divest the social critic of an artistic weapon as potent as irony, especially in virtue of its capacity to expose hypocrisy?

Clearly, Tolstoy himself is interested in social criticism; in *What Is Art?*, he practices it himself. He pretends that he doesn't understand the conventions of opera and ballet and describes them as a country bumpkin might for the purpose of defamiliarizing them in a way that renders them absurd. In this he means to attack the entertainments of the czarist aristocracy. But is Tolstoy being sincere when he adopts this posture? Again, his own theory may stand in the way of the kind of social criticism that he practices.[10]

He might respond that these excerpts from *What Is Art?* are not artworks and so are not problems for his theory. Yet, it is easy to imagine riffs like these as part of a short story—an intentionally humorous one—or even as a tale told by a wily peasant. Yet in such cases, Tolstoy could not categorize them as art by his own lights.

---

10. Also, given the premium that he places on the Christian message, it is not clear that he should lay down a blanket charge against ballet, since some ballets, like *Giselle*, advance overtly Christian themes as evinced by the forgiveness and redemption of Count Albrecht.

Tolstoy requires that artworks communicate an emotion that is individualized. And yet the emotion he prizes above all—Christian solidarity—risks being generic. Tolstoy commends the Christian message in *Uncle Tom's Cabin* in this respect. However, Tom's faith in that novel is extremely formulaic. Undoubtedly it is true in the fiction that Tom believes these Christian doctrines, but the way he expresses them sounds as if he is parroting a catechism. There is nothing individualized about Tom's theology; it is pretty much the standard party line. Some might say that it would not be out of place on a Christian greeting card.

Moreover, this may not simply be a problem with Stowe's novel; it would appear to be a potential pitfall for most attempts at producing explicitly Christian art, as is evidenced by many contemporary faith-based movies. They seem to gravitate toward the homiletic, even though they are sincere. And this raises another potential in Tolstoy's approach: How would he adjudicate cases where the emotion communicated is sincere, clear, and infectious, but not individualized, as is likely with much honestly intended religious art?

Indeed, there may even be a lurking tension in Tolstoy's account of art between the clarity requirement and the individualization requirement inasmuch as a certain degree of individuality may potentially come at the expense of clarity, where clarity is understood as being pellucid to one and all. Some sincere, highly individual, genuinely Christian art, like Robert Bresson's film *Diary of a Country Priest*, may be made with the intention to communicate genuine religious sentiments, but ones not readily accessible to everyone. Would Tolstoy regard this as counterfeit art? Obviously, this returns us to the problem raised by Christ's own parables.

In addition to these questions about Tolstoy's definition of art, there are also problems regarding his standards of evaluation. He assesses artworks to be good or bad in virtue of their possession or lack of sincerity, clarity, and individuality. However, we are talking about artworks; so, by definition, these must possess *some* degree of sincerity, clarity, and individuality. Thus, all artworks, properly so called, must be good irrespective of content. That is, all artworks are good to some extent. But this hardly seems to be an acceptable consequence. Surely, there are some artworks that are formally bad (absolutely obscure and unintentionally unfathomable). A theory, like Tolstoy's, that cannot accommodate this fact is certainly fatally flawed.

Tolstoy's theory also appears liable to the obverse criticism. It does not seem that formal defectiveness is simply a matter of a *lack* of formal goodness. Some works may be positively formally bad, without any redeeming formal qualities, whether in terms of clarity or individuality.

Indeed, there may be a systematic difficulty in terms of attempting to characterize kind terms, like good and bad, by means of degree terms like sincerity, clarity, and/or individuality. That is, the good/bad dichotomy appears to be a sharp yes/no, on/off distinction rather than a continuum. But if that is the case, degree concepts like clarity and individuality are not sufficient to define any strict opposition between goodness and badness. *Good* and *bad* seem to be logical contraries, but that is not consistent with their allegedly being matters of degree.

Tolstoy, of course, might attempt to repair these shortcomings by arguing that there is some definable threshold here over which artworks are categorically good and under which artworks are categorically bad. But it is hard to see how this threshold can be established in an indisputably nonarbitrary fashion.

Tolstoy's evaluative standards with respect to content undoubtedly strike us as alien, most particularly, with respect to his estimation of Christian art. This claim is crucially supported by two premises in his argument—namely, that the religion of an epoch defines the best feelings of that epoch and that Christianity is the religion of Tolstoy's and our epoch. Both premises appear controversial.

It is improbable that religions define the best feelings of their historical epochs. It stretches the imagination to the breaking point to think of a religion like that of the Aztecs—that embraced human sacrifice—as embodying the best feelings of its time in the sun. To maintain that religion always represents the best human feelings can only be sustained by adopting a question-begging definition of religion that would exclude Aztec worship, and comparable pious nastiness from the category of religion by stipulation. Tolstoy's claim on behalf of religion as a beacon to right feeling comes at the cost of either historical obliviousness *or* of a speciously biased, selective conception of religion that cherry-picks only the nice ones. But either way, the claim appears questionable.

Moreover, the assertion that Christianity is the religion of Tolstoy's epoch and presumably our own confronts a similar dilemma. It is obviously false if "Christian" has its normal extension, but circular if Tolstoy means it to refer to only the variants he approves of because they communicate what he antecedently regards as the best feelings of his and our moment.

Tolstoy begins his argument for Christian art with two premises: that if there is progress in human feeling, it is the function of art to abet it; and that there is progress in human feeling. I suspect that most of us can agree that abetting progress in human feeling can be a function of art, but I reckon that most are not convinced that it is the one and only function of art, nor that it has been or should be. Tolstoy might argue that it should be in order to account for the sacrifices made historically in order to support its production. But surely there are other explanations available here beyond telegraphing the best human feelings that, in turn, would warrant more functions for art to discharge than just one.

Moreover, with reference to the second premise, although most of us would probably agree that progress has been made in human sentiment, as evidenced by the extension of civil rights to certain racial and ethnic minorities, to women, and to LGBTQ people in significant parts of the world, we would also deny that it has been providential, as Tolstoy, a committed Christian, apparently believes. For Christians have faith in a foreordained eschatological redemption at the end of time (of history). But for the rest of us, whether or not there is progress in human sentiment is a contingent matter and not the necessary destination of the historical process. Unlike a believer such as Tolstoy, most philosophers nowadays deny that history has a teleological structure.

Arguably, progress has been made as a matter of fact, but regression is still always possible. Remember the Third Reich. And, furthermore, there is no guarantee that in the last instance, humane feeling will win the day. For example, to return to Tolstoy's later premises, religion, as commonly denominated, even as grasped by the simple folk, can be an agent of regression as well as of progress. Who can predict when religious violence will break out? Who can say with certitude that the future belongs to universal solidarity?

In any event, the unavoidable bottom line here is that moral progress is not an inevitable feature of the historical process, as Tolstoy's argument appears to presuppose. Art cannot be marshaled on the side of the inexorable march of history because *history* has no sides as such.

Perhaps Tolstoy's argument can be reconstructed in light of this objection. Since progress in human feeling is such a contingent, indeed, fragile matter, it may be argued there is a moral injunction that art function in its service. That is, given that moral progress is such an overriding goal for humanity, art must do whatever is in its reach to make it happen, if not directly as Christian art, then indirectly as universal art.

This once again raises questions about whether if art is capable of performing several important functions, there should be a categorical imperative for it to hew to only one of them. Tolstoy might say that in times when human solidarity is at risk, the urgency of the task mandates that art facilitate love. In other words, it's a matter of triage. But what about times when there is a modicum of avoidable strife? What pressure is there for art to stimulate amity then?

Of course, even when it comes to what Tolstoy calls universal art, we do not today believe that art's designated function is to engender comity among all. Avant-gardists commonly self-elect themselves as critics of the status quo, which, of course, puts them at odds, for instance, with not only contemporary capitalism but also the masses of consumers whose purchases keep the system running. Moreover, not only is this the consensus among what Tolstoy would have considered elitist artists, but the conviction has trickled down to popular artists as well. Rock star Bono of U2 claims that "the job of art is to be divisive."

The preceding objection to universal art may seem to fail to address Tolstoy's position from his perspective. That is, these counterexamples are not ones that would unsettle him, since he would not be troubled to consign the likes of Bono's music to the status of bad art. Yet they raise a question that may be recurrently problematic for Tolstoy's posture.

Tolstoy himself is a social critic, and social criticism seems like it is indispensable to his reformist intentions. But how can there be social criticism without some acrimony? Nor will the needful criticism simply be directed at the ruling classes, since the masses may be their docile followers and, for that reason, the proper object of critical rebuke, as well. In short, must not Tolstoy's system tolerate some divisiveness, since otherwise it seems to be self-defeating. But this complicates, if not undermines, pragmatically the case for the generality of universal art as a criterion of good art with respect to content. In concert with our earlier criticisms of Christian art, this raises serious questions about the grounds for Tolstoy's recommended standards of artistic evaluation with respect to content.

In addition, although Tolstoy has provided us with two ways of judging art—with respect to content and irrespective of content—he has not supplied us with any hint into the way in which we might go about coordinating these standards so as to make an "all things considered" evaluation of a given work of art. That is, how are we to combine these two standards in order to issue an overall judgment of the value of a selected artwork? Tolstoy gives us little or no guidance. What are we to say by way of a summary evaluation about a somewhat obscure, but not totally obscure, yet sincere and individualized work of committed Christian art? To the extent that Tolstoy has nothing to suggest about cases like this, his theory of evaluation is, among other problems, not sufficiently comprehensive.

Concluding Remarks

Given his unabashed revisionism, Tolstoy's definition of art deviates unsurprisingly from contemporary opinion about what counts as art. Tolstoy would probably consign most of what the art world today welcomes as art to the category of nonart (a.k.a. *counterfeit art*), and of that which passes Tolstoy's criteria for art status, most of it would be considered by him to be bad art.

Much modernist art like *Finnegans Wake* would not count as art due to authors' (like James Joyce's) forthright pronounced lack of a commitment to communication with the great body of humanity, whereas Tolstoy would be happy to disenfranchise most mass art from the category of art on the grounds that it is too formulaic and, therefore, nonindividualized.

Furthermore, many candidates for art status presently ignored by the art world would have to be reassigned to the canon, including perhaps, things like folk art, spirituals, and maybe even break dancing before it was commercialized or genuine Christian videos on YouTube, if there are any.

None of this reshuffling of the canon would probably disturb Tolstoy. He seems to have foreseen the world to come—our world of modernism on the one hand and mass art on the other—and found it wanting. He does not wish to interpret such a world; he intends his philosophy to change it. However, as we have seen, his theory may be at odds with this aim. It may pragmatically impede, for example, some of the very kinds of social criticism that his reformist program would appear to prescribe.

Tolstoy's commitment to Christian art and his argument on its behalf probably strike many contemporary readers as hopelessly dated. Yet, it is interesting to note that it may not be as old-fashioned as it may seem.

Yes, the explicit invocation of Christianity rings parochial. But if we change the terms of the argument somewhat, it is not clear that the result might not find favor with many progressives of various stripes. For instance, if instead of talking about the sentiment of Christian solidarity, we speak of encouraging the feeling of working-class solidarity or multicultural tolerance for every form of diversity, I suspect that many progressives—from socialists to small "l" liberals—would accept something like the historical imperative for their own cause that Tolstoy dragoons for his.

Moreover, they would, I think, be tempted to employ something like Tolstoy's argument, holding that art has a historical responsibility to abet the best emotions of their pertinent era—whether those be class solidarity, liberal tolerance, or a positive attitude toward multicultural diversity. Although eschewing Tolstoy's religious baggage, many progressives probably accept the proposition that art should be mobilized in the service of moral improvement, specifically in terms of improving empathy and equality among classes, races, sexes, sexualities, ethnicities, and so forth. They would most probably commend movies like *The Help* and *Pride* for engendering right feelings.

Many progressives may see improving sentiments of sympathy, tolerance, and acceptance among diverse groups of people as a historical mission that they must carry forward, in part by enlisting art in this endeavor. In this regard, Tolstoy's argument can be seen as a patent for many contemporary progressive arguments by movements with no commitments to Christianity, but with a faith in some or other utopia to come. Their difference, it needs to be stressed, with Tolstoy is one of detail—a question of what they regard as the emotions to be habituated in their own times, which it is art's vocation to promote as part of its historio-teleological essence.

The heirs of Tolstoy, that is, still walk among us.

This tendency, articulated so forcefully by Tolstoy, to submit art to a social agenda, although embraced even today by reformers of various allegiances, predictably has elicited a reaction formation, one that declares art to be altogether independent of the claims of society on art. That rejoinder posits the autonomy of art. One of the most influential statements in opposition to the kind of social approach that Tolstoy advanced was developed powerfully in the early twentieth century by the subject of our next chapter, Clive Bell.

Bibliography

Almyer Maude's translation of Tolstoy's *What Is Art?* (Macmillan/Library of Liberal Arts, 1960) was used for this chapter.

Bates, Stanley. "Tolstoy Evaluated." In *Aesthetics: A Critical Anthology*, edited by George Dickie and Richard Sclafani, 83–93. New York: St. Martin's, 1977.
———. "Tolstoy, Leo Nikolaevich." In *Oxford Encyclopedia of Aesthetics*, vol. 4, edited by Michael Kelly, 393–96. Oxford: Oxford University Press, 1998.
Diffey, T. J. *Tolstoy's What Is Art?* London: Croom Helm, 1985.
Jahn, Gary R. "The Aesthetic Theory of Leo Tolstoy." *Journal of Aesthetics and Art Criticism* 34 (1975): 59–65.
Matlaw, Ralph E., ed. *Tolstoy: A Collection of Critical Essays*. Englewood Cliffs, NJ: Prentice Hall, 1967.
Mounce, H. O., *Tolstoy on Aesthetics: What Is Art?* Aldershot, UK: Ashgate, 2001.
Silbajoris, Rimvydas. *Tolstoy's Aesthetics and His Art*. Bloomington, IN: Slavica, 1990.

CHAPTER 9

Clive Bell's *Art*

Art by Clive Bell was published in 1912. Bell was an English art critic. He was a member of the Bloomsbury intellectual circle, which included, among others, such figures as the novelist Virginia Woolf, the economist John Maynard Keynes, the biographer Lytton Strachey, and fellow art critic and painter Roger Fry. The group was named after the Bloomsbury neighborhood in London where they lived, and the group was culturally influential in Britain between the two world wars.

Bell's *Art* was an extremely important book. Apart from its philosophical impact, it was enormously influential in changing the artistic tastes of the English-speaking world, undoubtedly due to its exceedingly clear, crisp, well-written polemical style.

One way to initially place *Art* is as a defense of what we now call modern art—specifically, it can be read as a brief on behalf of neo-impressionism, such as, for example, the art of Paul Cézanne. But it also prepared sympathetic readers for the abstract art that was to come on the heels of neo-impressionism.

This art needed to be defended in the context of the early twentieth century because it departed from the way that the world looked and this caused widespread skepticism in a public that took verisimilitude to be the benchmark of art, properly so called. In these circumstances, Bell taught people how to appreciate the artistic value of art that was not dedicated to holding a mirror up to nature.

Art is a book that is primarily concerned with visual art—sculpture, but especially painting—rather than the arts in general (although some might claim a wider scope for the argument than Bell himself did). Bell's view, in contrast to Plato, is that visual art is not essentially a matter of imitation; instead, art is about form, that is, formal visual structure. By downplaying the importance of imitation and upgrading the importance of form, Bell was preparing the English-speaking world for the various modernist experiments in form, including eventually abstraction. From Bell's viewpoint, imitation, or accurately capturing the look of the world, is not what an artist *qua* artist essentially does. What a painter does is create form: balance, symmetries, interesting disequilibria, and so forth. This sort of aim does not require a picture in order to be carried out. Thus, *Art* is a seminal book because, among other things, it is tutoring the audience for art in how to appreciate abstract pictorial structures.

Bell's *Art* addressed the need to develop appreciative frameworks for the new forms of visual art that were beginning to emerge with increasing frequency from the work of Édouard Manet onward. This art was willfully abandoning the goal of imitating nature. A major factor in this shift from verisimilitude to, eventually, abstraction was indisputably the invention of photography.

As the nineteenth century turned into the twentieth, photography, and later cinematography, accounted for a shift in both theory and practice from painting as imitation to painting as abstraction. For if, as Plato claimed, art was a matter of holding a mirror up to nature, then photography threatened to do away with the vocation of painting since photography, it seemed, could automatically achieve virtually immediately what cost painters immense amounts of manual labor. Photography and then cinematography seemed to threaten to make painting—thought of as the process of capturing the appearance of things accurately—obsolete.

In a world where photography was becoming ever more accurate, painting appeared to have little role left to play. Just as the horse and buggy were rendered outmoded by the automobile, so photography and cinematography appeared to usurp the traditional role of painting. Painting simply couldn't compete if it defined itself in terms of verisimilitude. Thus, so to speak, painting needed to find some other occupation—something else to do—if it was to continue to command attention in the age of mechanical reproduction.

Part of the solution was modern art, a turn away from the commitment to verisimilitude in favor of strategies of distortive expression, aggressive pictorial invention, radical stylization, and abstraction. Visual artists abandoned the role of making slavishly realistic paintings. Viewers, however, had to find new ways of engaging this radically new art. And that was where a figure like Clive Bell entered the picture.

Bell plays a crucial role in this momentous transition because he teaches people a new way to appreciate visual art, one that downplays the mimetic or imitative approach and that encourages people to appreciate art in terms of form, or what he calls *significant form*.

The paintings that Bell primarily has in mind in *Art* are the neo-impressionist paintings of artists like Cézanne and Henri Matisse. These works still have representational motifs, though these paintings are not noteworthy most particularly for being imitations of what they picture. The figures in them are flattened and distorted for the sake of formal aims. Training viewers to appreciate these paintings in terms of formal design, in effect, readied audiences for the even more adventurous abstractions to come. Consequently, the publication of *Art* was a decisive juncture in the history of taste of the intelligentsia in, at the very least, the English-speaking world.

However, Bell himself would not have described the ambition of his book in this way. That is, he is not presenting *Art* simply as a way of responding to a change in the art of his time. He does not introduce himself merely as a critic who means to tell his audience how to negotiate the new art. Rather, he represents himself as a theorist or a philosopher. He intends to tell us about how art is and has been essentially for all times and all places. He is not saying that art changed last week, and that modern art would be a good thing for artists to do now that we have photography. If anything, he would say that photography makes us suddenly aware that art was never about merely imitating things. Everywhere there is genuine art there is and has been art that is devoted to form. Bell speaks in a philosopher's voice; he speaks *sub specie aeternitatis*.

In the last chapter, I noted that the expression theory of art arose as an alternative to the imitation theory of art, where the latter no longer appeared to be adequate to developments in the art world. Another alternative or successor theory to the imitation view is the sort of theory propounded by Bell; it is called formalism since it claims that the defining feature of art is form, or, as Bell puts it, *significant form*.

This emphasis on form enables Bell to appreciate things that other critics, wedded to the notion of art-as-imitation, could not, such as art from other cultures not committed to verisimilitude. Bell, for instance, is able to appreciate African masks—the kinds of masks that influenced Pablo Picasso—because of their formal qualities. He does not reject them as primitive, that is, as failed imitations; instead, he thinks that these tribal peoples were onto what art was really about. They were not caught up in the alleged Renaissance mistake of supposing that art is a matter of representation.

From his philosophical perspective of formalism, Bell rewrites the history of art in the West so that certain artists like Duccio and the Byzantine painters of icons get upgraded in virtue of their formal qualities, whereas DaVinci and Michelangelo are problematic: with their emphasis on verisimilitude, they seemed to be going in the wrong direction.

Bell does not present his view as a recommendation about what art can or should do now that photography is on the scene, although that actually may be an important element in the causal-historical factors accounting for the shift from representational art to modern art. Alternatively, what Bell can be taken as saying is that of what the new art makes us aware is precisely what art has always been about—from the cave paintings in Lascaux to the sand paintings of Native Americans through to Picasso. That is, art has always been about form, or, in his idiom, significant form.

Bell and His Predecessors

Before we start to look at the text of *Art* in detail, it would be useful to stand back and notice correspondences between Bell's theory and the theories we have encountered earlier so that we can see where Bell is coming from and start to make some connections. First, it should be clear that there is a strong correspondence with Hutcheson. Significant form plays the same role for Bell that uniformity amidst variety plays for Hutcheson, even though Bell does not believe that there is a discrete sense receptor that is responsive to the relevant stimulus.

For Bell, significant form is a structural feature of a work of art. In Hutcheson, certain structural features, that is, uniformity in variety, cause those feelings or sentiments that we call beauty. Bell does not like to talk about beauty because he thinks that in his own time beauty typically connotes sexuality or sexiness, so he avoids the term *beauty*. In its stead, he uses the notion of *aesthetic emotion*, which is pretty close to what Hutcheson and Kant talk about as the subjective experience of beauty or what is now often referred to as *aesthetic experience*.[1]

One difference between Hutcheson and Bell is that Hutcheson believed he could identify the exact structural features in an artwork that give rise to the subjective feeling of beauty by means of the uniformity-amidst-variety formula. Bell, in this respect, is much more like Kant, who denies that one can isolate the determinate conditions that provoke the aesthetic emotion by means of a specifiable concept, like the compound ratio of uniformity amidst diversity.

For Kant, the target of aesthetic judgment is purposiveness without a purpose or forms of finality. Similarly, Bell's notion of significant form is not reducible to a set of rules—rather, we know it when we see it. In other words, Bell, like Kant, does not think he can actually define a rule for eliciting that the aesthetic emotion. He just gives whatever it is that provokes the aesthetic emotion the technical name "significant form."

Yet significant form is reminiscent of Kant's form of finality in that it is the focus of the mental state called the "aesthetic emotion" by Bell, "aesthetic judgment" by Kant, and "aesthetic experience" by many contemporary philosophers. There can be little question but that Bell is descended from Kant, most especially from the first section of his *Third Critique*, the "Analytic of the Beautiful." (Whether Bell read beyond that is arguably doubtful.)

As already indicated, Bell is called a formalist, the name usually given to his philosophical position. He is called a formalist because he thinks that the object—the appropriate object—of aesthetic experience and the source of aesthetic emotion

---

1. It is interesting that Bell refers to this state as an "emotion," albeit an *aesthetic* emotion. Perhaps this shows the influence of Tolstoy. However, this choice is strange on several counts. The emotions typically are connected to human interests, but the aesthetic emotion, oddly enough, is disconnected from any such interests. Bell writes, "Art transports us from the world of man's activity to a world of aesthetic exaltation. For the moment we are shut off from human interests . . ." (p. 27).

Moreover, in mobilizing emotion talk, Bell appears to want to suggest the notion that there is a specific, unique feeling that is associated with exposure to art and only art. But this is problematic for two related reasons: nowadays, many are skeptical of the claim that emotions are associated to uniquely distinctive feeling states or qualia, *and*, in any event, there is even greater skepticism about the suggestion that exposure to artworks engenders an absolutely specific emotion (if it evokes an emotion at all). Thus, the descendants of Bell and his tradition are apt to speak of *aesthetic experiences* rather than of *aesthetic emotions*.

are the forms of the work of art, which he calls significant form. For Bell, something is art just in case it possesses what he calls significant form, and it is for this reason that this kind of theory is labeled a formalist theory. Bell is perhaps the paradigmatic formalist with respect to visual art.[2]

Arguably, formalism is descended from a notion that Kant introduced, namely, forms of finality or forms of purposiveness without a purpose. For the formalist, the target of aesthetic attention should be formal relations, and this is something that Bell thinks one can appreciate and apprehend independently of content. One can appreciate the various pictorial equilibriums between the groups of philosophers in Raphael's *The School of Athens*, for instance, without knowing anything about their doctrines.

Using Kant's vocabulary, Bell's notion of significant form is not a determinate concept—that is, it doesn't have any criteria. You know it when you confront it because it raises a certain feeling—the aesthetic emotion—in you, but there's no formula for arousing the aesthetic emotion. The Psychology Department cannot run tests on people to find out the rules you would need in order to construct an object in such a way as to elicit reliably the aesthetic emotion. It is all in the tasting, in other words.

We can also regard Bell as someone whose position on art is actually a way of insulating art from the kinds of criticisms Plato launched in his *Republic*. Plato wants to know what good art is for society—what benefit does it contribute to the commonwealth? Bell's answer is that this is not what art is supposed to do. Art is about instilling certain particular emotions, aesthetic emotions. Art is not about the everyday emotions Plato was worried about, that is, pity and fear, or any of the other garden-variety emotions that people encounter in everyday life. Art is actually something that raises you to an exalted emotional state, one that parts company with the everyday, the practical, instrumental, and/or means-ends relationships. Art casts you out of your self-absorption. It neutralizes your interests and interests in general.

In a way, Bell is on the opposite side of the debate from Plato, answering him by suggesting that Plato has misunderstood that which art is actually about. Art is about form; art is not about training the guardians or anyone else to rein in their appetites. Indeed, formalism historically has been a recurrently available countermove against censorship and claims that art is beholden to any kind of social imperative. Robert Mapplethorpe's photographs, for instance, were successfully

---

2. Arguably Eduard Hanslick is the paradigmatic musicological formalist. A literary version of formalism arose independently in the 1920s in Russia, while the American approach to literary criticism, called the New Criticism, evinced the influence of Bell's version of formalism. In terms of the fine arts, an expansion with nevertheless some connection to Bell's formalism was evolved by the critic/theorist Clement Greenberg, undoubtedly the most influential American art writer of the twentieth century.

defended in court against civic charges of pornography on the grounds of their formal value by art critics and historians.

Hutcheson and Kant both think of aesthetic experience as disinterested. Bell does not deploy the language of disinterestedness, but he clearly thinks that art, or at the very least the aesthetic experience, is free, in the sense that it is free from the concerns of life. For example, Bell says that "the contemplation of pure form leads to a state of extraordinary exaltation and complete detachment from the concerns of life" (p. 54).[3] So instead of "disinterested," Bell uses the phrase "complete detachment." He also says, "The form of significance of any material thing is that thing considered as an end in itself."[4] That is, the significant form of something is a feature of that thing as not connected to anything else.[5] It is intrinsically valuable.

Furthermore, Bell claims: "Be they artists or lovers of art, mystics or mathematicians, those who achieve ecstasy are those who have freed themselves of the arrogance of humanity" (p. 55). The word *ecstasy* is derived from the Greek *ekstasis*, which is being outside yourself. It's connected to the notion of detachment and disinterestedness as being outside of yourself and outside of normal human interests. It's a matter of transcending selfish interests. It's another term for that state that people try to get at with the notion of disinterestedness.

Moreover, "those who achieve ecstasy are those who have freed themselves from the arrogance of humanity. He who would feel the significance of art would make himself humble before it. Those who find the chief importance of art . . . in its relation to conduct, or practical utility . . . will never get . . . the best that it can give" (p. 55). That is, those like Plato who want art to be beneficial, and who "cannot value things as ends in themselves" misunderstand art categorically.

That is, utility, human business, ordinary passion—none of that has anything to do with the true appreciation of art. Like Kant and Hutcheson, Bell thinks the aesthetic experience is disinterested. But his position is also more radical than that. Indeed, he sounds much more like Schopenhauer. Why? Because Bell doesn't just think that disinterestedness is a feature of aesthetic experience; it's also the very point of aesthetic experience. That is, it is precisely why we have aesthetic experience. Bell says: "Art transports us from the world of man's activity to a world

---

3. All page numbers are from the edition of Bell's *Art* cited in the Bibliography.

4. This is a tricky claim since significant form *is* a means to something else, namely, aesthetic emotion. So, it is important that in this passage, Bell is talking about significant form *being considered* as an end in itself (even though it is not, strictly speaking, an end in itself). Slippage between talk about the end, aesthetic experience, being intrinsically valuable and the means to it, also being said to be an end in itself, is unfortunately common in discussions of aesthetic experience.

5. This notion that significant form is not connected to anything else will, as we shall see, provide Bell with the basis for claiming that the causes of significant form—like authorial intentions and historical factors—and the consequences or effects of artworks—including moral and political ones—are irrelevant to the engagement proper with artworks.

of aesthetic exultation. For a moment we are shut off from human interests, our anticipations and memories are arrested, we are lifted above the stream of life" (p. 27).

Often art is discussed in terms of escape. Both Schopenhauer and Bell think that art is an escape; it's an escape from ordinary life into a more exalted realm. That is why we seek aesthetic experience. On the other hand, for Hutcheson and Kant, disinterestedness is merely a condition for having aesthetic experiences; that is, you have to be somehow disinterested or detached or distanced in order to have these experiences. In other words, you have aesthetic experience only if you are disinterested—on condition of your being disinterested.

But Schopenhauer and then Bell, on the other hand, think that detachment itself is the very motivation for having aesthetic experiences. Putatively, we seek aesthetic experience specifically in order to be separated from or divorced from the practical, including the importunings of ordinary morality. For Bell, it is a specific kind of affect; it is an affect of release, a feeling of liberation. In this way, Bell is actually closer to Schopenhauer than other figures that we've examined in this book. For Bell, the function of artworks is to promote aesthetic experiences, and these are experiences remarkable for detaching us or enabling us to escape ordinary concerns.

If Schopenhauer is a watered-down and modified version of Kant, then Bell is a watered-down and modified version of Schopenhauer. This might not be so obvious because he writes in such plain, clear English without Schopenhauer's brooding Germanic, metaphysical dramatics. Call it Schopenhauer without Wagner. It is a velvet glove, with an implacably esoteric fist underneath.

Nevertheless, despite Bell's literary geniality, his ambitions should be apparent in the section entitled the "Metaphysical Hypothesis." There he is attempting to answer the question of why we're moved by certain arrangements of lines and combinations of lines. He says, "Occasionally when an artist, a real artist, looks at objects, the contents of a room for instance, he perceives them as pure forms in certain relation to each other and feels emotions for them as such. . . ." (p. 44).

That is,

> the emotion that the artist felt in his moment of inspiration he did not feel for objects seen as means but for objects seen as pure forms—that is, as ends in themselves. He did not feel emotion for the chair as a means to physical well-being, nor as an object associated with the intimate life of the family, nor as the place one sat saying things unforgettable . . . but as pure forms. (pp. 44–45)

Yet, why does it make any difference to see things as ends in themselves? Bell asks, "What is the significance of anything as an end in itself? What is that which is left when we've stripped the thing of all its associations, of all its significance?" and he answers that it is "ultimate reality" (p. 45). So, just as Schopenhauer thought that part of the pleasure of encountering works of art was the cognitive pleasure derived from seeing how things really are in themselves, now we have Bell making an extremely similar claim. Of course, it's expressed in a more urbane kind of English than Schopenhauer's German, and Bell is a lot more discrete about what constitutes ultimate reality. We don't have any Wagnerian interludes about the world as a throbbing orb of pain; nevertheless, there is agreement on this: that what an artist does, when an artist captures the form of a scene, is give you something like sight into how the world is in itself, apart from human associations, human passions, human needs, and practical human requirements.

Thus, there is a kind of straight line that goes from Hutcheson to Kant through Schopenhauer to Bell. Moreover, it is a tradition that stands in stark contrast to the lineage that extends from Plato, arguably through Hume, through Hegel and Tolstoy. Together these two lines of thought yield the fundamental dialectic that gradually emerges as the philosophy of art in the West: the ongoing debate between the claims of the autonomy versus the heteronomy of art, art's independence from versus it's participation in social life.

The Aesthetic Hypothesis

Although there is a way in which Bell can be seen as a product of the aesthetic tradition that benefits from the contributions of Hutcheson, Kant, and Schopenhauer, among others, there is a crucial way in which he differs from them. He is explicitly committed to providing a definition of art. There was, of course, a definition of art in Hegel's *Introduction*, but no great fanfare attended its presentation. In contrast, Bell introduces his definition with fireworks and a veritable marching band. This is of particular importance historically because after Bell (and probably as a result of his abiding influence), the ambition to define art becomes a major philosophical preoccupation, especially among Anglo-American philosophers in the twentieth century. Philosophers and the wider public really didn't care about defining art much before Bell, but after Bell, it eventually becomes a virtual cottage industry in the English-speaking world.

One immediate reason for Bell's interest in defining art is probably the influence of Tolstoy; as we shall see, at several points Bell shows an acute awareness of *What Is Art?* However, there is probably a deeper reason for Bell's concern with the definitional question and the concern of subsequent philosophers of art. And that concern can be summed up in the phrase "the avant-garde."

The radical experimentation of artists from the mid-nineteenth century onward so recurrently undermined fixed views of the nature of art that it seemed that a definition was just the sort of thing that was called for. One's intuitions were no longer reliable. Just as in baseball, you needed a scorecard to tell the players, in the art world, from Manet onward, it seemed that one needed a theory to identify the artworks. And this became the vocation of analytic philosophers of art in the twentieth century and beyond, with Bell being its best-known early advocate.

Bell makes clear that the definitional task is foremost in his mind in the opening chapter of *Art* when he declares that "either all works of visual art have some common qualities, or when we speak of works of art, we gibber" (p. 17). This is a bald demand for a definition of what we are talking about when we talk about *art*. If we can't say what is the common quality shared by all works of art—if we can't say what property all works of art have in common—then our discourse about art is all hot air. We are gibbering (which is the British way of saying "jabbering").

In order to avoid blather, what we have to ascertain is that "there must be some one quality without which a work of art cannot exist, possessing which in the least degree, no work is altogether worthless" (p. 17). What is this quality? What is the feature that makes something a work of art? If something is a work of art if and only if it possesses the property x, then Bell wants to know the identity of x, the unknown, lest we gibber.

Furthermore, Bell has a strategy for discovering x. He maintains that "the starting point for all systems of aesthetics must be the personal experience of a peculiar emotion . . . but all these emotions are recognizably the same kind." (pp. 16–17). That is, Bell presupposes that there is a consensus that everybody who knows about art experiences a peculiar or unique type of feeling when encountering artworks.[6] When you go into a museum or gallery and you contemplate the paintings, there is allegedly a special or unique state of mind that takes possession of you—at least if you belong to the cognoscenti.[7]

For example, if you are among the select company of art-sensitive individuals and you are in a gallery looking at a fire extinguisher, you won't get that special feeling. But when you look at Claude Monet's painting of a haystack next to the fire extinguisher, you will feel that peculiar sensation. Supposedly, there is a consensus among the right people about what that feeling is. It is hard to pinpoint— the French call it "*je ne sais quoi*" ("I know not what"). But you know it when you feel it, even if you can't actually define it with any precision. Bell calls it the "aesthetic emotion."

The aesthetic emotion is what all appropriately prepared viewers feel in the presence of genuine art. All those viewers recognize this feeling and agree that it consistently occurs with exposure to artworks. Bell does not think this is simply a

---

6. Bell obviously thinks that there is a connection between theory and criticism. He writes: "I will try to account for the degree of my aesthetic emotion. That, I conceive, is the function of the critic."

7. Although it needs to be stressed that this is a matter of sensitivity, not propositional knowledge; Bell confesses that he knows a brilliant mathematician who is so indifferent that he does not experience any distinction between exposure to a handsaw and to a genuine artwork. Some of this sensitivity is probably innate, but Bell, like Hutcheson, thinks it can be further cultivated.

plausible idea; he thinks it is self-evident. All the best opinions are on his side—that is, all the right people concur.

Moreover, if there is a feeling that is universally evoked in appropriately prepared viewers by works of art, then Bell thinks he is in a position to identify the property that makes something a work of art. Namely, use this unique feeling that correlates with all and only art to track whatever is giving rise to the feeling. All artworks supposedly give rise to these aesthetic emotions. If these effects are common to all and only artworks, there must be something common in the works that gives rise to the feelings. So, all you have to do is to employ that feeling as a tracking device.

In other words, for any authentic artwork, there is something in it that makes it an artwork. Whatever that something is, when you see the artwork, it is that feature that triggers the response of the aesthetic emotion in the subject. Here there is a straightforward analogy to Hutcheson's approach: discover the cause of beauty by locating the common feature in objects and performances that gives rise to feelings of disinterested pleasure. However, instead of the feeling being disinterested pleasure, Bell is talking about aesthetic emotions. What in artworks arouses aesthetic emotion? Whatever answers that question will tell us which feature of the work makes it an artwork.

So, what is the common feature of artworks that causes the aesthetic emotion? Bell offers a hypothesis (that is why the chapter is called the "Aesthetic Hypothesis"). He hypothesizes that the common feature is what is called *significant form*. The peculiar, art-specific emotion is the aesthetic emotion within the viewing subject. This is a peculiar feeling of exaltation, a feeling of being lifted out of the everyday. When we experience this emotion, we know we are in the presence of art. So, the art-making characteristic is whatever brings about the aesthetic emotion. And when we attend to the regularly recurring feature of the works that bring about this emotion, it is obvious that it is significant form. Therefore, significant form is the feature of the relevant object that qualifies it as an artwork.

Bell is not giving us a formula, like Hutcheson's unity amidst diversity. Bell is simply saying there is some structure in the work—which we can call significant form—that will bring about or cause an aesthetic emotion. The aesthetic emotion is a way of tracking down artworks, and once we have segregated out the artworks through their provocation of aesthetic emotions, we can see what they all have in common. Supposedly what they all have in common is significant form. What is significant form? It is an arrangement of lines, colors, spaces, and vectors that elicit the aesthetic emotion.

For example, a painting of Christ's crucifixion may be divided down the middle by Jesus on the cross with equal numbers of disciples on either side of their savior. The balance achieved by this disposition of figures would exemplify significant form. The significant form of a painting is its internal logic or internal structure, and this organization of elements is that which causes aesthetic emotion.

Significant forms are arresting configurations of shape and line that give a painting its unity, including, for example, gestalt-like qualities of closure. And exposure to the stimulus of significant form excites aesthetic emotion, the true experiential test of art status, in us.

Some proof of the existence of this hypothesis might be that if you could isolate another body of artworks with which you're not heretofore familiar, say Oceanic art, then you will find that that body of artworks both elicits the aesthetic emotion while also displaying significant form. Bell thinks that you may actually confirm this by exposing yourself to art forms with which you are not familiar, but which are regarded as the products of recognized artistic traditions such as tribal African masks, and then observing both that the masks trigger the aesthetic emotion in you and that they possess significant form. On the other hand, things that are not artworks putatively will not incite aesthetic emotions, nor will they manifest significant form. So, *ex hypothesi*, significant form is what causes the art-identifying aesthetic emotion in the subject; thus, significant form is the property in the object that constitutes it as a work of art.

The method here looks very empirical. Gather together the works of art. Notice that they arouse a regularly recurring mental state in the appropriate viewers. Ask yourself what common property or properties the pertinent works have which are apt to account for this systematically occurring state. Note the result; it is significant form.

This method is intended to rest upon something like an analogy with the way in which one would go about discovering the nature of sweetness. Sweet things elicit certain sensations that everyone can identify. Pick out all the things that elicit this sensation and then see what else they have in common—that is, in addition to their disposition to provoke sensations of sweetness. Presumably, that will be some determinate chemical structure. Bell is suggesting a similar procedure for isolating the essence of art.

So, there is the putative aesthetic emotion felt by those who experience artistic painting in the proper circumstances. That is, there is a certain feeling or experience you have when looking at a painting or a sculpture that is unlike the emotions you undergo at any other time. That is analogous to the experience of sweetness mentioned above. What the researcher then does is to use that experience—that supposedly unique experience—to zoom in on the recurring features of the artworks that give rise to it. Whatever features of the relevant objects that give rise to the aesthetic emotions will be that which make artworks art.

And as we know, Bell infers that that is significant form.

So, Bell's argument is as follows:

(1) A unique class of effect has a unique class of correlated causes.
(2) The unique class of constantly correlated causes of the unique class of effect x is the essence of x.

(3) Art possesses a unique class of effect—the aesthetic emotion.

(4) So, art has a unique, constantly correlated class of causes—which we have discovered is a matter of significant form.

(5) Therefore, significant form is the essence of art. (Or, something is an artwork if and only if it possesses significant form.)

Now, there are a couple of immediate objections that someone might raise to the aesthetic hypothesis, which Bell stands ready to answer. The first objection is that the methodology is too subjective; it begins with certain feelings, the so-called aesthetic emotions. But aren't feelings just too subjective a basis on which to ascribe art status? The grounds for the aesthetic hypothesis are too idiosyncratic. There's no way of confirming it. You have your feelings; I have my feelings. And that's that.

Bell puts the objection this way:

> it may be objected that I am making esthetics a purely subjective business, since my only data are personal experiences of a particular emotion. It will be said that the objects that provoke this emotion vary with each individual, and that therefore a system of aesthetics can have no objective validity. (p. 18)

The worry here is that we will not be able to gather together the relevant artworks if we rely on the subjective responses of disparate viewers. The aesthetic emotion may be ignited in you by exposure to A and in me by B, where you are not moved by B, and I am not moved by A. This would be a matter of conflicting tastes and, allegedly, there are no adjudicating disagreements in taste.

Bell concedes that the aesthetic emotion is subjective. It's subjective in a sense with which we're already familiar: the aesthetic emotion is something that happens inside the subject. Where else would an emotion arise except inside the subject? But though the aesthetic experience is subjective, in the sense that it occurs within the subject, that does not entail that it is either arbitrary or idiosyncratic or that it is beyond all methods of proof. Rather, Bell suggests a way in which one could actually go about proving that a work has the capacity to elicit the aesthetic emotion even from spectators who, at least initially, deny that they feel it with respect to a given work.

How can one do this? Bell maintains that you can do this directly by influencing the way that your disputant sees the artwork in question. Suppose that you say painting A engenders an aesthetic emotion, and your interlocutor denies this. Bell contends that you do not have to settle for the peaceful coexistence of two conflicting testimonies. You can try to direct your disputant to attend to various parts of the painting, noting their relationships to other parts. You can show how the figures in red of the left side of the picture counterbalance the figures in blue on the right side. By pointing to various symmetries in the work, for instance, you can induce an aesthetic emotion in your interlocutor, thereby experientially convincing her that the painting has significant form and, thus, is an artwork. You may say, "Look here, now look there, and now back here again," in an effort to jump-start an aesthetic emotion by making salient the elements and relationships that constitute the significant form of the painting.

Likewise, you can put two things next to each other—after the fashion of the old-time side-by-side slides, art-appreciation lecture—in a way that draws the viewer's attention to certain features of the organization of the painting, either by comparison or contrast with another painting.

Or you might use powerful descriptive, metaphorical, and/or figurative language in order to get somebody to see some qualities that he might not be familiar with or see without assistance. If you're a dance critic, you might call the movement "milky" or you might call the movement "jittery," and just by giving that vivid description, you might enable a spectator to see some quality of the choreography that she did not notice previously.

In other words, where there are initially diverging subjective reactions to a piece, we can actually resolve the debate by literally helping our disputant to undergo an aesthetic emotion by directing his attention to the artwork in question in a way that foregrounds or highlights its significant form, thereby making it available demonstratively to an interlocutor so that it can enable the piece to set its powers to work on him. Our elicitation by demonstration of aesthetic emotion in our interlocutor, in turn, confirms intersubjectively our assessment of the painting as a work of art.

We can call this procedure demonstrative/experiential criticism—criticism that proceeds by inducing through demonstration an experience in the viewer by directing her attention to the work in a certain way. This sort of criticism can be contrasted with interpretive criticism which strives to tell you the propositional meaning of a work.

Some of our best practicing critics are demonstrative/experiential critics. But this sort of criticism not only is the prerogative of the professional. We all may employ demonstrative/experiential criticism in our daily commerce with friends and acquaintances. For when we have disagreements about the art status of a work, Bell argues, it is not the case that we have no other option but to state our opposing subjective views. We can convince others by inducing the relevant subjective feelings in them by mobilizing the resources of what I have called "demonstrative/experiential criticism." In this way, we can persuasively lead others to corroborate the intersubjective art status of the works we maintain to be artworks.

Bell's first response to the worry that since aesthetic emotions are subjective, they will be unable to provide an objective basis for a theory of art insofar as feelings cannot be disputed is that disagreements over whether or not a work elicits aesthetic emotions *can be adjudicated* demonstratively. But he also wants to point out that the disagreements that people have over which particular works elicit the aesthetic emotion do not, in any case, undercut his theory.

Why not?

Because although the people disagree about whether *particular* paintings do or do not evoke the aesthetic emotion, everybody who is art-sensitive supposedly agrees that all genuine artworks do evoke the peculiar emotion that Bell labels "*the* aesthetic emotion." So, there's general agreement by everyone that the aesthetic emotion is what marks off artworks. That is, anyone who's claiming that something is an artwork is doing it in virtue of the fact that it elicits this aesthetic emotion.

But this allows that there may be problems of application. In other words, we may disagree at the level of applying the theory but not at the level of the theory itself. The point that Bell is trying to make here is that disagreements of the sort we might have about whether something elicits the aesthetic emotion do not compromise the theory that the aesthetic emotion is the hallmark of art. The problem of disagreement over what works elicit aesthetic emotion occurs at the level of practice or application, not at the level of the general theory of art.

Bell writes:

> Yet, though all aesthetic theories must be based on aesthetic judgments, and ultimately all aesthetic judgments must be matters of personal taste, it would be rash to assert that no theory of aesthetics can have general validity. For though A, B, C, D are the works that move me, and A, D, E, F the works that move you, it may be well that x is the only quality believed by either of us to be common to all the works on his list. We may all agree about aesthetics, and yet differ as to the presence or absence of the quality x. (pp. 18–19)

Moreover, as we have seen, Bell contends that at the level of application, there are intersubjective ways to adjudicate demonstratively disputes over whether or not works possess x, that is, whether or not they engender aesthetic emotions by means of significant form.

Bell's theory then is that significant form is the essential feature of art; he specifically has in mind fine art, painting, and sculpture. This is the rival to the view that art is a matter of imitation or representation—the sort of theory that we encountered in Plato's *Republic*. There imitation was understood as analogous to holding a mirror up to objects.

But significant form is a property that paintings can possess whether or not they mirror anything. Think of abstract paintings by Piet Mondrian. They have significant form, but they don't imitate the look of anything. Likewise, the drip paintings by Jackson Pollock do not represent anything. Yet they are art. Why? Bell, although unfamiliar with those works himself when he wrote *Art*, would say: because they possess significant form.

Of course, Bell doesn't want to deny that many paintings do represent things. But he wants to say that the fact that they represent things is really irrelevant to their standing as genuine artworks. Rather it's their formal design that qualifies them as artworks. Whether the paintings represent a crucifixion or children's games, the content is irrelevant. It is their symmetries, echoing forms, and comparable design features that constitute their arthood.

An analogy with music may be helpful here. There are certain pieces of music—for example, program music—that tell a story, that represent things, like Felix Mendelssohn's incidental music to *A Midsummer Night's Dream*. It tells a story, but what's exciting about it as music is the rhythms, the melodies, the repetitions, the crescendos, and the like—in short, its musical forms. It's not that you can't hear Puck's wings fluttering at a certain point. What's central is actually the sonic qualities—the sonic forms and melodies and rhythms. So even though the music here does represent something, that's not what makes it worthwhile to listen to as music. It's not the story it tells that makes you want to hear it. It's the formal qualities of the music.

Similarly, Bell wants to take an analogous position with respect to paintings. Paintings may in fact represent things, but it's not the fact that they represent things that's crucial to their status as art. It's the manner, the form, the structure of the painting that are significant. Bell readily acknowledges that it is true that many, maybe most, paintings historically have represented things. Yet, he maintains that representation has always been strictly irrelevant to their status as works of art. That is, *at best*, representation has always been irrelevant to the art status of paintings.

However, on the downside, representation can also be an obstacle to apprehending a candidate as a work of art because the representational content of a piece can distract our attention away from its significant form in ways that block the elicitation of the aesthetic emotion. Indeed, in works of art, the representational content may even serve to mask the painting's lack of significant form. So, *at worst*, representation can enable nonart to masquerade as art.

Bell writes:

> Let no one imagine that representation is bad in itself; a realistic form may be significant, in its place as part of the design, as an abstract. But if a representation form has value, it is as form, not as representation. The representative element in a work of art may or may not be harmful; it is always irrelevant. For, to appreciate a work of art we need bring nothing with us from life, no knowledge of its ideas and affairs, no familiarity with its emotions. (p. 27)

After arguing that all forms of representation other than the representation of three-dimensional space are irrelevant to art status, Bell contends

> that there is an irrelevant representative or descriptive element in many great works of art is not the least surprising. . . . Representation is not of necessity baneful. . . . Very often however, representation is a sign of weakness in an artist. A painter too

feeble to create forms that provoke more than a little aesthetic emotion will try to eke that little out by suggesting the emotions of life. To evoke the emotions of life he must use representation. Thus a man will paint an execution, and, fearing to miss with his first barrel of significant form, will try to hit with his second by raising an emotion of fear or pity. (pp. 28–29)

What Bell is getting at here can be illustrated by the following diagram of a spectator looking at the painting *The Death of Marat*, which painting, in turn, refers to an actual historical event that occurred in the real world, the world outside the painting—namely, the assassination of the French revolutionary leader Marat.

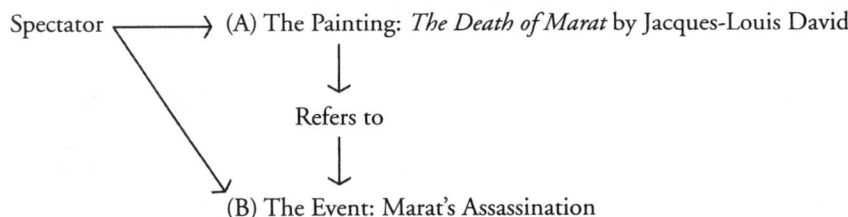

In a nutshell, Bell's worry is that with a representational painting like David's, the spectator may likely be looking in the wrong place. To appreciate the painting as art, the viewer should be attending to (A) *The Death of Marat*. But the danger with representation is that with such paintings, the spectator will be contemplating (B) the real-world event of the assassination of Marat. Attention to (A) in terms of its significant form will engender the aesthetic emotion, whereas thinking about (B) will arouse everyday emotions such as indignation or pity. These everyday emotions may well distract attention from the significant form of the painting, encouraging us instead to dwell on the actual historical event, thereby robbing the viewer of an occasion to undergo the aesthetic emotion.

Or, in a lesser painting, the pictorial provocation of everyday emotions may obscure the fact that the piece in question is altogether without significant form and, therefore, is not an artwork at all.

Bell's argument here is underwritten by a certain view of the emotions. Emotions are directed toward objects. You are angry with the government; you hate your in-laws; you fear Ebola; you envy Einstein. In these examples, the government is the object of your anger, your in-laws the object of your hatred, Ebola the object of your fear, and Einstein the object of your envy. All emotions have objects. According to Bell, the object of the aesthetic emotion is significant form.

Moreover, each emotion is governed by certain standards of appropriateness. The criteria of appropriateness pertaining to fear is the dangerous and the threatening. That is, the appropriate objects of fear are particular things that are dangerous or threatening. Ebola is dangerous and is an appropriate object of fear. A wet noodle, all things being equal, is not dangerous (supposing it is not radioactive) and is not, for that reason, an appropriate object of fear.

On Bell's view, the appropriate object of the aesthetic emotion is significant form. With representational painting, what the painting represents—what it refers to—is not the appropriate object of attention, since it will not yield the aesthetic emotion. It will yield an inappropriate everyday emotion such as indignation or pity. Representational paintings, for this reason, have the emotional potential to block the appropriate response of viewers to painting as an art.

Another way of putting the point is to argue that everyone admits that the proper object of our attention when viewing a painting is the object before us, the painting itself. The danger with representational painting is that it will draw our attention away from the proper object of our attention to what the painting is about—to what it refers to—such as Christ driving the moneychangers from the Temple. This then will result in our emotions being displaced from their appropriate object (the significant form of the work), which instead is swamped by the everyday emotions appropriate to the content of the painting, such as feeling allegiance to Jesus, which is an inappropriate mode of emotional transaction with a painted work of art *qua* art.

Bell's argument can begin by positing that emotions have objects, some of which are appropriate and some of which are inappropriate. The object of the emotion with respect to painting is either the painting itself or the events or persons portrayed that are represented by the painting. If the events or persons portrayed in the painting are the objects of the spectator's emotion—Bell calls these *suggested emotions*—they are inappropriate. Suggested emotions are inappropriate because they take the wrong objects as their focus of attention. The representational components of the painting are at best irrelevant to aesthetic attention in the sense that they do not interfere with paying attention to significant form, the appropriate object of the art of painting.

Nevertheless, with representation, there is the persistent danger that you'll be looking in the wrong place. The emotions that are suggested by the painting—that are specifically suggested by the representation—are the wrong kinds of emotions. Why? Because they're worldly emotions; they're everyday emotions. They're emotions that take as their objects gods and goddesses, and victories and defeats, and villains and heroines; but that is not what painting as painting is about. Painting as such is about the painterly forms and the structure of the picture plane—their significant form. That and that alone will give rise to the unique sort of preferred emotion, namely an aesthetic emotion.

In the best case, representation in a painting is irrelevant. However, sometimes representation is problematic insofar as it distracts attention from the significant form. Even worse, it may cover over the fact that the painting lacks significant form by eliciting a surfeit of nonaesthetic—a.k.a. everyday emotions.

To summarize Bell's argument formulaically:

(1) Artworks elicit emotions.

(2) Certain of the emotions elicited by artworks are appropriate to artworks, and other emotions are inappropriate.

(3) If the emotions that are elicited by artworks are inappropriate, then the features of the artwork that give rise to them are at best irrelevant.

(4) Emotions have objects.

(5) Emotions have appropriate objects.

(6) The objects of emotion with respect to artworks are either (a) the painting itself or (b) the events and/or persons portrayed (represented) by the painting.

(7) If the events or persons portrayed in a painting are the objects of the emotion, then the objects of the emotion are inappropriate and, therefore, the emotion is inappropriate.

(8) With respect to the representational components (the representational features) of a painting, the events or persons portrayed (represented) are the objects of the emotion.

(9) Therefore, with respect to the representational components of a painting (its representational features), the objects of the emotions are inappropriate and, therefore, the emotions here (what Bell calls suggested emotions) are inappropriate.

(10) Therefore, the representational components of a painting (the representational features of artworks) are at best irrelevant for aesthetic attention. (That is, the representational components of the painting better be irrelevant, lest they interfere with the appropriate emotional response to the painting.)

Instead, the features of the painting that are relevant for aesthetic attention are the formal elements—a.k.a. its significant form—which engenders the appropriate sort of emotion, the aesthetic emotion.

As I've said, this view is called formalism. It is formalist obviously in the positive sense, in that it specifies that the form and the structure of the picture plane is the object of appropriate aesthetic attention. All you have to do is pay attention to the way the lines, the shapes, the colors, and the vectors are all structured and organized. It is also formalist in the negative sense that this argument precludes having any interest in the painting other than as painted form. The connection to the world and everyday life is thereby severed. So, in cases of representational painting, you're not supposed to dwell on what the painting represents but only on its form. Indeed, the historical context of the painting and the purpose the artist intended it to serve are irrelevant to appreciating the painting, since undergoing the aesthetic emotion is solely dependent on its manifest (significant) form; what you see, that is, is what you get (indeed, just exactly what you should get, get it?).

So when you travel in Italy you and walk into a church or a gallery where you see examples of sculptures of, say, the four virtues, or representational paintings of various sins, although you might think that these are invitations to meditate on the virtues or vices, from someone like Bell's point of view, this kind of art content is merely a pretext for the artist to invent visual shapes. The art is not really the virtue of modesty as portrayed by a statue that you should be contemplating in the presence of the artwork; rather, you would be better advised to look at the way the folds of the drapery establish a visual rhythm in the sculpture, for therein lies the significant form of the work, the feature which Bell hypothesizes makes it an artwork. To dwell on the so-called content of the work would be a category mistake, an error with respect to the kind of thing an artwork is.

A Critical Examination of the Aesthetic Hypothesis

The first chapter of *Art* advances the aesthetic hypothesis, which is meant to answer the question of what art is, and, of course, it does so by suggesting that art is whatever has significant form. Bell thinks he can discover what has significant form by asking himself which works evoke the aesthetic emotion because there's allegedly a kind of constant correlation between artworks and the aesthetic emotion. He gives you the impression, as noted previously, that what he's doing is something like discovering what causes sweetness.

With sweetness, we start with certain reactions—that such and such tastes sweet—and then we go on to analyze what in the relevant objects imparts this sensation. This enables us to discover the molecular structure common to all the things that give impressions of sweetness. The idea, then, is that the aesthetic emotion is to significant form as sweetness is to whatever the molecular structure is of things that give rise to the feeling of sweetness.

But is this analogy convincing? We can define the molecular structure that gives rise to sweetness independently of the sensation of sweetness. And we can use that way of identifying the pertinent molecular structure to test our hypothesis about that which causes the impression of sweetness by exposing people to that very molecular structure and seeing whether they say it's sweet.

But you can't do the same thing, though, with significant form. Why? Because significant form, unlike the molecular structure that gives rise to sweetness, is not independently specifiable apart from the aesthetic emotion. Almost all we know about it is that it causes aesthetic emotion. So, we have no way of saying or establishing what significant form is apart from the emotion it allegedly raises. Therefore, we cannot independently choose a specimen with significant form and test to see whether or not it evokes aesthetic emotion, since we would have to know that it evoked aesthetic emotion in order to choose the specimen in the first place.

That is, we have no way of running a test for whether significant form systematically causes the aesthetic emotion since we have no way of independently identifying significant form apart from the provocation of the aesthetic emotion. Thus, for example, we can't construct significant forms according to a certain formula to see if things meeting that formula always give rise to the aesthetic emotion. Put technically, we have no independent variable to manipulate.

Why? Again, simply because we don't know what significant form is apart from the fact that it supposedly evokes the aesthetic emotion. So, unlike the relationship between the molecular structure of whatever gives rise to sweetness and the sensations of sweetness, the relationship between significant form and aesthetic emotion is untestable. But even more problematic than its untestability is its uninformativeness.

We suppose that significant form provokes aesthetic emotion. So, we say aesthetic emotion is caused by significant form. But that is equivalent to saying significant form is that which evokes aesthetic emotion, which is both uninformative and circular.

This may seem not quite right. After all, we supposedly know something about the aesthetic emotion. It is a form of exaltation or ecstasy. But this is not sufficient to differentiate the aesthetic emotion for other forms of exaltation or ecstasy. There are also religious exaltation and ecstasy that also are said to release us from everyday, earthly concerns.

Suppose I am positioned before a painting of the Blessed Virgin and Jesus, and I feel ecstasy, a freedom from the mundane, and an intimation of the transcendental. How could Bell discriminate between whether I was feeling the aesthetic emotion or some deeply reverential emotion?

It appears that Bell would have to say that it is an aesthetic emotion just in case it was aroused by the significant form of the painting. But then the aesthetic emotion cannot be defined independently of significant form while, at the same time, significant form cannot be defined except in terms of the aesthetic emotion. Thus, the two concepts are uninformative because they are circular—each invokes the other in the course of its definition; neither can be defined independently of the other.

The situation recalls a famous example from Molière. Imagine that you want to know what causes sleep, and somebody tells you that what causes sleep are certain dormitive powers. Then, of course, you ask: What are dormitive powers? Suppose that the answer you get is: dormitive powers are those that cause sleep.

Now, have you learned anything by being told that what causes sleep is that which causes sleep? Clearly not, nor can you test these dormitive powers in order to see whether or not they cause sleep because you have no independent idea about what these dormitive powers are—about what constitutes the dormitive powers; you only know their effect—that they cause sleep.

But isn't the relationship between these putative dormitive powers and sleep, on the one hand, and significant form and aesthetic emotion, on the other hand, pretty much the same? Thus, for the same reason, the latter relationship is untestable, even though it may look like a standard causal hypothesis. And it is also uninformative, since we cannot know whether a state is one of aesthetic emotion without knowing if it is a response to significant form, while simultaneously being unable to determine whether the stimulus is a matter of significant form without knowing whether it has given rise to an aesthetic emotion in the appropriate conditions. The definitions of significant form and aesthetic emotion are defective because they are circular. And insofar as those definitions are utterly egregiously uninformative, they cannot provide any insight into answering the question "What is art?"[8]

One of the most radical features of the aesthetic hypothesis is Bell's argument to the effect that representation in a painting is always irrelevant. A critical premise in that argument is the seventh: "If the persons and events portrayed (represented) in the painting are the objects of the emotion, then the objects and the emotions elicited from said objects are inappropriate." In Bell's idiom, they are suggested emotions.

The alleged justification of this is that the persons and events referred to by the representational component of the work are outside the painting itself, and it is obviously the painting itself to which we should be attending. The emotions we mobilize with respect to the representational components are only suggested by the painting because they are really elements that are not, so to speak, inside the painting. Marat, for instance, is not *inside* the painting *The Death of Marat*.

So, if we are stricken with grief when we stand before *The Death of Marat*, we are grieving for the actual death of Marat, the real-world assassination of Marat, which, it goes without saying, is not inside the painting. Charlotte Corday killed Marat in the real world, the world outside the painting. The representational components of the painting refer us to this real-world event. But if we start grieving about this real-world event, then we are no longer attending to the painting. Our attention is directed to the wrong place, a place outside the painting, and thus the ensuing emotional response is an inappropriate emotional response to the painting. To respond to the painting in such a way that we will be moved appropriately, we should contemplate David's construction of the picture plane, his arrangement of forms in pictorial space.

Yet this seems strange. Does it really make sense to say that being moved to grief by a painting of a political leader's assassination is inappropriate? Responding

---

8. The *aesthetic emotion* should not be confused with something like the alleged "Stendhal syndrome"—the rapid heartbeat, dizziness, fainting, and even hallucination associated with exposure to artistic masterpieces. The aesthetic emotion is not this specific, nor has the supposed Stendhal effect even been corroborated to exist empirically.

to it with jealousy would be affectively inappropriate; yet responding with grief appears just right. Consider religious paintings. Reverence appears to be an appropriate response to them. Reverence, in most cases, seems to be the very point on which such paintings are predicated. Admittedly, the Madonna does not inhabit the paintings that are about her. But surely responding to a religious painting with reverence is *prima facie* an appropriate way of responding to a religious painting.

In response, Bell is apt to say that though reverence may *appear* to be appropriate in these cases, we see that it is not once we realize that the reverence response is directed at something that is *outside* the painting. Even if reverence seems to be the intended response to the historical context of the painting, it is not. Artistic intentions and historical context are also *outside* the painting. But is this kind of argument persuasive?

A great deal will depend on how we are going to determine what is outside of a painting, since that will make the difference in terms of what is and is not—or what should and should not be—the focus of our attention. For Bell, the only thing that is inside the painting, it seems, is its significant form. He appears to presume this. He offers no argument to establish it. And it appears unlikely that one can maintain this position without begging the question.

Moreover, how will Bell deal with the fact that reverence would not seem to be an inappropriate response to a prayer, even though the saint one is addressing is not literally in the words we recite.

On Bell's view, the significant form of the painting seems to be the only inhabitant of the "inside" of the work. But, from an unbiased perspective, there seem to be a lot of things "inside" the painting that can lay claim to our attention. For example, some paintings contain stories.

Consider Pieter Bruegel's *Fall of Icarus*. It represents a moment in the story of Icarus, the Greek youth whose father gave him wings of wax that enabled him to fly. Although Icarus's father warned him not to fly too close to the sun, Icarus ignored this advice. Flying high, the sun melted his wings. Icarus fell to earth, landing, in Bruegel's picture, in the sea, sinking headfirst into the water with only his legs visible on its surface.

It does not seem forced to say that this narrative is inside the picture. It is being represented by the picture. Isn't the story in the picture?

Bell would argue undoubtedly that the story of Icarus is not part of the significant form of the painting. But, in fact, in this painting, it is virtually impossible to appreciate the form of the painting unless you know that the painting is a representation of the story of Icarus.

The dominant visual elements in the painting involve a farmer in the foreground plowing his field. Icarus is, in effect, "hidden" in the background with only his legs visible in a splash. Bruegel's idea seems to be that historic events may go unnoticed at the moment they occur, and he finds a wonderful formal device for underlining this theme since we, like the farmer, are at first oblivious to the plight of Icarus. Moreover, knowing the story of Icarus is precisely what allows us to appreciate the decentered visual form of the painting—the fact that its focal point is eccentrically placed. That is, without engaging with the narrative, we would not grasp the significant form of the picture.

The reason you need to know the story is that the part of the picture that represents Icarus falling in the water is not visually prominent; indeed, it is, as they say, "hidden in clear sight." But without noticing it, you cannot appreciate the actual pictorial structure of the painting. Thus, if what is *in* the painting is whatever is indispensable to the structure of a painting, then sometimes narratives—as in the case of Bruegel's *Fall of Icarus*—are *in* the painting. And if narrative elements can be *in* the painting, then other representational elements can be as well.

Narrative and other representational elements may be indispensable for isolating structural configurations and, therefore, they must be *in* the relevant paintings. They cannot be meaningfully said to be outside the painting, especially if they are essential to the viewer's isolation of the significant form of the painting. And, if they are indeed *inside* rather than *outside* the painting, then they are appropriate objects of our emotional response.

Of course, you may feel that this discussion of what is "inside" and "outside" the work is more confusing than it is productive and, for that reason, better forgotten. But much of the thunder of formalism will disappear if talk about what is "inside" and "outside" works of art is dropped (which, I might add, would not necessarily be such a bad thing).

Another problem with Bell's aesthetic hypothesis recalls a problem that we encountered with Hutcheson's account of beauty and Tolstoy's account of good art irrespective of content. For Hutcheson, everything that possesses some degree of unity—which amounts to everything that we can individuate—is beautiful in his sense to some degree, while for Tolstoy, something qualified as art has to be good irrespective of content, just because it meets the criteria for art status (it to some degree possesses sincerity, clarity, and individuality). That is, for Tolstoy all art is to some extent necessarily good irrespective of content. Bell's aesthetic hypothesis is obviously beset with the same sort of difficulty.

For, in order to be art, a candidate must possess significant form. Any work intended to be art, but defective formally, simply would not count as a genuine artwork. All genuine artworks will have significant form and, hence, will be good. But certainly, this is counterintuitive. You view a painting—a painted canvas hanging on the wall of an art gallery—that is a formal mess. Surely, the correct appraisal is that it is a bad work of art, but not that it is not a work of art at all. What would such a painting be if it were not a work of art?

Yet it is not clear that Bell has a place in his account for bad works of art. They all must possess significant form, which entails that they are good. Although it would be nice to live in a world where there is no bad art, we cannot get there by defining it out of existence.

A final problem worth mentioning about the aesthetic hypothesis takes note of the fact that it is an attempt to define art in terms of its manifest properties. Significant form addresses the eye. It is something that the art-sensitive folk can see. In this, formalism is like alternative theories of art such as the imitation theory and the expression theory. In those philosophies, as well, the essential properties constitutive of visual art—imitation, on the one hand, and expression, on the other hand—were features that one could discern perceptually. However, philosophers have become increasingly convinced that the essence of art is not something that, as Arthur Danto put it, the eye can decry.

Danto's beloved intuition pump to this conclusion was Andy Warhol's *Brillo Box*, a handmade simulacrum of the sort of carton that boxes of Brillo pads were packed in and in which they were delivered to local grocery stores. To all intents and purposes, Warhol's *Brillo Box* is indiscernible from the ones manufactured by Proctor and Gamble. That is, they look exactly the same. From a distance, supposedly, you cannot tell one from the other. However, one of them is an artwork (Warhol's), and the other is not (Proctor and Gamble's). Thus, whatever determines art status—whatever defines art and differentiates it from nonart—is not something that one can see.

Danto's argument from indiscernabilia undermines any attempt at a theory or definition of art that aspires to locate the essence of art in some perceptually available, manifest feature such as imitation, expressiveness, and, for our present purposes, significant form.

This should also be evident from Danto's example, although in a way that he does not exploit. The Brillo cartons that Warhol took as his source material were themselves highly designed. From an unprejudiced viewpoint, they have significant form. However, most of us, I suspect, would hesitate to consider them art. Bell, of course, was a revisionist in terms of what he was willing to call art. But, considering that most industrially produced, commercial products nowadays are highly designed—often perhaps achieving what Bell would accept as significant form—would he be happy to accept it all as *art*?

The Metaphysical Hypothesis

We have spent a great deal of time discussing Bell's aesthetic hypothesis. The reason for this is straightforward. The aesthetic hypothesis is the best-known and most influential part of *Art*. Indeed, I suspect it is the only section of the book that most people read. It is invariably the part that is anthologized, and it has been anthologized quite often, whereas the book as a whole was until recently out of print. Nevertheless, there is more to *Art* than the aesthetic hypothesis. There is also what Bell calls the "metaphysical hypothesis."

The aesthetic hypothesis maintains, among other things, that significant form engenders the aesthetic emotion, which itself involves feelings of exaltation. Yet isn't there something mysterious about that? Why would a mere configuration of lines—apart from their representational content—provoke ecstasy? Obviously, comparable questions might be raised with respect to absolute music. However, it may appear even more unfathomable when it comes to the disposition of lines and shapes on canvas. Note that even if you do not accept the aesthetic hypothesis and its attempted definition of art, Bell is still right that sometimes we are moved by painterly forms. And that would appear to call for an explanation. So, the metaphysical hypothesis would still have some claim to interest, even if the aesthetic hypothesis did not.

The metaphysical hypothesis is Bell's answer to the question Why do certain arrangements and combinations of form move us so strangely? He asks, "Why are we put into an ecstatic state, why are we lifted from the stream of life by being exposed to certain combinations of lines, colors, and spaces?" (p. 43). His answer to this appears to be that in making the artwork, the artist creates a visual array that possesses significant form.

The artist produces this significant form in order to express her feelings—the feelings she had when encountering what Bell calls "material beauty," which often involves what we would *natural beauty*. The artist translates that experience into significant form and when we nonartists experience it, the artwork arouses in us a comparable aesthetic experience.

So supposedly, in a way that unavoidably reminds one of Tolstoy, the reason that we are moved by significant form—the explanation of why we have the aesthetic emotion—is that the artist has expressed by means of some configuration exemplifying significant form her feeling when encountering natural beauty, and that then that form arouses the aesthetic emotion in us.

Nevertheless, that can't be the whole story. Why not? Because Bell asks the question of why we are moved by significant form and the *we* here means why all humans are moved and the answer just suggested is not an answer for all humans. The answer so far only tells us why we nonartists are moved by significant form. But why are artists moved in the first place? Why are they moved by material beauty?

Bell tries to explain this in a way that he acknowledges is extremely speculative. He writes that "occasionally when an artist, a real artist looks at objects, the contents of the room for instance, he perceives them as pure form in certain relation to each other and feels emotions for them as such. These are his moments of inspiration" (p. 44). So why is the artist moved? The notion of *pure form* is key. When the artist perceives things as pure form, the artist begins to see things as ends in themselves, in other words, not connected to networks of cause and effects, or of purposes.

Earlier I alerted you to the similarity between Schopenhauer and Bell in terms of their conception of art as a release from the world of affairs. But there seems a further similarity in their views of the artist's relation to her subject matter. Bell's version is obviously extremely toned down, but Bell's notion is highly reminiscent of Schopenhauer's. For Bell, what is striking about the artist's vision is that she encounters things in nature as pure forms, by which Bell has in mind things not connected in means-ends relationships. And that is what, so to speak, lifts the artist out of the stream of life or, as Schopenhauer would have put it, out of the stream of striving.

What we have here is something like Schopenhauer-lite, with references to ultimate reality included. That is, reality as viewed outside the connective tissue of causes and effects, of purposes, means, and utilities. Bell does not enlist Platonic Forms, but he is talking about something like the order of visual relationships between objects as perceived outside of the networks of causation and purpose, which somehow affords us that which Bell refers to as a sense of ultimate reality (p. 46). And this then accounts for why the significant form encountered by the artist in nature has the effect of eliciting in the artist an aesthetic emotion which then the artist, so to say, is able to arouse in spectators by his own creation of comparable significant forms.

Clearly, this is a highly speculative suggestion that perhaps provokes more questions than it can answer, including why a glimpse of ultimate reality would elicit the aesthetic emotion. Does this require a more explicit commitment to some notion of human bondage to the world as will? And who would grant that?

But another question that cannot be dodged is whether the metaphysical hypothesis is consistent with the aesthetic hypothesis. Why even ask this?

According to the metaphysical hypothesis, artists appear to be able to experience aesthetic emotion with respect to what Bell calls material beauty, that is, with respect to things in real life as opposed to art. Yet won't that then undermine the aesthetic hypothesis?

Remember the aesthetic hypothesis is supposed to pick out all and only artworks. And artworks necessarily possess significant form. What's significant form? Significant form is what raises the aesthetic emotion. But according to the metaphysical hypothesis, we learn that artists have aesthetic emotions with respect to material beauty, which possesses something like significant form, only in the world outside art, including nature. So, if that's true of the artists, doesn't that contradict Bell's theory that what marks works of art is significant form with its power to arouse aesthetic emotion?

For artists, the array of objects on a table, as in the case of still lifes, or the disposition of hill and dale, as in the case of landscapes, can also lead to the aesthetic emotion in virtue of their possession of pure form—material beauty's equivalent to significant form. Thus, significant form doesn't seem to do what Bell advertised it would do, namely, to select out all and only the artworks, since for artists, dining room tables laden with fruit and viands and landscapes may also possess significant form.

Bell boldly promised to save us from gibbering, jabbering, and blathering. Has he succeeded?

Art and Ethics

As we have seen, Bell defines an artwork in terms of its possession of significant form, its capacity to elicit the aesthetic emotion. An artwork is good in proportion to its quotient of significant form. The aesthetic emotion it provokes is a form of ecstasy, taking us out of the stream of ordinary experience. It is an emotion unlike all others; rather than binding us to the earthly world of affairs, it liberates us from them. Since the aesthetic emotion is distinct from ordinary emotions, it is distinct from every moral emotion, as we undergo them daily in virtually every encounter with others. Thus, if and when moral emotions—or, for that matter, immoral emotions—are aroused by a work of art, they are irrelevant to its engagement and evaluation. Only form and the emotions it engages are what matter.

Discounting the appropriateness of morality in assessing the value of artworks in favor of formal considerations is a recurring commitment of formalism. In this, formalism represents a rejection of a simple moralistic approach to art—views that see artworks as bad to the degree that they promote morally unsavory emotions and/or evil actions. Recall Plato.

One might suspect that insofar as Bell rejects simple moralism, regarding morality as irrelevant to the appreciation of an artwork, he would think that there is no issue about justifying art—the practice of art—morally. However, he accepts the responsibility to justify art; he agrees that the aesthetic activity requires an ethical justification, as, he says, does every other branch of human activity. In other words, he in effect takes up Tolstoy's challenge to vindicate art and includes a fairly elaborate demonstration, arguing that art not only is morally valuable but also has the greatest moral value.

In fact, Bell is notorious for writing the following: "Art is, I am sure, one of the most valuable things in the world—so valuable, indeed, that in my giddier moments I have been tempted to believe that art might prove to be the world's salvation" (p. 32).[9]

---

9. There is a tendency among some modernists to think of art as a replacement or alternative to religion—or maybe as the religion of post-Enlightenment, disenchanted humankind. Possibly, Bell, in this quotation, is echoing this sentiment. His exact position may be hard to locate here, however. He also writes: "Art and Religion are, then, two roads by which men escape from circumstance to ecstasy. Between aesthetic and religious rapture there is a family alliance. Art and Religion are means to similar states of mind." In this case, it

Bell's argument for the moral value of art depends on the supposition that there are things that are intrinsically good—things that are ends in themselves rather than things that are instrumentally good because they are the means to further goods. Bell does not provide an argument for the existence of intrinsic goodness, but rather assumes it, although there are arguments available to that conclusion (including Aristotle's to the effect that there cannot be only instrumental goods; that would entail an intolerable regress; hence, there must be some foundational goods from which the instrumental goods are derived).

But if there are things that are intrinsically good, how are we to go about identifying them? Bell recommends that we use the method of isolation as articulated by the philosopher G. E. Moore, a particularly influential thinker for the Bloomsbury Group. Moore proposed a thought experiment as the means to discover what is intrinsically good. Imagine some end existing disconnected from everything else. Does it retain its goodness when so isolated? Would it still be valued positively if it were the only thing in existence? If the candidate meets this test, it will be intrinsically good. Why? Because if it depended on the existence of something else, some other end, it would be an instrumental good and not an end in itself.

Like G. E. Moore, Bell maintains that the only candidates that survive the method of isolation are mental states, certain states of mind. Apparently, nothing would possess value without minds to value it, but minds, or at least certain states of mind, could be valued as ends in themselves, even in the absence of everything else.

Of course, art is connected with a certain state of mind, namely the aesthetic emotion. Moreover, the aesthetic emotion seems to be the sort of mental state Moore and Bell think of as ends in themselves, perhaps because the aesthetic emotion is divorced from worldly affairs and instrumental striving. That is, the aesthetic state of mind is not valuable as a means to something else. It is valuable for its own sake.

Furthermore, if something is conducive to what is intrinsically good, then presumably, it is good. Therefore, since artworks engender aesthetic emotions, they are good. Bell also appears to presuppose that if something is good, then it is ethically justified. (Perhaps Bell thinks that ethical justification just follows from goodness.) So being good, artworks are ethically justified. This much gives Bell an ethical justification for art. But as already noted, Bell wants to prove more; he wants to demonstrate that there is no greater means to goodness than art.

In order to do this, he assumes that if something is conducive to the highest intrinsic good (that is to say, the best mental states), then it has the greatest moral value. Moreover, he maintains that aesthetic emotions are the highest intrinsic goods because they are the best mental states, the most intense and the purest

---

doesn't sound as though Bell thinks of art as a successor to religion. It sounds as though he is assuming their coexistence.

(putatively being independent of the exigencies of life). Aesthetic emotions are induced by aesthetic or art-making qualities of artworks—that is, by significant forms noteworthy for their potency and directness of effect. Therefore, the aesthetic or artistic qualities of art are constitutive of the highest moral value. But since these aesthetic qualities are the essence of art, properly so called, Bell concludes that there is no greater moral value than that which attaches to the artistic qualities of artworks or, for short, *art* as such.

Although Bell denies that the arousal of ordinary moral/immoral emotions are relevant to our commerce with artwork, mired as they are in the quotidian demands of life, art itself is ethically justified—indeed, most highly justified—because of its connection to intrinsic goodness, specifically, to the highest intrinsically good mental states, the aesthetic emotions.

We can outline Bell's argument thusly:

(1) There are intrinsic goods.
(2) If anything survives the method of reflective isolation, then it is intrinsically good.
(3) Only certain states of mind survive the method of reflective isolation.
(4) Therefore, only certain states of mind are intrinsically good.
(5) Aesthetic emotion is such a state of mind.
(6) Therefore, aesthetic emotion is intrinsically good.
(7) If an action or object is conducive to that which is intrinsically good, then it is good.
(8) Artworks are conducive to aesthetic emotions.
(9) Therefore, artworks are conducive to that which is intrinsically good.
(10) Therefore, artworks are good.
(11) If something is good, it is ethically justified.
(12) Therefore, artworks are ethically justified.
(13) If something is conducive to the highest intrinsic good (i.e., the best mental states), then it has the greatest moral value.
(14) Aesthetic emotions are the highest intrinsic goods (they are the most intense, purest mental states).
(15) Aesthetic emotions (the highest intrinsic goods) are brought about by the artistic qualities of artworks (significant form).
(16) Therefore, the artistic qualities of art have the greatest moral value.

One problem with Bell's argument is that it moves rather freely between talking about individual works of art—the things that prompt aesthetic emotions—and the practice of art as a collective endeavor. However, this gap might be bridged, at least logically, by talking about the essence of art, significant form, as the locus of the capacity to ignite aesthetic emotion.

A deeper problem, however, is the putative move from something's being good to something's being ethically justified. That is, for argumentative purposes, bracket all the problems in the argument that may arise before the eleventh premise. Consider only premise (11).

In premise (11), Bell presumes that if something is good, then it is ethically justified. Maybe Bell believes that this is an analytic truth, that it follows by definition. But, in fact, this is false.

Something may be good but, nevertheless, not be ethically justified. Exercise—taking a morning jog—may be good, but it does not ethically justify going jogging when one's child is choking to death on his breakfast cereal. Not even intrinsic goodness, if one believes in such things, is automatically ethically justifying.

I conjecture that Bell and Moore would both agree that philosophizing is intrinsically valuable since it involves supposedly vaunted mental states, but philosophizing stolidly while one's spouse sinks under the waves for the third time is not ethically justified. If one is going to assess something good, or even intrinsically good, to be morally good, one needs to take heed of its consequences. The reason for this is obvious since something good or even intrinsically good can have bad moral consequences in context.

Maybe Bell thinks that he has the authority of G. E. Moore to support him. But he does not. In his *Principia Ethica*, Moore explicitly states:

> It is, in fact, evident that however valuable an action may be in itself, yet owing to its existence, the sum of good in the Universe may conceivably be made less than if some other action, less valuable in itself, had been performed. But to say that this is the case is to say that it would have been better that the action should not have been done. (Moore, pp. 147–48)

That is, if the bad consequences of good and even intrinsically good actions and states of affairs disrupt the overall economy of goodness in the universe, they are not morally defensible—they are not ethically justified. Perhaps Bell just forgot the utilitarian side of G. E. Moore.

Nevertheless, in any event, it is not simply that Moore has not got Bell's back. The problem is that ethical justification is inextricably connected to consequences and that talk of goodness—and even intrinsic goodness—does not obviate this fact about moral judgment.

Moreover, the preceding observation not only compromises premise (11) and that which it is thought to imply; it also subverts premise (13) and that which is supposed to follow from it. That is, Bell will be blocked from his conclusion that art is the greatest moral value. Art on Bell's account seems neither ethically justified nor the royal road to the most exquisite moral value.

Salvation, it would appear, if at all, lies elsewhere. And, in any event, Tolstoy would not have been impressed.

Concluding Remarks

Clive Bell played a significant role in the development of taste in the English-speaking world by educating art lovers in how to appreciate modern art. Before Bell, most were predisposed to assume that verisimilitude was essential to being a visual artwork. Yet, as a result of his efforts, many connoisseurs, at least, were converted to the idea that what made a painting a work of art was not that it held a mirror up to nature, but something else—its form. In teaching viewers the way to engage with neo-impressionism, he readied them for the deviations from imitation to come as advanced art raced toward abstraction into the twentieth century. Bell made an immense difference in the way in which people—especially art lovers—thought about art, preparing them for the future.

However, Bell's influence on the philosophy of art among Anglophone philosophers was at least as profound as his influence on the taste of the educated viewership of visual art. Arguably, Bell encouraged philosophers to think of the construction of a definition of art as their first order of business. Moreover, the kind of theory that he forged—defining art in virtue of the type of mental state that art is putatively designed to facilitate—is still alive and well, going by the label "the aesthetic theory of art."

Of course, contemporary proponents of this view no longer speak of *aesthetic emotions*, preferring instead the idiom of *aesthetic experiences*. But generally, these experiential states are characterized as intrinsically valuable ones in a manner that parallels Bell's account of aesthetic emotions.

Similarly, the aesthetic theorist of art beckons the audience to attend to the artwork itself and to discount, as outside of the work, the intention of the artist (the intentional fallacy) and the historical context of the artwork's provenance (the genetic fallacy). And needless to say, for the aesthetic theorist of art, as for Bell, the moral, political, religious, utilitarian, cognitive, social, and other mundane consequences of artworks are irrelevant to the appreciation of art *qua* art.

Not all aesthetic theorists share Bell's formalism. They stay clear of notions like significant form. But they do concur with his view that art is autonomous, dedicated to affording an experience that is separate and divorced from ordinary human interests, including socially significant ones.

If Bell's theory of art points toward future developments in twentieth-century Anglo-American aesthetics, it also emerges from tendencies coalescing from the eighteenth century onward. From the discourse on beauty from figures like Hutcheson and Kant, the concept of disinterestedness becomes increasingly important as a way of attempting to characterize what we call aesthetic appreciation.

Moreover, as early as the 1820s, some commentators, like Victor Cousin, began to associate engendering disinterest, variously defined, as the essence of art, resulting in ideas like "art for art's sake" and aestheticism, and, even more radically, in Schopenhauer's conception of art as a categorical break from the world of everyday interests, desires, and striving. Bell, we can see, domesticates Schopenhauer's celebration of the autonomy of art by camouflaging, if not thoroughly removing, much of his wilder metaphysical speculations.

Undoubtedly, many Anglo-American philosophers, including even aesthetic theorists of art, will be surprised to find themselves accused of belonging to the lineage of Schopenhauer, but the impress of Schopenhauer's thinking on Bell's is, I believe, incontestable. Much of Bell is Schopenhauer minus the extravagance.

I also predict that many contemporary philosophers of art will question my assertion of Bell's influence on them, insofar as they will explicitly deny that they are aesthetic theorists of art. And it is true that the number of card-carrying aesthetic theorists is small.

Yet their influence has been great. A number of their doctrines, like the intentional fallacy, the genetic fallacy, the intrinsic value of aesthetic experience, the autonomy of art from ethics, politics, and so on are taken as commonsense intuitions by many in the field of the philosophy of art, which "intuitions" are appealed to, often as counterexamples, in debates as though they, the "intuitions," are so obvious as to be indisputable.

Yet these so-called intuitions are really fragments of a theory that was taught to many contemporary philosophers in their early arts education under the title of the New Criticism, an appreciative practice of which the aesthetic theory of art is the rationally reconstructed, theoretical foundation.

In the Introduction to this book, I recalled Keynes's suggestion that the intuitions invoked by many businessmen are really nothing more than snatches of the theories of some dead economist, vaguely remembered. The same can be said of a large number of the intuitions of contemporary philosophers of art who, truth be told, are recycling intuitions as commonplaces which are actually fragments of the aesthetic theory of art as that evolved from Hutcheson through to Bell and contemporary versions. In this respect, these intuitions comprise something like the unconscious of contemporary aesthetics. And just as psychoanalysis is supposed to attempt to relieve the grip of unconscious fixed ideas by retracing their formation, part of the project of this book has been to unravel the historical trajectory of these convictions in order to question their naturalness and inevitability.

There is a narrative to this book. It notes how the philosophy of art began by considering the arts as an integral part of the societies in which they evolved. Even Hume believed that art was, for example, beholden to ethics. But beginning in the Enlightenment, perhaps due to obsession with analyzing everything into discrete parts, the notion of the autonomy of art began to take hold and to increasingly take control of the discussion within the philosophy of art. The field soon began to divide into two camps—those who regarded art as autonomous, like Bell, versus those who defended the cultural embeddedness of art as invested with a social mission—a view represented by Hegel and Tolstoy.

This controversy, which is reflected in the chapters of this book, then continued throughout the twentieth century and remains a major arena of controversy even today.

I have concluded my account of its earlier stages with the discussion of Bell because with Bell, due to his forceful and clarion presentation, I think the autonomy of art thesis got its most influential and attractive polemic—one that captured the "intuitions" of philosophers and ordinary art lovers alike in a way that made it the default position in much of the dialectic to come.

Bell ends our story—albeit an interim report—in that he sets the stage for one of the leading debates that still commands the attention of philosophers of art in our own times: the last century and the dawn of the present one.

Bibliography

The edition of Clive Bell's *Art* used in this chapter was published in 1958 in New York by Capricorn Books.

Bywater, William G. *Clive Bell's Eye*. Detroit, MI: Wayne State University Press, 1975.
Carroll, Noël. "Clive Bell's Aesthetic Hypothesis." In *Aesthetics: A Critical Anthology*, edited by George Dickie, Richard Sclafani, and Ronald Roblin, 84–94. New York: St. Martin's, 1989.
Danto, Arthur. "The Artworld." *Journal of Philosophy* 61 (1964): 571–84.
Dean, Jeffrey T. "Clive Bell and G. E. Moore: The Good of Art." *British Journal of Aesthetics* 36 (1996): 135–45.
Dickie, George T. "Clive Bell and the Method of *Principia Ethica*." *British Journal of Aesthetics* 5 (1965): 139–43.
Ekman, Rosalind. "The Paradoxes of Formalism." *British Journal of Aesthetics* 10 (1970): 350–58.
Feagin, Susan. "Roger Fry and Clive Bell." In *Key Thinkers: Aesthetics*, edited by Alessandro Giovannelli, 113–25. London: Continuum, 2012.
Gould, Carol. "Bell, Clive." In *Oxford Encyclopedia of Aesthetics*, vol. 4, edited by Michael Kelly, 251–54. Oxford: Oxford University Press, 1998.
———. "Clive Bell's Aesthetic: Tradition and Significant Form." *Journal of Aesthetics and Art Criticism* 35 (1994): 433–43.
———. "Clive Bell on Aesthetic Experience and Aesthetic Truth." *British Journal of Aesthetics* 34 (1994): 124–33.
Guyer, Paul. *A History of Modern Aesthetics*. Vol. 3, *The Twentieth Century*. Cambridge: Cambridge University Press, 2015.

Lake, Beryl. "A Study in the Irrefutability of Two Aesthetic Theories." In *Aesthetics and Language*, edited by William Elton, 107–13. Oxford: Basil Blackwell, 1954.

Lang, Berel. "Intuition on Bloomsbury." *Journal of the History of Ideas* 25 (1964): 292–302.

Meager, R. "Clive Bell and Aesthetic Emotion." *British Journal of Aesthetics* 5 (1965): 123–31.

Moore, G. E. *Principia Ethica*. New York: Dover, 2004.

Read, Herbert. "Clive Bell." *British Journal of Aesthetics* 5 (1965): 107–10.

Envoi

I have concluded this selective history of the philosophy of art in the West with Clive Bell's *Art*. Coming at the beginning of the twentieth century, it sums up with genuine philosophical panache the earlier sentiments of the art for art's sake movement and the aestheticism of Walter Pater, James McNeill Whistler, and Oscar Wilde. Thus, it also sets the stage—decidedly to the advantage of autonomism—for the debate in the coming decades about the relation of art to society. Autonomism maintains this edge in its later refined reincarnations such as the aesthetic theory of art, most ably defended by Monroe Beardsley.[1] The persuasiveness of autonomism has seemed so compelling that it has come to function as something like the "unconscious" of the Anglophone philosophy of art, grounding such "intuitions" as a knee-jerk faith in the belief in art's essential immunity to political criticism. Such convictions, however, are being hotly contested today by many philosophers of art who, it is hoped, will profit from contemplating this history of how the claims of autonomy emerged from the presumption of heteronomy and continues to be locked in dialectical confrontation with it.

---

1. See Noël Carroll, "*Les Culs-De-Sac* of Enlightenment Aesthetics: A Metaphilosophy of Art," *Metaphilosophy* 40 (2009): 157–78.

Index

1984, 267

Absolute Beauty, 111, 112
accessory beauty, 158, 174
Addison, Joseph, 101
adherent beauty, 174, 175
aesthetic emotions, xvii, 278–80n4, 283–95, 299–305
aesthetic experience, xii, xvi–xvii, 61, 164n8, 166, 169, 170, 177, 181, 183n13, 185, 191, 195n19, 197, 228, 235, 236, 238, 240–43, 252n6, 278, 280, 281, 286, 299, 305, 306
aesthetic hypothesis, 282, 284, 286, 293, 295, 297–300
aesthetic ideas, 184, 185, 187–90, 207
aestheticism, 149, 197, 306, 309
alazon, 2, 3, 14
allopathic medicine, 87–89
Analytic philosophy, 199, 283
Anglophone philosophy, xiii, xvii n4, xx, xxi, 305, 309
Antigone, 37, 75, 76, 81, 85, 219
Antimony of Taste, 192
Apollonian, 243, 244
Aquinas, Thomas, 91
Aristophanes, 2, 13, 14, 34, 55, 246
Aristotle: xi–xv, 58–98; vs. Plato, 25n8, 52, 56, 58; vs. Hutcheson, 99, 101, 130, 110, 111, 113, 114, 118n4, 119, 121; vs. Hegel, 210, 214
Art (by Clive Bell), 275–77, 283, 288, 293, 298
art for art's sake, 17, 19, 86n14, 149, 197, 306, 309
Artaud, Antoine, 77n10
asceticism, 240
Astaire, Fred, 129
autonomism, xx, xxi, 149, 238, 243, 309

Bacchae, 71, 85
Baudelaire, Charles, 246, 249n1, 261

Beardsley, Monroe, 243, 309
beautiful: Plato, 1, 2, 4–10, 14–20; Hutcheson, 99–105, 107–10, 112–24; Kant, 156–63, 165, 167, 173–75, 177, 181, 183–87, 189, 192, 194–96
beauty as the symbol of morality, 190
beneficial pleasure, xiv, 4, 9, 10, 56, 58n2, 77
Berlioz, Hector, 246, 249n1, 258
Bloomsbury Group, 275, 302
Bono, 271
boredom (Schopenhauer), 228, 234, 242
Brave New World, 267
Brillo Box, 267, 298
Bruegel, Pieter, 296, 297
Buñuel, Luis, 265
Burke, Edmund, 101, 177

catharsis, xiv, 52, 69, 84–98
Cézanne, Paul, 275, 276
Chaplin, Charlie, 260
characters, 63, 66, 68–71, 73, 76, 81–83, 85, 86, 89, 97
Checker, Chubby, 129
Chekhov, Anton, 70
Christ, Jesus, 218, 219, 242, 260, 284, 291
Christian art, 218n9, 260, 269–73
Christmas Carol, A, 260
Cicero, 128n1
Citizen Kane, 188
classical stage of art (Hegel), 215–18
closure, 72, 74
Clouds, 13–14, 34
Collingwood, R. G., 248, 257
comedy, 2, 13–14, 35, 49, 51n14, 60, 62–63, 65–69, 145, 174, 266
communication (Tolstoy), 247, 249, 252–58, 262, 264, 265, 267, 272
Comparative Beauty, 111
consciousness (Hegel), 200–203, 205–10, 213–17, 219–21, 224–25, 230–33, 235–37

311

constructivism, 71n8
Continental philosophy, 199
Cousin, Victor, 306
Critique of Judgment, xvi, 155–57, 173, 200
Critique of Practical Reason, 156
Critique of Pure Reason, 155, 156, 220
cubism, 1
Cunningham, Merce, 264
czarist Russia, 246–47, 250n3, 268

Dada, 1, 264, 265
Dalí, Salvador, 265
David Copperfield, 260
David, Jacques-Louis, 212, 290, 295
DaVinci, Leonardo, 277
Death of Marat, The, 290, 295
definition of art, 7, 212, 223, 250, 256–57, 262, 263, 268, 269, 272, 282, 298, 299, 305
dependent beauty, 173–76
Descartes, René, 6
desire (Schopenhauer), xvii, 233–35, 240, 242, 306
Diary of a Country Priest, 269
diction, 69
Diderot, Denis, 36
diegesis, 32, 33, 63, 68, 69
Dionysian, 243, 244
disinterested pleasure, xv, 102, 108–11, 114, 116, 117, 121, 151, 157, 158, 172, 173, 186, 192, 194, 238, 284
disinterestedness, xii, xv–xvii, xix, 101, 102, 137, 141, 158, 160, 161, 173, 183, 185, 194, 195, 197, 238, 280, 281, 305
divine madness, 14–17, 19, 20, 22, 23, 237
Don Quixote, 139, 260
Dubos, Baptiste, 248
Duccio, 277
Duchamp, Marcel, 223, 224
dynamical sublime, 177–82

ecstasy, 15, 20n6, 240, 244, 280, 294, 299, 301
egoism, 102, 240, 241
Einstein, Albert, 119n5, 290
eiron, 2, 14

Eisenstein, Sergei, 71n8, 253n7
emotions: Plato, 31, 48–50, 52–56; Aristotle, 59, 61, 66, 68, 70, 76, 83–86, 88–97; Tolstoy, 247, 248, 254–57, 259, 261, 262, 266, 273
empiricism, 99, 101–4, 126, 129, 130
end of art, the, 220–22
Euripides, 71, 244n8, 246
exemplary necessity, 162, 168, 172, 195
expression (Tolstoy), 247–49, 254–57, 264
expression theory of art, xii, xviii, 247, 248, 257, 277, 298

Fahrenheit 451, 267
Fall of Icarus, 296, 297
fear: Plato, 20, 29–33, 49, 50, 52, 55; Aristotle, 59, 61, 66, 68–71, 75, 79–98
form of finality, 166, 167, 170, 278
form of purposiveness, 166, 167, 195
formalism, xii, xvii–xx, 149, 197, 277–79, 292, 297, 298, 301, 305
free beauty, xix, 4, 158–60n4, 163n7, 164n8, 165, 168, 171–76, 180, 181, 184, 185, 191, 194, 195, 238, 251
functional definition, 61

genetic fallacy, 305, 306
genius, 185–87, 189, 237, 248
Giselle, 268n10
Glass, Philip, 126
Goethe, 85, 246
grand tour, 176
guardians, 28–31, 33–37, 40, 48, 64, 279
Guyer, Paul, xx

Hanslick, Eduard, 279n2
Hegel: xi–xiii, xvi, xvii, xx, 199–26; vs. Tolstoy, 247, 259
Hesiod, 11, 17, 18, 28, 29
heteronomy, xiii n2, xix, xx, 227n1, 282, 309
Hippias, 2–6, 10, 14
Hippias Major, xiv, 1, 2, 6, 10, 14, 56, 58n2, 103, 211n5

Hirt, Aloys, 211
Hobbes, Thomas, 26, 102, 110
homeopathic medicine, 87–89
Homer, xiv, 11–13, 15–20, 22, 28, 30, 31, 34, 58, 67, 149
Horace, 144, 148
Hume, David: xi–xiii, xv, xvi, xix, 126–54
Hutcheson, Francis: xi, xii, xv–xvii, xix, 99–124; vs. Hume, 126, 127, 129, 130, 134–37, 140, 141, 153; vs. Kant, 157–60, 169n10, 185

Ideal Critics: Hume, 133, 135–53; Kant, 157, 168, 173
Idealism, 200, 226
identification, 20n6, 28, 31, 32, 34–39, 59, 60n1, 82, 118, 137, 138, 248
Iliad, 13, 22, 150
imitation: Plato, 25, 35–38, 40, 41, 43, 45–49, 55; Aristotle, 58, 59, 62–67, 69–71, 77, 78, 84, 93, 95, 97
imitation theory of art (Manet), 248, 277, 298
indifference-to-existence test, 161n5, 168, 194, 195
inner sense, 106, 120, 130
intentional fallacy, 305, 306
intuitions, 190, 191, 207, 213, 243, 282, 306, 307, 309
irony, 4, 16, 265, 268

kalon, 1–4, 10, 56, 58n2, 103, 209, 211
Kandinsky, Wassily, 225
Kantian, xvi, xvii, 151, 157, 159, 180, 182, 188, 195, 197, 200, 230, 251, 252n6
Karloff, Boris, 36, 266
Keynes, John Maynard, xii, 275, 306

Langer, Susanne, 248
Lascaux, 277
Laws (by Plato), 16n5, 51n14
Lee, Christopher, 36
Leibniz, 158n3
Les Misérables, 260
Locke, John, 99, 102
Lockean, 102, 107

Longinus, 176n11, 187n15, 248
Lyotard, Jean-François, 177n12

Mad Magazine, 141
Malevich, Kazimir, 225
Mapplethorpe, Robert, 279
mass hero, 71n8
mathematical sublime, 177, 178, 180, 181
Matisse, Henri, 276
Mendelssohn, Felix, 289
metaphor, 5, 16, 51n14, 120, 187, 188, 190, 191, 196, 197, 232, 267, 287
metaphysical hypothesis, 281, 298–300
Michelangelo, 106, 277
mimesis, 25, 32–34, 39, 40, 44, 50, 53n15, 55, 56, 58, 60, 63, 65n5, 68, 69, 77, 78, 111
Mind (Hegel), 201–203, 217, 221
Moby Dick, 267
Modern System of the Arts, xix, 113
Modest Proposal, A, 265, 268
Molière, 260, 294
Mondrian, Piet, 225, 288
Moore, G. E., 302, 304
Mozart, 8, 196
Myth of Gyges, 26

neo-impressionism, 275, 276, 305
New Criticism, 279n2, 306
Nicomachean Ethics, 78, 90
Nietzsche, xiii n2, 86n14, 195n19, 227, 243, 244
noumenal, 180, 193, 199, 200, 228, 229, 231

objectification, 232, 233, 236, 238–40, 242
Oceanic art, 285
Odyssey, The, 13, 22, 30, 67
Oedipus Rex, 72, 73, 80, 81, 85, 91, 174
Old Comedy, 2, 14
Original Beauty, 111
Ovid, 144–48

paradox of taste, 127, 128, 132, 133, 144, 192
paradox of tragedy, 84

Pater, Walter, 309
perfection, 6, 158, 165, 174, 211, 212, 259
pessimism, 228, 233, 244
Phaedrus, 16
phenomenal, 180, 193, 200, 210, 228–30, 232
photography, 276, 277
Picasso, Pablo, 187, 277
pity: Plato, 29–31, 49, 50; Aristotle, 59, 61, 66, 68–71, 75, 79–89, 91–95, 97, 98
Plato: xi–xv, xvii, xix, 1–7, 10–16, 18, 20–22, 25, 26, 28–42, 44–56; vs. Aristotle, 58–60, 62–65, 75–79, 84, 86, 89, 91–93, 95, 96, 98
Platonic Forms, 300
Platonic Ideas: Plato, 42; Schopenhauer, 236–39, 242, 243
plot, 60, 61, 64, 66, 67, 69, 70, 71, 75, 77–86, 93, 97
poesis, 61, 101
Pokémon, 131, 132, 136
Politics (by Aristotle), 84, 86, 87
postmodernism, 140, 177n12
Price, Vincent, 36
Principia Ethica, 304
principium individuationis, 229, 241, 244
principle of sufficient reason, 228–32, 234, 236, 237, 242
purposiveness without a purpose, 159, 166, 167, 170, 184, 187, 278, 279

Raphael, 246, 279
Rationalist Aesthetics, 158n3, 165, 185
reflective judgment, 169, 178, 184, 197
Reich, Steve, 126
Reid, Thomas, 248
Relative Beauty, 111–13, 123
representation (Schopenhauer), 227–33, 240, 242
Republic, xiv, 1, 6, 10–13, 20n6, 21, 25, 26, 28, 30–34, 48, 54–56, 58, 59, 62, 63, 65n5, 77, 204, 279, 288
reversal of fortune, 80, 81, 83, 88, 95, 97, 134
romantic stage of art (Hegel), 215, 217–20, 225

Romeo and Juliet, 187, 214
Rossi, Antonio, 176

Saint Paul, 204
Sappho, 68
Sartre, Jean-Paul, 225
School of Athens, The, 279
Schopenhauer: xi–xiii, xvii, xix, 227–44; vs. Bell, 280–82, 300, 306
sensus communis, 162, 168, 193, 200
Serrano, Andres, 261
Shaftesbury, Earl of, 101, 102
Shakespeare, 67n7, 113, 189, 214, 246
significant form, xvii, xviii, 276–80, 284–301, 303–5
Socrates, xiv, 1–34, 39, 41, 58, 77, 186, 201, 211n5
Socratic, 4, 6, 17, 19, 25, 34, 68, 244n8
Socratic fallacy, 6
spectacle, 50, 69, 77, 83, 239
Spinoza, 232n4
Spirit (Hegel), 201–3, 205, 207–10, 213–22
standard of taste, 126–29, 132–35, 142–44, 146, 148, 153, 168, 209
Star Trek, 44
Steele, Richard, 101
Stendhal syndrome, 295n8
sublime, 145, 156, 173, 174, 176–85, 187n15, 196, 216, 248
supersensible, 126, 178, 180, 182, 184, 185, 193, 200
Surrealism, 47, 264, 265, 267
symbolic stage of art (Hegel), 215–18
Symbolism, 40, 246, 265, 267

Tacitus, 144–46, 148
taste: Hutcheson, 100, 101, 104–8, 111, 114–17, 120; Hume, 126–53; Kant, 157–64, 166, 168, 171, 173, 176, 184–86n14, 189–96
Teletubbies, 147
television (TV), 11
Tennessee Walker, 174
Theogony, 29
thing-in-itself, 200, 241
Timaeus, 22
Tokyo Story, 131, 132, 136

Tolstoy, Leo, xi–xiii, xviii–xx, 246–73
tragedy: Aristotle, 59–77, 79–97;
    Hegel, 219
Triumph of the Will, 261
Tzara, Tristan, 264

Uncle Tom's Cabin, 260, 269
unconscious bias, 194, 195n19
uniformity amidst variety, 112–15, 120, 121, 123
uniformity and diversity, 165, 278

Velasquez, 187

War and Peace, 246, 267
Warhol, Andy, 267, 298
What is Art?, xviii, 246, 247, 249, 268, 282
Whistler, James McNeill, 309
Wilde, Oscar, 309
Wittgenstein, Ludwig, 7
World as Will and Representation, The, 227–44